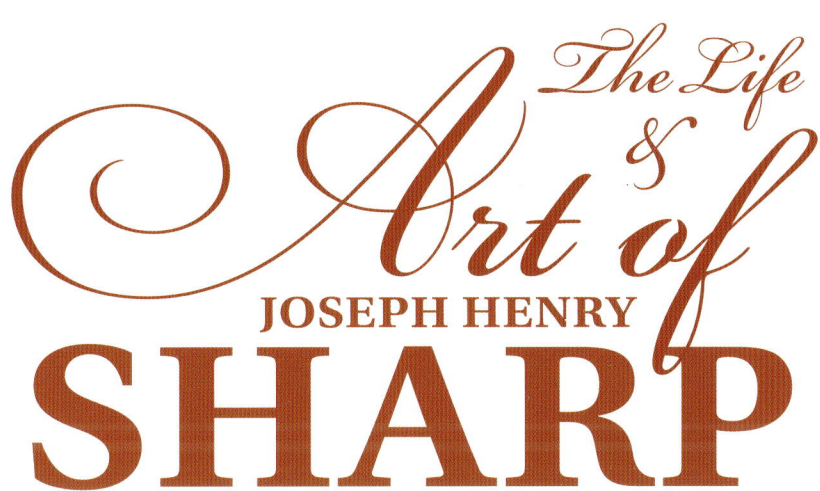

The Life & Art of

JOSEPH HENRY

SHARP

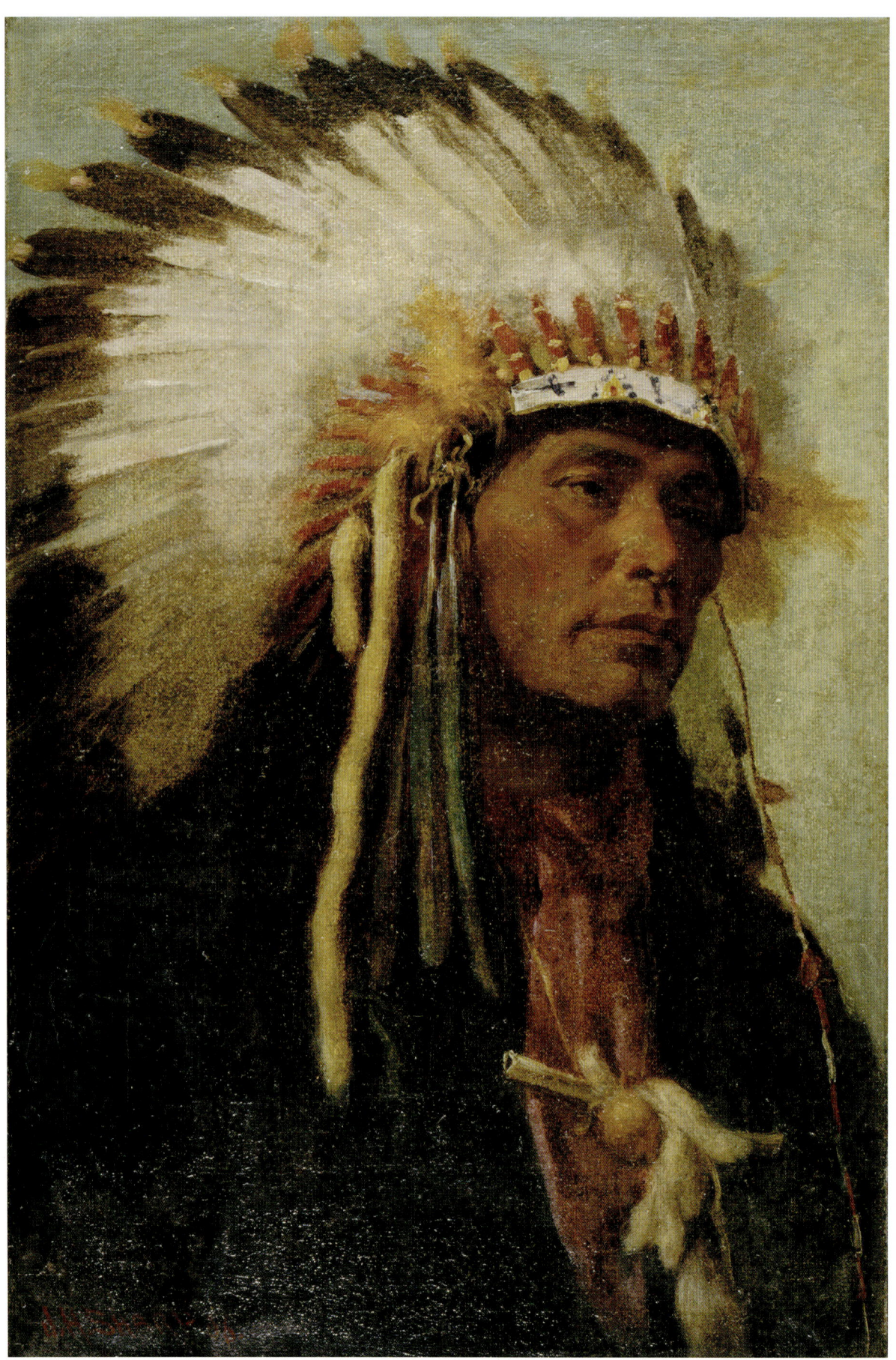

WHITNEY WEST

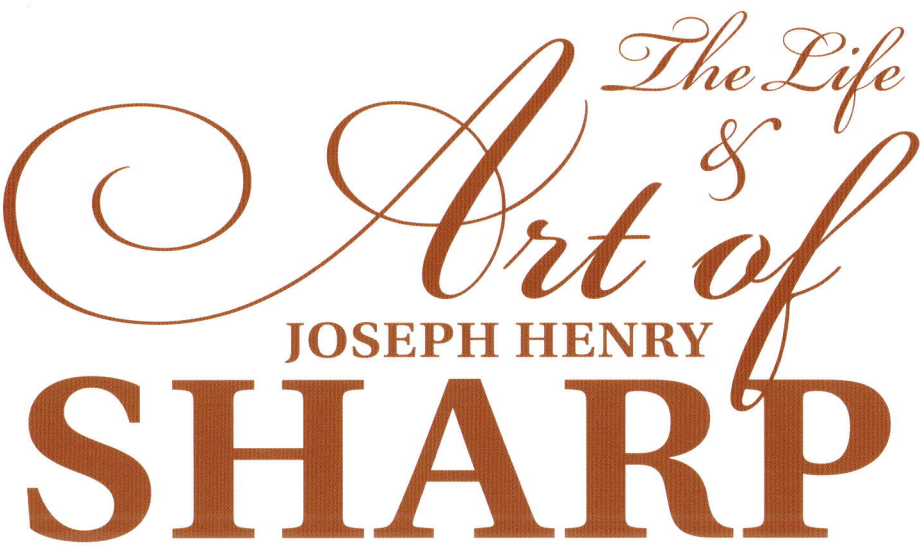

The Life & Art of JOSEPH HENRY SHARP

PETER H. HASSRICK

WITH MARIE WATKINS, SARAH E. BOEHME, AND KELIN MICHAEL

INTRODUCTION BY KAREN B. McWHORTER

Buffalo Bill Center of the West
in association with
The Lunder Research Center at the Couse-Sharp Historic Site

**BUFFALO BILL
CENTER
OF THE WEST**

Buffalo Bill Center of the West
720 Sheridan Avenue, Cody, Wyoming
centerofthewest.org

FOR BUFFALO BILL CENTER OF THE WEST
Project Manager: Sylvia Huber

Designer: Jessica McKibben, Cody, Wyoming
Editor: Steven Baker, Oklahoma City, Oklahoma
Indexer: Amron Gravett, Wild Clover Book Services, San Louis Obispo, California

978-0-931618-72-7
Printed in South Korea

JOSEPH HENRY SHARP
ONLINE CATALOGUE

SharpArtCatalogue.com

The Joseph Henry Sharp Online Catalogue complements and expands upon the publication, *The Life and Art of Joseph Henry Sharp*, by providing thorough documentation of known Joseph Henry Sharp works in public collections. Through research on about 750 works, entries will include color images, title, alternative titles, date, medium, size, inscriptions and provenance (when available), exhibition history, and a scholarly analysis written by authors of the publication.

The Online Catalogue will launch in the Fall of 2019. Systematic updates will be ongoing as new information comes to light.

The site has been made possible through a generous donation from The Ricketts Art Foundation.

Record 500 — *Concha*

Record 13 — *Strikes His Enemy Pretty—Crow*

Record 56 — *Crucita—A Taos Indian Girl*

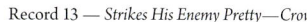

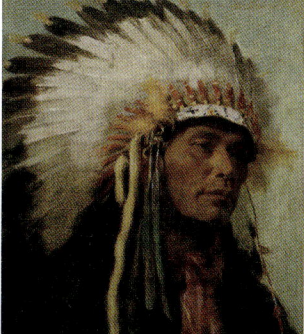

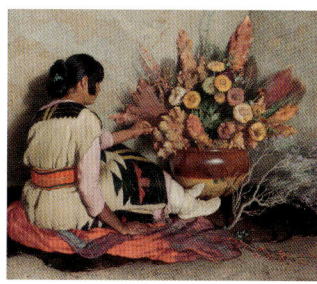

Record 501 — *The Agency Store*

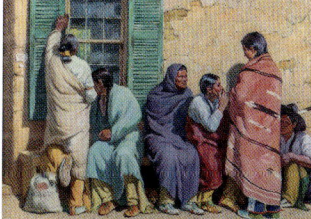

Record 239 — *Sunset Dance—Ceremony to the Evening Sun*

Record 17 — *John and Jerry Chanting*

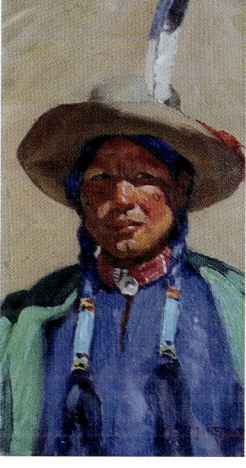

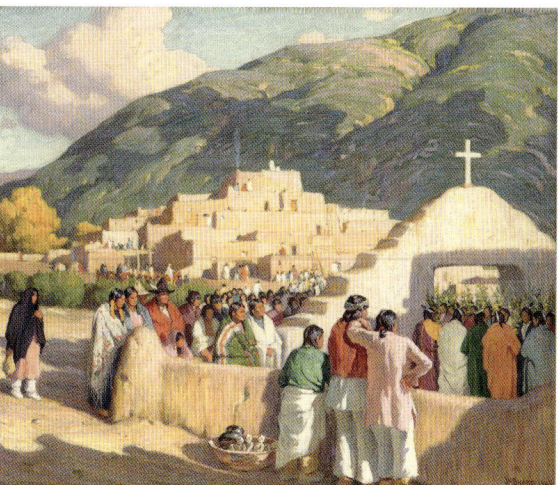

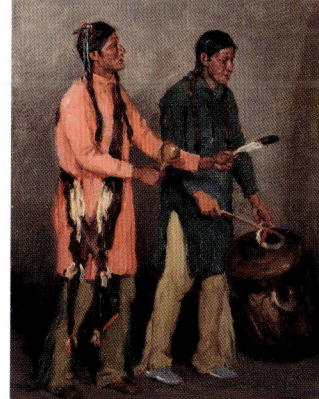

DEDICATION

This book is dedicated to Sylvia Huber for all of her hard work and exceptional coordination of the *Whitney West* series.

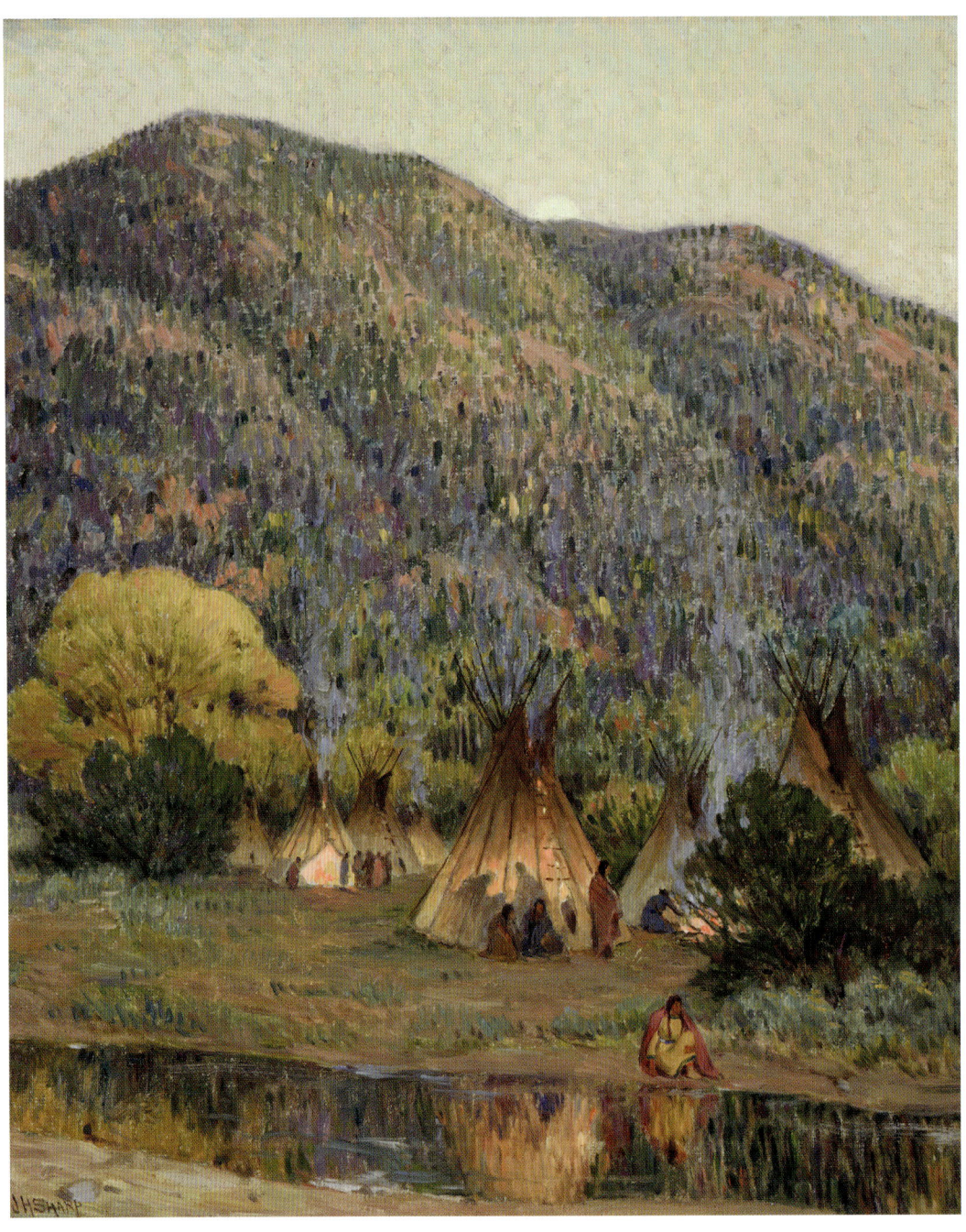

JOSEPH HENRY SHARP, *Indian Village*. ca. 1920, oil on canvas, 23 ½ x 20 in.
Cincinnati Art Museum, Cincinnati, Ohio. 2003.102

CONTENTS

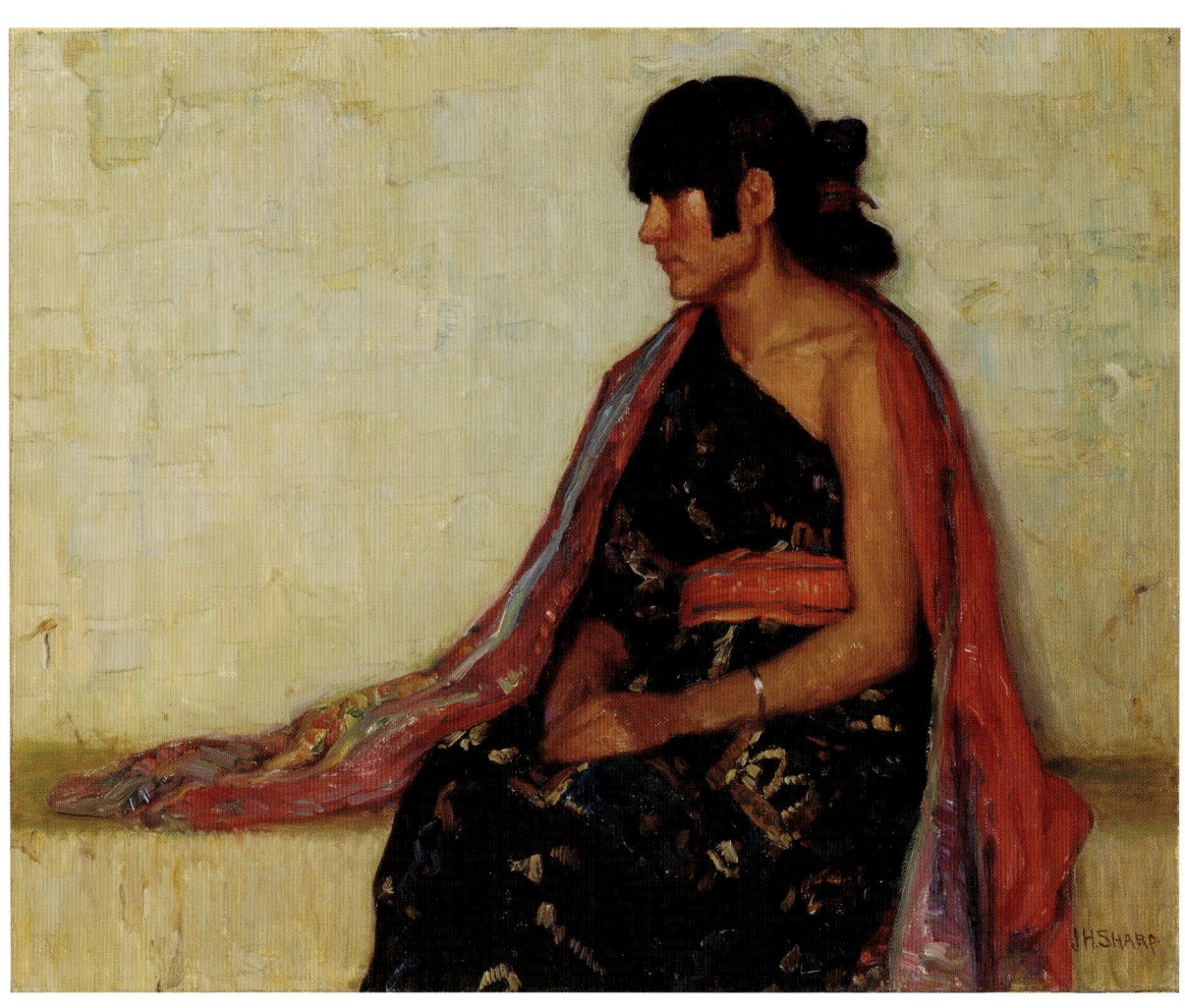

JOSEPH HENRY SHARP, *Crucita—Old Hopi Dress.* ca. 1933, oil on canvas, 16 x 20 ⅛ in. Buffalo Bill Center of the West, Cody, Wyoming. Gift of Mr. and Mrs. William S. Moorer. 25.65

FOREWORD

Peter Seibert
Executive Director & CEO
Buffalo Bill Center of the West

In many respects, the life of Joseph Henry Sharp epitomizes the story of the West. From the plains and mountains of Montana to the shadows of the Sangre de Christo Mountains in New Mexico, Sharp sought to capture both a natural and a historic world that was changing both for him and his generation. His imagery of Native Americans captured a thoughtfulness and reflection in the subject's eyes that can only lead one to conclude that they, like we the viewers, were pondering the future of the changing American West.

During his life Sharp's work formed the basis of a 1949 retrospective exhibition at the Gilcrease Museum in Tulsa, Oklahoma, and numerous institutions and private collections now hold his paintings. Today, in an arguably unique achievement among American western artists, one of his western homes and one of his studios are operated as museums: the first, his impressive Taos studio, by our collaborators in this project, The Lunder Research Center at the Couse-Sharp Historic Site in Taos, New Mexico; and the second, his charming Montana cabin, the Absarokee Hut, by this institution—the Buffalo Bill Center of the West in Cody. Visiting them enables one to better understand the rich body of work that Sharp produced.

Having worked at several museums that owned Sharp paintings, I am always amazed at both the wide range of his subjects and the quality of his works. Once during a community appraisal event, I spotted a painting across the room that spoke to me. The depiction of a pensive Native American could only have come from the brush of Joseph Henry Sharp. The owner had found it at a yard sale in Taos and knew nothing of the artist. For me, it was a great discovery of an important work by this artist but also proof that, even amongst the detritus of bottles and broken picture frames in a yard sale, Sharp's work can continue to catch the attention of new generations.

This project brings together the best in thoughtful research and writing on the life of this artist. The book and online catalogue of Sharp works in public collections, part of an ongoing set of periodic publications known as the *Whitney West*, seek to sustain and enhance research and study of great western American artists.

PREFACE

Peter H. Hassrick
Director Emeritus and Senior Scholar
Buffalo Bill Center of the West

In 1986, right in the middle of my twenty-year tenure as director of what is today the Buffalo Bill Center of the West, I had a surprise call from an admired friend and generous supporter, Forrest Fenn of Santa Fe. Fenn had long been a devotee of the Montana and New Mexico painter Joseph Henry Sharp (1859–1953). Three years earlier he had completed the first definitive book on Sharp, *The Beat of the Drum and the Whoop of the Dance: A Study of the Life and Art of Joseph Henry Sharp*, and had amassed a vast collection of archival resources to accomplish that worthy task. He had also, as a celebrated dealer in western American art, sold countless Sharp paintings and gathered a large group of Sharp-related artifacts. It was concerning this last activity that he had picked up the phone to call me. Among the Sharp treasures he had assembled was the handsome log cabin residence, known as the Absarokee Hut, that Sharp and his wife, Addie, had built in 1905 at Crow Agency in southern Montana. Fenn was nervous about its longevity on the reservation and was looking for a new, permanent home for the historic structure. The Buffalo Bill Center of the West owned approximately thirty-five original works by Sharp, and I considered Fenn's offer to donate the cabin as a most welcome—in fact, a once-in-a-life-time—opportunity. The cabin reflected the unfettered sense of adventure that the young Sharp couple had once embarked upon in service to art, to preserving in paint the identity of countless Northern Plains Indian people and their remarkable lifeways, and to expanding the scope of American art beyond its eastern comfort zone. I immediately accepted Fenn's proposal and arranged for a truck to pick up and transfer the cabin to Cody the very next week.

Fenn eventually donated a set of Sharp's papers to the McCracken Research Library, along with many fascinating artifacts that had once decorated the cabin. The cabin was professionally and lovingly restored and then placed in its own special garden next to the Whitney Western Art Museum. It stands there today as a tribute to Sharp's place in the northern Rockies and the largess of generous patrons such as Forrest Fenn.

This publication and the accompanying online database of Sharp works held in public collections are an offshoot of those events more than thirty years ago. They substantiate the remarkable quest undertaken by the artist and his family to venture west in search of unexplored places, subjects, and insights. As Sharp told his hometown newspaper in 1894 after his first meaningful trip into the Southwest, "Any one willing to sacrifice a few modern comforts and rough it through the mountains and Indian pueblos of New Mexico can experience a novel life, fully repaying the time and trouble." Sharp's enduring vision was subsumed in a life in art among people whom he recognized as the "real Americans" and began in earnest when, around 1899, he realized that "the Indian is becoming a factor for distinctly American pictures." And to become a part of that movement, he dedicated himself both to making a historical record of individuals in paint and to documenting the quotidian life of Plains and Southwestern indigenous people. In the latter endeavor, Sharp set himself apart from his contemporaries. As one critic noted in 1908, "Mr. Sharp has succeeded in doing what few white men have done—getting an insight into the real home life of the Indian. His Indians are not the austere, mock-heroic types that are painted by artists who work chiefly from imagination."

Sharp stepped outside the bounds of many traditional western artists. Unlike his contemporaries Frederic Remington and Charles Russell, Sharp undertook serious art training both in Cincinnati and in the European art centers of Antwerp, Munich, Paris, and Madrid. He painted scenes of women and men with equal fervor, never diminishing the former with sexist inferences as Russell was wont to do in the 1890s. Even when he settled primarily in the West after 1900, Sharp continued to exhibit his work in major exhibitions and institutions in art centers from Boston to Pittsburgh and from New York to San Francisco. He played an important role in founding and sustaining the Society of Western Artists in the late nineteenth century and in the inception and perpetuation of the famous Taos Society of Artists. He remained steadfastly loyal to his traditional Beaux Arts style and techniques but ventured outside those parameters frequently enough with Impressionist and Post-Impressionist works to keep from being stigmatized or limited in expression.

As Sharp embarked on his career as a full-time painter of Indians in 1901, he published a biographical sketch that addressed his achievements to date and assessed his fundamental character. It recounted that "Mr. Sharp is a typical American, full of tact and energy; ever on the alert for the new, beautiful and healthful in art: of a nervous temperament, and is a fine example of a self-made man." At Sharp's funeral more than fifty years later, his fellow Taos artist Ernest Blumenschein recognized Sharp's facility as a painter, observing that through "his indefatigable labor [he] developed his technical skill to a point where he could put up his easel and paint with great speed whatever his eye could see. . . . He was the reporter, the recorder of absolute integrity of the American Indian. . . . He will go down in history with Russell and Remington." Sharp would have been gratified with this conclusory assessment.

———————————

Extensive research of Joseph Henry Sharp's body of work has revealed that some titles and/or dates of creation may differ from those currently in use.

Titles and dates of creation for works illustrated in this publication are based on the first discoverable date of exhibition or illustration and the title used at that time. The titles and dates that have been shared with us by institutions, if and when they differ from our research or method are indicated in brackets in the Joseph Henry Sharp Online Catalogue.

ACKNOWLEDGEMENTS

Peter H. Hassrick
Director Emeritus and Senior Scholar
Buffalo Bill Center of the West

This volume, part of the *Whitney West* series, provides a careful and fresh evaluation of Joseph Henry Sharp's life and work. Many important and profoundly useful treatises have been published on Sharp, including Forrest Fenn's definitive books, *The Beat of the Drum and the Whoop of the Dance* (1983) and *Teepee Smoke* (2007), along with Thomas Minckler's *In Poetic Silence* (2010). Added to that are Sarah E. Boehme's book on Sharp's Montana home, *Absarokee Hut* (1992), and Marie A. Watkin's doctoral dissertation on Sharp's early patrons (2000). These books have been augmented by the Center's remarkable and rich archival collection of Sharp Papers graciously donated to the Harold McCracken Research Library in 1986 by Forrest and Peggy Fenn. These have collectively provided inspiration and insights that have been invaluable in the fulfillment of this dream to revisit Sharp and his contributions to the American art canon.

Throughout this project, the Buffalo Bill Center of the West has supplied the necessary resources and support through the Whitney Museum of Western Art curatorial division, including especially Karen McWhorter and Nicole Harrison; the remarkable Harold McCracken Research Library staff, especially Mary Robinson, Karen Preis, Karen Roles, and Mack Frost; the museum's enlightened leadership of Bruce Eldredge and Peter Seibert, its trustees, and the Whitney Advisory Board. Most important of all, this book and the associated online catalogue could not have been produced without the dedication and savvy of my indefatigable assistant, Sylvia Huber.

We are proud to have been associated in this project with our donor and collaborator The Lunder Research Center at the Couse-Sharp Historic Site of Taos.

We gratefully acknowledge the generous contributions of the following organizations and individuals, without whom this project would never have come to fruition.

The Ricketts Art Foundation of New York, Joe Ricketts, founder
The Jerry Blank Family Foundation of Miami, Florida
The Gerald Peters Family Foundation of Santa Fe, New Mexico
William D. Weiss, The Community Foundation of Jackson Hole, Wyoming
Ben Chapman of Cody, Wyoming
Anne Young of Cody, Wyoming
Ray Harvey of Paradise Valley, Arizona
Lisa Wirthlin of Salt Lake City, Utah
Duffy and Tina Oyster Foundation of Dallas, TX

We are grateful to the following image lenders to the publication: American Museum of Western Art—The Anschutz Collection, Claire Mosier, Museum Librarian and Historian, and Darlene Dueck, Curator; Bair Family Museum, Elizabeth M. Guheen, Director and Chief Curator; Big Horn County Historical Society, Randy Schoppe, Director; Billings Public Library, Gavin J. Woltjer, Library Director; Buffalo Bill Center of the West, Harold McCracken Research Library, Sean Campbell, Imaging Manager; Butler Institute of American Art, Pat McCormick, Registrar/Archives; Cincinnati Art Museum, Julie Aronson, Curator of American Paintings, Sculpture and Drawings, and Anne Buening, Curatorial Assistant; C. M. Russell Museum, Emily Crawford Wilson, Curator, Brenda Kornick, Collections and Exhibitions Director, and Kathryn Kramer, Renner Research Center Manager; Denver Art Museum, Meg Erickson, Curatorial Assistant, and Renee B. Miller, Rights and Reproductions Coordinator; Eiteljorg Museum, Johanna M. Blume, Interim Curator of Western Art, History, and Culture, Christa Barleben, Registrar; Emfietzoglou Gallery Museum, Athens, Greece; Gerald Peters Gallery, Ana Archuleta, Art Assistant to Gerald Peters; Gilcrease Museum, Diana M. Cox, Intellectual Property and Copyright Manager; Huntington Museum of Art, Linda Sanns, Registrar; The James Museum of Western & Wildlife Art, Jason Wyatt, Collections Manager; The Lunder Research Center at the Couse-Sharp Historic Site, Davison Packard Koenig, Executive Director/Curator, and Regina Scherffius, Program Manager; Montana Museum of Art and Culture, Jeremy Canwell, Curator of Art; Musée d'Orsay, Musée du Louvre, Museo Nacional del Prado, Museum of Modern Art, Art Resource, Jennifer Belt, Associate Permissions Director; Museum of Wisconsin Art, Andrea Waala, Registrar; National Art Gallery—Alexandros Soutzos Museum, Athens, Greece; National Cowboy and Western Heritage Museum, Kera Newby, Digital and Manuscript Archivist; National Gallery of Art, Peter Huestis, Division of Imaging and Visual Services; New Mexico Museum of Art, Michelle Gallagher Roberts, Deputy Director; Pennsylvania Academy of Fine Arts, Anna Marley, Curator of Historical American Art, and Alex Till, Assistant Registrar; Phoebe A. Hearst Museum of Anthropology, Leslie Freund, Collections Manager, and Martina Smith, Cultural Policy Specialist; Phoenix Art Museum, Adriana Milinic Fanning, Digital Assets Manager; Lainey Jacobson Reynolds-Keene; Smithsonian American Art Museum, Riche Sorenson, Rights and Reproductions Coordinator; Sotheby's, London, Harry Edmonds, Department Assistant; Stark Museum of Art, Sarah E. Boehme, Curator, and Katherine Barry, Registrar; Syracuse University Libraries, Nicole Westerdahl, Reference and Access Services Librarian; and Taos Art Museum at Fechin House, Christy Schoedinger Coleman, Executive Director and Cindy Atkins; Thomas Minckler Fine Arts, Thomas Minckler; Yellowstone Art Museum, Lisa Ranallo, Registrar.

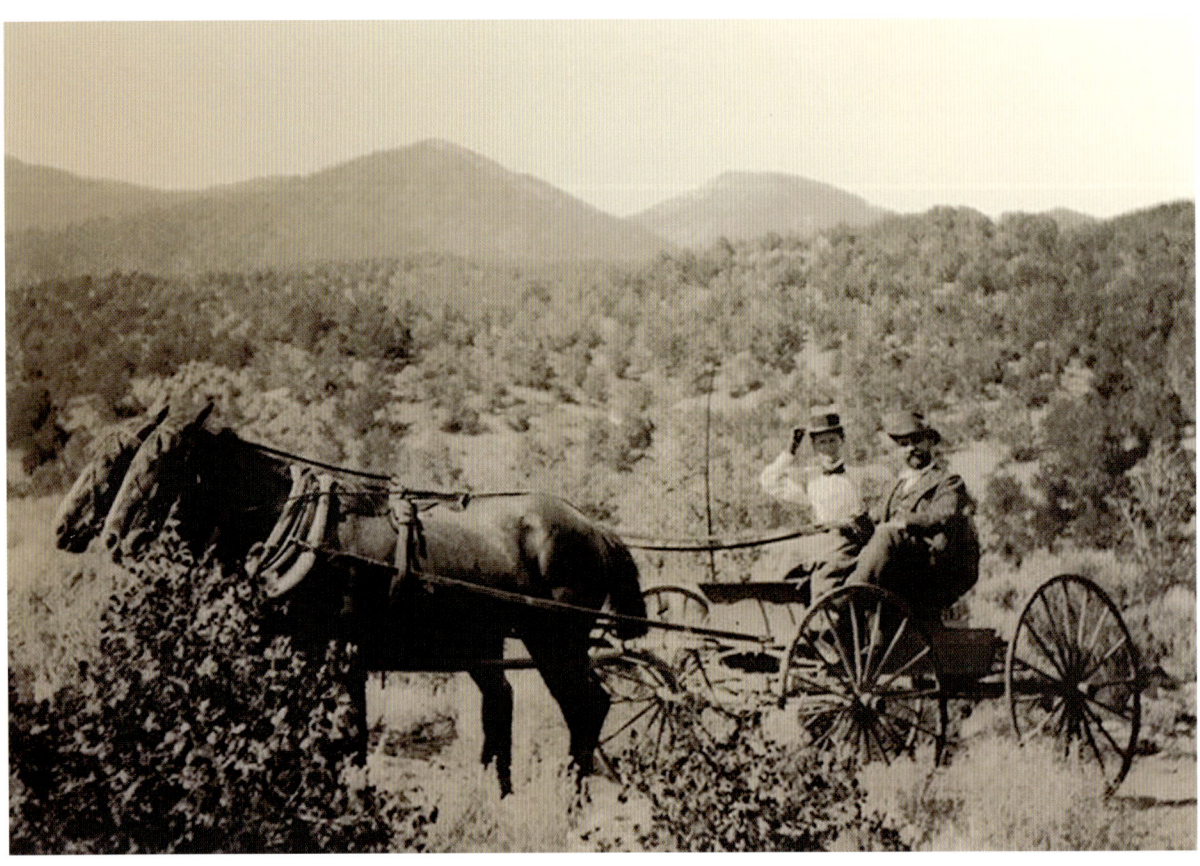

Addie and Sharp in horse-drawn wagon. photograph, b&w
TIA Collection, Santa Fe, New Mexico

INTRODUCTION

Karen B. McWhorter
Scarlett Curator of Western American Art
Whitney Western Art Museum
Buffalo Bill Center of the West

JOSEPH HENRY SHARP'S PURSUIT OF INSPIRATION

Taos, New Mexico, is nearly eight hundred miles from Crow Agency in southern Montana. Even the most direct route between the two locales would make for a lengthy road trip. The Rocky Mountains span the distance and extend well beyond in both directions, limiting the number of possible travel itineraries one might consider. But, like a series of massive cairns set in place by some primordial giant, the cordillera reassuringly points the way. Today, a scenic drive from New Mexico to Montana can be navigated with relative ease by car (and, certainly, easier still by plane). In the late nineteenth century, before the advent of the automobile and its widespread use in the American West, the burgeoning railroad network facilitated the journey. By the 1860s, lines spread like arteries throughout the western region and were an integral mode of transportation. One could ride the rails, shoulder to shoulder with other pioneering souls, to any number of growing communities west of the Mississippi and, beyond city centers, jump on a branch line to more remote destinations. Past the tracks' farthest reaches, however, hearty travelers had little choice but to bump along rutted roads via buckboard, horseback, or the stage.

Artist Joseph Henry Sharp (1859–1953) was one such hearty traveler who frequently undertook the trip between Taos and Crow Agency, often adding a third leg to Pasadena, California. Despite the laborious nature of travel throughout the American West at the turn of the century, no journey was too long or arduous for Sharp, an inveterate wanderer with an adventurous spirit. Sharp was the type to describe traversing 150 mountainous miles by wagon in just one week as a "wonderful experience."[1] Not all his western excursions were so taxing, though; Sharp passed many comfortable commutes in the buffet, smoking, or library cars of the Great Northern or the Atchison, Topeka and Santa Fe (AT&SF) railways. In 1916 he reflected that, for many years, he had

---

1 J. H. Sharp (hereafter JHS) to J. H. Gest from Browning, MT, August 24, 1903, Beinecke Rare Book and Manuscript Library, Yale University, New Haven.

spent $150 to $200 annually in fares on the AT&SF alone.[2] At that time, a ticket from Pasadena to Santa Fe was around $30, and from Denver to San Francisco $80. Bearing in mind these prices and acknowledging that Sharp frequently traveled on other lines as well, one gets a good sense of Sharp's peripatetic lifestyle. But travel was not just enjoyable and entertaining for Sharp; it was the means by which he honed his artistic talents and found the ideal subjects to match his skill.

Had Sharp spent his career close to home in the Midwest—had he been a little less ambitious and adventurous—he might have enjoyed success as a portraitist and art instructor, a post he took up in 1892 and for which he was well suited. Perhaps his main influence would have remained his early mentor Frank Duveneck, from whom he might have adopted a secondhand academic style based on the Munich mode. Had Sharp stayed in the Midwest, his aesthetic and subjects may have wholly reflected European trends. But Sharp did not stay in the Midwest. Instead, he sought the world as his classroom, and ultimately endeavored to create uniquely American art. As the authors of this catalogue convincingly suggest, Sharp's sojourns in Europe proved instrumental in the artist's development, and his later residencies in Montana and New Mexico were transformative.

Abiding a teacher's schedule during the early chapters of his professional career, Sharp traveled predominately during the summer, venturing west for the first time in 1883 and then with frequency for a decade beginning in 1893. In 1903, he and his wife, Addie, established residence on Crow Agency, a jumping-off point from which to visit communities among the Northern Plains tribes, commune with artists working in the region, and explore the windswept, yet starkly beautiful terrain of Montana, the Dakotas, and Wyoming. The two would arrive in time for Crow Fair in the fall and stay on through early winter, at which time they would depart for California. They spent summers in Taos.

And so, like birds undertaking a reverse migration, the Sharps spent colder months in the North and warmer months in the Southwest. The biting chill of Montana winters did not dissuade Sharp, but rather inspired him. Undeterred by subzero temperatures, he worked to perfect snow scenes and Indian portraits in firelit tipi interiors, two picture types for which he would become famous. Without distraction, he painted at an almost feverish pace and produced enough work to populate group exhibitions throughout the United States and circulate solo shows. Sharp's compulsion to create prevailed over shivering hands and congealing paint, until the early 1920s when the harsh climate began to take too great a toll on the artist's declining health.

From his first trip to New Mexico, it became clear that the Southwest would provide a lifetime of inspiration. The region's appealing qualities were many: the beauty of the Sangre de Cristo Mountains and surrounding arroyos and desert; the milder climate (perhaps mild only in comparison to Montana); a greater number of willing and more affordable models; and a growing artists'

---

2 JHS to William Haskell Simpson, Atchison, Topeka and Santa Fe Railroad, July 26, 1916, MS 22, Joseph Henry Sharp Collection, McCracken Research Library, Buffalo Bill Center of the West, Cody, WY. Gift of Mr. and Mrs. Forrest Fenn (hereafter JHSC).

community. The latter of these attractions he helped create; Sharp was a founding member of the famed Taos Society of Artists, the first significant association of American artists working in the West.

In both Montana and New Mexico, Sharp traveled throughout the countryside in search of fodder for his canvases, but also seeking outdoor adventure [PLATE I.1]. A plein air painting excursion would often also involve a cast or two in a trout stream or an invigorating hike. Sharp's life was a string of long, fulfilling days. He rarely stood still, except to paint, and was actively recreating outdoors into his seventies. Sharp was an energetic and curious man, whose interest in all things new and exciting kept him traveling around the world and crisscrossing the American West. As he went, he collected souvenirs, made sketches, and took notes and photographs to draw upon for inspiration when he returned to one of his studios. Sharp amassed an especially large collection of Plains Indian and Pueblo material culture. He treasured these artifacts for more than their practical application as props for his paintings. For him they represented the ingenuity of their makers, peoples whose traditional ways of life were becoming increasingly threatened. Like many artists of his and earlier eras, Sharp shared the belief that the West as he knew it was drastically changing in the face of immigration and industrialization. His perceptions of the region and its peoples were informed by popular representations by authors such as James Fenimore Cooper and artists such as George Catlin (whose mission to preserve the likenesses of Native peoples on canvas Sharp emulated) and Henry Farny. He later witnessed firsthand the adversities faced by the indigenous cultures of the Northern Plains and the Southwest.

Sharp's affinity for collecting art and artifacts was shared by many of his predecessors and peers, including Frederic Remington and Alexander Phimister Proctor, and later by W. H. D. Koerner. Each of these artists actively amassed personal collections of western memorabilia, portions of which now reside at the Buffalo Bill Center of the West in Cody, Wyoming (the Center), alongside substantial holdings of their artwork. Part of Sharp's carefully curated collection and one of his studio buildings—his "Absarokee Hut" from Crow Agency, now relocated and refurbished—are also at home at the Center. Together, the Center's four "studio collections" provide invaluable insights into the creative processes of the artists who built them and are counted among the museum's most unique assets. They include an extraordinary array of artwork, collected artifacts, studio furnishings, personal effects, and archival material.

This latest volume of the *Whitney West* series and a complementary online database of Sharp's work in institutional collections constitute a project that was inspired in part by the Center's holdings of Sharp's artwork, possessions, papers, and Montana cabin. Much of this trove was donated to the Center by Sharp scholar Forrest Fenn of Santa Fe, author of the sweeping biography *Teepee Smoke: A New Look into the Life and Work of Joseph Henry Sharp* (2007). As part

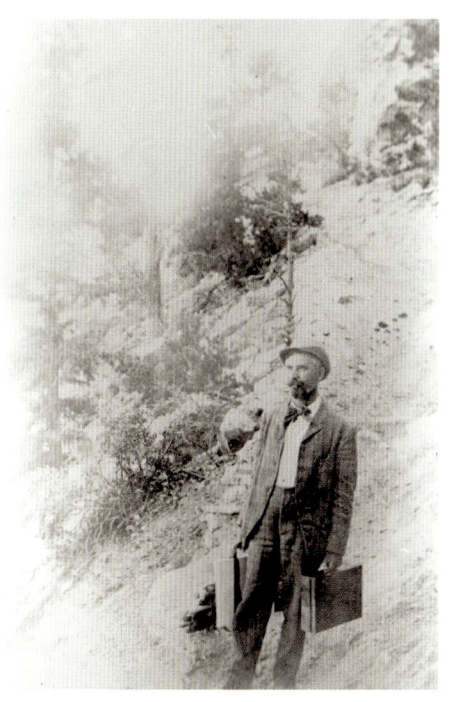

UNKNOWN
PHOTOGRAPHER

J.H. Sharp on Bright Angel Trail, Grand Canyon, 1906

Harold McCracken Research Library, Buffalo Bill Center of the West, Cody, Wyoming. JHSC. Gift of Mr. and Mrs. Forrest Fenn. MS22.2.6, P.22.38

of the Center's ongoing efforts to promote scholarship focused on art of the American West, this project builds on Fenn's expertise and research by providing fresh perspectives on Sharp's life and career. Special attention is paid to Sharp's artistic process, which involved diverse workspaces and influences. Peter H. Hassrick, the Center's Director Emeritus and Senior Scholar, spearheaded this important and timely undertaking and invited three fellow art historians to lend their expertise.

Marie Watkins traces Sharp's education, begun in Cincinnati and continued in Europe. Readers will learn that Sharp became a well-regarded teacher early in his career but was also a committed and lifelong student of his craft. Sponge-like and eager, Sharp soaked up lessons about beauty and art in museums and academy halls, through personal interactions with teachers and fellow artists, and by studying aesthetic principles of varied cultures and eras. Sharp possessed an open mind and an empathetic appreciation for the world and all its difference and was inspired by art as diverse as European Old Master paintings, Chinese ceramics, and Indian artwork and artifacts.

Peter Hassrick's contribution to this catalogue clarifies elements of Sharp's training, patronage, and early inspiration, and untangles apocryphal accounts of his start as an "Indian painter." Hassrick also contextualizes Sharp's "multifarious studios," describing the practical and philosophical importance of ateliers for artists working at the turn of the century, and illustrating how Sharp conformed to and defied conventional uses of a workspace. Each of Sharp's studios possessed a unique character, reflecting a different facet of the artist's persona; he worked in makeshift sites in the West just as nimbly as he did in commodious luxury in the Midwest and Europe. He painted *en plein air*, working from a retrofit sheep wagon amid sage-covered prairies or, alternatively, from a comfortable chair in one of his own backyards—a lush garden with soaring hollyhocks in Taos or the often-snowy tract stretching toward the Little Bighorn River at Crow Agency. Sometimes Sharp's studio was a buffalo hide teepee set up on his property. Studio walls could hardly contain him, yet each workspace Sharp occupied during his career in its own way aided his work and provided an enriching atmosphere in which to create.

Sarah Boehme closely examines one of Sharp's homes, the rustic log cabin he built in Montana in 1905. The Absarokee Hut has stood on the Center's campus in Cody since 1986, when Forrest Fenn donated the historic building to the museum. Thanks to Fenn's generosity and foresight, summertime visitors can tour the restored cabin filled with Sharp's belongings, crossing its threshold into the artist's world. In her essay, Boehme describes the cabin's decor and the artist's collections, which he thoughtfully gathered and artfully displayed. She traces the cabin's history—its construction, improvement, and eventual sale. Sharp's Absarokee Hut was simply built and comfortably appointed; its design and furnishings were chosen with care by the artist. His interests and influences were on display in the eclectic assemblage decorating the studio's walls and surfaces. But more than a workspace or a *Wunderkammer*, the Absarokee Hut was a hub, a central location that granted Sharp proximity to the subjects which inspired him.

Kelin Michael offers further insight into Sharp's biography, suggesting ways in which the artist's schooling in Europe and in the Midwest influenced his later paintings of western American subjects. Europe's fine art academies cast a long shadow in the nineteenth century, their considerable influence stretching to Cincinnati, where Sharp began his studies. Michael points out that many midwestern artists whom Sharp admired as a young man were themselves products of European instruction. They returned to America and shared with their students, including Sharp, the skills and styles to which they had been introduced abroad. Sharp was thus exposed to European trends from his earliest days in art school. His own stints of overseas study would provide him a more intimate understanding of contemporary and historical European art and strengthen his technical abilities as a painter. These early experiences were foundational and provided for Sharp a toolkit on which he drew throughout his career.

Sharp's travelogue would impress even the most avid adventurers today, and when one considers the greater challenges facing long-distance explorers in the nineteenth and early twentieth centuries, it is hard not to appreciate the artist's fortitude. Fueled by wanderlust and a desire to leave a lasting legacy, Sharp traveled the world, from Munich to Madrid to Montana, from San Francisco to Santa Fe and farther still. And though the open road seemed to summon him with each change of season, Sharp built studios in the places that held the greatest significance and offered the greatest artistic opportunities. Taos, New Mexico, and Crow Agency became the homes to which the itinerant artist would consistently return.

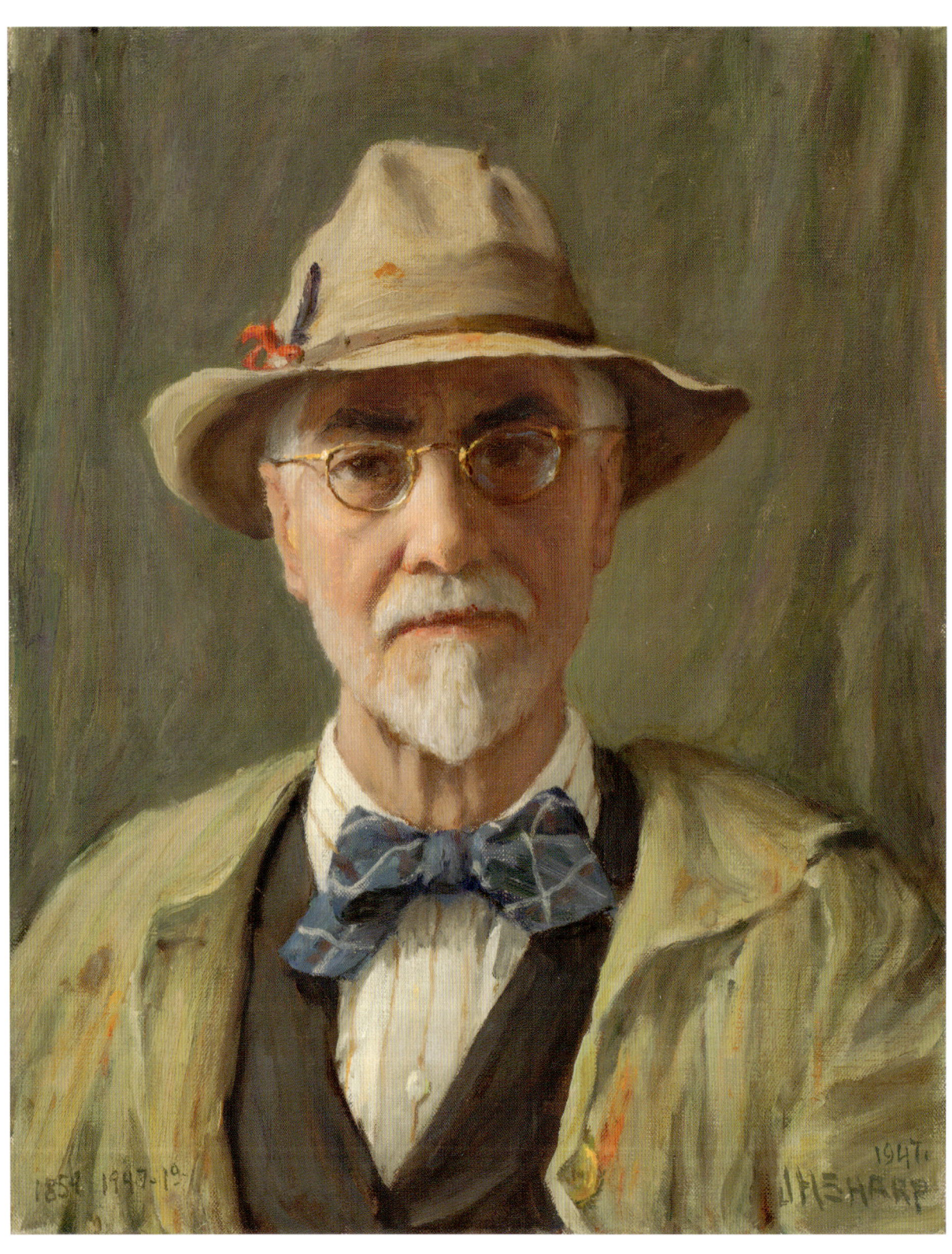

JOSEPH HENRY SHARP, *Self-Portrait*. 1947, oil on canvas, 24 ⅝ x 20 ⅝ in.
Gilcrease Museum, Tulsa, Oklahoma. Gift of the Thomas Gilcrease Foundation, 1955. 0137.323

MARIE WATKINS

THE CALL OF THE WEST
THE ART OF JOSEPH HENRY SHARP

In 1893 skipped for the West—Never regretted it!

Joseph Henry Sharp, 1948

Joseph Henry Sharp [PAGE 2] chose Montana as his first home in the West, living on the Crow Agency Indian reservation in order to harmonize his life with his art. Taos would follow as his second western home. Sharp's several thousand representations of Native peoples form an integral part of both western narrative painting and ethnological portraiture. "Painter of Indians" became his brand identity. This epithet, however, is simplistic, if not misleading. He was also a prolific landscape and still-life painter. While migrating between primary residences in Montana and New Mexico, he painted the same sites over and over in different seasons and in different lights in a constant dialogue with nature. He never passed an opportunity to stop at places and visit with people. He sketched, scribbled, drew, and painted on whatever surface was at hand. Working with an ever-present cigar in hand, Sharp often painted on cigar box lids, using them as a handy substrate in the West's far-flung plains and mountain ranges.

His incessant creative energy mixed well with an exhaustive travel schedule. Typically in haste, he sought new faces and places to paint, cultivated new relationships, and searched out new markets to show and sell his art. A curiosity to understand cultures other than his own, coupled with wanderlust, often took him outside his usual western travel circuit. The compulsion to paint and draw wherever possible drove him to discover and appreciate the cultures that he encountered. Through the years he added Alaska, Hawaii, Europe, North Africa, Asia, and South America to his growing travelogue. At age seventy-seven, he wrote a fellow artist that if he were young again, he "would go to China for 5 years at a stretch" to paint ethnic groups as he had traveled earlier among Native American tribes. "Chinese art [is] not only the greatest of all," he wrote, "but their artisans & craftsmen [are] beyond compare."[1] The Asian souvenirs he brought back were intended to be arranged in still-life motifs, primarily

---

1 JHS, Taos, NM, to Joe Scheuerle, October 13, 1936, Joseph Scheuerle Letters, owned by Thornton Boolean, microfilmed by the Archives of American Art, Smithsonian Institution, Washington, DC (hereafter AAA).

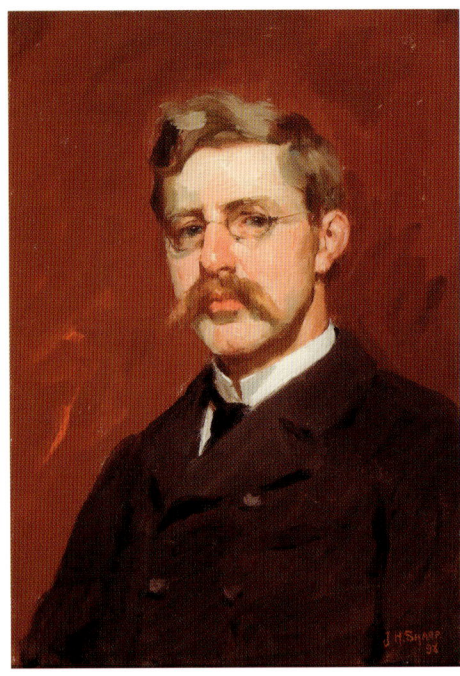

floral.[2] The exuberant bouquets that came from his Taos and Pasadena gardens provided an opportunity to explore color harmonies and patterned arrangement while examining nature more intimately than possible in the vast western spaces. An unrepentant realist with no interest in early Modernist modes, Sharp painted nearly every artistic genre, but the West was his work's constant heartbeat.[3]

Underpinning Sharp's art is his strong academic training, which he began at the age of fourteen at the McMicken School of Drawing and Design.[4] His mother, Elizabeth, and hometown philanthropist Nancy Norton of Ironton, Ohio, recognized his developing artistic abilities and encouraged his enrollment.[5] As a result of increasing deafness from a childhood swimming accident, Sharp dropped out of the local public school in his early teens and went to work in a nail factory where the noise further depleted his hearing. At this point, an art career seemed a viable option for a more successful livelihood, as art provided an alternative means of communication. Eventually permanently deaf, Sharp could speak, but he chose to carry a small notepad to communicate with others and to sketch, a custom he practiced throughout his life.[6]

Sharp proudly pronounced McMicken the only art academy west of New York and Philadelphia, and he arrived at the school during Cincinnati's

2 For a comprehensive discussion of Sharp's still lifes, see Thomas Minckler, *In Poetic Silence: The Floral Paintings of Joseph Henry Sharp* (Tucson: Settlers West Galleries, 2010). "Exhibition at Kreimer's," *Cincinnati Enquirer*, November 1933, Cincinnati Art Museum Archives, Cincinnati, Ohio (hereafter CAMA).

3 There are rare examples of Sharp's possible attempts at Post-Impressionism and early Modernism.

4 The McMicken School of Drawing and Design was established in 1869. It became a department of the University of Cincinnati in 1871 and then, in 1884, was transferred to the Cincinnati Museum Association, joining the newly founded Art Museum in Eden Park. In 1887 the name of the school (no longer affiliated with the University of Cincinnati) officially changed to the Art Academy of Cincinnati.

5 Meetings and telephone conversations with members of the Lawrence County Historical Society, Ironton, Ohio, summer 2010. Norton Scott, great-grandson of the Nortons, donated Sharp's portrait of Nancy Norton to the Lawrence County Historical Society's Grey House Museum. He puts the date of the painting circa 1889–1892, when his great-grandmother was between sixty-five and sixty-eight years old. "Painting," *Ironton Tribune*, May 15, 1990, p. 1A; Mike James, "Historical Society Acquires Painting," *Ironton Tribune*, March 22, 1991, p. 2A; R. Norton Scott to Jim Heald, May 11, 1990, Lawrence County Historical Society.

6 Carolyn Reynolds Riebeth was a child when she met the Sharps at Crow Agency in 1902. Her father, Samuel Guilford Reynolds, served as agent of the Crow Indian Reservation in Montana from 1902 to 1910. The Reynolds family and the Sharps became good friends. Riebeth visited and remained in contact with them throughout their lives. Her discussion of life at Crow Agency from 1902 to 1910 provides unique insight into the Sharps' lives at this time and life at Crow Agency. Carolyn Reynolds Riebeth, *J. H. Sharp among the Crow Indians, 1902–1910: Personal Memories of His Life and Friendships on the Crow Reservation in Montana* (El Segundo, CA: Upton and Sons, 2003), esp. 27, 131, 137.

   Regarding Sharp's ability to communicate, Riebeth added that Sharp did not lip-read with most people, though he could with Addie. She recalled that Sharp spoke freely "in a soft, careful monotone." See Riebeth, *J. H. Sharp among the Crow Indians*, 20–22, 137. Also, she noted that she did not believe that Sharp knew sign language, though she had observed Sharp interacting with "finger motions" with an Indian. Because the various Indian tribes spoke only their own language, they used sign language to communicate with others (see 19–20).

self-professed "Golden Age," when the former frontier town was known as the Queen of the West.[7] The city's nicknames quickly multiplied as it garnered national attention for its cultural and intellectual life. "Athens of the West," "Paris of America," and "London of America" signified the city's desire to promote civic pride and establish a cultural identity. Cultural institutions offered traditional art education and training, local artists established distinguished reputations, patrons built notable art collections, and art galleries opened.[8] Sharp took advantage of all this regional art center had to offer and would become the city's favorite son and chief ambassador.

The ambitious art student joined an outstanding group of contemporary Cincinnati painters, including Robert Frederick Blum, Kenyon Cox, Joseph Rodefer DeCamp, Frank Duveneck, Henry Farny, Elizabeth Nourse, Edward Potthast, Henry Ossawa Tanner, and John Twachtman. Duveneck led the Cincinnati art community with his emphasis on realism and life classes with nude models. In time, Duveneck [PLATE 1.1] became Sharp's mentor and friend. Eventually they traveled together and copied "old master" paintings in Europe. Their 1895 visit to the Prado led to Sharp's passion for Velazquez. His copies of the Spanish Baroque artist's works [PLATE 1.2] led to references to Velazquez in his later genre paintings and self-portraits.[9] Years later Sharp recalled their "pilgrimage to the shrine of Velazquez . . . which was of inestimable value."[10]

Sharp's study abroad was not unique but followed a pattern well established by aspiring American artists. Firsthand knowledge of the "great masters," study with contemporary leading masters, and rigorous academic training enhanced their skills and reputation. Sharp traveled to Europe three times, enrolling as a Cincinnati student in 1881–82 at the Royal Academy of Fine Arts Antwerp and in 1886–89 at Munich's Royal Academy of Fine Arts, and for a faculty study in 1894–96 at the Académie Julian and the Académie Colarossi in Paris.[11]

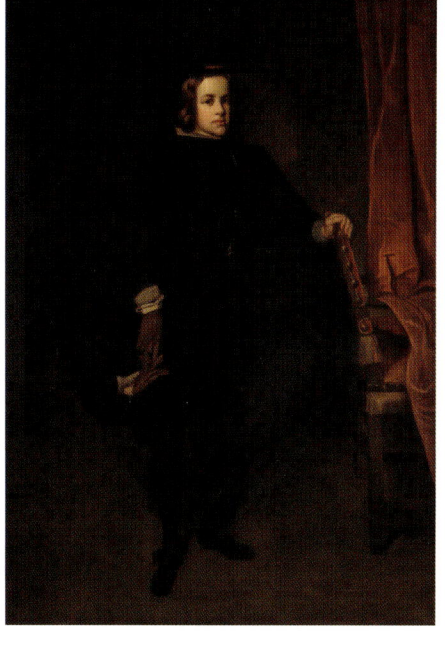

[PLATE 1.2]

JOSEPH HENRY SHARP

Study of Prince D. Baltasar Carlos by Diego Velázquez

ca. 1895, oil on canvas,
81 ⅝ x 46 ⅛ in.
New Mexico Museum of Art,
Santa Fe, New Mexico. Gift of
Joseph Henry Sharp before 1932.
2015.6

---

7 "Them Was the Days," *American Scene* 15 (Autumn 1974): 13. The name "Queen of the West" was popularized by Henry Wadsworth Longfellow's 1854 poem "Catawba Wine."

8 For a discussion of the history of the arts in Cincinnati, see Robert C. Vitz, *The Queen and the Arts: Cultural Life in Nineteenth-Century Cincinnati* (Kent, OH: Kent State University Press, 1989). Julie Aronson, ed., *The Cincinnati Wing: The Story of Art in the Queen City* (Athens: Ohio University Press, 2003), demonstrates with its ample illustrations the critical importance of this regional art center to American art.

9 While still in Europe, Sharp and Duveneck sent their "copies after Velazquez" to the Cincinnati Art Museum. The paintings arrived on October 21, 1895, and were hung in the museum on October 27, receiving high praise. The artists donated these paintings to the museum, but they were deaccessioned in 1945. "Among the Artists," *Cincinnati Enquirer*, October 21, 1895, p. 7; "Among the Artists," *Cincinnati Enquirer*, October 27, 1895, p. 8.

10 JHS to J. H. Gest, May 28, 1903, CAMA.

11 Sharp broke up his Munich studies, returning briefly to Cincinnati in mid-July 1887, then arriving in New York on the SS *Westernland*. He sailed again for Europe in late September to continue his studies in Munich. The manifest of the SS *Alaska*, manifest with the port of departure Liverpool, England/Queenstown, Ireland, records Sharp returning to New York on June 10, 1889.

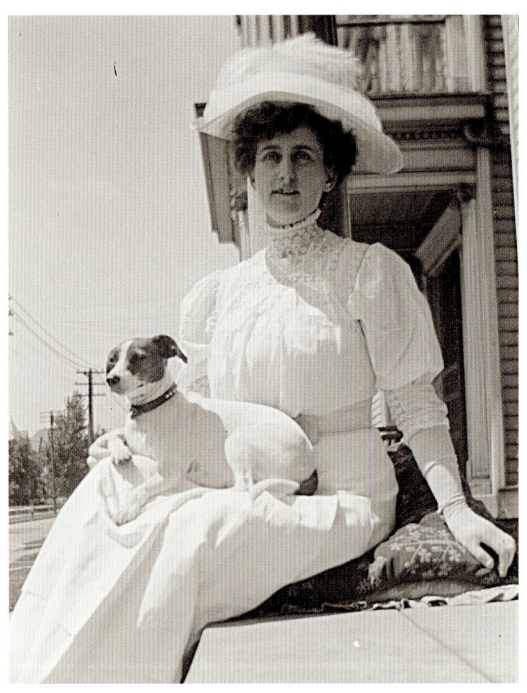

[PLATE 1.3]

JOSEPH HENRY SHARP

Addie in hat holding small dog

undated, photograph, b&w
C.M. Russell Museum,
Great Falls, Montana.
Gift of Robert Luhn

During the summer break of 1883 Sharp first traveled to the American West to paint Indian subjects, pursuing a childhood aspiration sparked by reading James Fenimore Cooper. Aware of the developing market for Indian subject matter and his colleague Henry Farny's recent success, Sharp sought his advice, but found he opposed the plan. In the end Farny provided information on Pueblo Indians and the Penitentes, an unsanctioned Catholic lay organization, clearly pointing Sharp toward the Southwest and far away from his own Plains Indian painting territory.[12] Just as the U.S. government carved up Indian lands, artists were divvying up Indian groups as subject matter. In persuading Sharp to search for new subjects in the Southwest, Farny inadvertently contributed to the founding of the Taos Society of Artists in 1915, the group of artists who would, along with Modernists who visited the region, reshape the national image of the Southwest.

Sharp made his way to Santa Fe, then on to Albuquerque, Tucson, California, and the Pacific Northwest. Under the headline "A Cincinnatian in California," the *Cincinnati Enquirer* wrote at length about "the talented young artist of this city," thus beginning of the paper's loyal support and chronicling of his lifelong western ventures.[13] Sharp established an early reputation in his hometown of Cincinnati. Impressed with the student's work habits, the local press applauded his "quick, keen air of a broker. He is always in a hurry, hustling wherever he is, and has nothing of the languid, procrastinating disposition generally attributed to artists."[14]

It was during the 1880s that Sharp also met his future wife, Addie Josephine Byram (1863–1913) [PLATE 1.3], who had undertaken serious study in Cincinnati and in Germany to become a concert pianist.[15] The couple married on June 16, 1892, in her hometown of Liberty, Indiana, and they honeymooned in Annisquam, Massachusetts. When they returned to Cincinnati in the fall, Sharp took a position as an instructor at what was by then called the Art Academy of Cincinnati and soon became a teacher popular with students.

---

12 Farny had been to the Southwest and had recently done work at Zuñi for illustrations in Frank Hamilton Cushing's 1883 series of three articles in *Century Magazine*.

13 "A Cincinnatian in California," *Cincinnati Enquirer*, September 9, 1883, p. 16. As early as 1878 (*Cincinnati Daily Gazette*, May 1878), the Cincinnati newspapers began to introduce Sharp's work to the community, a harbinger of the success he would achieve and sustain as a professional artist for the next seventy years.

14 Undated newspaper article, Research files from author's doctoral dissertation, 2000 (hereafter ADD). Addie chronicled her husband's career and their shared life in two scrapbooks that she filled with newspaper and journal clippings, social invitations and programs, photographs, and calling cards.

15 An 1892 Ironton news article wrote of Addie Byram, who was by then married to the hometown artist, as a "commanding person of excellent education, as most of her life has been passed in musical studies and she spent four years under the best masters in Germany." ADD.

The following summer the Sharps joined friend and fellow Cincinnati artist John Hauser in Santa Fe. Addie remained in Santa Fe while the two men explored the New Mexico Territory, but this was the last time she stayed behind until 1910 when illness prevented her from joining her husband. She became Sharp's constant companion and often acted as his spokesperson and interpreter. Occasionally during their travels she gave piano recitals at Indian boarding schools.[16]

Sharp and Hauser embarked on an arduous travel agenda, driving a bone-rattling buckboard to the northern New Mexico pueblos of Tesuque, Pojoaque, San Ildefonso, Santa Clara, San Juan, and Taos.[17] This exploration marked the beginning of Sharp's ardent affair with the Southwest that lasted until his death. As he long remembered the trip, he left Cincinnati as an emerging artist searching for his way and returned with a clear purpose, having found his niche. Much of what he saw and learned on this initial tour of Pueblo life and Penitente practices would be recalled in later compositions throughout his career and would lead to individual and institutional patronage.[18] The photographs that Sharp took among the southwestern Pueblos led to his first major artistic triumph, *The Harvest Dance* [SEE PLATE 2.2]. Composed from reference photographs, a technique he would employ throughout his career, the multifigure painting of dancers demonstrates a thorough understanding of the conventions taught in academy schools.

An October 1893 *Harper's Weekly* publication of Sharp's essay "The Pueblo Indian Dance," and his accompanying illustration *The Harvest Dance of the Pueblo Indians* from several months earlier, facilitated the artist's growing reputation, and the hometown newspapers continued their backing of the young artist. Under the headline "Return of the Adventurer from the Wilds of New Mexico—Strange Customs and Superstitions of a Neglected Corner of America," a *Times-Star* reporter saluted Sharp as an artist-explorer from the "land of the Comanche and Apache in the wilds of New Mexico in places where few white men have ever ventured."[19]

---

16 ADD.

17 According to Sharp's account, the artists were in residence at San Juan for a week, making sketches while "waiting for the big dance and feast that came off today." The dateline of July 10, however, does not correspond to feast days or dances at San Juan Pueblo. Tewa, Tiwa, and Keres feast days are saint's days in the Catholic calendar, so they do not move around like the ceremonies at Zuñi and Hopi. The artists could have seen a corn dance at San Juan Pueblo (today known as Ohkay Owingeh) on June 13 and 24, at San Ildefonso on July 25, at Taos on July 25 and 26, and Santa Clara on August 12. The article concluded that the artists "made engagements with several [Native Americans] to pose at Santa Fe this week." Before returning to Santa Fe, they traveled on to Taos Pueblo. Sharp, however, would be back in Cincinnati before San Geronimo Day, the annual feast day at Taos Pueblo celebrated on September 29–30.

18 The *Enquirer* reported that "Mr. Sharp brought home a large number of sketches. He has acquired a wonderfully real idea of the country and the natives. His sketches breathe the atmosphere of [New] Mexico. He has some large, very strong study heads and other sketches of Indians in every occupation of life." "Art and Artists," *Cincinnati Enquirer*, December 3, 1893, p. 20.

19 "An American Crucifixion: Return of the Adventurer from the Wilds of New Mexico—Strange Customs and Superstitions of a Neglected Corner of America," *Cincinnati Times-Star*, September 2, 1893, sec. 1, p. 7.

The newspaper portrayed Sharp as a heroic pioneer who left behind eastern comforts and security for hardships, unpredictability, danger, and gunplay, seeking the rewards of "picturesque" Indians and rugged landscapes. This was a self-image he persistently promoted throughout his career, sometimes tongue-in-cheek. In an 1893 article he told of sagebrush that would "thrive on a hot stove" and declared that one remained a tenderfoot in the Southwest "until he can eat cactus and shoot corns and stone bruises off with a forty-five caliber Colt's revolver."[20]

Newspaper caricatures also spoofed Sharp and his western travels. Although they hit the mark in their day, they strike readers today as racially offensive. One caricature, drawn by Sharp's friend and former student Joe Scheuerle, depicts the artist running for his life, easel and umbrella in hand, as a trio of stereotypical hostile Indians, clad in warbonnets and breechclouts, stomp on his palette. One shoots a pistol, another brandishes a tomahawk, while yet another wonderingly touches the wet paint on the palette [SEE PLATE 2.10]. The caption added humor for the era's readers: "Art Club members are hoping he will have his handsome scalp and luxurious whiskers when he returns [to Cincinnati]."[21] In fact, dispossessed Plains Indians lived peacefully on reservations, in relative poverty, yet the savage stereotype persisted and enhanced Sharp's tales of risking life and limb. In his paintings, however, the artist rarely depicted Native Americans with weapons or as hostile. In his portraiture and narrative works, the subjects are dignified human beings, loving family members, community members engaged in daily pursuit of work and leisure, and practitioners of religious rites, all with a culture of their own.

Among the reflections he shared with the press upon his return in 1893, Sharp predicted that the Southwest he had witnessed would disappear in five years. Aware of the profound cultural transformation the region was experiencing, he brought back as many Indian artifacts as he could pack to use in future paintings. Like an Old World explorer who had carried back exotic New World treasures to his royal patron, Sharp emptied his leather trunk to an utterly astonished reporter in his studio. The reporter delightedly enumerated the treasure chest's contents:

> "studies of Indian faces and dreary scenes of sage deserts and mountains. A hundred photographs covertly taken were scattered about, while war bonnets, dance bonnets, peace pipes, saddles, boots and spurs, pistols and guns, bows and arrows and quivers, buckskin dresses and long-fringed leggings, moccasins and war clubs, turquoise beads and bright bone necklaces, purses woven of porcupine quills, gaily colored and solid silver armlets and rings were tumbled about."[22]

When some of these curios appeared in one of Sharp's subsequent shows, a

---

20 J. H. Sharp, "At the Pueblo Games: An Artist's Experienced in New Mexico; Life among the People," *Cincinnati Tribune*, July 14, 1893, p. 4:4.

21 ADD.

22 "An American Crucifixion."

critic remarked that the inclusion of Indian artifacts significantly contributed to the exhibition's success.[23] Sharp's collection of authentic Southwestern Indian objects evoked a whole and complete culture for the eastern audience while masking the complexities of contemporary Native life.

In *The Virginian* (1902), Owen Wister refers to such collections of objects as "trophies of the frontier."[24] Sharp acquired artifacts by purchase and trade, and these fragments of a conquered culture aestheticized cultural difference for hometown consumption. Nonetheless, Sharp became a knowledgeable collector of Indian objects, and his enthusiasm reflected an appreciation of the artistic skills of Native peoples whom he regarded as the "real old masters."[25] Whatever case may be made for Sharp's acquisitiveness and the effects of his selection, he was still an artist with pragmatic needs. Color, texture, form—these and other artistic aspects of the items he found motivated his critical eye in acquisition. Many objects that he put to practical use became signature features in his repertoire, but such use inevitably provided misleading information when they were deployed as studio props in fabricated pictorial settings.

In contrast to the sensationalism of local newspaper articles, Sharp wrote an informative article for *Harper's* in which he described a Pueblo corn dance. An armchair traveler could experience a religious ceremony and "a striking scene of gorgeous color" encompassing the intriguing dress of the participants and the "rhythmic chanting" and "monotonous thump-thumping of the drum."[26] Although Sharp could not hear the music, he felt the vibrations of the drums and could distinguish some low sounds.[27] As a result of his deafness Sharp was an acute observer who would have

23 ADD.

24 Owen Wister, *The Virginian* (New York: Penguin Books, 1988), 249. Objects taken from massacres (e.g., Sand Creek) and battlefields, including grisly human parts, might be seen as trophies, and they were publicly paraded as such (objects from Sand Creek in Denver). Also, at establishments like Jake Gold's Old Curio Shop in Santa Fe, objects were made for sale in the souvenir market at that time. Jonathan Batkin, "Tourism Is Overrated: Pueblo Pottery and the Early Curio Trade, 1880–1910," in *Unpacking Culture: Art and Commodity in Colonial and Postcolonial Worlds*, ed. Ruth B. Phillips and Christopher B. Steiner (Berkeley: University of California Press, 1999), 286–92.

25 JHS to Butler, September 28, 1925, Joseph G. Butler Papers, Butler Institute of American Art, Youngstown, OH (hereafter BP).

26 J. H. Sharp, "The Harvest Dance of the Pueblo Indians of New Mexico," *Harper's Weekly* 37 (October 14, 1893): 981–83. This title should be "The Pueblo Indian Dance." Less than a year later, Sharp penned another brief article for *Harper's* with an accompanying illustration: J. H. Sharp, "The Pueblo Turquoise Driller," *Harper's Weekly* 38 (June 9, 1894): 549. The illustration, *The Turquoise Driller*, is a work scene. Seated on a blanket with a rudimentary stick drill by his side, a young Pueblo man intently inspects a stone. Leah Dilworth writes that the Pueblo turquoise drillers were among the most common images in southwestern tourist publications. Dilworth, *Imagining Indians in the Southwest: Persistent Visions of a Primitive Past* (Washington, DC: Smithsonian Institution Press, 1996), 141. The texts and the accompanying illustrations represented aspects of Pueblo life that Sharp observed. These images of Southwestern Indian crafts and dance performances also reflected the developing tourist market, which equated primitivism with authenticity.

27 Sharp told Riebeth that he could not hear the "big bass drum at Indian dances, nor the native dance drums that it accompanied," though he could feel the reverberations. Riebeth, *J. H. Sharp among the Crow Indians*, 19.

been more attuned to body movement.[28] With the dance freed of its musical component, he translated the pure movement and grace onto his canvas. Witnessing unspecified "religious festivities of the Pueblos," Sharp became captivated with Native dance, which would become an integral part of his stock in trade.

In spite of their photographic sources, *The Harvest Dance* and the *Harper's* illustration are pastiches.[29] Here Sharp sought to capture the spirit of the dance, valuing emotional impact more than detailed accuracy. In contrast to his portraits of individuals, in large compositions he constructed a generic event, not an ethnological document. These dance images emphasize the figures; their settings could be any of the Tewa Pueblos he visited. In the full-color oil, Sharp added high-profile buildings not only to strengthen the composition but possibly to make the setting look like Taos. No other Pueblo has such tall structures.[30] The adobe buildings frame a public religious spectacle that is central to the Pueblos' social cohesion.

The Harvest Dance created a sensation at the Cincinnati Art Club's Fourth Annual Exhibition in May 1894.[31] Nearly two thousand people attended the opening-night gala at the Cincinnati Art Museum. Critics compared the event to "first nights" in London and Paris, believing they had witnessed an American artistic renaissance. Newspapers urged the museum to acquire *The Harvest Dance*:

> "If this remarkable picture, the only one of its kind ever painted by a Cincinnati artist, is not sold here at home, it will undoubtedly find a sale in Paris, where paintings characteristic of Western life are always eagerly sought."[32]

Undoubtedly the journalist knew of Sharp's imminent two-year faculty leave to study in Paris.[33] At the exhibition's end, the Cincinnati Art Museum

---

28 When living at Crow Agency, Addie Sharp responded to Carolyn Reynolds's dismay that Sharp could not hear her playing the piano, "Oh, but he likes to watch my hands." Riebeth, *J. H. Sharp among the Crow Indians*, 56.

29 In the article "The Pueblo Indian Dance," Sharp wrote that his illustration "represents the Corn or Harvest Dance." The summer dances are not necessarily harvest dances in the literal sense, as some happen before crops are ripe. They are, however, corn dances. Nevertheless "Harvest Dance" is not a completely unreasonable title, and perhaps more marketable than "Corn Dance."

30 In looking at both versions of *The Harvest Dance*, it may be too easy to get hung up on Sharp the "ethnographer" and forget Sharp the savvy artist. After all, the choice of Taos as setting may itself have been a factor in marketing. The uniqueness and recognizability of the north building complex is a clue for any viewer who has visited Taos Pueblo that lets them feel that they're a part of the scene—insiders, as it were.

31 "At the Art Museum," *Cincinnati Times-Star*, May 17, 1894; "High Art," *Cincinnati Enquirer*, May 18, 1894, p. 5; "The Art Club Exhibition," *Cincinnati Commercial Gazette*, May 20, 1894.

32 "High Art Exhibition by Home Artists," *Cincinnati Times-Star*, undated, ADD.

33 Shortly before Sharp's departure to the Southwest for the summer, the *Cincinnati Enquirer* announced that the Art Academy of Cincinnati had awarded him a two-year faculty leave to study in Paris, beginning at the end of the following school year. "In the Art World," *Cincinnati Enquirer*, May 18, 1893, p. 6. Sharp's faculty study in 1894 was the last awarded by the school, as the Panic of 1893 ushered in a national economic depression affecting local operating budgets. The collapse of the Philadelphia and Reading Railroad and the National Cordage Company, two of the country's largest employers, rippled out to the rest of the economy, closing more than 15,000 businesses. Ohioans were hit particularly hard in this economic crisis, with 50 percent unemployment among industrial workers. The depression ended in 1897.

trustees purchased the painting, in part to encourage local artists.[34] Sharp was working hard to establish himself in the art world with a major canvas and a new subject, and the museum purchase was solid validation of his efforts. As one wag wrote, "Once in a long while a prophet is honored in his own country, even in Cincinnati."[35] On July 28, 1894, Sharp, Addie, and her sister Louise Byram sailed on the *Maasdam* for Antwerp.[36]

Sharp had made his way to Paris by December.[37] There Sharp met fellow Cincinnati faculty member and sculptor Clement Barnhorn. Three Cincinnati Art Academy alumnae, Elizabeth Nourse, Willie Betty Newman, and Eudora (Dollie) Hereford, had also made their way to Paris to study and exhibit their work. Of the seven thousand Americans then living in Paris, one in seven were artists, including this Cincinnati circle. In the late nineteenth century, Paris was the undisputed art capital, the place to make one's reputation, where artists aspired to show in the Salon.[38] Within this arena of fierce competition, Sharp saw three of his works hanging in the 1896 Salon alongside the best contemporary French art of the time.[39] That year Sharp regaled fellow Julian academy students Ernest Blumenschein (1874–1960) and Bert Phillips (1868–1956) with stories of his earlier travels to Taos and the painting opportunities that awaited artists there. Four years later, Blumenschein and Phillips followed Sharp's advice, and in due course their adventures led to the development of an art colony in Taos.

After two years of European study, the Sharps steamed into New York harbor on the SS *City of Rome* on August 31, 1896. Stowed in the

---

34 "The Art Museum," *Cincinnati Commercial Gazette*, March 1, 1894.

35 A group of Cincinnati businessmen bought Edward Potthast's *Dutch Interior* for the museum at the conclusion of the exhibition. See "The Dutch Interior," *Cincinnati Commercial Gazette*, June 3, 1894. The article "Street Talk" in the Enquirer pronounced Potthast's painting "more representative of the growth of art in the city than Sharp's." Possibly the newspaper may have been stirring up a story. Of course, it is conceivable that some trustees didn't care for *Harvest Dance*, and the paper ran with that.

36 Addie Sharp studied French while abroad. Byram continued her voice studies. The *Cincinnati Enquirer*, on February 16, 1896 (p. 18), reported under the heading "Music," that "Miss Louise Byram, of Liberty, Ind, who will be remembered as a vocal student in this city a few years ago, is completing a finished education abroad. She has been studying under Mme. Forster at Prague. Several of the Austrian art critics have named her 'The Little Patti.'" Also, in Addie's scrapbook, an unidentified 1896 news clipping reported that Byram was in vocal training in Vienna. Riebeth remarked that Byram not only spoke German well, but dreamed in the language. See Riebeth, *J. H. Sharp among the Crow Indians*, 59.

37 Judging from a sketch dated August 29, 1894, Sharp must have met Duveneck and a group of expatriates from his art school in the fishing village of Chioggia, near Venice, shortly after his arrival in Europe. Working *en plein air*, in an ambiance so different from home, Sharp joined the long lineage of artists interpreting the Venetian light reflecting off the water and canals and onto the colors of fishing boats, markets, and streets. He fell seriously ill in Chioggia, however, and was counseled to postpone study at the Académie Julian. Not heeding that advice, he made his way to Paris by December. The date of Sharp's arrival there is unconfirmed. J. H. Gest to Clement Barnhorn, October 20 or 30 (day unclear), 1894; J. H. Gest to JHS, November 6, 1894, both in CAMA; "Art and Artists," *Cincinnati Enquirer*, November 11, 1894, p. 19.

38 See Kathleen Adler, Erica E. Hirshler, and H. Barbara Weinberg, *Americans in Paris, 1860–1900*, video (London: National Gallery, 2006); David McCullough, *The Greater Journey: Americans in Paris* (New York: Simon and Schuster, 2012).

39 The Salon that year accepted the oils *Devant St. Antoine* and *Portrait de Mme S* and the pastel *La paresseuse*.

cargo hold was *Devant St. Antoine* (1895; private collection) (*Study for Devant St. Antoine* [PLATE 1.4]), along with other paintings, sketches, and collected objects. *Devant St. Antoine's* celebrity preceded her arrival with critical notice in the press. The Salon-exhibited life-size nude was proof of Sharp's international critical acceptance. Unequivocally, the painting demonstrated Sharp's devotion to craft, technical virtuosity, and mastery of the human figure. He could now add "academic painter par excellence" to his credentials. Avant-garde movements, however, had begun to undercut the academy's dominance, and a new aesthetic was beginning to replace traditional, academic values. For a while, Sharp experimented with a variety of styles, media, and subject matter. But by the turn of the twentieth century, he knew who he was as an artist and where he was headed. For the next forty-five years, Sharp proved himself again and again an academic artist, and showed that he and his art were relevant.

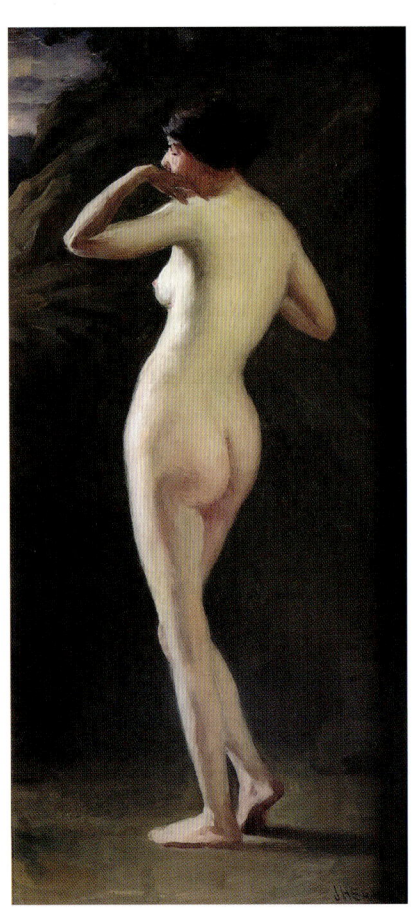

Once home, Sharp did not bask long in the critical accolades. According to the press, the first thing the artist did was to go to the zoo to see the Sicangu Sioux from the Rosebud Reservation who had contracted to perform dances and cultural shows there.[40] Ready to pick up where he had left off in 1893, Sharp resumed a frenetic pace of teaching, portrait commissions, and Art Club activities, and pursued an intense exhibition schedule, with showings in his studio, the Cincinnati Art Museum, the Art Institute of Chicago, the Society of Western Artists, the Carnegie Institute, and a juried selection of work for the forthcoming Tennessee centennial.

On June 16 the Sharps left for Taos and added Colorado to their travel plans, inching closer to Farny's painting territory. Whereas Farny need not have feared competition from Sharp ten years before, now was a different story. The Cincinnati papers kept Sharp's name in the news, reporting on his journey and interviewing him upon his return. They were thrilled by his portraits and landscape sketches, intended, he said, "mostly as studies in the working up of more elaborate paintings of Indian life in the west."[41]

Two days before fall classes began on September 13, the Sharps returned to Cincinnati, with the artist scheduled to teach a life class for women students only. A month later the Society of Western Artists selected four of his summer paintings, all of which displayed the rigor of his classical training.[42] Critics, along with the museum-going public, singled out the "startling" nocturne *The Lament for the Dead* (1897)

---

40 "Art Notes," in ADD.

41 "Artist Henry Sharp Home from New Mexico with a Fine Collection of Sketches," *Ironton Register*, 1897; "Doings in the Realm of Art," *Cincinnati Enquirer*, August 29, 1897; *Cincinnati Enquirer*, September 19, 1897, p. 20.

42 Also shown at the exhibition were *Do-ree-tah, Pueblo Indian Maid, A Taos Mountain Buck*, and *John, of Taos*.

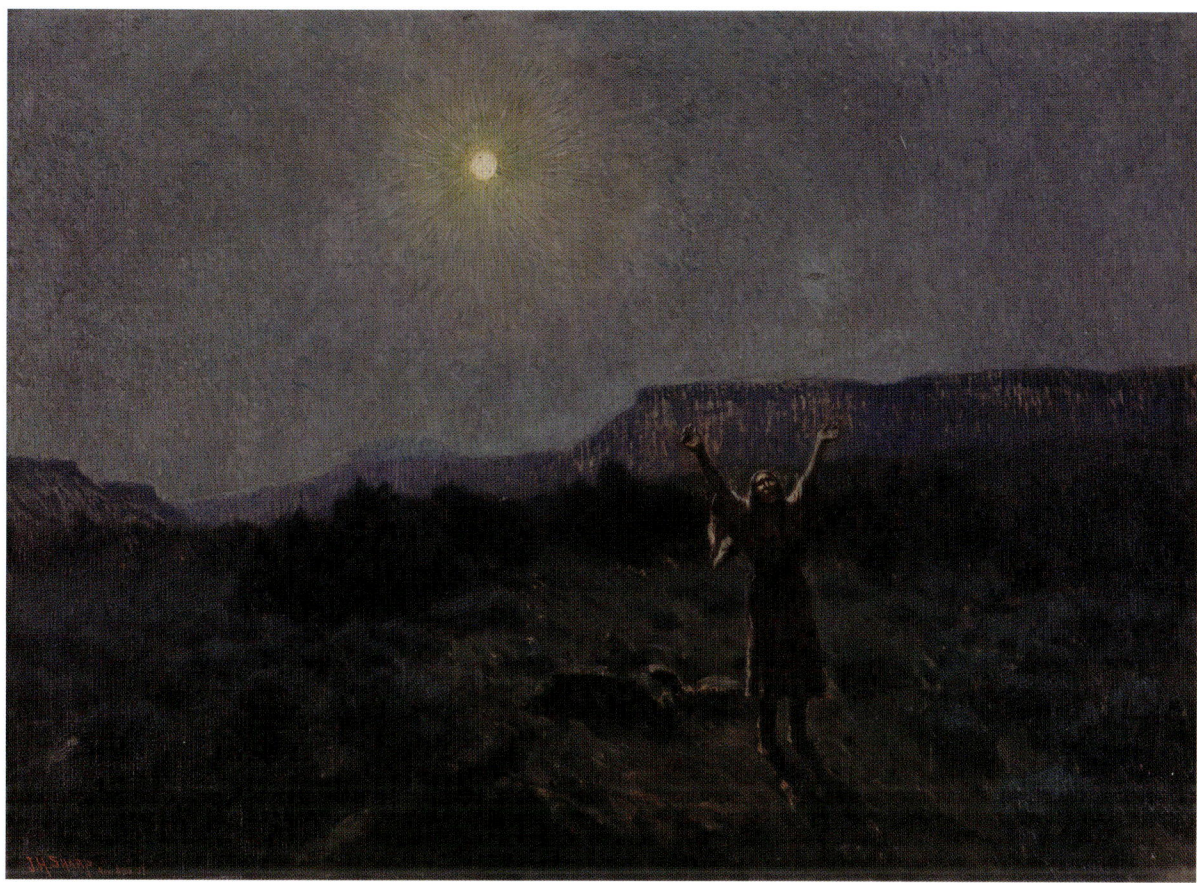

[PLATE 1.5]

JOSEPH HENRY SHARP

The Lament for the Dead

1897, oil on canvas,
33 ¼ x 47 ⁵⁄₁₆ in.
Cincinnati Art Museum,
Cincinnati, Ohio. X1939.133

[PLATE 1.5], which marked a shift from Sharp's previous, sparkling, sunlit southwestern compositions. With Post-Impressionist broken color and short brushstrokes Sharp created "the mysterious feeling" of a "weird moonlight scene . . . that tells a peculiarly pathetic story" of the mourning ritual practiced by a frantic, grieving widow who "wanders over the plain at night."[43] This critical acclaim marked the beginning of Sharp's nocturnes and burial motifs. The "vanishing Indian" trope is ubiquitous in American cultural history, as is the grieving widow.[44] This imagery in part reflected contemporary Anglo-American cultural practice of a strict, public mourning etiquette in which women were regarded as "true vessels of grief."[45]

In addition to showing oils, pastels, and watercolors, Sharp added monotypes to the year's artistic output. He exhibited a collection of sixty such works at Cincinnati's Traxel and Maas Gallery in December 1897

---

43 ADD.

44 Brian Dippie, *The Vanishing American: White Attitudes and U.S. Indian Policy* (Lawrence: University Press of Kansas, 1991). Examples of grieving Indian widows include Joseph Wright's *Indian Widow* (1784), Karl Bodmer's *Burial Ground of the Mandans*, and John Mix Stanley's *Chinook Burial Grounds*.

45 The classic example of the grieving widow is David's *Andromache Mourning Hector*, which Sharp would have encountered as a student in Paris. Maureen DeLorme, *Mourning Art and Jewelry* (Atglen, PA: Schiffer, 2004), 51. See also Briony D. Zlomke, "Death Became Them: The Defeminization of the American Death Culture, 1609–1899," PhD dissertation, University of Nebraska–Lincoln, 2013; Bernadette Loeffel Atkins, *Widow's Weeds and Weeping Veils: Mourning Rituals in 19th Century America* (Gettysburg, PA.: B. L. Atkins, 2002).

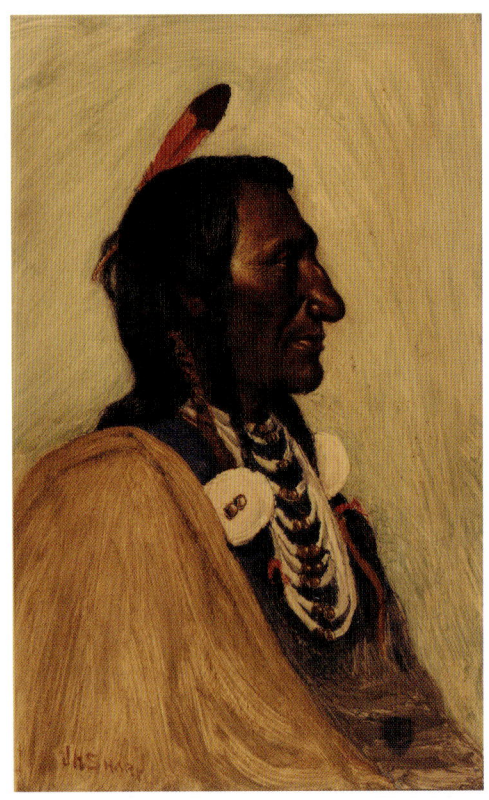

[PLATE 1.6].[46] The art of the monotype resurged among American artists in the late nineteenth century, and Sharp devoted substantial effort to the medium. He was "one of the most indefatigable workers of this monotype field of late," according to a Cincinnati paper in 1897.[47]

Besides participating in jovial informal evening gatherings for creating monotypes with other members of the Cincinnati Art Club, Sharp exhibited monotypes in art galleries, museums, and art societies from 1897 to 1902. Attuned to the medium's current popularity and its potential for commercial and aesthetic possibilities, he showed these works in both urban and rural venues from the East to the West, receiving much critical attention for them.[48] In Denver, fellow artist, friend, and affluent community leader Blanche Dougan Cole called Sharp the "best monotypist" in America and arranged a popular showing of his monotypes, the first exhibited in the city.[49] Sharp, too, reached out to friend and Cincinnati colleague Henry Ossawa Tanner (1859–1937), the African American painter then living in Paris, to help find a dealer to manage his monotypes in the European market.[50] Sharp was as tireless in promoting and selling his art as he was creating it.

After another demanding year of departmental administrative and teaching responsibilities, private commissions, exhibition venues, business trips to the East Coast to visit the offices of *Century Magazine* and Copley Print Company, the Sharps departed for summer work in Taos in June 1898, in a much better mood than the previous summer. "Come out & have some bacon, canned tomatoes & tea with us!" Sharp wrote Gest, inviting him to partake in their rugged, less sophisticated western life.[51] The local Cincinnati newspapers continued their support of Sharp, stretching the truth in referring

---

46 In the exhibition catalogue, the gallery announced that "Mr. J. H. Sharp has completed a series of Monotypes, illustrative of Indian Character and Life, based upon his studies in the far West during several years. The subjects embrace Heads, Figures, and Landscapes."

47 "Sharp's Monotypes of Indian Life and Character," in ADD.

48 As early as 1897, Sharp owned a monotype press. A few months after the successful Traxel & Maas exhibition, the artist traveled to New York and Boston to market his monotypes with the prestigious *Century Magazine* and Copley Print Company, respectively. Along with his Indian works, Sharp included European landscapes and seascapes from his studies abroad.

49 *Denver Daily News*, undated, ADD. Sharp was pleased with his critical reception and the sale of more than twenty monotypes in Denver. Cole—like Addie, an Indianan—moved to Denver and maintained a social and working friendship with the Sharps for many years. Los Angeles became her permanent residence in 1903.

50 Henry Ossawa Tanner, Jerusalem, Olivet House, to JHS, January 29, 1899, ADD.

51 JHS to J. H. Gest, June 7, 1898, CAMA. On their way to Taos, the Sharps stopped in Omaha, Nebraska, to deliver the genre painting *Rainy Day* for the Trans-Mississippi and International Exposition, where the Indian Congress and Buffalo Bill's Wild West were appearing. The Omaha World's Fair ran from June 1 to November 1, 1898. It seems an unusual marketing decision for Sharp to show *Rainy Day*, rather than a work with Indian subject matter, as midwesterners would have connected more personally with the latter imagery than an eastern audience would have. Perhaps Sharp still hadn't determined his artist's voice and thought Indian paintings alone were too risky an undertaking.

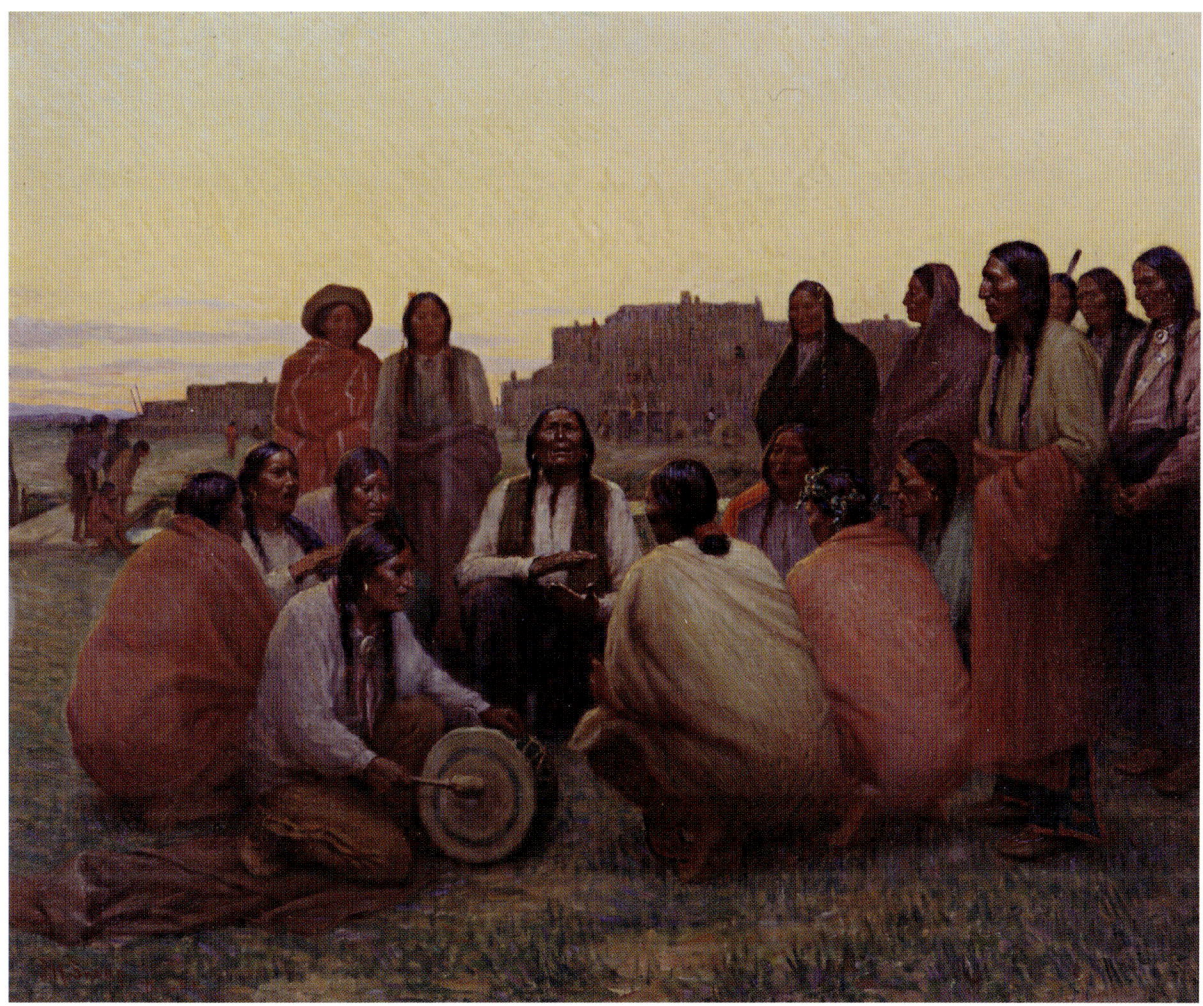

to his summer journey as an "annual trip" to Taos, and they continued shaping a unique artistic identity for him in the West and among Indians.[52] Returning to Cincinnati with a burgeoning portfolio, Sharp missed the fateful arrival of Phillips and Blumenschein in Taos by days. After returning home, Sharp completed *The Evening Chant* [PLATE 1.7], his next major success.

According to the *Cincinnati Enquirer*, the first view of the "large masterpiece" was a private showing in February 1899 in Sharp's studio for the Woman's Club, a formidable force in the local art scene. More than seventy women attended the opening.[53] From there, *The Evening Chant* traveled the Society of Western Artists' circuit, to much acclaim. It appeared as the frontispiece with Sharp's accompanying essay "The Chant" in the March *Brush and Pencil* journal. Sharp had launched his career as one of the premier painters of American Indians.

[PLATE 1.7]

JOSEPH HENRY SHARP

The Evening Chant

ca. 1899, oil on canvas,
29 x 36 in.
Courtesy of the Phoebe A. Hearst
Museum of Anthropology and
the Regents of the University of
California, Berkeley, California.
17-671

---

52 J. H. Sharp, "An Artist among the Indians," *Brush and Pencil* 4, no.1 (April 1899): 2. Several months after the news article, Sharp wrote that his first travels to the Indians of the Southwest was in 1893 and that he continued to spend three to four months each summer with them, which was also misleading.

53 "Reception," *Cincinnati Enquirer*, February 19, 1899, p. 32. According to the article, Sharp had just completed "The Chant," which he had worked on intermittently during the previous two years. Other "Indian pictures" were also displayed.

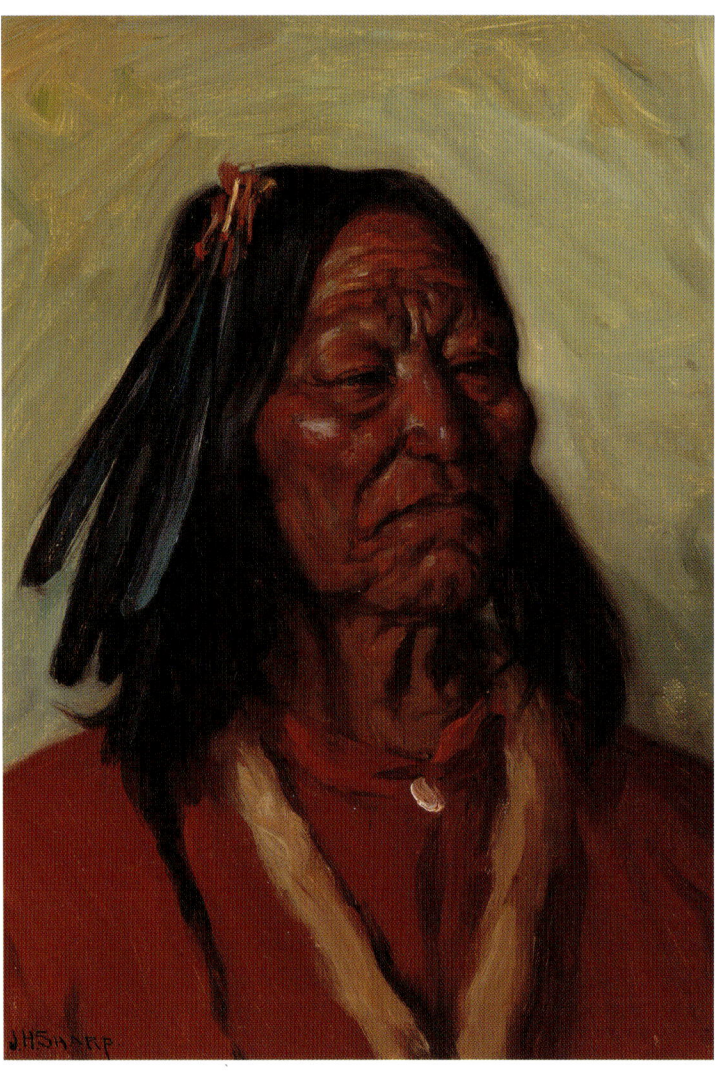

[PLATE 1.8]

JOSEPH HENRY SHARP

Bull Thigh, Cheyenne

ca. 1905, oil on canvas,
16 ⅝ x 12 ¾ in.
Gilcrease Museum, Tulsa,
Oklahoma. Gift of the Thomas
Gilcrease Foundation, 1955.
0136.506

When Sharp's 1899 summer break rolled around, he made a life-changing decision: he turned north. The local media promptly took notice that Sharp had gone to the plains. "Until very recently few painters had the temerity to invade this field so distinctly for years Farny's own," one reporter wrote, perhaps anticipating a row or hoping to create one.[54] A decade later, Sharp explained that through his firsthand western observations, he became aware of the "longevity of the southwestern Indian. I found that his northern prototype would soon become extinct and I decided to put into my canvases representations of their present day and time. I went north because I realized that Taos would last longer."[55] He echoed his predecessor George Catlin's (1796–1872) obsession captured in the expression "If I do not paint them no one ever will."[56] Making documentation of the disappearing Plains culture an artistic mission, Sharp set out to paint as many portraits as he could. He also painted Plains Indians customs, ceremonies, and costumes in ways that met with anthropological approval, as these paintings also found their way into anthropology exhibitions and collections. The newspapers narrated the Sharps' summer journey "among the Indians in Montana and Dakota, where their time was divided between the Crows, Northern Cheyennes and Sioux."[57] Sharp closed out the century with the usual art classes, commissions, and exhibition venues.

This work attracted the attention of one of his most ambitious collectors of that time, Joseph G. Butler Jr. When the Youngstown, Ohio, industrialist and philanthropist purchased a portrait of Oglala Fire for seventy-five dollars [SEE PLATE 2.1], the transaction marked the beginning of twenty-seven years of patronage and comradeship. A lay historian and collector of American art and memorabilia, Butler had begun acquiring Indian portraits for their historical value. He intended his Indian Gallery to serve as an enduring tribute to the "vanishing American," a distinctively

54 ADD.
55 Jon de Lack, "J. Henry Sharp-Painter of Indians," *Society*, November 6, 1913, p. 11.
56 "Babcock," 1920, CAMA.
57 "For Woman's Eye," *Cincinnati Enquirer*, September 24, 1899, p. 36.

American concern at the time. By 1906 Butler had acquired from Sharp forty oil portraits and one oil sketch of a Crow camp.

Sharp rang in the new year in 1900 with impressive new patronage and opportunities. The entrepreneur and philanthropist Andrew Carnegie purchased *Spotted Bird Who Sings* (ca. 1900; location unknown). Butler bought seven more portraits in January, adding another three in October. Other business magnates soon added other Sharp portraits to their collections. The National Jury for the Paris World's Fair accepted *Bull Thigh, Cheyenne* [PLATE 1.8]. Ethnologist Alice Fletcher, who spoke on "Indian story and song" at the Folklore Society in Cincinnati, began a friendship with the Sharps that would lead to prominent patronage from the Smithsonian Institution and from feminist and philanthropist Phoebe Apperson Hearst. Sharp's streak of success continued as he and Addie made their way to Crow Agency and Pine Ridge, South Dakota, for the summer.

Drawing on his staggering output during the past summers in the West, Sharp opened an exhibition of eighty-five Indian paintings in the Cincinnati Art Museum on October 7, 1900, scheduled to travel to Detroit and St. Louis. Concurrently, Pittsburgh hosted a smaller exhibition of his works that the artist coordinated to show later in Philadelphia. When it seemed his exhibition schedule could not be more demanding, the Cosmos Club invited him to show at its exclusive scientific and social men's club in Washington, DC. Soon after that, Dr. A. L. Benedict, director of the Ethnology Building of the forthcoming Pan-American Exposition in Buffalo, contacted Sharp to exhibit his paintings there.

The Cosmos Club showcased ninety-three portraits in December 1900, the largest collection of Indian portraits seen in Washington, DC, since John Mix Stanley's Indian Gallery in 1851.[58] This venue introduced Sharp to a network of anthropologists with whom he interacted throughout the rest of his career. A prominent club member, William Henry Holmes, an artist, geologist, anthropologist, archaeologist, and museum director, was then head curator of the Department of Anthropology at the United States National Museum. He purchased eleven portraits for the Smithsonian Institution.[59] The Smithsonian bestowed authority on Sharp's paintings as ethnological documents. The Washington press praised them, with some newspapers advocating purchase of the entire collection for its ethological value. "The artist has chosen for his subjects some of the finest types of the aboriginal American," the *Post* observed, "and his work is notable for the character in his faces, not necessarily noble, but full of strength and individuality."[60] A *Washington Star* critic concurred that the paintings were "very attractive to

---

58 Catlin exhibited his Indian Gallery in 1837.

59 Holmes selected three Cheyenne portraits (*Little Wolf the Younger*, *Yellow Wings*, and *Strong Left Hand*); four Sioux (*Wolf Ear*, *Chief Spotted Elk*, *Hand*, and *Two Dogs*); two Pueblo (*Do-ree-tah* and *Running Horse*); and two Crow (*White Swan* and *Chief Two Leggings*).

60 "Portraits of Indians: Notable Works of J. H. Sharp on Exhibition at Cosmos Club," *Washington Post*, December 18, 1900, ADD.

scientist and artist alike, as well as all lovers of Indian life and character."[61]

Before the ink had dried on the Smithsonian's acquisition, Sharp wrote to Gest, "What do you think about my getting all I can ('ad') out of the sale to U.S.?"[62] He realized it was not enough to be an artist, but that he needed to promote his art as well. Little did he realize when writing to Gest, however, that the Smithsonian's acquisition would be cited in virtually every article, essay, and book written about him. In 1907, as Sharp was holding a second Smithsonian show, news headlines referred to him as "Uncle Sam's official painter of Indians."[63] Four years later, Holmes wrote to Sharp that "I regard you as among the first, if not the very first painter of Indian portraits in the country."[64] Sharp never forgot the importance of this first institutional benefactor. "That purchase started my reputation," he wrote in gratitude in 1948.[65]

Exactly one year after Sharp's big break in DC, a show-stopper headline appeared in the *Cincinnati Enquirer*: "Fortune Comes with Fame." Phoebe Hearst had finalized "a deal" that would "agitate art circles."[66] The philanthropist had purchased a selection of Sharp's paintings, some shown at the Pan-American Exposition and others from his studio, for the anthropology department she had helped to found at the University of California. *Evening Chant* she kept for herself to hang over her desk in the *San Francisco Examiner* building.[67] She proceeded to make a five-year contract with Sharp, agreeing to buy fifteen paintings per year, and established what would turn out to be a warm friendship with the Sharps. Hearst's initial acts of patronage became pivotal in Sharp's career, allowing him financial freedom and securing his recognition as the principal turn-of-the-century painter of American Indians.[68] At the end of the spring 1903 term, Sharp submitted his letter of resignation to the Cincinnati Art Academy, and Crow Agency became the Sharps' permanent address.[69] The Sharps lived at the Server Hotel until they completed their cabin, "Absarokee Hut," in November 1905. Cincinnati, however, remained an umbilical cord of patronage, exhibitions, art supplies, and friendships.

61 "Art Notes," *Washington Star*, December 22, 1900, ADD.

62 JHS, Cincinnati, to J. H. Gest, January 16, 1901, CAMA. Sharp well knew the prestige, power, and influence of the Smithsonian, as several years later he asked Holmes if he would write "a letter appreciating the value of such a work, with some sort of idea of your knowledge and appreciation of my work to artistic and ethnological value etc. it might be of great aid. I will promise it will in no way be used in any sort of an illegitimate 'ad.'"

63 "Uncle Sam's Official Painter of Indians," 3 Jan 1907, *Leslie's Weekly*; "Examples of Indian and Western Paintings," Pasadena, CA, clipping, n.d., both in ADD.

64 W. H. Holmes to JHS, January 3, 1911, Joseph Henry Sharp, Curatorial Files, National Museum of American Art, Smithsonian Institution, Washington, DC.

65 JHS to Dr. John Ewers, August 8, 1948 Joseph Henry Sharp, Curatorial Files, National Museum of American Art, Smithsonian Institution, Washington, DC.

66 "Fortune Comes with Fame," *Cincinnati Enquirer*, December 11, 1901, ADD. Today we use agitate in a negatively charged manner; the writer here meant "excite."

67 Hearst also kept *The Great Sleep* and later donated both paintings to Berkeley's Anthropology Department. *Grave in a Cotton Wood Tree* is also part of the Berkeley collection and may have originally been placed in Hearst's private gallery.

68 "A Successful Artist," ADD.

69 Sharp's letter of official resignation to J. H. Gest, May 28, 1903, CAMA.

The Sharps continued to be habitués of Crow Agency in the fall and early winter, as "the North [is] too green to paint" in the summer, Sharp wrote.[70] Pasadena, where family members resided, was their home in late winter and early spring, and they went to Taos in the summer. There were always side trips along the route, especially the Grand Canyon, where Sharp painted alongside countless other artists drawn to rendering its grandeur and availing themselves of its lucrative sales potential. "Old Thomas Moran was often there," he fondly recalled in 1949 to a couple that had just purchased one of his small Grand Canyon landscapes, "and we used to hustle—fascinating to try to paint."[71]

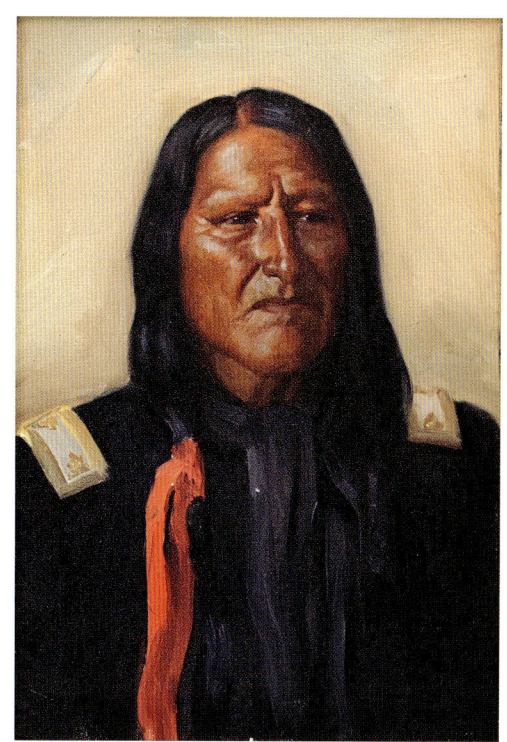

Of Sharp's painting locales, Crow Agency is the one that most enhanced his reputation as an "Indian painter." Crow Agency served as a home base from which to seek out the surviving warriors in the neighboring Indian agencies of the Blackfeet, Sioux, Cheyennes, Shoshones, and Arapahos. This meant traveling by stage or wagon 50 to 150 miles to remote places where he, often joined by Addie, would spend weeks at a time. Determined to paint as many Plains Indians as he could, he declared that he would paint all the "old fighters" whom death didn't take first.[72] Eventually Sharp painted more than two hundred men who had fought in the Battle of the Little Big Horn [PLATE 1.9]. Many of the half-length portraits, designed to emphasize the models' physiognomy and dress, included on the canvases' backing detailed biographical anecdotes about the sitters. The reviewer for the *Cincinnati Observer* recognized the individuality of Sharp's portraits: "In his work Mr. Sharp occupies a field alone. He went out among the Indians themselves, and painted not incidents or types, but individuals."[73]

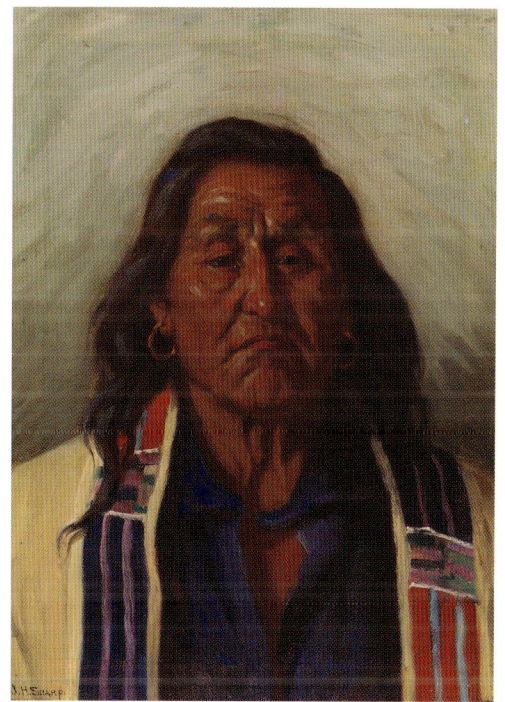

Sharp's models, too, turned a critical eye on his portraits. Crow chief Deaf Bull, among others, had the final word on their authenticity. As Sharp recounted: "I hung all my Indian portraits around the walls—Deaf Bull happened in, went around,—stopped rather defiantly a bit, in front of each one—finally came to his own portrait, looked at it a bit pointing his finger at it, said, 'there is the only real Indian in the lot, the rest are cowards'; turned and stalked out."[74]

---

70 JHS, Sheridan, WY, to Scheuerle, April 15, 1909, AAA.

71 JHS, Sheridan, WY, to Scheuerle, April 15, 1909, AAA.

72 JHS, Santa Fe, NM, to Butler, March 14, 1904, BP.

73 *Cincinnati Observer*, November 9, 1901, ADD.

74 JHS notes from photocopies, n.d., Joseph Henry Sharp Collection, Gilcrease Museum Library and Archives, University of Tulsa, Tulsa, OK.

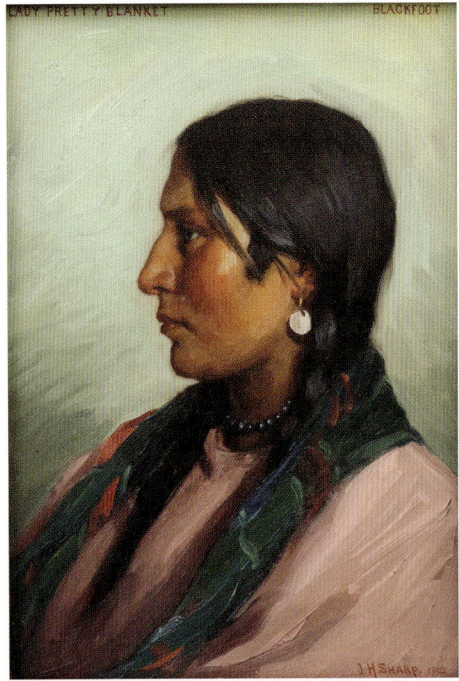

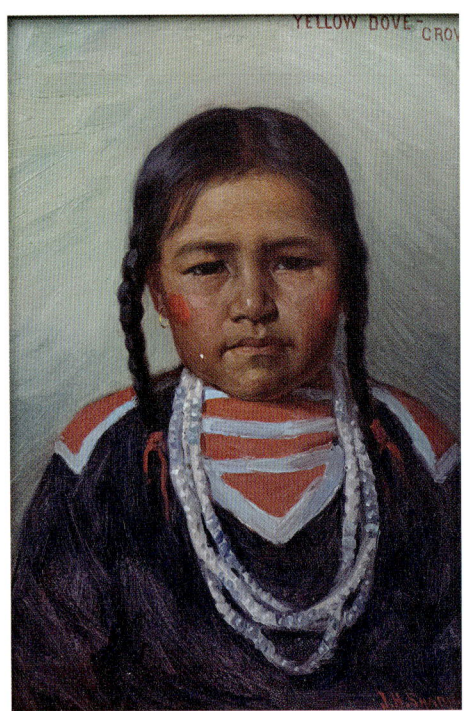

[PLATE 1.11]

JOSEPH HENRY SHARP

*Lady Pretty Blanket—
Blackfoot*

1902, oil on canvas, 13 ¾ x 9 ¾
Courtesy of the Phoebe A. Hearst
Museum of Anthropology and
the Regents of the University of
California, Berkeley, California.
17-202

In Sharp's portrait of him, Deaf Bull appears as, if not an art critic, certainly an imposing individual [PLATE 1.10].

Unquestionably, the portraits were salable commodities; some of the more popular images Sharp painted several times. Nonetheless, these portraits and others, of women and children [PLATE 1.11 AND PLATE 1.12], remain an outstanding achievement in that they link individuals with future generations and provide a rich history of actual personalities Sharp encountered in the Indian communities.

The past loomed over the present in Sharp's landscapes as well. As models for his portraits became scarcer, landscapes were becoming a more important part of his repertoire. Absarokee Hut looked "over the scene of Custer's massacre" [PLATE 1.13], as the newspapers liked to report, but Sharp avoided the word *massacre*, whereas he frequently used *battlefield*.[75] As a result, these paintings became more than landscapes—they incorporated themes that resonated in both western American history and popular culture.[76]

Among his immediate surroundings, Sharp found another subject that appealed to his audience—indigenous burial and mourning practices. The scaffold graves punctuating the Crow Agency horizon in all directions became a motif he repeatedly explored. *The Great Sleep* [PLATE 1.14], which ultimately hung in Hearst's office, is an austere winter-scape framed by barren trees. A critic who saw the painting at the Carnegie Galleries in Pittsburgh in 1900 supplied a narrative reminiscent of the death of a knight errant: "An Indian brave, the hero of many battles, lying upon his lofty bier, his blanket wrapped about him and his bow and arrows at his side. The bleakness of the scene, the leaves lying brown and sere upon the ground, the snow upon the distant mountain sides and the whistling wind through the bare leafless trees give to the painting a profoundly solemn aspect."[77]

Among his depictions of mourning rituals, Sharp developed several multifigured compositions that depict the wrapped corpse placed on a travois to be taken away for burial and the final inventory of the person's life, the transfer and division of property. Each of these activities is a profound occasion that portrays honor, worship, and familial affection. For the emotional orchestration of this funeral practice in these works, Sharp laid out a frieze-like panorama with an off-center tipi towering above the distant horizon. The bleak winter scene with broken patches of snow

75 *New York Globe*, January 6, 1907, ADD.

76 *St. Louis Art Review*, January 1907; *Indianapolis News*, May 21, 1908; *Kansas City Star*, January 17, 1909, ADD.

77 "Art Gems at the Carnegie Galleries," *Pittsburgh Commercial-Gazette*, December 26, 1900.

cover adds to the picture's solemnity. *Dividing the Chief's Property* [SEE PLATE 3.4] draws on art historical precedents of the classical past and pays homage to some of Benjamin West's history paintings, such as *Agrippina Landing at Brundisium with the Ashes of Germanicus* (1768; Yale University Art Gallery).

After their move to Crow Agency, the Sharps continued their frenetic lifestyle, rushing here and there among the Plains reservations and pursuing summer work in Taos and often the southern pueblos of Laguna, Acoma, and Zuñi as Sharp produced more and more paintings. One ambitious exhibition schedule included a showing of one hundred paintings in Los Angeles in May 1904, followed by a trip to St. Louis with a portrait of Crow chief Old Dog for the Louisiana Purchase Exposition.[78]

Although Sharp was an artist of landscapes in all seasons, he liked the technical challenges of painting the Montana snow, not the least of which was painting in frigid temperatures with cold fingers and handling semisolid paint that spread like peanut butter. In the dead of winter, Sharp traveled about the agency in a sheepherder's wagon christened the "Prairie Dog," a mobile studio acquired from rancher and patron Charley Bair.[79] The *Cincinnati Times-Star* ran a 1909 layout titled "No Steam-Heated Flat Artist" to emphasize his enduring pioneer spirit. Sharp, thickly bundled in overcoats, hat, and gloves, posed with his easel in front of the Prairie Dog and a snow-covered backdrop [SEE PLATE 2.21].[80] In 1916, with temperatures dipping to thirty-three below zero, Sharp, with his deadpan delivery, warned his

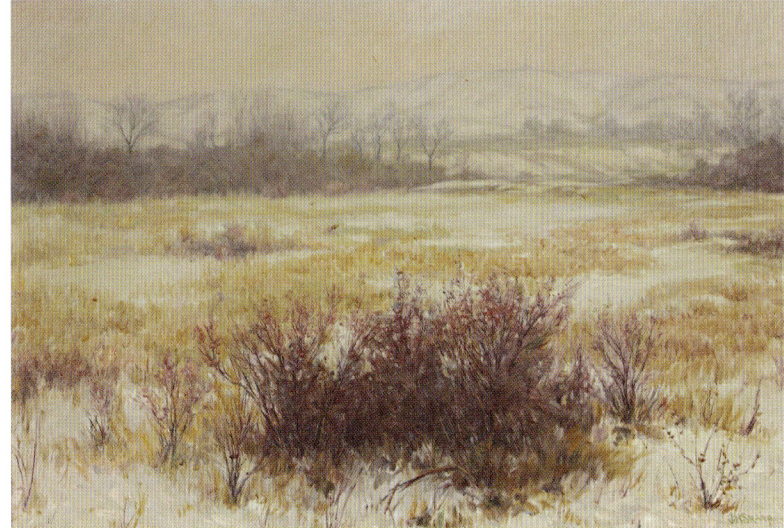

[PLATE 1.12]

JOSEPH HENRY SHARP

Yellow Dove—Crow

ca. 1899, oil on academy board, 13 ¾ x 9 ½ in.
Courtesy of the Phoebe A. Hearst Museum of Anthropology and the Regents of the University of California, Berkeley, California. 17-13

[PLATE 1.13]

JOSEPH HENRY SHARP

Custer Battlefield

ca. 1906, oil on canvas, 24 x 36 in.
Billings Public Library, Billings, Montana. L1998.008-PBL

---

78 Sharp became ill in St. Louis. For most of his life, he was prone to bouts of gastrointestinal disorder, some associated with "painter's colic" (i.e., lead poisoning) and nervous exhaustion. "You know I have to either work or sleep," Sharp once remarked. Often working up to fourteen hours a day, he was happiest and least anxious making art. JHS, Crow Agency, to J. H. Gest, September 26, 1906, CAMA.

79 Lee Rostad, "Charley Bair: King of Western Sheepmen," *Montana The Magazine of Western History* (Autumn 1970): 53. Charley Bair, Sharp's best patron in Montana, gave Sharp the sheepherder's wagon. Bair was legendary in Montana. A self-made man, he was known as the "King of Western Wool Growers" because he was the most successful sheep grower with the largest individually owned ranch in North America. Sharp recalled to Thomas Gilcrease: "I had a sheep & cattle herders commissary wagon—took everything out except stove. Put in sky and side lights, 6 x 12 ft. inside and could stand or sit to paint. Haul it to different localities and get several canvases each place. Painted night and moonlight also—good big lantern behind me. Generally worked outside until cold froze the paint, then in & fired up." JHS notes from photocopies, n.d., Joseph Henry Sharp Collection, Gilcrease Museum Library and Archives, University of Tulsa.

80 "No Steam-Heated Flat Artist," *Cincinnati Times-Star*, January 9, 1909, CAMA.

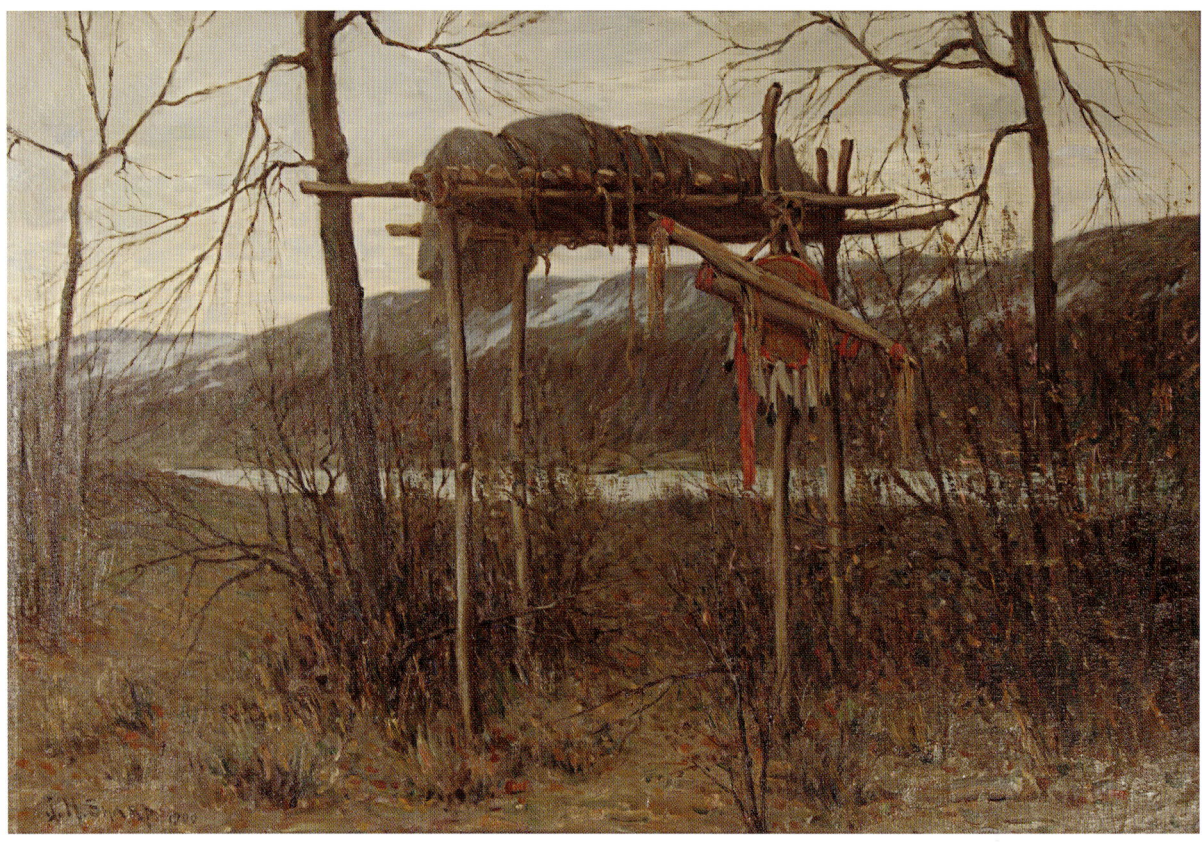

[PLATE 1.14]

JOSEPH HENRY SHARP

The Great Sleep

1900, oil on canvas, 22 x 33 in.
Courtesy of the Phoebe
A. Hearst Museum of
Anthropology and the Regents
of the University of California,
Berkeley, California. 17-204

Cincinnati patrons that "snow scenes will cost more" next time around.[81]

When time allowed, Sharp liked to paint side by side with Fra Dinwiddie Dana, a former student and fellow artist who resided with her husband at their 2Λ Ranch in Parkman, Wyoming, about sixty-five miles from Crow Agency. Dana offered not only serious criticism that Sharp sorely missed from his Cincinnati colleagues but also a respite from the pressures of work. Gleefully he wrote to a friend, "No Indians at Danas."[82] His happiness at this "glorious ranch and country" with "lovely people" spills over into the freedom of two loosely brushed 2Λ Ranch compositions.[83] A cool bluish cast of deepening shadows in the snowpack plays against the scintillating yellow haystacks in *Winter Landscape with Haystacks* (a la Monet) [PLATE 1.15].

Despite all of his plein air experiences, Sharp still maintained in 1906 that he couldn't "sail into a big landscape canvas yet with so much courage as I do a small head."[84] Two years later he continued to "find [landscapes] very interesting, & very *difficult* too, to get or do what you want to."[85] Through painting winter after winter for more than a quarter century, however, Sharp came to understand how to capture the various textures

81 JHS, Sheridan, WY, to J. H. Gest, January 18, 1916, CAMA.

82 JHS, Taos, NM, to Scheuerle, August 27, [1914 or 1915], AAA.

83 JHS to Scheuerle, August 27, [1914 or 1915], AAA.

84 JHS, Crow Agency, to J. H. Gest, January 22, 1906, CAMA.

85 JHS, Crow Agency, to Scheuerle, October 20, 1908, AAA. Sharp wrote that because of the
    lack of Plains models, he had "turned a great deal to landscapes, the last few years."

and color of snow for realistic winter scenes. Colors, from warm yellow-oranges to cool bluish violets, reflected the lighting, time of day, and nearby objects. Snow was his subject, sometimes painted with bold and vigorous strokes and sometimes rendered with light and feathery exercises in tonality.

Continuing to push the boundaries of his artistic comfort zone, Sharp began to experiment with firelight scenes at Crow Agency. Warm, mellow, intimate interiors contrasted with the cold, crisp winter days on the vast plains. "I am interested in firelight things now," he noted to Cincinnati colleagues in 1905, "& have a little teepee interior rigged up in studio, where I can pose model by lamplight & work by daylight. Awfully hard but lots of fun & interesting."[86] Within a year, at his much-anticipated December opening at the gallery

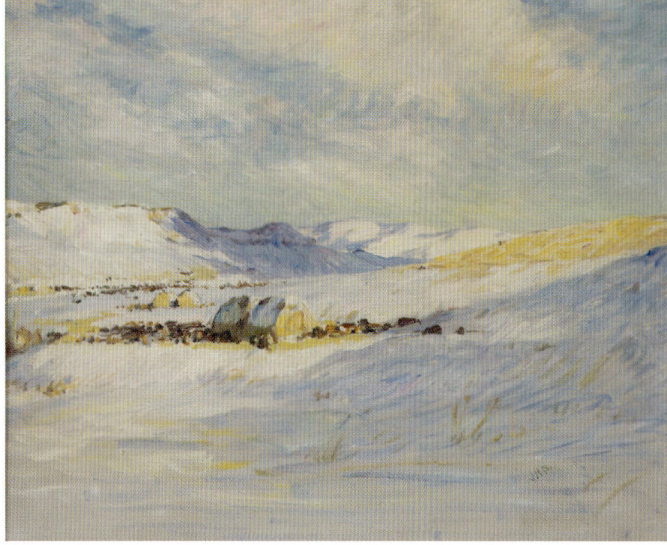

Fishel, Adler and Schwartz, on Fifth Avenue in New York, Sharp debuted landscapes, portraits, and burial scenes, along with the sentimental *A Gift for Her Brave* [SEE PLATE 2.20]. Bathed in soft firelight from an unseen source, the tender image of a mother cradling her child seated on the ground repeats a long tradition of Nativity iconography, but here set within a tipi furnished with cozy animal hides. The reflecting glow of the swaddling circling the baby's head creates a halo effect.

During his and Addie's summer sojourns in Taos, Sharp continued to try his hand with firelight images.[87] Initially disappointed, he wrote to Gest on August 7, 1908, "I painted a few heads, but they did not interest me after the northern fellows. Then in old lumber room I tried a few heads & figures by firelight, but under such circumstances the result was not the best, so I gave up such work until I can get a studio & decent place & light to work in."[88] That very day, the Sharps purchased their home in Taos, which he referred to earlier as their "first love and stamping ground."[89]

Then, in late October, Sharp happily wrote to Scheuerle, with whom he shared a love of the West, that he had "started an entire new note in my work." Having had second thoughts about the Pueblos as subjects and in firelight, he "finally tried sunlight, nude studies, heads under trees & in the sun, 6½ x 8½ small, & found them very interesting that way, & by

---

86 JHS, Crow Agency, to Mr. Koch, 1 January 1905, CAMA. Henry J. Koch (1849–1932) was the cashier at the Cincinnati Art Museum, where he worked from 1899 to 1926. A student of natural history, he wrote a book on his international hunting experiences.

87 Possibly Sharp was influenced by seventeenth-century Dutch genre scenes illuminated with candlelight and hearth light, and by the works of French Baroque painter Georges de la Tour from his European studies as a student.

88 JHS, Taos, to J. H. Gest, August 7, 1908, CAMA.

89 JHS, Taos, to J. H. Gest, June 15, 1906, CAMA.

firelight."[90] Interesting, indeed! Firelight images would become a signature style. As Sharp had foretold to Butler in 1904:

> Now that I have more time, I shall devote much of it to compositions & pictures of the poetry & legends as well as the home life of the Indians at present. There is a vast field & beautiful subjects for fine pictures as well as of historical & ethnological value. Of course, I will make portraits of the most important living men the principal aim. The other is important too, & the material I gather for such pictures will come in fine by and by when I am done with the old fighters, or when they are no more.[91]

With the element of light from fire, Sharp tapped into something primal, a dialogue between light and darkness that reached back to early humans who created and viewed cave paintings by firelight.

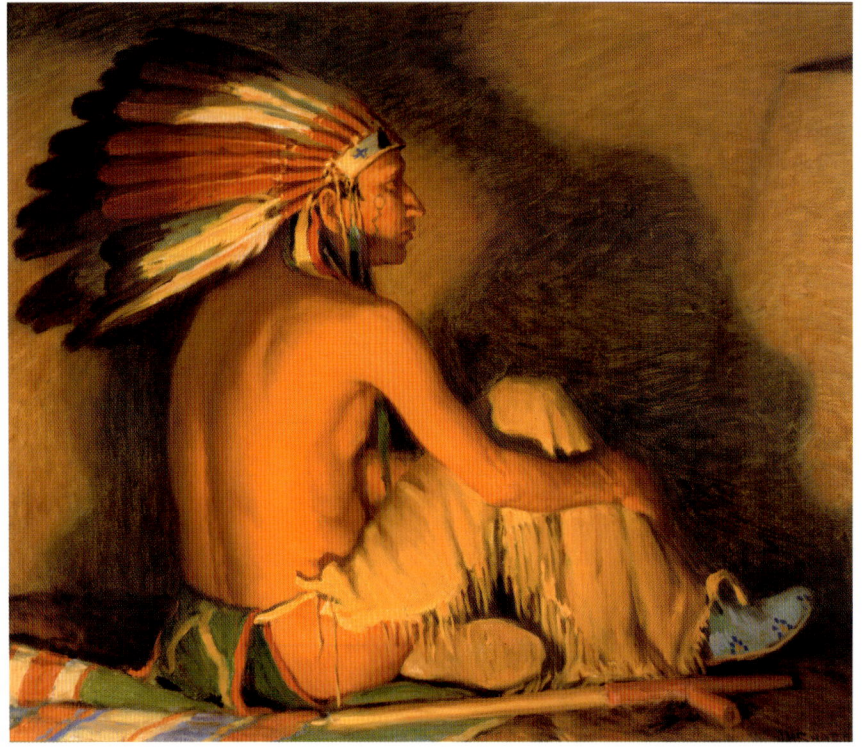

[PLATE 1.16]

JOSEPH HENRY SHARP

Hunting Son—Firelight

ca. 1925, oil on canvas, 23 x 30 in. National Cowboy and Western Heritage Museum, Oklahoma City, Oklahoma. Gift of Dorothy Duran Garrett, in Memory of Mr. and Mrs. Archer Leslie. 1992.16

Thereafter, exhibition lists consistently contained *firelight* in titles and included untitled firelight compositions. In essence, the compositions are genre scenes keyed by a selection of still-life objects from the artist's artifact collection. The shallow stage setting created an illusion of close proximity. Perhaps part of the appeal is the ability afforded the viewer to gaze covertly inside these private interiors. In deep silence, seated models, with faces glowing orange before a fire, sometimes hold objects—from pipes to shields to bows to warbonnets—in nostalgic reveries of past days and contemplation of what is to come [PLATE 1.16]. Narratives in other works are more dynamic with drummers, arrow makers, singers, and group ceremonies.

Firelight imagery proliferated in Sharp's Taos studio compositions. He added fireplaces in adobe interiors and campfires in tipis. In September 1909 the Sharps purchased an abandoned *oratorio*, a family chapel, that shared a common wall with the home of fellow artist Eanger Irving Couse and his wife, Virginia; this was converted to his studio, later known as the

90 JHS, Crow Agency, to Scheuerle, October 20, 1908, AAA.
91 JHS, Santa Fe, NM, to Butler, March 14, 1904, BP.

"Studio of the Copper Bell."[92] Most likely, the limited and dark space of this first studio persuaded him to acquire a three-room home in July, which he converted into a two-storied studio with a large northern window. In the second studio's west room, outfitted with a Pueblo-style fireplace, Sharp designed an architecturally interesting window that was square on the inside and round on the outside [PLATE 1.17]. This window and fireplace are seen in the backdrop of countless Taos genre paintings, and the setup developed into a virtual brand image. The cooler natural light from the window and the warmer artificial light from the adobe fireplace complemented each other in his ongoing exploration of light [SEE PAGE 138]. On the truss in the newly added loft, Sharp hung numerous Indian objects from his collection [SEE PLATE 2.36], available for reference while he painted intricate details that would connote historically accurate compositions for many viewers. In 1921 Cincinnati art critic Mary L. Alexander observed, "There are some unusually fine firelight canvases in the show, and while Mr. Sharp is always enthusiastic about the painting of firelight, this year's exhibition finds him a little more than usual."[93] Firelight paintings remained best sellers for three decades.

Typically, the Sharps made a point to return to Montana by October, especially after Crow Fair, an agricultural celebration, was inaugurated in 1904. The fall of 1908 was true to form, proving to be Sharp's most productive time to sketch, paint, and photograph. "I'll be busy every daylight hour," he wrote, "& up half the night at dances for next 10 days, as

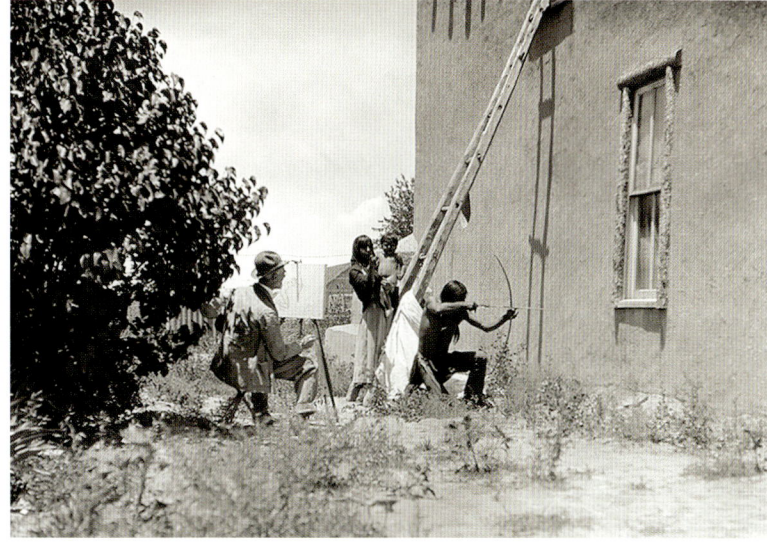

[PLATE 1.17]

UNKNOWN
PHOTOGRAPHER

Sharp's Taos Studio

ca. 1925, photograph, b&w
The Couse-Sharp Historic Site,
Taos, New Mexico

---

92 On September 29, 1909, the Sharps purchased the abandoned chapel from the archbishop of the Diocese of Santa Fe. Juan de Luna built it as a family chapel around 1835, and his son Juan Rafael Luna sold it to the diocese in 1853. In 1912 Sharp hung a Spanish-style bronze bell, which he purchased at Taos Pueblo for a hundred dollars, between the adobe pillars above the front door. He christened his chapel workspace the "Studio of the Copper Bell." *Taos Valley News*, June 1, 1912. The bell, dated "Diciembre 28, 1868," in Roman letters with serifs, is dedicated to "Maria Conception." A decorative raised cross appears on the side above the inscription. The bell's rim, 20¾ inches in diameter, has a flattened portion on one outside area, which appears to indicate that the bell was struck from the outside rather than with a clapper. Francisco Lujan, reported to have been born in Embudo, New Mexico, may have been the bell caster. Bells are attributed to Lujan as late as 1868. Itinerant bell casters like Lujan worked in northern New Mexico, traveling from village to village wherever their services were needed. Typically, Lujan would set up shop in the town plaza and work with discarded local copper or bronze. According to local tradition, residents added jewelry and money as offerings for a successful cast and tone. Ernie Leavitt, anthropologist and museum curator, interview with author, summer 2006, Taos, NM.

93 Mary L. Alexander, "Sureness and Snap to Indian Pictures That Sharp Paints," *Cincinnati Times-Star*, November 25, 1921.

Indians are coming in fast for the big camp & fair next week."[94] The Indians set up tipis along the banks of the Little Big Horn River about half a mile from the agency and Sharp's cabin. That was where Sharp habitually kept himself in October in order to capture traditional Indian life as Indians from other agencies came together. Many of them dressed in traditional clothing for the festivities, including dances and races. The Indians would parade across the ford and wind through the agency in their finery [PLATE 1.18].

"I got some good motifs for pictures during camp—painted some at night & moonlight," Sharp informed Gest.[95] A popular subject derived from

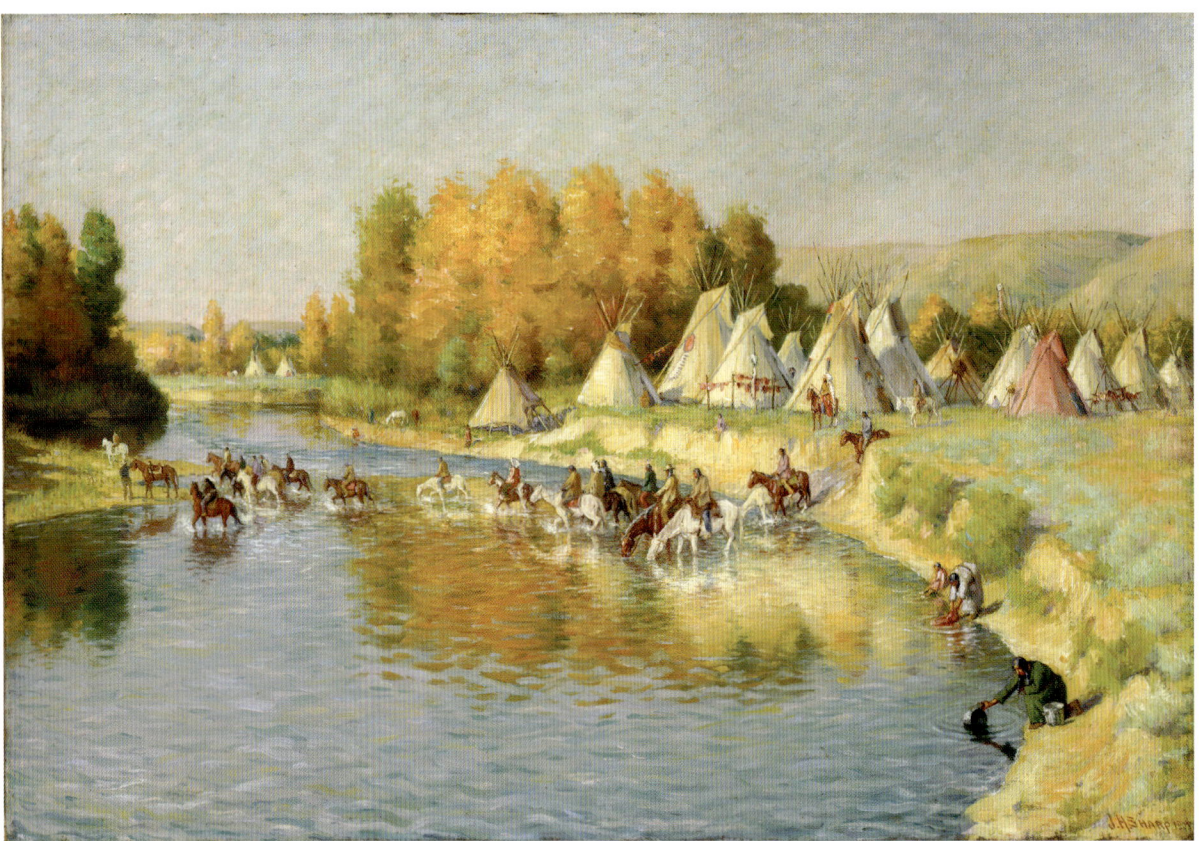

[PLATE 1.18]

JOSEPH HENRY SHARP

Crows Fording the Little Horn; [Encampment of Crow Indians]

1908, oil on canvas,
26 ⅞ x 40 ⅛ in.
Smithsonian American Art Museum, Washington, DC.
Bequest of Victor Justice Evans.
1985.66.362,159

Crow Fair was the tipi nocturne [SEE PLATE 4.4]. Otherwise banal views of tipi encampments are transformed into serene scenes of pure visual, if not nostalgic, pleasure for the viewer who wished to return to the glow of an imagined past. In the soft luminescence and shadows, time stood still.

But time didn't stop. Sharp told Scheuerle in 1909 that "the Shoshone & Arapahos have no costumes at all, & their celebrations & dances are nothing. The agent stopped the Blackfeet dances 3–4 yrs ago, so we have not been up there."[96] From Sharp's aesthetic standpoint, like the views of many

94 JHS, Crow Agency, to J.L. Hubbell, October 1, 1908, Box 74, Folder "Sharp," Lorenzo Hubbell Papers, Special Collections, University of Arizona.

95 JHS, Crow Agency, to J. H. Gest, November 17, 1908, CAMA.

96 JHS, Sheridan, WY, to Scheuerle, April 15, 1909, AAA. Others noted the loss of American Indian material culture, including Superintendent Ernest Jermark of Pine Ridge Reservation, who in 1929 remarked to an advertising executive seeking "Indian relics" that he should contact traders because "they're the only people with ceremonial garb and relics anymore."

anthropologists of his day, the contemporary Plains Indians
provided little visual interest unless wearing old-styled clothing
and performing traditional rituals. Sharp believed he was
painting and preserving the "real Indian" in his art, in contrast
to what he viewed as exploitative enactments for movies.
Later relocated to Taos, Sharp continued to paint a remarkable
number of Plains narratives from his early studies, sketches,
photographs, artifacts, and perhaps above all his cherished
memories, though now primarily using Taos models.

The Sharps' lives and livelihood took a battering at the end
of Crow Fair 1908, though Sharp wrote, "We are very happy *all*
the time."[97] Always one to find a consoling prospect even under
dire circumstances, he was apparently in denial about Addie's
debilitating health. Finding his wife's decline difficult to accept,
he talked as if nothing had changed and wrote repeatedly that she was getting
better and made plans, perhaps unrealistically, for their future together. Addie,
who had been unwell during their Taos summer, had "worked herself to a
frazzle" at Crow Fair and fallen gravely ill with a recurring respiratory ailment
and, likely, mental illness. Nonetheless, Sharp believed Addie was improving
in mid-November, but his worry about her "prevented good results" in his
work at Crow Fair.[98] In about two weeks' time, there would be no work at
all. Contact with a coal cinder critically damaged Sharp's left eye, an injury
that required him to refrain from painting for nearly two years and that
would plague him the rest of his life. Medical bills for both Addie and Joseph
mounted and drained their resources.

Even in the midst of these calamities, the Sharps continued their
established work migrations, his surfeit of amassed paintings continued on
to exhibitions, and they closed on the property to convert to a studio. Before
their imminent departure for Crow Fair in 1909, Sharp received a much-
needed "dandy good letter . . . full of enthusiasm and the 'Call of the West,'"
from Scheuerle, whose comradeship gave him courage to confide to his friend
his and Addie's ongoing anguish: "Her will power and strength that held
her & me up so beautifully through the many long months gave out, & she
has had a severe nervous prostration. . . . But we'll both soon be out of the
woods, & we'll cut the last year out and start over again."[99] Regarding his fear
of losing his eyesight, he wrote: "Can you realize what it is to be *blind* in one
eye for near a year, the other over weak from the strain & the nerves going [to
keep you from] . . . the most beautiful & paintable thing in the world & not
work. To never have that anticipating feeling when squeezing paint tubes—
the hope that you may really truly paint something good this time?"[100]He
concluded that the two were leaving to go north to see his doctor and
afterward to Crow Agency. This would be Addie's last call on Absarokee Hut.

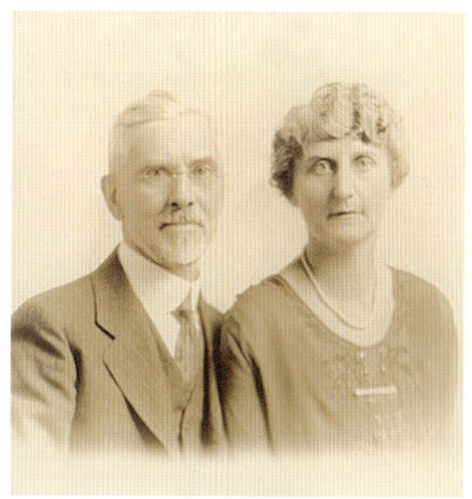

[PLATE 1.19]

UNKNOWN
PHOTOGRAPHER

J. H. Sharp and Louise B. Sharp

1922, passport photograph,
sepia tone
TIA Collection, Santa Fe,
New Mexico

---

97 JHS, Crow Agency, to J. H. Gest, November 17, 1908, CAMA.

98 JHS, Crow Agency, to J. H. Gest, November 17, 1908, CAMA.

99 JHS, Taos, to Scheuerle, October 3, 1909, AAA.

100 JHS, Taos, to Scheuerle, October 3, 1909, AAA.

In June 1910 the Sharps returned to Taos to continue the studio renovation and repairs to their home, but within three weeks' time Addie suffered a complete collapse and went to Los Angeles for medical care. Sharp was also contending with an ongoing gastrointestinal illness and chronic fatigue. Three years later, in April 1913, Addie died of pneumonia at age forty-nine, a month after her release from a private Pasadena sanitarium. Two years later, in March 1915, Sharp married Addie's younger sister, Louise, who had been a constant presence in their lives and had faithfully helped the Sharps over the past several years during their illnesses. Louise continued to be Sharp's support, now as his spouse, sharing with him thirty-eight years of companionship and travel [PLATE 1.19].

Whether Sharp drew inspiration from tragedy we don't know. He did what he did best, however: paint relentlessly, schedule exhibitions to showcase his work, travel. In September 1914, to considerable praise, Sharp opened a solo show at the Palace of the Governors in Santa Fe, where "admiring hundreds" came for the opening.[101] Then he focused on the two competing California Expositions to be held in 1915: the Panama-California Exposition in San Diego and the Panama-Pacific International Exposition in San Francisco.[102]

Critics immediately noticed and applauded a change in Sharp's work. Cincinnati art critic J. H. Earhart, noting that Sharp had been off the exhibition circuit with recent paintings because of an eye injury, was impressed with the artist's new canvases: "His work is now matured and possesses great dignity and depth of purpose."[103] Earhart thought *The Stoic* and *Grief* (1912; location unknown) "splendid examples" of the "humanity that he treats of and aims to paint as his mental vision sees them—as people who have hearts and souls."[104] Possibly these paintings offered spiritual salve to the hardships and anguish he and Addie were suffering. In these large canvases the artist made lone Plains Indian males the focus. The partially nude figures in part represent repackaged classicism from his academic training. The male in *Grief* could be any man bowed by overwhelming sorrow. With *The Stoic* [PLATE 1.20], there is no doubt that the subject is a Plains Indian. Along a worn path leading to a mesa in the far distance, a life-size Herculean figure clutches a staff to keep him upright as he drags four horse heads attached to buffalo hide tethers threaded through cuts in the man's back muscles, to demonstrate his courage and endurance in the grievous loss of a son or other close relative. Arguably an ethnographic document with Sharp's detailed explanation of this ritual on the canvas backing, the painting is also a narrative history painting in the academy tradition, depicting the universal themes of the human spirit—heroic quest, struggle and sacrifice, and the

---

101 "Lovers of Art Throng Palace of Governors," *Taos Valley News*, September 15, 1914. *The Stoic* and *The Gamblers* showed with the SWA in Chicago from December 31, 1913 to January 25, 1914.

102 *Crucita—A Taos Indian Girl* (ca. 1913) appeared in San Francisco (February 20, 1915–December 4, 1915), and *The Stoic* (1912), *The Broken Bow* (1912), *The Gamblers* (1912), *Grief* (1912), and *Pottery Decorators* (ca. 1913) in San Diego (January 1, 1915–January 1, 1917).

103 J. F. Earhart, "Sharp's Paintings, A Notable Exhibit," *Cincinnati Times-Star*, November 19, 1912, CAMA.

104 Earhart, "Sharp's Paintings, A Notable Exhibit."

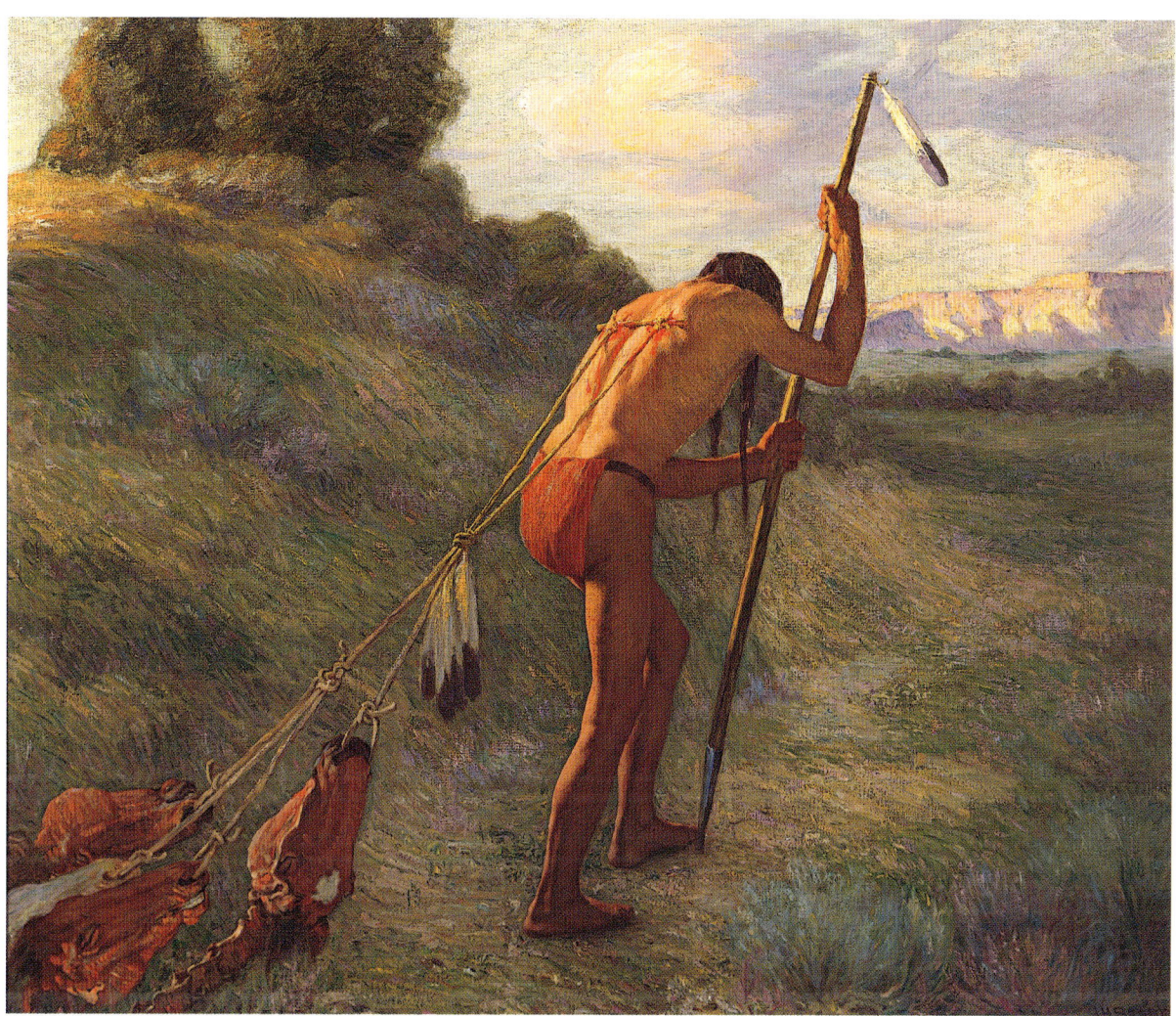

virtues of courage, loyalty, and honor. Neither of the figures look for comfort.

Taos had given the artist new directions and new models. Of the many exhibited works that express Taos culture to the viewer, *Crucita—A Taos Indian Girl* [PLATE 1.21] showed at the National Academy of Design in the spring of 1913 and later at the San Francisco Exposition. Crucita, of Taos Pueblo, wearing a meticulously detailed dress, likely a dance costume, sits on the floor of Sharp's adobe chapel studio on one of his favorite Plains props, a buffalo hide, and artfully arranges a bouquet, a profusion of accurate floral details in a ceramic vessel.[105] She holds the slender flower stalk like a paint brush before her floral composition. However, Crucita seems hardly more important than the still life, which would become a main genre in his

[PLATE 1.20]

JOSEPH HENRY SHARP

The Stoic

1912, oil on canvas,
52 ½ x 61 ½ in.
Collection of the New Mexico Museum of Art, Santa Fe, New Mexico. Gift of Joseph Henry Sharp, 1917. 395.23P. Photo by Blair Clark

105 Sharp inscribed on this painting that Crucita wore a Hopi wedding dress. Historical photos indicate that this may be an error. Such dresses were ubiquitous in the Tewa and Keres Pueblos, at Zuñi, and possibly at Hopi because of the Hopi-Tewa connection at First Mesa. It is a dance costume, not everyday wear. The dress may have been purchased from a Fred Harvey shop, and that was the sales pitch, since many tourists put Hopi high on the list of places to visit. I thank Dr. James Moore for supplying this information. Michael B. Stanislawski, "Hopi-Tewa," in *Handbook of North American Indians*, vol. 9 (Washington, DC: Smithsonian Institution, 1979), 587–602; Edward P. Dozier, *Hano: A Tewa Indian Community in Arizona* (Fort Worth: Harcourt, Brace, Jovanovich College Publisher, 1966).

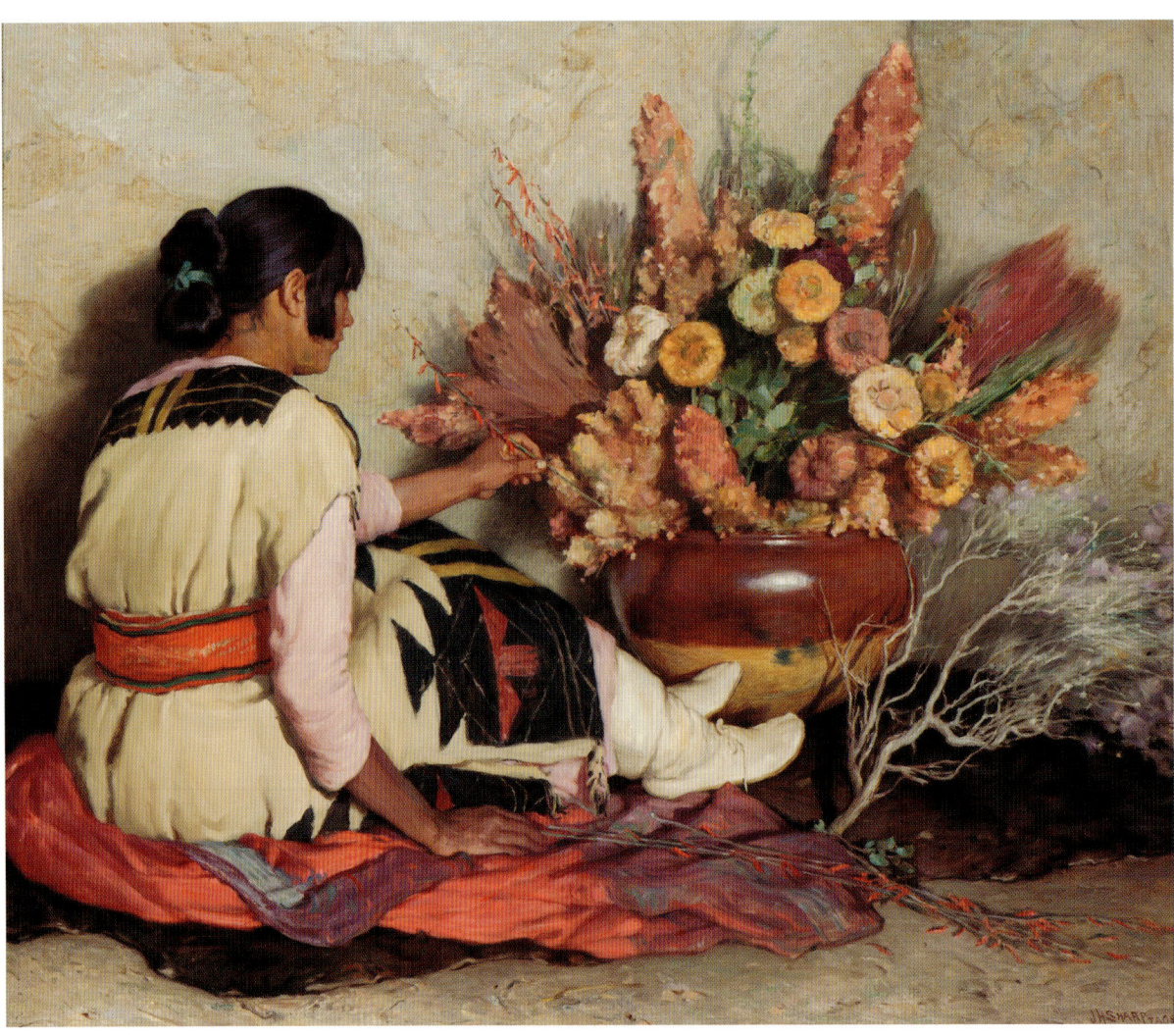

[PLATE 1.21]

JOSEPH HENRY SHARP

Crucita—A Taos Indian Girl

ca. 1913, oil on canvas,
47 ½ x 55 ½ in.
Gilcrease Museum, Tulsa,
Oklahoma. Gift of the Thomas
Gilcrease Foundation, 1955.
0137.2194

later years. The flowers are nonnative as is the activity of floral arranging. Sharp elides the Anglo and Pueblo cultures in this painting, perhaps hinting to the informed viewer that this is indeed artifice. With a remarkable range of textures and surfaces, the artist demonstrates that realistic impressions can be a part of artifice, and he indicates that Crucita, as a model, is part of the contemporary Taos economy and environment in this seeming slice of everyday life. As Sharp would have been aware, the association of women and flowers has an art historical pedigree reaching back to the ancient world, representing spring or the sense of smell, or both. In Sharp's own past, however, he had possibly seen in Paris the pairing of women and flowers in the works of Gustave Courbet, Frédéric Bazille, and Edgar Degas (among others), part of an international artistic production of women in conjunction with bouquets.[106] Crucita may be the first Native American portrayed in this genre.

106 Examples of women paired with a floral still life include Gustave Courbet, *Young Woman Arranging Flowers (the Trellis)* (1862); Frederic Bazille, *African Woman with Peonies* (1870); Edgar Degas, *Portrait of Estelle Musson Degas* (1872) and *A Woman Seated beside a Vase of Flowers (Madame Paul Valpinçon?)* (1865). Among Sharp's contemporaries who painted in this genre were Sir Lawrence Alma-Tadema, Albert Lynch, Francis Coates Jones, John William Goddard, Anders Zorn, and Henry Brown Fuller.

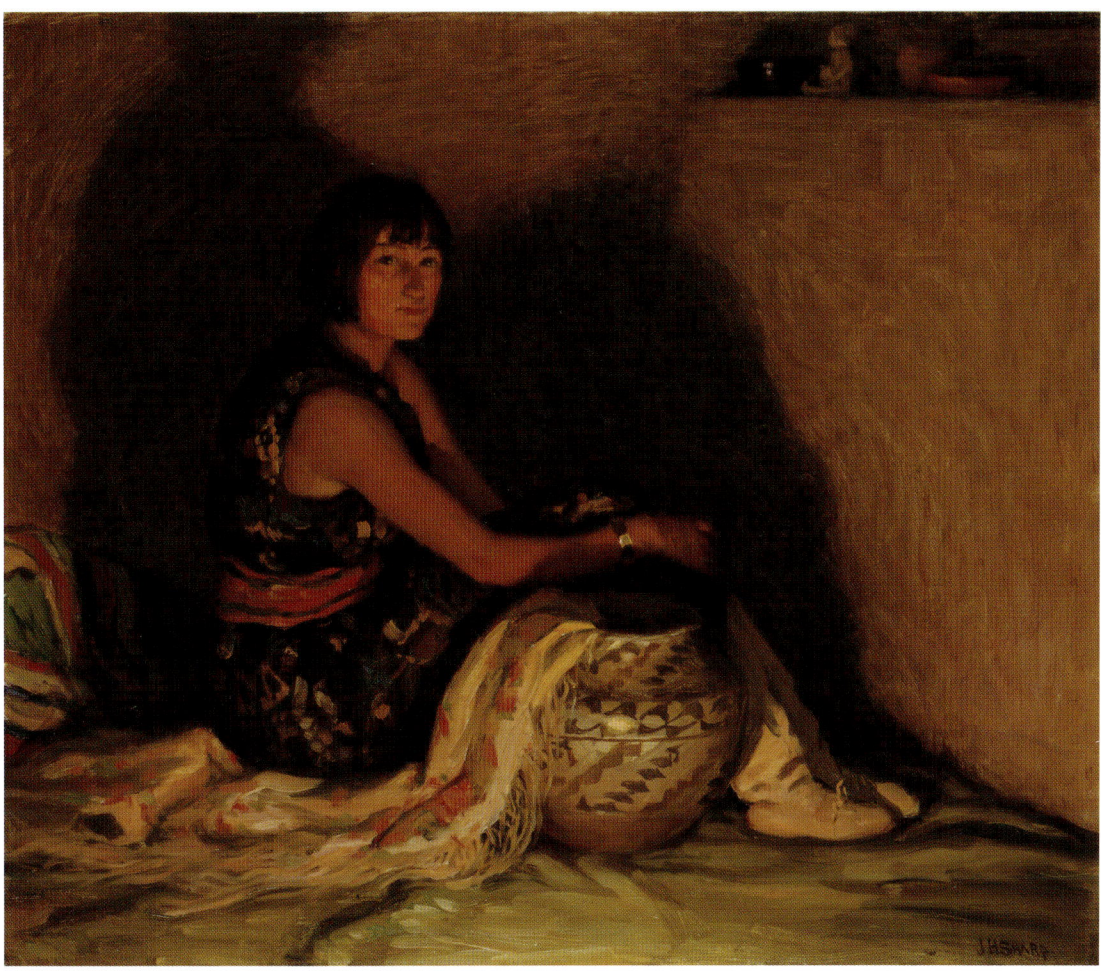

From her first steps as a model for Sharp in 1913, Crucita would dominate his female imagery and motifs.[107] In the paintings in which she appears, she is variously posed solo, part of a couple, as a family member, or among a group of women; seated on the ground, floor, or *banco*; in an adobe interior, garden, or Taos valley; in firelight or sunlight; decorating pottery, shelling corn, or arranging flowers; and in juxtaposition with a variety of ceramic vessels, woven baskets, or textiles. One Cincinnati reviewer summed it up well in the 1930s: "What would a collection be without the lovely Crucita!"[108] Her daughter Leaf Down followed in her footsteps [PLATE 1.22].

[PLATE 1.22]

JOSEPH HENRY SHARP

Leaf Down

1928-1929, oil on canvas,
19 ¾ x 23 ½ in.
Denver Art Museum,
Denver, Colorado. Gift of Anne
Waring Maer. 1999.291

---

107 James Moore established that Crucita Gomez is the sister of Geronimo Gomez (Star Road). See Elsie Clews Parsons, *Taos Pueblo* (Menasha, WI: George Banta Publishing Co., 1936; reprinted, New York: Johnson Reprint, 1970), 56. (Parsons spells the name "Crusita.") Although there were other Crucitas at Taos, it makes sense that she would have modeled, as this was usually something that resulted from family connections and both her brother and husband were models. Also, models tended to continue working for particular artists; for example, Albert Martinez and Joe Gomez for Berninghaus, and Ben Luhan for Couse. Crucita's mother was Juanita Suazo (Suaso?). Her Tiwa name, Pæõ, translates as Deer Leaf, so "Leaf"-something might not be far-fetched for a granddaughter. Juanita was married to a Gomez, but the name isn't in Parsons, *Taos Pueblo*; probably Ignacio or Francisco Gomez (San Geronimo Cemetery record, http://www.kmitch.com/Taos/cems/geronimocem.html). Crucita married Juan de Jesus Martinez (White Sun) on February 8, 1892. The couple had two daughters and a son.
108 News fragment, ca. 1930s, CAMA.

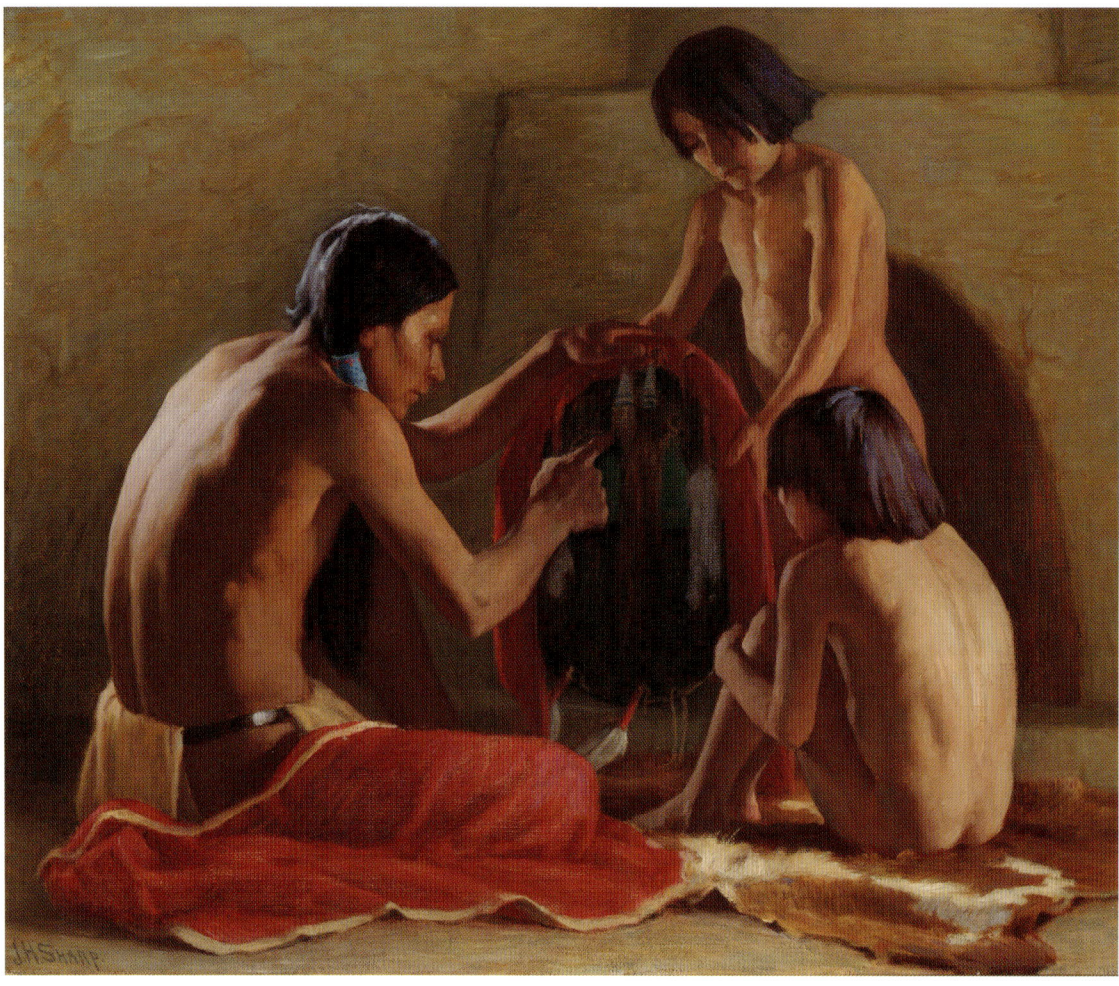

[PLATE 1.23]

JOSEPH HENRY SHARP

The Old War Shield

ca. 1915, oil on canvas,
34 ¾ x 40 ½ in.
Gilcrease Museum, Tulsa,
Oklahoma. Gift of the Thomas
Gilcrease Foundation, 1955.
0137.310

Offering a contrast to the novel female imagery, *The Broken Bow* [SEE PLATE 2.24] was also exhibited in San Diego. In this narrative of father and son bonding, the father is teaching a specific skill to his young son: the mending of a bow. The setting is Sharp's chapel studio, with the father seated on the buffalo hide on the floor and the boy on the *banco* against the adobe wall. The models are dressed from his collection of Northern and Southern Plains Indian artifacts. For all its detailed depiction of attributes of various tribes, *Broken Bow* presented a romantic image of an ideal Indian that appealed to audiences' stereotypes.

Family pictures would become a staple motif. With the opening of Sharp's second Taos studio in 1915, a young child named Alberto took center stage as a model in his Cincinnati exhibition of Indian and western painting at the Hotel Gibson in late November. "One finds Alberto everywhere and in every way," art critic Mary Alexander observed. *The Old War Shield* [PLATE 1.23], which Sharp would show the following year at the National Academy, rephrases the *Broken Bow*, the narrative now staged with the adobe fireplace as backdrop and a war shield from his "curios," as he liked to call them, replacing the bow. The father points to a place on the war shield, with two young sons listening intently to the history lesson. Employing a asymmetrical triangle formula that the artist favored, the father in three-quarter back view anchors the left base, the seated son in similar position at the right, and the head of the older son forming the apex.

From the mid-1910s through the 1920s, Sharp painted some of his finest figural compositions and critical successes in Taos. Paralleling his fresh start was the formation of the Taos Society of Artists (TSA) [PLATE 1.24]. The artists' student years in Paris remained their lodestone for creating a similar site in Taos in their search for inspiration for a pure American art form.

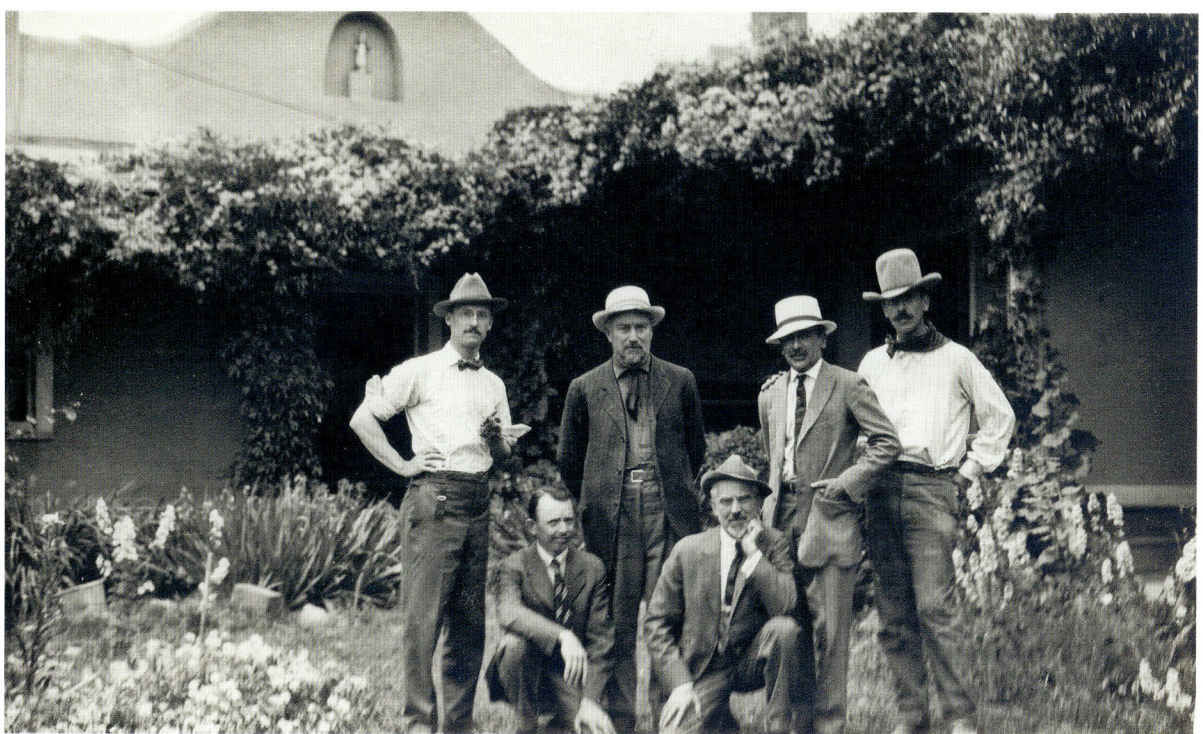

In July 1915, Sharp's hope of "a Taos colony à la Barbizon" became reality.[109] A charter member, Sharp worked faithfully with the society through its ups and downs until it disbanded in 1927. The TSA members were united in finding a national stage by mounting traveling exhibitions to establish a market for their southwestern imagery, and in doing so, they established the first art colony in the Southwest. They forged friendships and engaged in rivalries. Each had a unique philosophy and style that sometimes lead to professional disagreements and outright personal clashes. They challenged, motivated, and supported one another and as a result produced some of their best work. In the process they redefined the course of American art. Sharp had returned to the place where he had begun as a student all those years ago—to paint in the Southwest.[110]

Unlike fellow TSA members Ernest Blumenschein and Walter Ufer, Sharp rarely painted sociopolitical imagery. At the end of the decade that changed briefly. A series of paintings took on the problems of assimilation: *Indian Medicine or Black Robe* (1916), *Ration Day at the Reservation* (1919)

[PLATE 1.24]

UNKNOWN PHOTOGRAPHER

Founding Members of the Taos Society of Artists

undated, photograph, b&w
The Couse-Sharp Historic Site,
Taos, New Mexico

---

109 JHS, Taos, to J. H. Gest, June 15, 1906, CAMA.
110 Robert White, *The Taos Society of Artists* (Albuquerque: University of New Mexico Press, 1998).

[PLATE 1.25], *Young Chief's Mission* (1919), and *The Oil Promoter* (1920) brought critical attention.[111] Of the three, *Ration Day* is as tough and political as any French painting. This painting focuses on the wreckage of a nomadic people whose culture once centered on hunting bison but who are now forced to live on reservations and draw rations—food substitutions not only foreign to their diet but of poor quality.[112]

Sharp would have witnessed "ration days," when annuities were paid the Indians in goods, while living at Crow Agency and in his movement about the other agencies in the area. He also would have seen "payment days," when Indians came to the agencies for money annuities. In contrast to the valiant "old time fighter" he had painted, Sharp portrayed the contemporary, "agency Indians," the latest historical role assigned them by the federal government.[113] His second studio, which had a bison skull hanging above the traditional Taos turquoise-blue door frame, stands in as the agency distribution building in the shallow, stage-like setting. The composition fuses carefully detailed material culture from his props with stock poses from paintings and photographs of nearly twenty years earlier. Unlike the subjects of his portraiture, the individuals here, primarily women, have generalized features and impassive faces. Perhaps this generic style was deliberate, intended to symbolize the harshness of reservation life on the Plains. The Indians wait quietly, some in groups and others by themselves. A pall of sadness hangs over the gathering as the viewer's eye moves from the lower left, where the woman sits in a contemplative pose with chin cupped in hand (a melancholy trope) to a woman bent over Crow flour sacks she is organizing, to a standing group in hushed conversation, to a woman leaning against the wall. A dog curled up with tucked tail is the punctuation to this statement of the despair and indignity of reservation life. The symbolic device of a bison skull, a gloss on the extinction of a way of life, further emphasizes the consequences of assimilation awaiting the Indians who would walk across that threshold to obtain their government rations. The open door to the agency signified access to white civilization, sequestered behind the thick adobe walls.

The empathy expressed in the painting, however, is in stark contrast to the words Sharp wrote on the back of *Crow Camp, Montana* (ca. 1919; Gilcrease Museum). The Indians camped out at the agency in anticipation of their rations, he noted, and, upon receiving them, spent the next few days feasting and using up their allotment. This cultural behavior was incongruent with the values, priorities, and goals of Sharp's lifestyle of budgeting, saving, and practicing financial responsibility. Nonetheless, the

---

111 In regard to the 1919 works, Sharp wrote Butler that "artist friends who have so far seen them unhesitatingly pronounce them the best I have done." Butler added these paintings to his collection.

112 Vine Deloria Jr. and Raymond J. DeMallie, *Documents of American Indian Diplomacy: Treaties, Agreements, and Conventions, 1775–1979* (Norman: University of Oklahoma Press, 1999): 978.

113 JHS to J.L. Hubbell, October 6, 1908, Lorenzo Hubbell Papers, Special Collections, University of Arizona; *A Catalogue of Indian Portraits in the Collection of Joseph G. Butler, Jr., Youngstown* (Youngstown, OH: Vindicator Press, ca. 1907), 22.

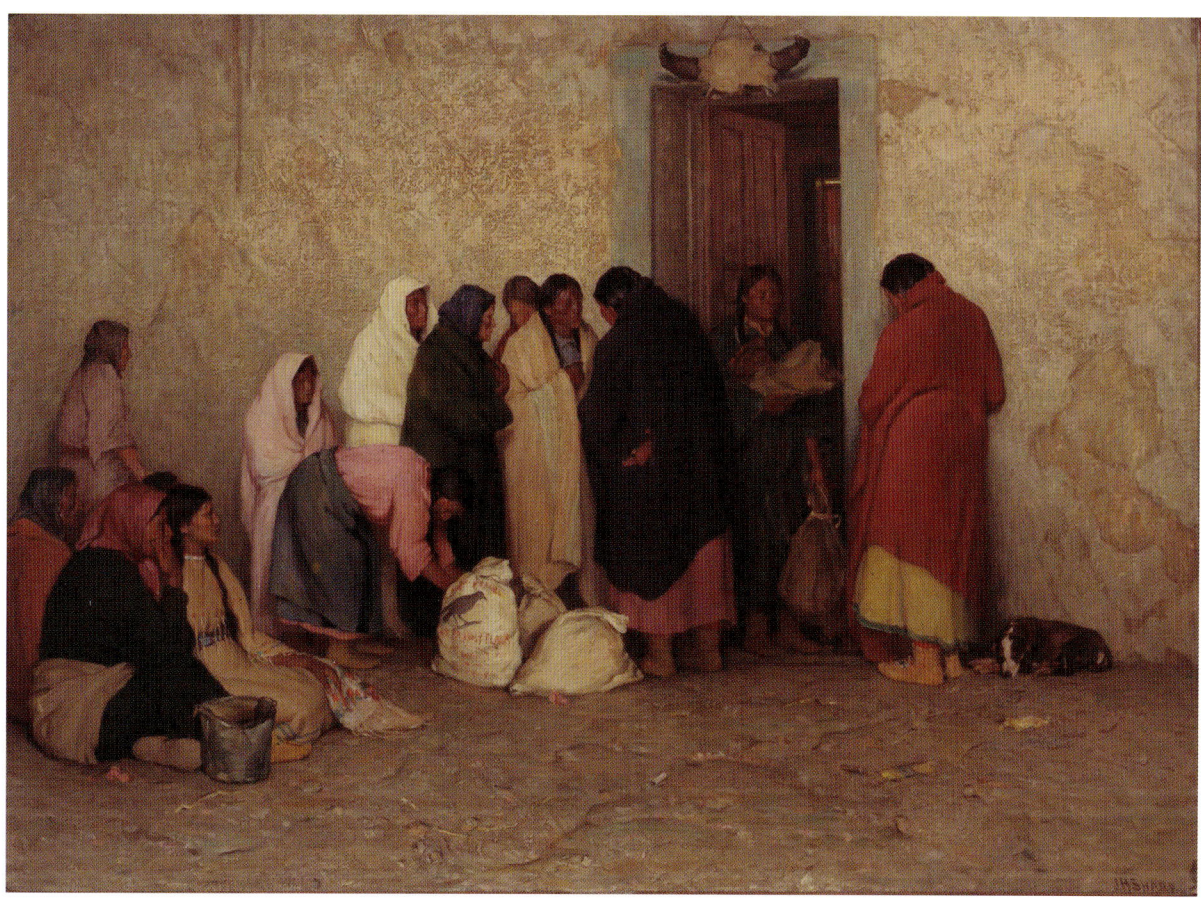

[PLATE 1.25]

JOSEPH HENRY SHARP

Ration Day at the Reservation

1919, oil on canvas, 40 x 55 in.
Butler Institute of American Art,
Youngstown, Ohio. 921-O-504

questions of what Sharp's true positions were on Indian policies and what sort of relationships he had with the Indians he knew are perplexing.

Also new in Sharp's compositions by 1915 was the painting of Hispanic subjects, which other TSA members occasionally painted. Primarily, Sharp's works have Penitente associations. During his first trip to Taos, he remarked that the Penitentes were "a subject for lifetime" and he proposed "to devote years to it." He fell short of that early goal, however, and did not begin to paint this imagery until the 1920s. *The Old Santos Mender (Old Penitente)* [PLATE 1.26] and *Chemayo* [*sic*] *Weaver, an Old Penitente* (1925, location unknown) were part of his 1925 Exhibition of Indian Paintings at Traxel Art Galleries.[114] The artisans in both paintings have the casual, unposed appearance of a snapshot as they are absorbed in their work in their shops, unaware of our voyeuristic viewing.

Just short of a decade later, Sharp turned again to Penitentes, but the large canvas *The Passing of a Penitente* [PLATE 1.27] was a religious painting that would have pleased his European academic instructors and perhaps was an acknowledgement of Carl von Marr, a Munich teacher. Sharp had listed a photo of Marr's monumental painting *The Flagellation* (1889; Museum of Wisconsin Art) as number one among the pictures to be shown at the Woman's Club in 1899. Marr worked on this painting between 1885 and 1889, the period when Sharp studied with him.

---

114 There are two paintings entitled *The Old Santos Mender*, 1925 and 1949.

[PLATE 1.26]

JOSEPH HENRY SHARP

*The Old Santos Mender
(Old Penitente)*

1925, oil on canvas,
36 ¾ x 31 ¾ in.
Gilcrease Museum, Tulsa,
Oklahoma. Gift of the Thomas
Gilcrease Foundation, 1955.
0137.2088

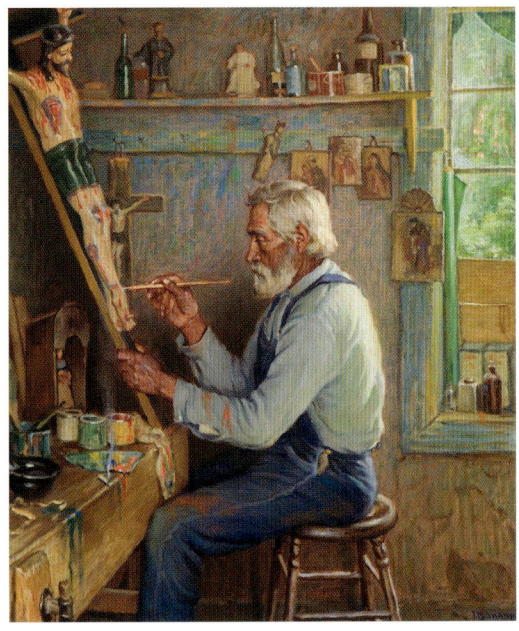

Sharp set the Penitente ceremony in his studio chapel, which he claimed had once been a Penitente chapel. Oral tradition in Taos refers to this building as a *Penitente morada*, though Juan de Luna built the structure around 1835. Most likely, the chapel served as a Luna family chapel. At some time, however, Penitente services appear to have taken place there. Blood spatters appear on the *vigas*, or beams in the center of the nave near the altar area. During Holy Week rites, penitents would, as Sharp depicted, lash their backs with whips as they knelt before the altar. The inclusion of the well-dressed man on the left *banco* indicates that the practice was not class-bound in the community. Sharp noted that the candlesticks on the altar were original from a Penitent *morada*.

From the 1920s on, Sharp made another innovative turn in his subject matter, by painting works of contemporary Taos, some with a droll sense of humor. In *Studio Visitors*, *Three Taos Indians*, and *Sunset Dance—Ceremony to the Evening Sun*, Sharp addressed the multiculturalism and increasing tourism in Taos. He noted to a patron in the fall of 1919, "A good many tourists here this year, but no business like last year. They spend all the $ for gas and grub."[115] He was becoming annoyed by their intrusions into his open studio. However, this was not always his attitude, as the backstory of *Studio Visitors* shows [PLATE 1.28]. Bawling Deer (Frank Martinez), a popular model (seated on the bench in the painting) brought three Apache friends visiting Taos for San Geronimo Day celebrations to his workplace, Sharp's studio. Sharp, delighted as the visitors viewed his unfinished painting of Bawling Deer, conceived of a composition and began to make "quick pencil sketches."[116] Although Sharp wrote that "*all* posed at one time for the painting" and that "in order to keep the models interested, I had to change the picture on the easel at the regular intervals of rest," the two figures in profile resemble models in other of his paintings. All four figures are clad in clothing from his collection. Bawling Deer's Sioux shirt is the

---

115 JHS, Taos, to Butler, September 2, 1919, BP.

116 Indians at Crow Agency viewed his ongoing work. Critiques from professional critics or the public are not unusual and have a long art history pedigree. Sharp may have been aware of this motif in such nineteenth-century works as Francois Biard's *Four O'clock at the Salon* (1847), several Daumier caricatures, and fellow American William Sidney Mount's *The Painter's Triumph* (1838).

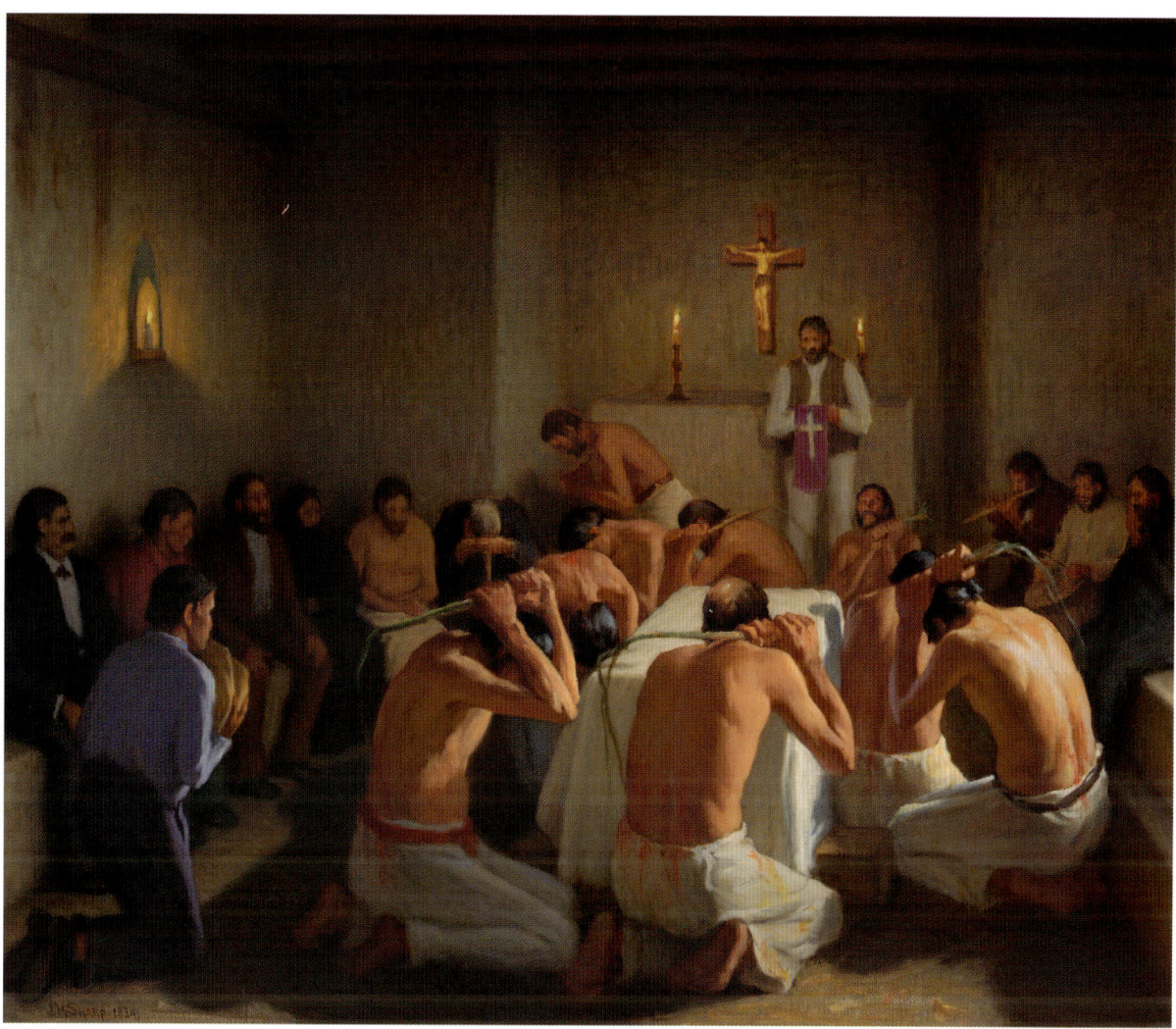

[PLATE 1.27]

JOSEPH HENRY SHARP

The Passing of a Penitente

1934, oil on canvas,
34 ½ x 40 ¾ in.
Gilcrease Museum, Tulsa,
Oklahoma. Gift of the Thomas
Gilcrease Foundation, 1955.
0137.307

same as the one he wears in the unfinished canvas on the easel.[117] Bawling
Deer, who has put on his modeling shirt, is amused with his friends'
critical reactions to his employer's work.

From the studio interior, Sharp moved his models to the streets
of Taos. In *Three Taos Indians* [PLATE 1.29], the subjects stand before
a windowed storefront that looks like a tourist shop. A woven Indian
basket, a string of dried Indian corn, and a black olla line the entrance to
the unseen shop entrance. The objects are as much a "portrait" of Taos to
the tourist as are the Indians themselves. The men, in different states of
dress, look as if they have come from a modeling job; presented as types,
they are treated as dispassionately as the objects. The left figure, in profile,
wears beaded, fringed buckskins with a blanket wrapped around his waist,
beaded moccasins, and feathers in his braided hair; the middle, full-frontal
figure is cowled from head to shins in a white blanket, likely purchased
from the town's J. C. Penney, as was common; and the right figure, hair

117 From Sharp's note accompanying the painting. *Studio Visitors* was reproduced on the
   program cover for the exhibition "J.H. Sharp's Exhibition of Indian Paintings and Western
   Landscapes" at Traxel Art Galleries, November 30 to December 11, 1926.

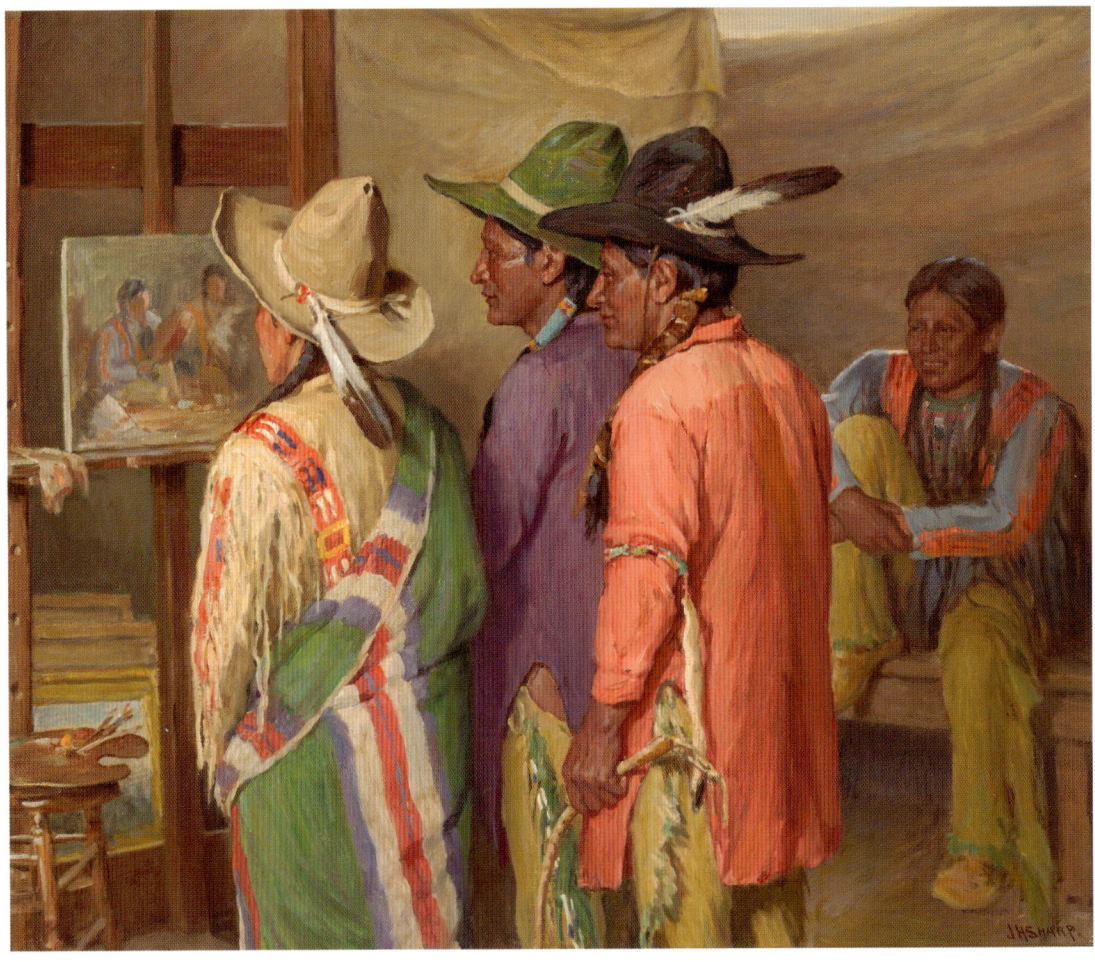

in braids adorned with a feather, stands bare-chested in *contrapposto* with leather moccasins, captured in the odd act of simply holding a blanket. There is no readable action or narrative to engage the viewer.

An opened camera case rests on the ground to the left of the buckskin-clad model's feet and a burning cigarette with a rising trail of smoke in front of his feet appears to have been quickly thrown down as he and his two companions posed for the tourist (or the viewer) preparing to snap a photograph.[118] In this performance, one can almost hear "Actors take your positions, please!" as the three Indians, with apathetic expressions, patiently wait to hear "Cut!" and go on their way.

Sunset Dance—Ceremony to the Evening Sun [PLATE 1.30] takes us to what has become another must-see tourist location, Taos Pueblo, especially on feast days, September 29–30, with San Geronimo Day the foremost attraction. No visitors are present in this Indian-only composition. The scene appears timeless. Sharp, however, has markedly included in the foreground center a basket filled with clay figurines, Tesuque rain gods, and a black olla resting at the feet of an individual. The ceramics were

---

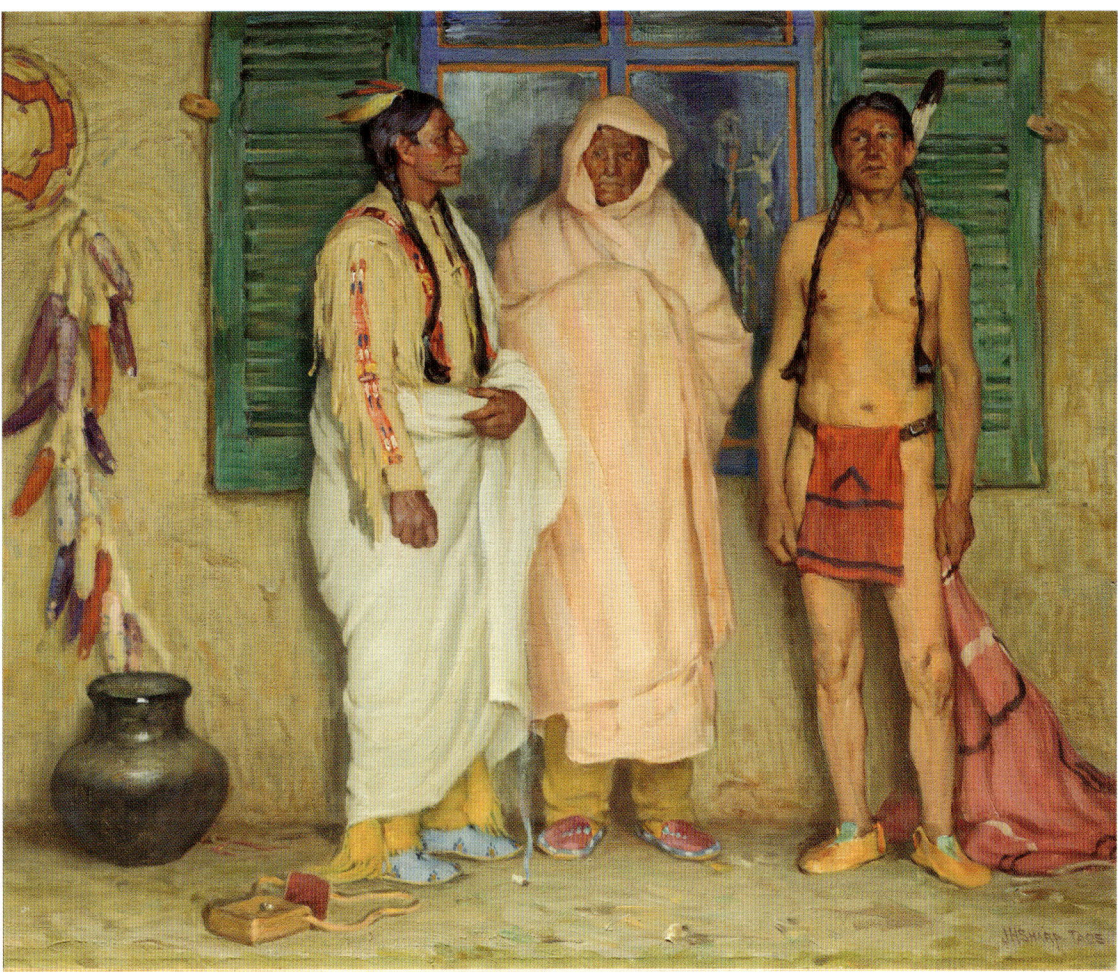

[PLATE 1.29]

JOSEPH HENRY SHARP

Three Taos Indians

ca. 1925, oil on canvas,
25 ¼ x 30 ¼ in.
American Museum of Western
Art—The Anschutz Collection,
Denver, Colorado. 0312

commodities that catered to the burgeoning southwestern tourist market. In particular, the rain gods were made in the thousands, beginning in the 1880s. These objects, along with the clothing the figures wear, appear again and again in Sharp's paintings. Although he has painted a contemporary scene for the initiated, perhaps he is also acknowledging that he and his art are complicit in transforming Taos into a tourist town and that his paintings, too, are commodities produced to be bought and sold, no different from the pottery in the basket.

In spite of the painting's title, the setting of the composition is possibly the afternoon of September 29, and the people are going to vespers, which marks the beginning of San Geronimo celebrations. The time is autumn, as signaled by the yellow cottonwood tree. The shadows would correspond with the time of vespers between 4 and 6 pm. Sharp has somewhat exaggerated the height of the south complex for compositional purposes as he balances the church and the pueblo, using the architecture as a metaphor for the relationship between the church and traditional practices. While some have interpreted Sharp's positioning of the cross as imposing a Christian viewpoint on Taos Pueblo, the church's presence in the pueblo was centuries old, and as with all the pueblos, in Taos, Christianity and traditional practices were interwoven. The church and the pueblo are

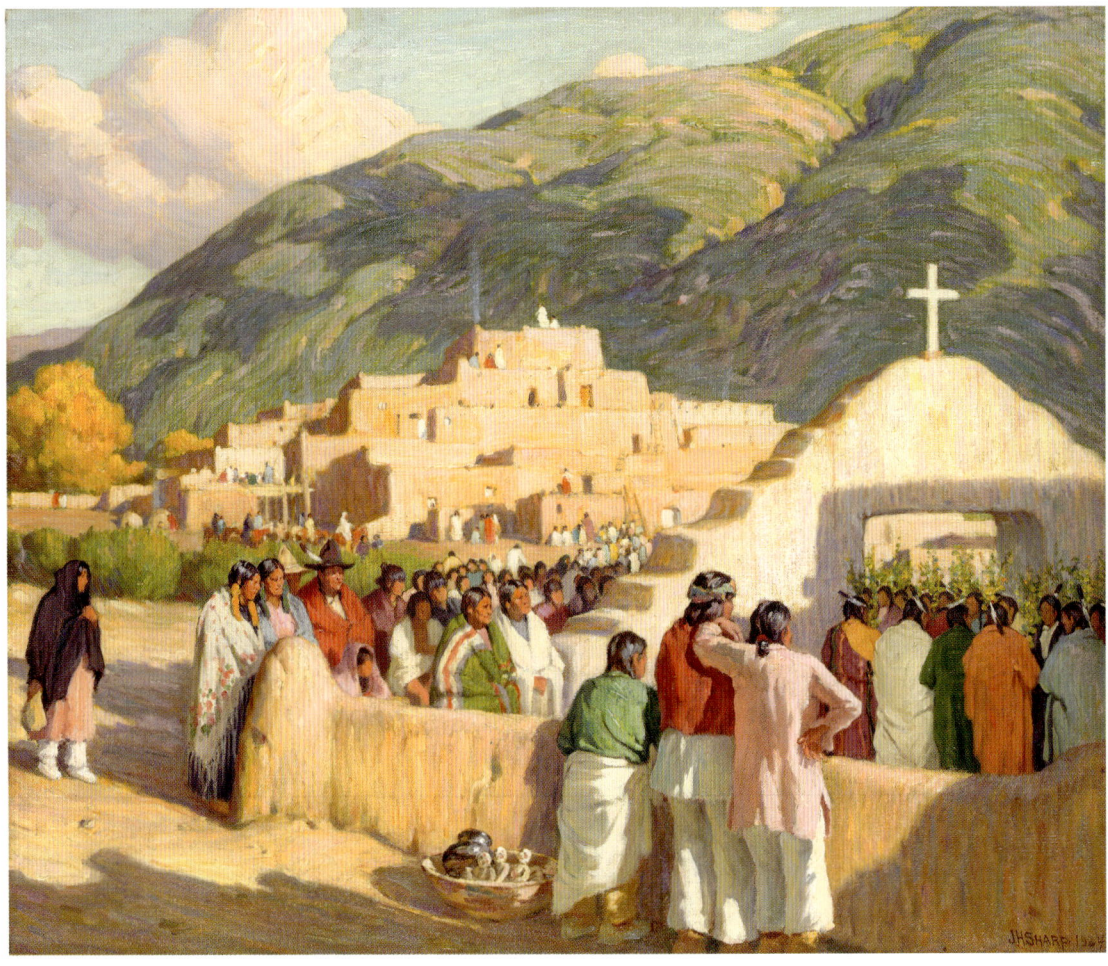

[PLATE 1.30]

JOSEPH HENRY SHARP

Sunset Dance—Ceremony to the Evening Sun

1924, oil on canvas,
25 1/8 x 30 in.
Smithsonian American Art
Museum, Washington, DC. Gift of
Arvin Gottlieb. 1991.205.15

approximately of equal height. In fact, the smoke rises higher than the cross, if we consider these two metaphors as comparable, not church dominant. It seems that Sharp is portraying church and Pueblo as coequal.[119]

As Sharp wrote to Butler in the fall of 1919, "The older I grow the harder I work."[120] He wasn't exaggerating. Through the 1920s Sharp continued to produce one canvas after another of Montana and Taos genre paintings, Indian portraits, firelights, and landscapes, along with still lifes, and maintained an active exhibition schedule. His work provided happy memories for patrons and tourists of their cultural discoveries in Taos, much as travelers had purchased Canaletto's eighteenth-century Venetian works on the Grand Tour. Sharp's paintings generated from the 1920s to the 1940s are a visit to Taos with the artist as our tour guide. Sunny street scenes with Indians coming to and fro or paused to chat outside his front gate on Kit Carson Road allowed patrons to retrace their steps on the dirt road to his studio and garden they had visited [PLATE 1.31]. He painted Taos's nooks and crannies—whatever was close at hand for him. It was his life at home in Taos.

Other Taos imagery expands beyond the Pueblo and the inhabitants and

119 I thank Dr. James Moore for graciously sharing these observations and his knowledge about the celebration of San Geronimo Day and its depiction in Sharp's and other TSA artists' work.
120 JHS, Taos, to Butler, September 2, 1919, BP.

ceremonies that visitors would have seen on their itinerary there. Colorful landscapes proliferate, with and without an Indian presence, whatever the buyer might want. Taos Valley, Twining, Hondo Canyon, Taos Canyon, Lucero Canyon, and Taos Mountain were all places he relished visiting in his treks in the out-of-doors to scenes like that depicted in *Indian Village* [PLATE 1.32]. Landscape had much to say to Sharp and it gave him a new way of seeing. Like the saturated white of snow in Montana, the jeweled tones of the mountains at Taos held a special place in Sharp's heart.

Like the French peasants in popular nineteenth-century imagery, Indians seemed to live outside contemporary time and were a link to a preindustrial past. Sharp tapped into this appeal. In such works as *Gift Dance Drummers* [PLATE 1.33], a Puvis de Chavannes idyll without the sensuality and nudity, Pueblo life appears untroubled. The gathering of Pueblo families in groups portrayed in the painting suggests harmony and an alternative to contemporary urban society.

By 1930 an active septuagenarian, Sharp had found the essentials for a meaningful and satisfactory life. Although he was looking back on his life, he did not feel that most of it was over. In fact, the opposite was true: he was examining himself as he made another fresh start. Sharp wrote to Scheuerle in 1936 openly expressing these sentiments and summing up his artistic endeavors of that decade:

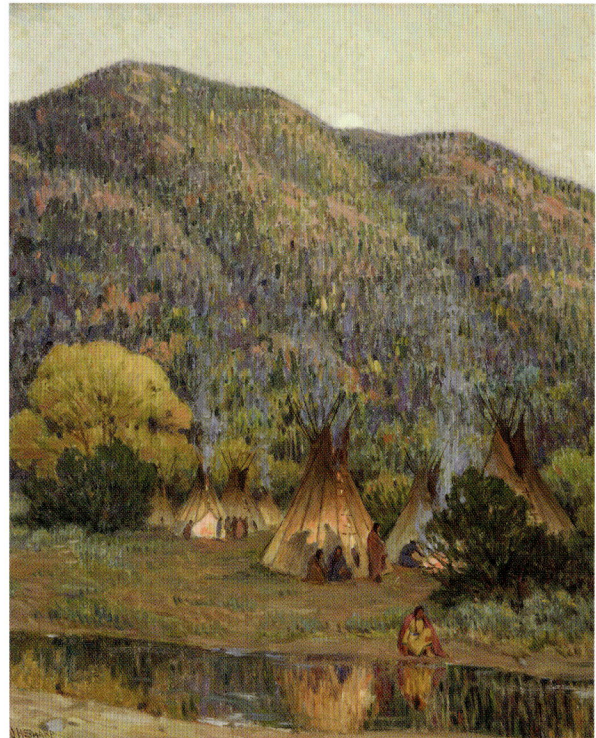

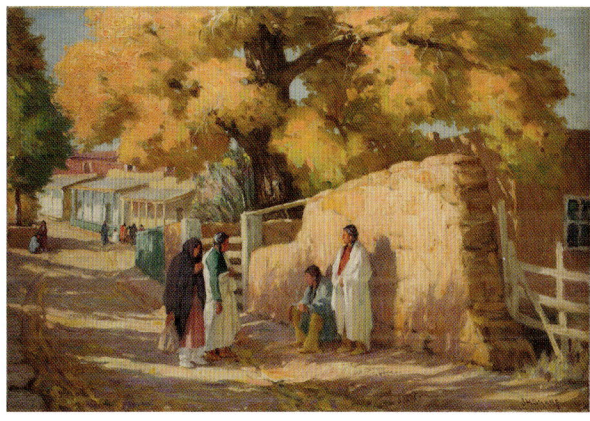

[PLATE 1.31]

JOSEPH HENRY SHARP

Summer Visitors

ca. 1926, oil on canvas,
16 x 24 in.
Denver Art Museum,
Denver, Colorado. 2013.115

[PLATE 1.32]

JOSEPH HENRY SHARP

Indian Village

ca. 1920, oil on canvas,
23 ½ x 20 in.
Cincinnati Art Museum,
Cincinnati, Ohio. 2003.102

> Do you know I hadn't painted an Indian for over two years until this spring. . . . I just got tired of them after over 40 yrs. of it. Besides these Indians (tho' they wear their hair like the Northers) are not so interesting as those old fighters & meat-eaters with fire water when they could get it—with all that, I never had a disagreeable experience with them in my life! I've been painting a good deal of landscapes, still life (mostly flowers on big scale) & marines.
>
> I've been been out in the mts. & canons last 2–3 weeks painting aspens—glorious! Haven't quite as much steam at 77 as 40–50–60, but work more hours than any of the young cubs around here and what is more satisfaction, I've done just as good & *better* work last 2–3 yrs than ever.[121]

121 JHS, Taos, to Scheuerle, October 13, 1936, AAA.

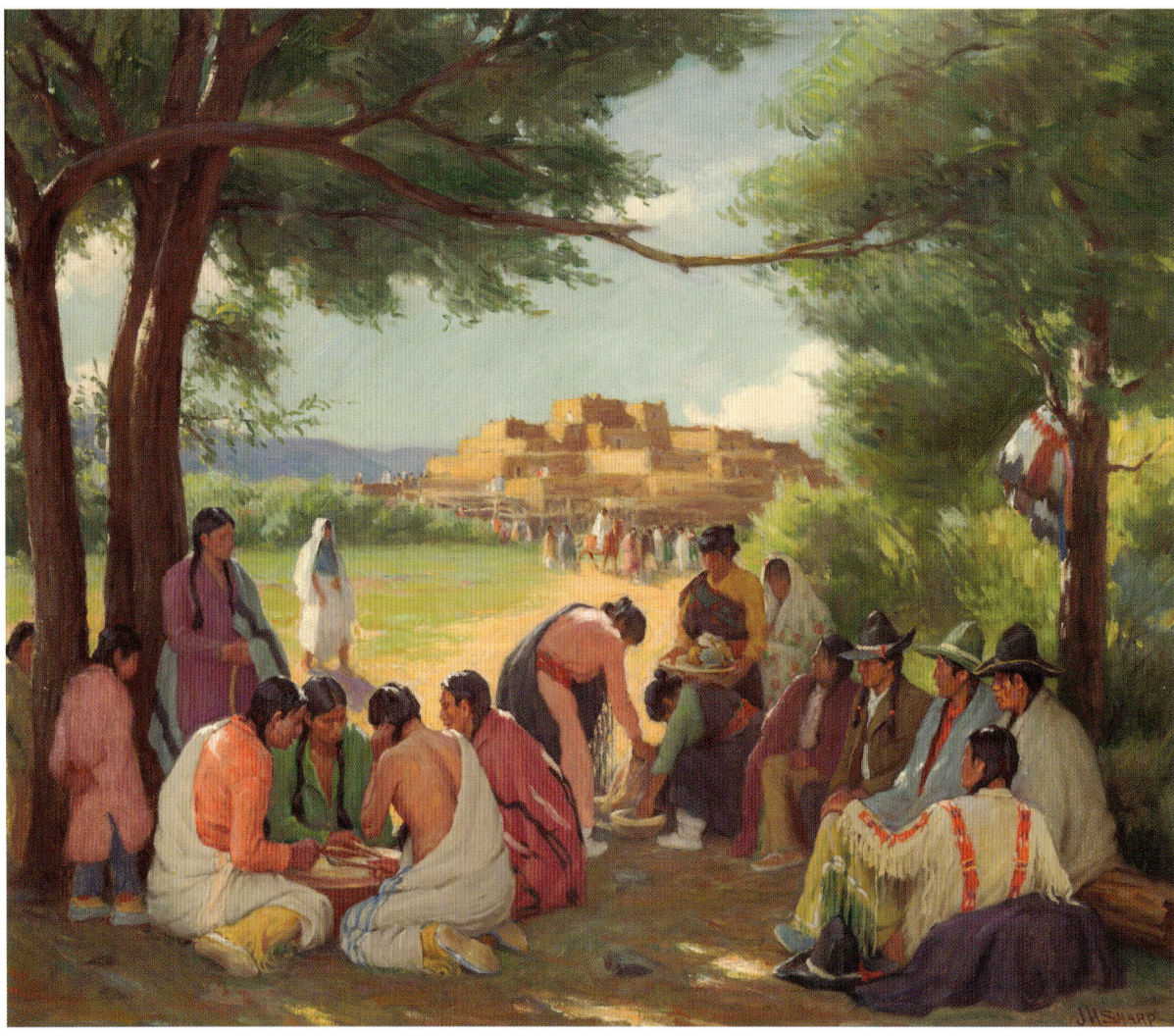

It comes as a surprise that Sharp is no longer interested in the subject matter that made his reputation as the foremost "Indian painter" of his generation. In a follow-up letter to Scheuerle, it is apparent that Sharp, "who had just gone up in a Goodyear Blimp," was maintaining his sense of adventure but was simply burned out on Indian imagery:

Just got tired—now I have to go back to [Indians] this summer. Almost cleaned out of *salable* stuff, so have to make some firelight & war bonnet potboilers! I have a lot of heads of the fine old fellows yet, but people (this generation) are only interested in a curious way, not as purchasers. Very few of the present generation know anything of the Indian, the romance, dignity & beauty of their life, & care less. In a way, all these cowboy stunts, with Indians or not makes it all kind of common & curio stuff—they have it in every town out west that has a hotel or place for trailers![122]

Over the preceding decades, Sharp had watched the world change around him. Like everyone else, he had made it through the Great

122 JHS, Litchfield Park, AZ, to Scheuerle, April 15, 1937, AAA.

Depression, but he was writing in 1937, when the so-called Roosevelt recession took the steam out of the economic recovery. He had also seen the transition from railroad to automobile tourism and auto camping, which might explain his comment about people being "interested in a curious way, not as purchasers." One's identity is shaped by timing as well as place, and there comes a time when you see that the "world" has changed but you no longer can.

One destination out of reach for most of the mainland U.S. public was access to Hawaii, an exotic dream locale in the 1930s. Dazzling Hawaiian watercolors and oils, primarily marines, with some florals, became a respected and productive subject matter [PLATE 1.34]. In March 1930 Sharp mailed a humorous Honolulu postcard to the *Taos Valley News* teasing, "Come in, the water's fine," knowing temperatures were cold in northern New Mexico.[123] He added that Hawaii was the "most beautiful part of the world we have seen." The following February, Sharp exhibited a collection of Hawaiian and Taos paintings at Gump's Fine Art Gallery in Waikiki. In 1935 Kreimer and Brother Co. in Cincinnati held an exhibition of "Hawaiian and Taos Paintings" that also included works from a Japanese trip. Mary Alexander, who reviewed the show, noted:

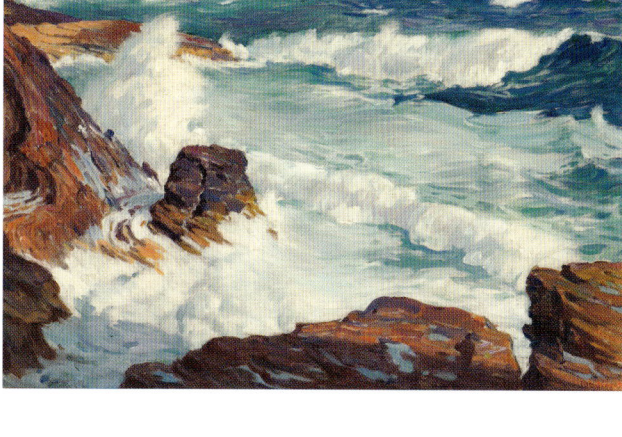

[PLATE 1.34]

JOSEPH HENRY SHARP

A Scene Near Diamond Head, Honolulu, Hawaii

1930-1938, oil on canvas, 35 ⅝ x 40 ⅝ in. Gilcrease Museum, Tulsa, Oklahoma. Gift of the Thomas Gilcrease Foundation, 1955. 0137.306

> One of the finest and most novel features is the series of water colors done on the coast of Hawaii; these are the most attractive and colorful paintings Mr. Sharp has ever exhibited, and the pleasure he has taken in doing them is as evident as that he has taken in doing his floral pieces and landscapes. His flower studies and landscapes are painted with the same serious and thoughtful care for the actual objects and their effect in arrangement and light as his Indian paintings.[124]

Sharp did return to Indian imagery. As Alexander wrote, "He is to us always our beloved Indian painter and in the benevolent way is bound up in the romance and the folklore of the Indian." In particular she thought *John and Jerry Chanting* [PLATE 1.35] "exceedingly well painted."[125] John and Jerry—Hunting Son (John Gomez) and Elk Foot (Jerry Mirabal)— were a popular modeling duo among artists and, like Crucita and Leaf Down, posed for Sharp for years in innumerable motifs

Despite his temporary disillusionment with painting Indians, he knew how he wanted to be remembered, and it wasn't as a marine or still-life

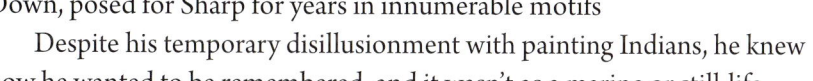

123 "The Artist's Colony Corner," *Taos Valley News*, March 6, 1930.

124 Mary L. Alexander, "The Week in Art Circles," *Cincinnati Enquirer*, November 12, 1935, CAMA.

125 Alexander, "The Week in Art Circles."

artist. "I want to be known as a *TAOS* painter since I discovered it and told the other boys," he bristled to a historian who wanted to include him in a *Who's Who of California* in 1941. "Most of my painter life has been spent in New Mexico, Montana, and the Northwest Indian country."[126] The 1940s was proving another busy decade and he was still fighting for his

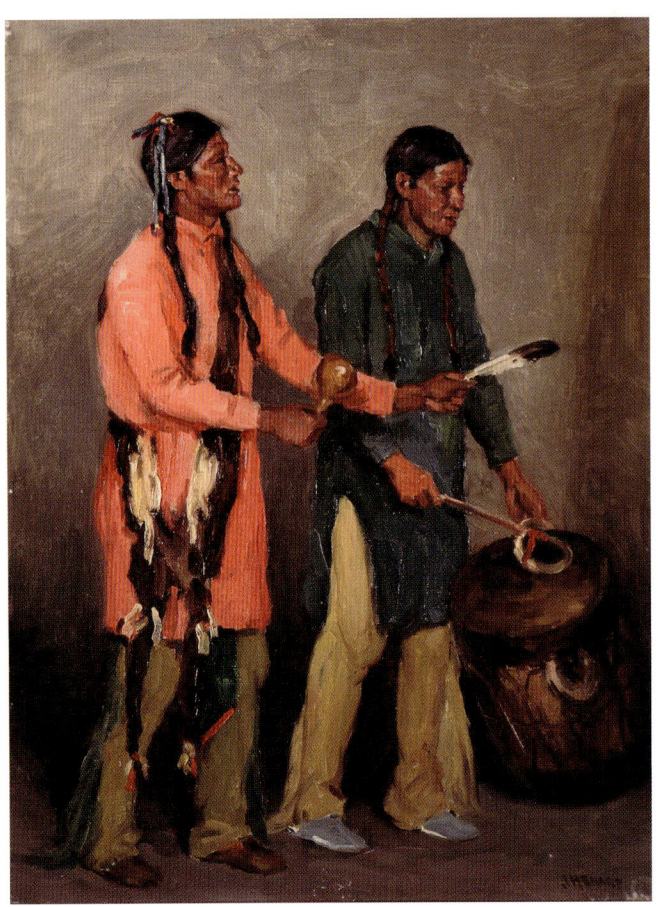

[PLATE 1.35]

JOSEPH HENRY SHARP

John and Jerry Chanting

ca. 1935, oil on canvas,
24 ¼ x 18 ¼ in.
Buffalo Bill Center of the West,
Cody, Wyoming. 24.65

legacy. He wrote a patron in 1943, "I feel the years rushing by and beginning to 'put my house in order.'"[127] The artist offered the patron a deal on one of the versions of *The Great Mystery* [PLATE 1.36] for half price, along with an eighty-dollar carved framed. Sharp had always been particular about frames and continued in the 1940s to buy from Newcomb-Macklin Co., commenting that he "would have sold more pictures if I had frames for them."[128] To another client he wrote that he continued "to work in the studio 3–4 hrs. every am. that I'm not working outside—not with so much steam & energy, but enough." Then cheekily he added, "We celebrate our birthdays together—her's Oct 7, & mine Sept 27th—same cake & don't have to blow out so many candles!"[129]

The following summer Sharp wrote a gallery owner off the cuff: "Did I tell you I sold all my remaining old Custer Battle & other Chiefs & warriors of the N.W. and several of the *large* ones to the Gilcrease Foundation, Okla. 75 of those old portraits now, the other 200 painted 30–45 yrs. ago are in Museums or some such institutions where they remain without transfer or re-sale, & I am satisfied."[130] Sharp had secured his artistic legacy with oilman Thomas Gilcrease, his most important patron in the latter part of his career. Almost 250 paintings and numerous artifacts, including his beloved trademark hat, are part of this collection, the largest holder of his paintings.

Sharp was hardly "satisfied," however. He continued describing his plans to the dealer: "Now this year will concentrate on the rest of things in Studio to dispose of. Other sales last year good. Expect it to continue, as with return of gas many old patrons & others from Tex. Okla & N.M. were in Taos & had $ to spend!" He worked too hard, too long, to

126 JHS to Ferdinand Serrett, November 12, 1941, CAMA.

127 JHS to Ferdinand Serrett, November 12, 1941, CAMA.

128 JHS, Taos, to Mrs. C. R. McKenzie, El Paso, September 16, 1946, ADD.

129 JHS, Santa Fe, NM, to Miss Martha E. Nickles, Cincinnati, OH, October 9, 1944, ADD.

130 JHS, Pasadena, to Mrs. McKenzie, March 26, 1946, ADD.

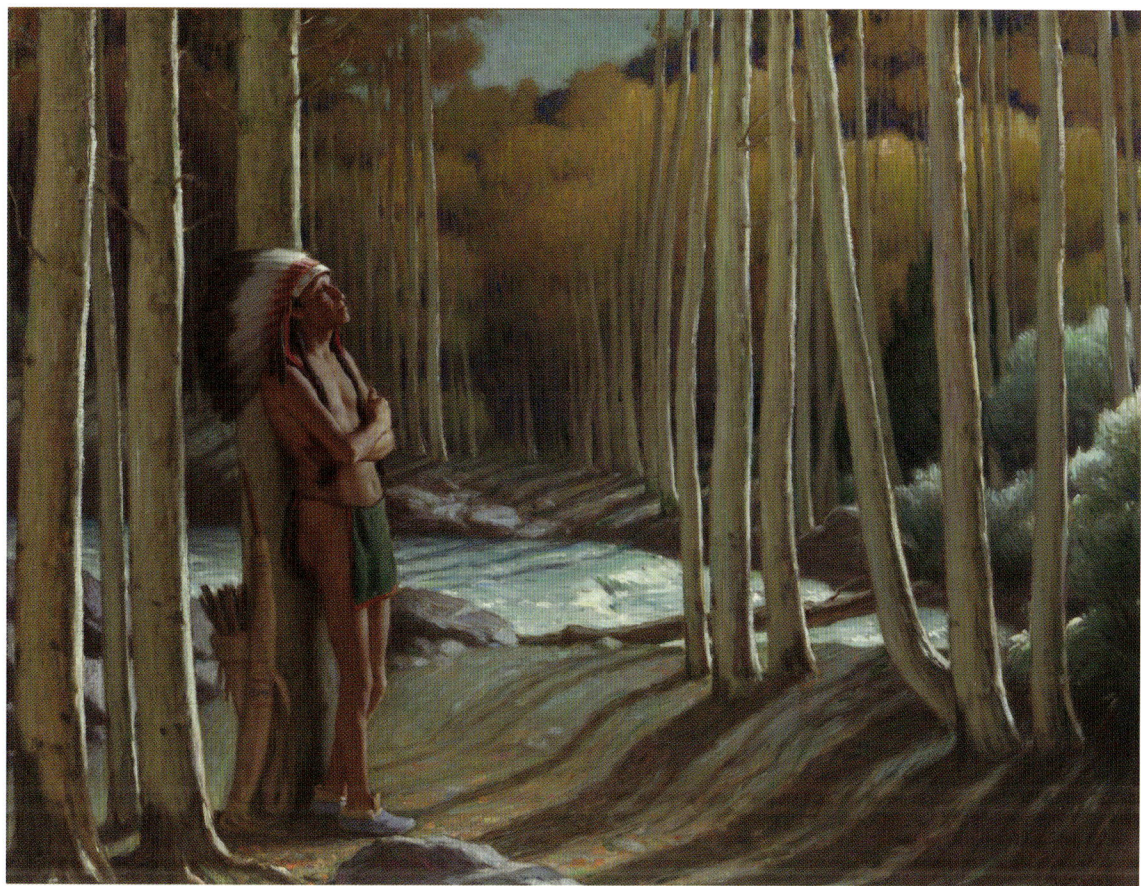

[PLATE 1.36]

JOSEPH HENRY SHARP

The Great Mystery

ca. 1929, oil on canvas,
35 ⅞ x 45 ¹⁵/₁₆ in.
Gilcrease Museum, Tulsa,
Oklahoma. Gift of the Thomas
Gilcrease Foundation, 1955.
0137.325

stop marketing his work. He had time left. A year before his death, he
corresponded with a client advising how to hang her painting:

> "You may have to re-arrange your pictures and wall space—we do
> it in studio & house. To get full benefit it should be put in a *full*
> light—not *against* a window. Have some one hold the picture up
> in various places on the walls & *see* when it fits in before changing
> any permanently. It is as hard to frame & place a painting as it is to
> paint them!"[131]

To use one of Sharp's favorite verbs, he *hustled* until the very end. Sharp
died on August 29, 1953.

In his later years, he supplied biographical information to a relative who
wanted to write an article about him. This is how he summed up his life:

> "In your article—don't go up in the air—'Uncle Henry' is not
> eminent, or a great artist & all that—he's just worked hard & had
> a lot of fun doing it, & will have more. Aunt Addie & Aunt Louise
> *deserve* 50–50 for anything we have accomplished. I've fallen short
> of my aims—probably not ten canvases in 60 yrs. work that are
> anyways near satisfactory."

Despite this humble self-assessment, Joseph Henry Sharp gave us much to
contemplate, admire, and question in his inexhaustible seventy-year career.
His paintings were many things to many people and continue to be so today.

---

131 JHS, Taos, to Mrs. Krohn, September 3, 1952, ADD.

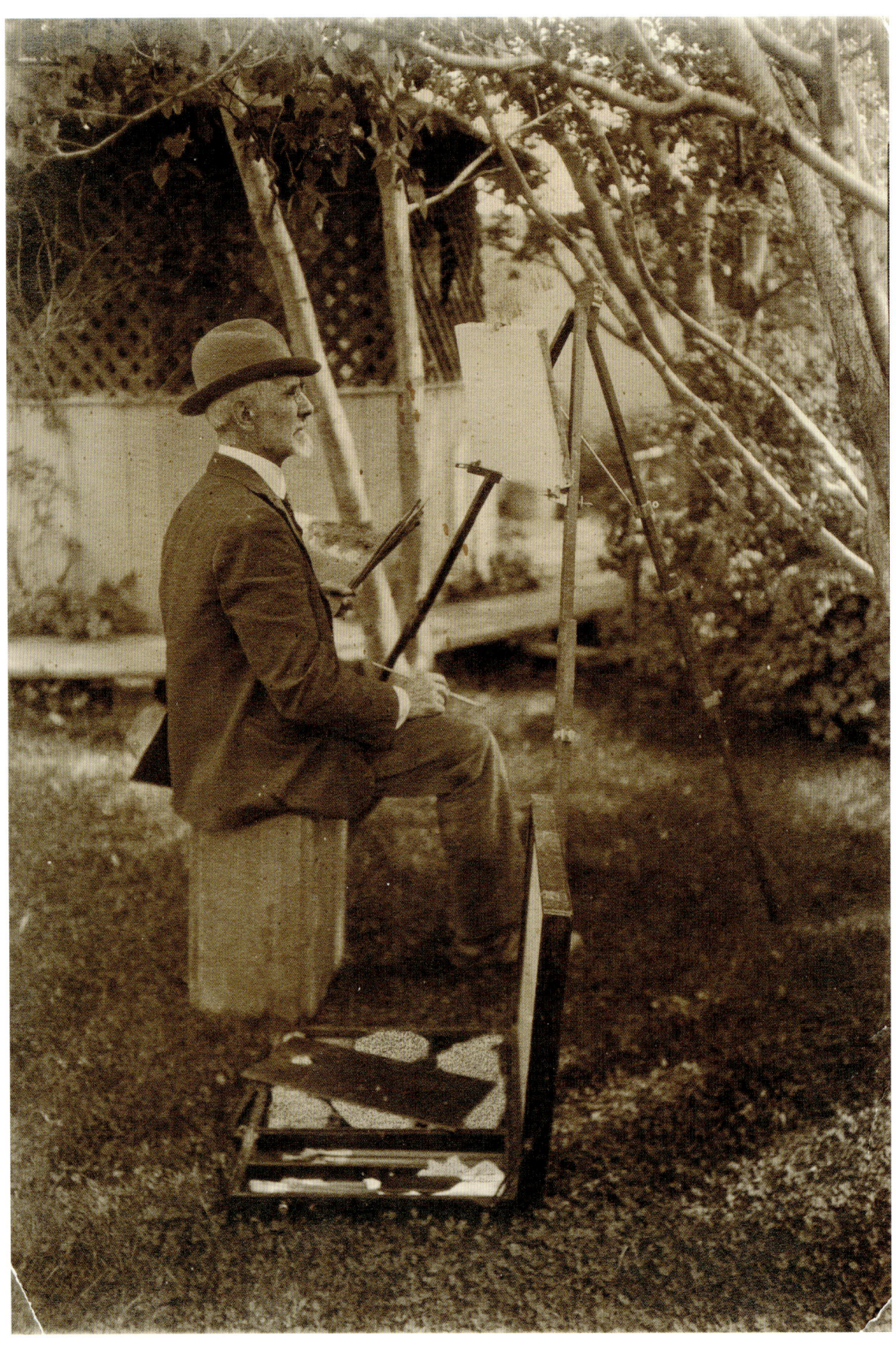

UNKNOWN PHOTOGRAPHER, *Sharp Painting in the Field*. 1920, photograph, b&w
Harold McCracken Research Library, Buffalo Bill Center of the West, Cody, Wyoming. JHSC. Gift of Mr. and Mrs. Forrest Fenn. P.22.23.1

PETER H. HASSRICK

THE STUDIOS OF JOSEPH HENRY SHARP

The history of artist Joseph Henry Sharp's multifarious studios is as complex and fascinating as any part of his illustrious and lengthy career as an artist. In 1948, when the artist was eighty-nine years old and appeared much as he had when he produced his rare, late self-portrait [PAGE 2], he penned a letter to the esteemed Smithsonian ethnologist John C. Ewers, recounting his genesis story as a painter of American Indians. He told Ewers about the time, as a boy of six or seven, he had first encountered Indians in rural Ohio where he grew up, how "exciting and interesting" it was and what a "deep impression" it made on him. He then wrote that his whole saga as a painter of Indians had begun in the late 1890s when he "had a little studio at the McMicken School" in Cincinnati. There, he said, he painted his first serious Indian portrait, one of a Sioux man named "Ogalalla Fire,"[1] and an art collector from Youngstown, Joseph G. Butler Jr., purchased it and started Sharp on his road to fame. "This decided me," he wrote Ewers, "and in 1893 [I] skipped for the West—never regretted it!"[2]

This narrative, though compelling, is a bit confusing. Sharp said Butler's *late* 1890 purchase had caused him to go west for the first time, yet he also asserted that he initially split for the West in 1893. Moreover, there was no McMicken School in the 1890s as it had ceased to exist in 1889. The following essay may help to set the record straight, because wherever that "little studio" was and however it connected to his artistic and philosophical course are profoundly significant elements in the developing story of Sharp as an artist.

The McMicken School of Drawing and Design was founded in 1869 for the "promotion of taste and design in the industrial arts," and was one of the first established departments of the University of Cincinnati.[3] Sharp enrolled there in 1874 as a fourteen-year-old

---

1 "Ogalalla Fire" has several spelling variations. The foregoing appears to have been the preferred spelling among Henry Farny and his Cincinnati artist friends, including Sharp. Some newspapers spelled it "Ogallalla Fire" (unidentified clipping, ca. 1899, JHSC). At other times, but not consistently, Sharp used a shortened version, "Oglalla Fire." The name of the Lakota Sioux band from which the man's first name is derived is commonly spelled "Oglala."

2 JHS to Ewers, September 20, 1948, JHSC.

3 "Art Academy History," Art Academy of Cincinnati, https://www.artacademy.edu/about-aac/history/history.php.

boy and stayed there, at least intermittently, until 1887. He was probably a student there in 1879 and may have had a small studio there that year when he painted a work titled *An Artist's Attic* (1879; location unknown), probably a view of a garret workspace, and submitted it to the art wing of the Cincinnati Industrial Exposition.[4] In 1882, following a year of study in Antwerp, he set up his first real Cincinnati studio at 30 W. Fourth Street in the Ogden Building, which was known for hosting artists. Although he was probably enrolled briefly at the McMicken School in 1885, most of his time in the next few years was spent back in Europe. When he returned for an extended period in the late 1880s, he is thought to have moved once again to the Ogden Building and reestablished his studio there. It would have been impossible for Sharp to have had a studio at the McMicken School in either the early or late 1890s, since it had been converted into the new Art Academy of Cincinnati, next door to the Cincinnati Art Museum, in 1887.[5]

After his marriage to Addie Byram in 1892, Sharp took up teaching life drawing at the Art Academy. In that same year, according to one of the standard sources on Cincinnati's art scene, *The Queen and the Arts*, Sharp employed the model for his first Indian portrait, *Ogalalla Sioux Indian Scout* [PLATE 2.1], a Sioux man who "was passing through the city."[6] But this source and Sharp's memory are equally flawed. The portrait in question was actually not painted until 1898 (as it is dated on the canvas), and Sharp completed the oil not at the McMicken art school but in his large studio in downtown Cincinnati. By the late 1890s, the date Sharp gave Ewers as his debut in the West, Sharp had been west twice, once in 1883 and again in 1893, so the portrait could not have served as an impetus for sending the artist to the frontier. And as for Oglala Fire being stranded in town or just passing through, he in fact had been in Cincinnati since at least 1881 and continued to reside there as late as 1901.[7] Oglala Fire was the primary model for Sharp's mentor, Henry F. Farny. Known to Farny as "Joe," Oglala Fire was also Farny's studio assistant and man servant and the janitor at the Cincinnati Art Club, an organization founded in part by Farny and Sharp in 1888.[8] Butler did buy Sharp's *Ogalalla Sioux Indian Scout* in 1899, probably from a joint exhibit of the Society of Western Artists in Cincinnati. He paid

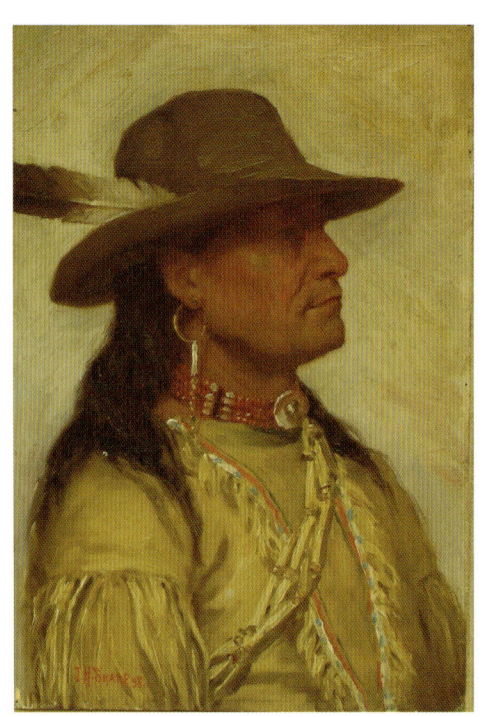

[PLATE 2.1]

JOSEPH HENRY SHARP

Ogalalla Sioux Indian Scout

1898, oil on canvas, 13 x 9 in.
Butler Institute of American Art,
Youngstown, Ohio. 913-O-505

---

4 *See Art Catalogue, Industrial Exposition* (Cincinnati, 1879), no. 254. The whereabouts of the work is unknown.

5 *Art Catalogue, Industrial Exposition*, no. 254.

6 Vitz, *The Queen and the Arts*−, 181.

7 Farny used Oglala Fire as a model in his painting *End of the Race* (1881; Rentschler Collection, American Heritage Center, University of Wyoming) and in a 1902 portrait, *Chief Ogallala Fire* (private collection).

8 See Susan Labry Meyn, *Henry Farny Paints the Far West* (Cincinnati: Cincinnati Art Museum, 2007), 64, 139; and Denny Carter, *Henry Farny* (New York: Watson−Guptill, 1978), 32.

seventy-five dollars for the painting.[9] Sharp had already sold one major western painting, *The Harvest Dance* [PLATE 2.2] for five hundred dollars to the Cincinnati Art Museum in 1894, so Butler's initial purchase was certainly nothing exceptional.[10]

In 1899 Sharp divulged the real inspiration for his selection of the West and Indians as subjects for his art. It had to do with Farny and the ambiance of Farny's Cincinnati studio. In what might be regarded as a national debut, an article in the art magazine *Brush and Pencil* in 1899, Sharp referred to himself as "an artist among the Indians." In the second paragraph of this account of his western muse, Sharp said, "I must pay

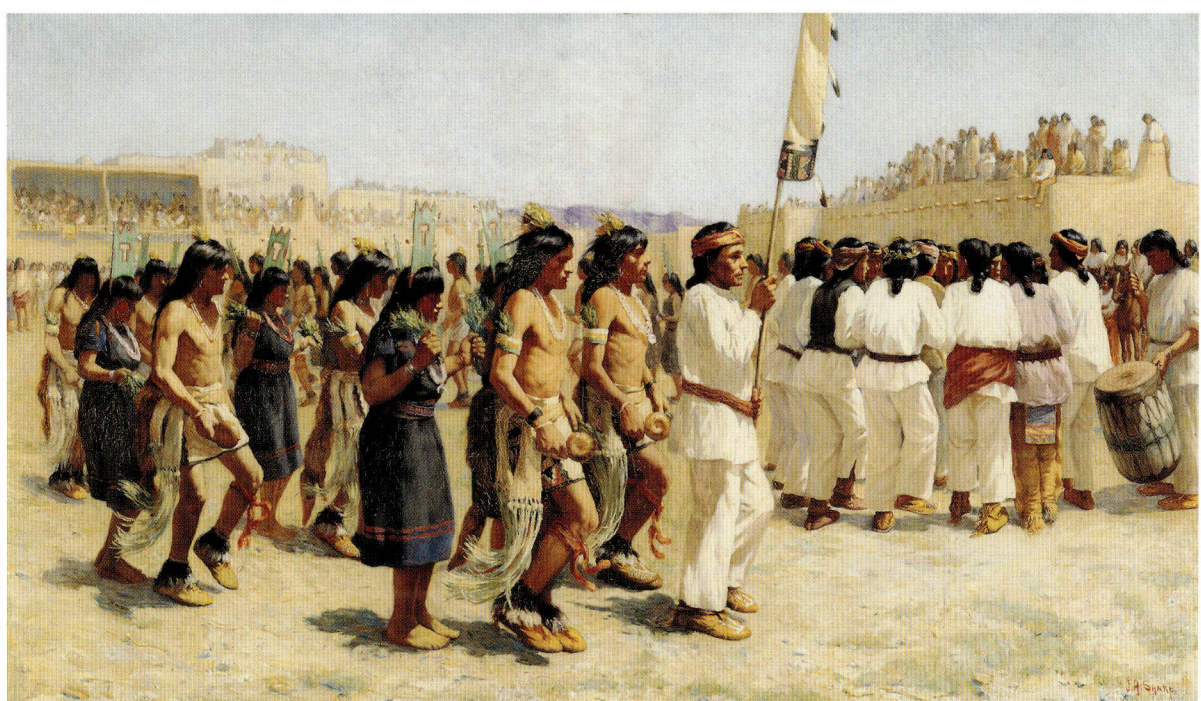

tribute to Mr. Henry F. Farny, not only a pioneer in this field, but one of the most successful delineators of Indian life and character."[11] Sharp reported that he had made his first productive trip to the West when he visited New Mexico in 1893. Farny had preceded him into the West by more than a dozen years, in 1881, when the older artist made his initial excursion to Fort Yates in North Dakota to paint among the Standing Rock Sioux. Twelve years Sharp's senior, Farny quickly established himself as the pictorial champion of the Northern Plains Indian people. "Farny has struck an artistic bonanza," wrote one reporter upon his return.[12] What struck most of Farny's acquaintances was not just the paintings of Native people that began to appear on his easel but the Sioux artifacts he brought home with him. Another reporter referred to the artist's collection as "a

[PLATE 2.2]

JOSEPH HENRY SHARP

The Harvest Dance

1893-1894, oil on canvas,
27 11/16 x 48 5/8 in.
Cincinnati Art Museum,
Cincinnati, Ohio. 1894.10

9   Sharp's sales ledgers, 1899; untitled article about the exhibit, both JHSC.
10 Sharp's sales ledgers, 1894, JHSC.
11 Sharp, "An Artist among the Indians," 1.
12 "Studio Studies," *Cincinnati Commercial Tribune*, December 1, 1881.

great quantity of Indian loot," but more thoughtful assessments considered the objects "his treasures."[13] Deeply proud of his acquisitions, Farny proclaimed that he would "soon put them on exhibit on Fourth Street," by which he meant his studio in the Ogden Building.[14] Sharp rented his first major studio in the same building the next year and no doubt envied and soon sought to emulate Farny's space.[15]

Artist studios functioned in a number of different ways in Sharp's day. They were first and foremost workspaces where, in Sharp's case, the painter labored over his canvases. In addition, though, they provided a place for artistic interaction, and Sharp would have profited greatly from interfacing with the likes of Farny and their close mutual friend and mentor Frank Duveneck in the Ogden Building. Furthermore, each selected artifact that decorated the studio and helped fill those canvases invited individual reaction, sometimes becoming "the central subject that gathers round it the most gratifying and entertaining talk."[16]

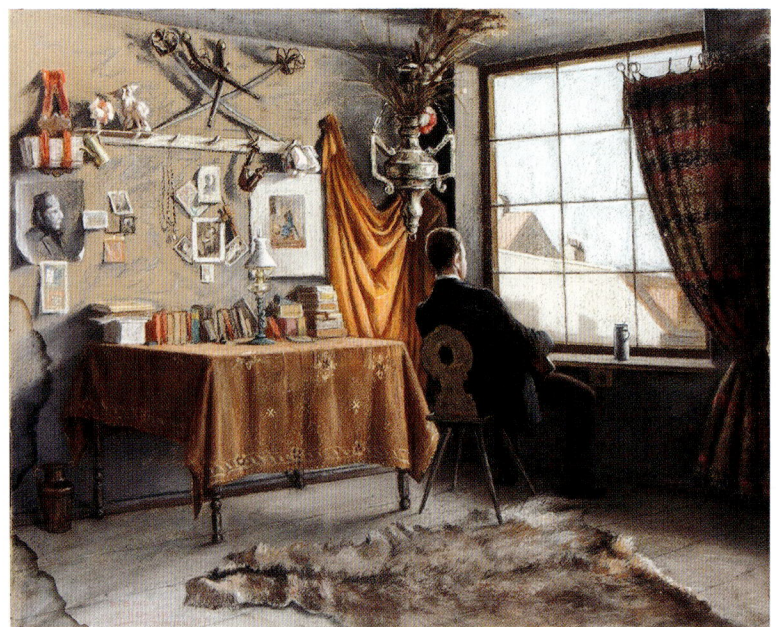

[PLATE 2.3]

JOSEPH HENRY SHARP

My Studio, Munich

1888, pastel, 22 x 23 in.
TIA Collection,
Santa Fe, New Mexico

Many artists used their studios as commercial spaces as well. During the 1890s, Sharp was particularly adept at marketing his work through his studio. He hosted large and successful exhibitions there in 1894 and 1896, for example, interspersed with commercial gallery shows.[17] For the 1894 studio display, as a reporter described it, the space was converted into "an exhibition room, and on its walls are over one hundred canvases and watercolors."[18]

But for all artists of the period, the studio represented the quintessence of the individual artist's personality. Here was a place, organized and decorated by the artist, that revealed his or her particular aesthetic and cultural persona. In 1888, while studying with Carl von Marr in Munich, Sharp had a studio that he proudly decorated with objets d'art he collected in and around Bavaria [PLATE 2.3]. When he returned to Cincinnati the next year, these objects entered his studio at 30 W. Fourth Street. The

---

13 "Mr. Farny among the Sioux," *Cincinnati Daily Gazette*, November 8, 1881; "Lo! The Poor Indian," *Cincinnati Inquirer*, November 8, 1881.

14 "Lo! The Poor Indian."

15 Forrest Fenn, *Teepee Smoke: A New Look into the Life and Work of Joseph Henry Sharp* (Santa Fe: One Horse Land and Cattle Co, 2007), 38.

16 "Studio Studies."

17 See *Studio of J. H. Sharp* (April 1894), *Exhibition: Studio of J. H. Sharp* (November 1896), and *Exhibition of Paintings* (Traxel & Maas Galleries, April 1894), JHSC.

18 "Art and Artists," unidentified clipping, April 1894, JHSC.

community considered the collection as one of Cincinnati's true "treasure troves." He was praised for possessing a discerning eye in collecting European bric-a-brac and an adventurous spirit for having preserved such exotic artifacts. The reviewer referred to his studio as "a very interesting place of rendezvous for those who have an intensified hankering after the beautiful in art and the genuine in curios."[19] At a time prior to Sharp's concentration on painting Native people of the West, this European, Old World milieu was the artistic identity that he wished to present.

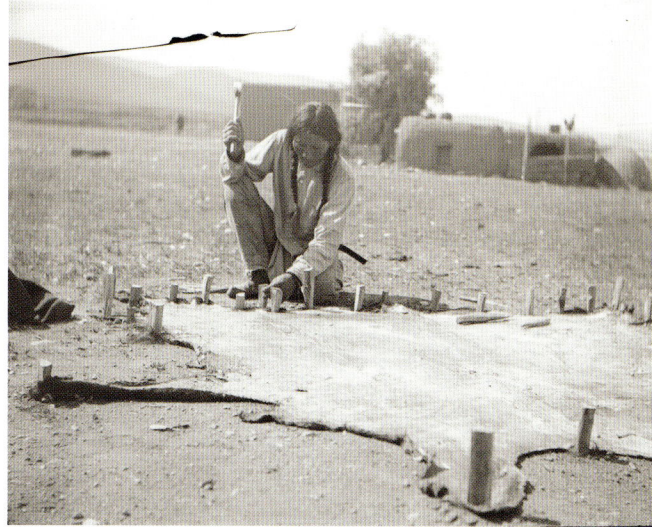

After 1893 Sharp's artistic personality and focus began to shift to a far more American scene. He said that from the moment he started studying at the new Cincinnati Art Academy in the late 1880s, he had "wanted to paint Indians." And he would probably have moved in that direction had it not been for a powerful impediment in the person of Henry Farny. "Farny was doing them [Indians]," he wrote, and "dissuaded me by telling of hardships & dangers & made me feel I didn't exactly have a right to paint Indians—after a couple of years or so when he saw I was determined to go west, he gave me books on Pueblo Indians, & particularly the Penitentes of N. Mex, & wanted me to take that up."[20] When he visited New Mexico in 1893, Sharp was essentially following Farny's directive. Ultimately, though, he defied Farny's earlier, professed territorial claim on the Northern Plains tribes and traveled in 1899 to paint among the Crow and Northern Cheyenne, as well as the Pueblos near Taos and Santa Fe.

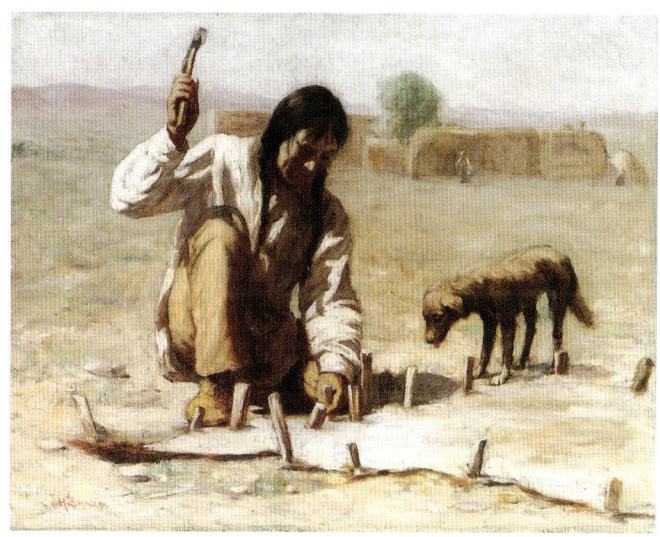

[PLATE 2.4]

JOSEPH HENRY SHARP

Stretching the Hide

1894, photograph, b&w
C. M. Russell Museum,
Great Falls, Montana

[PLATE 2.5]

JOSEPH HENRY SHARP

Stretching the Hide

1894, oil on canvas,
10 ⅝ × 13 ¾ in.
Private Collection, Image courtesy
of Sotheby's, New York, New York

As early as the fall of 1893, Sharp's studio walls began to fill with Indian relics in emulation of Farny's collection. Festooned with Pueblo artifacts, his workspace, according to the *Cincinnati Enquirer*, "vividly suggested his recent journey. He spent most of the summer months in [New] Mexico. It would seem as if a whole tribe of Indians . . . could camp right in his front studio without bringing any baggage or even a change of clothing with them, and not miss any of their necessities for living."[21] These artifacts would help

19 "Treasure Troves," *Cincinnati Commercial Tribune*, 1889, clipping, JHSC.

20 JHS to Robert Taft, April 1939, Robert Taft Collection, Kansas Historical Society, Topeka, Kansas..

21 Unidentified clipping, *Cincinnati Enquirer*, fall 1893, JHSC.

Sharp prepare for an important 1894 exhibition of his work, some from New Mexico and others from studies he had made in and around Cincinnati.[22]

Photographs he took at the Pueblos also began to fill the drawers in his studio [PLATE 2.4]. He consulted these images closely when composing paintings such as *Stretching the Hide*, of 1894. A newspaper reviewer who saw Sharp's exhibition at the Traxel and Maas Galleries proclaimed *Stretching the Hide* [PLATE 2.5] to be "one of the most delicate bits of color in the exhibition," suggesting that Sharp collected color field studies to work from, as well.[23]

In the summer of 1894 the Sharps sailed for Europe where the artist took up studio space at the Académie Julian in Paris. His intention was to become proficient in portraiture and to visit the ateliers of some of the French masters of the day. But it was a representation at another studio, that of the Spanish Baroque painter Diego Velázquez, that intrigued him most. Interrupting his stint in Paris, he and Duveneck took a side trip to Madrid to visit the Prado Museum. They both delighted in Velázquez's famous painting of his studio, *Las Meninas* (1656; Museo del Prado, Madrid), in which he pictured himself painting the king and queen of Spain as well as their daughter, La Infanta, Margarita. Relishing Velázquez's use of mixed light sources and virtuoso brushwork, they copied several of the Spanish master's works over a number of weeks' study.[24] The Prado also housed paintings by Rembrandt and Caravaggio, two fellow Baroque masters of light, but Sharp and Duveneck were primarily interested in Velázquez. Rembrandt was an advocate of metaphysical light and Caravaggio used it primarily for dramatic effect. Velázquez, however, explored light as a way of defining form and experimented with the effects of indoor and outdoor light. Those qualities were what the two American painters most appreciated.[25]

On returning to Cincinnati in the fall of 1896, Sharp moved into a new, possibly larger studio in the Ogden Building. He used the space to host an exhibition, this time featuring his European works exclusively. "The

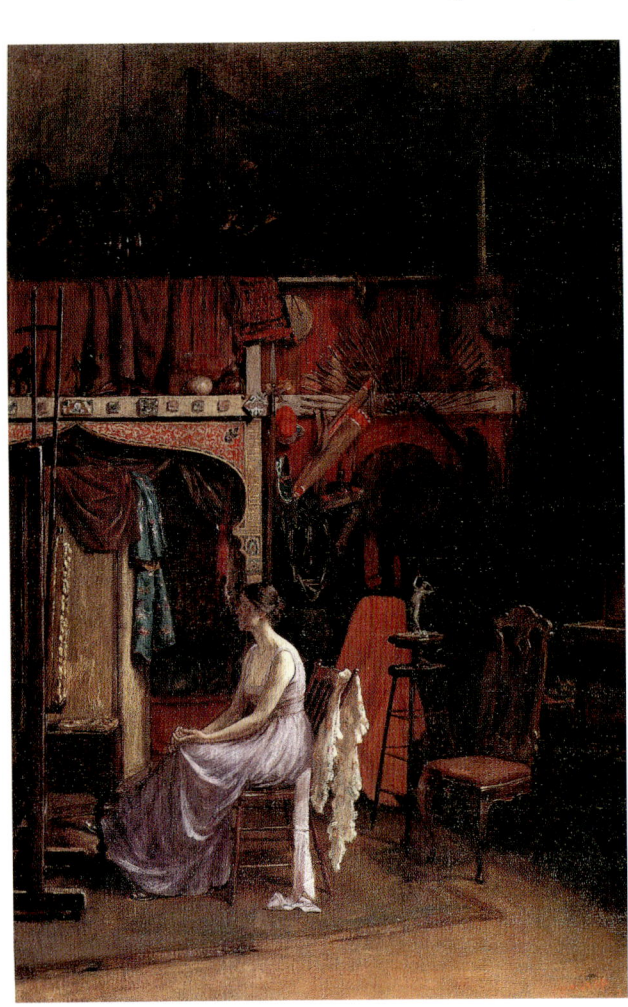

[PLATE 2.6]

JOSEPH HENRY SHARP

In the Studio

1897, oil on canvas,
32 ¾ × 22 ¼ in.
Collection of the Huntington
Museum of Art, Huntington,
West Virginia with funds provided
by the Winslow Anderson
Endowment

22 *Exhibition of Paintings, April 1894: J. H. Sharp* (Cincinnati: Traxel and Maas Gallery, 1894).

23 "Four Walls of Pictures," *Cincinnati Commercial Tribune*, April 22, 1894.

24 A photograph of Addie posing in Sharp's Cincinnati studio in about 1896 includes his large oil copy of one version of *La Infanta* (C. M. Russell Museum).

25 According to unidentified clippings in JHSC, the two artists exhibited a selection of these copies in the Cincinnati Art Museum upon their return to the United States in late 1896.

new studio of Mr. J. H. Sharp has been visited with much pleasure and interest by the artist's friends and admirers," wrote one local reporter.[26] That studio was a source of immense pride for him and was alluring enough to Sharp's followers that he painted a portrait of the space with Addie in the act of contemplating one of his canvases [PLATE 2.6]. In photographs taken in the same period, Sharp himself was inserted, but the background filled with a combination of European objets d'art and Indian artifacts remained essentially the same [PLATE 2.7].

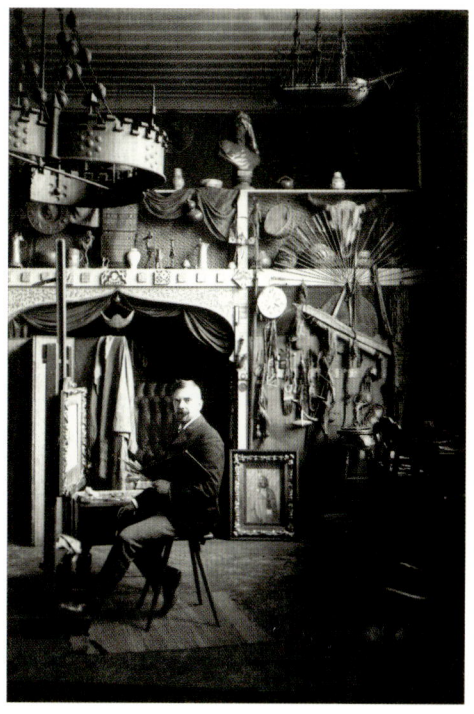

Although Addie is prominently positioned in the painting of the studio, Sharp's agenda was really to present himself through the portrayal. Arranged and picturesquely situated, this studio proved to be more than a mere creative space. Sumptuousness implied dignity, the exotic aura signified cosmopolitan sophistication, and the proper massing of materials offered a confirmation of good taste. Addie was added to the composition as a personal gesture but also as a feminized decorative adjunct to help make the space more attractive and the art more salable. This approach mirrored that of Sharp's contemporary and fellow Munich Academy student William Merritt Chase, seen in such paintings as *A Friendly Call* of 1895 [PLATE 2.8].

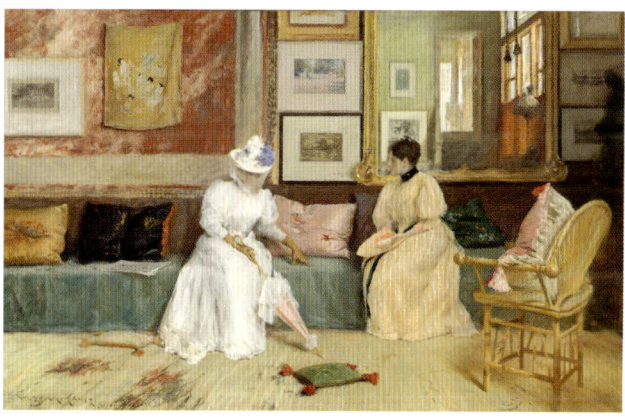

By 1898, Sharp's promising career was lauded regionally, and his studio with its bravado spirit broadly recognized. The people of Denver, for example, read about it in an article that appeared in the *Rocky Mountain News*: "He is a learned as well as a devoted collector of bric-a-brac, and his wide travels in both Europe and America have enabled him to fill his studio with specimens both rare and unique, and which are hallowed with the interest of association. Only those who, like Mr. Sharp, have traveled outside the beaten track are enabled to show true judgement and artistic interests."[27]

But Sharp's peripatetic nature kept him unmoored. By 1899 he had found a compelling alternative to the luxuriance of his Cincinnati studio, the Far West. Before embarking on his summer travels that year, he presented himself in the national press as a second-generation George Catlin, an artist among the Indians. "The Indian is becoming a factor in American pictures," he wrote that spring, "and Western artists in

[PLATE 2.7]

UNKNOWN PHOTOGRAPHER

Joseph Henry Sharp in His Cincinnati Studio

1896, photograph, b&w
Harold McCracken Research Library,
Buffalo Bill Center of the West, Cody,
Wyoming. JHSC. Gift of Mr. and
Mrs. Forrest Fenn. P.22.95

[PLATE 2.8]

WILLIAM MERRITT CHASE

A Friendly Call

1895, oil on canvas, 30 ⅛ x 48 ¼ in.
National Gallery of Art, Landover,
Maryland. Chester Dale Collection.
1943.1.2

---

26 Unidentified clippings in JHSC; catalogue for the fifty–four–work display, *Exhibition: Studio of J. H. Sharp, 1896.*

27 "Artists' Club Will Show Sharp's Monotypes," *Rocky Mountain News*, December 12, 1898.

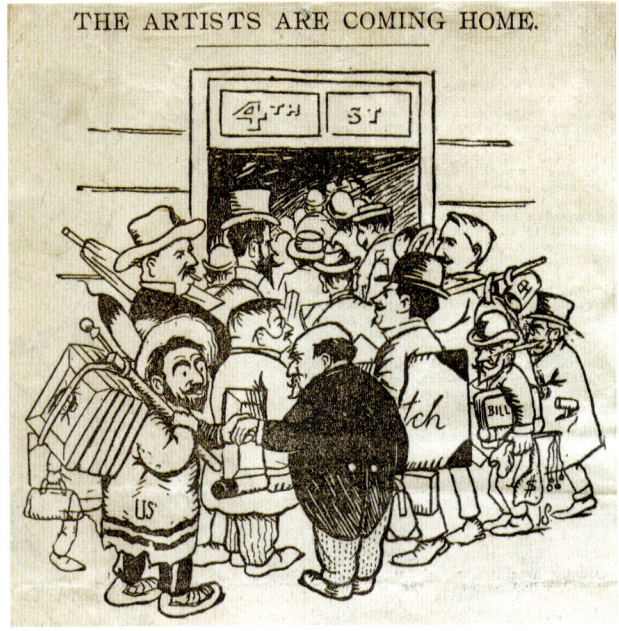

THE ARTISTS ARE COMING HOME.

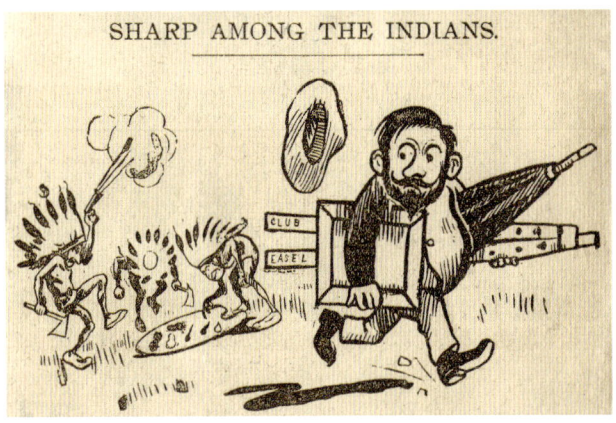

SHARP AMONG THE INDIANS.

[PLATE 2.9]

JOE SCHEUERLE
(b. Austria, 1873–1948)

Sharp among the Indians

Cincinnati newspaper, cartoon
Harold McCracken Research
Library, Buffalo Bill Center of the
West, Cody, Wyoming. JHSC.
Gift of Mr. and Mrs. Forrest Fenn.
MS22.4.1.22.02

[PLATE 2.10

JOE SCHEUERLE
(b. Austria, 1873–1948)

The Artists Are Coming Home

Cincinnati newspaper, cartoon
Harold McCracken Research
Library, Buffalo Bill Center of the
West, Cody, Wyoming. JHSC.
Gift of Mr. and Mrs. Forrest Fenn.
MS22.04.02.16.00

particular seem to be grasping his importance as a picturesque motif."[28] Two cartoons that appeared in a Cincinnati newspaper that year singled Sharp out as a restless adventurer. One titled "Sharp among the Indians" [PLATE 2.9] reinforced the imagined dangers that Farny had warned him about, while a subsequent one, "The Artists Are Coming Home" [PLATE 2.10], pictured him attired in an Indian trade blanket with a passel of paintings on his back and an eagle feather in his hat, all signifying that Farny's admonitions had proven to be much exaggerated.

Out west, though, in Taos during the summers of 1897 and 1898, Sharp's accommodations and studios could be described as rudimentary. They were often crudely improvised in the field, near what he referred to as his accommodations, "a small adobe house at or near the Indian pueblo."[29] Yet, in a most gratifying way, he was becoming a fixture and daily attracted dozens of Pueblo men, women, and children to his doorstep.

One of the Taos men who especially appealed to Sharp was Soaring Eagle [PLATE 2.11]. Sharp referred to him as "my favorite model." Although Soaring Eagle seemed to have had a weakness for whiskey, he was in Sharp's view a perfect choice for his canvas. By this, Sharp meant a "real, picturesque Indian." Sharp described him as "a pure type of Indian in face, beautiful in figure, stolid, and as inquisitive as a child in character." Such Indians, in Sharp's mind, were quickly disappearing and would not last a generation or two longer.[30] That assessment was then, as not seen earlier in the decade, somewhat racially tinged given the artist's clearly expressed stereotypical vision of Native people as a childlike, vanishing race.

Photographs of Sharp's sitters during the summer of 1898 in Taos reveal that most of his work was done outside his adobe house under the warm, bright New Mexico sun. He took several shots of one of his Pueblo models, Concha, and there in the brilliant sunlight produced an especially vibrant, early and rare watercolor [PLATE 2.12 AND PLATE 2.13]. Sharp seemed dazzled by the shadows and chromatic intensity provided by his plein air observations. And as for his model, here was a man who was both

28 Sharp, "An Artist among the Indians," 1.
29 Sharp, "An Artist among the Indians," 4.
30 Sharp, "An Artist among the Indians," 1–2, 6.

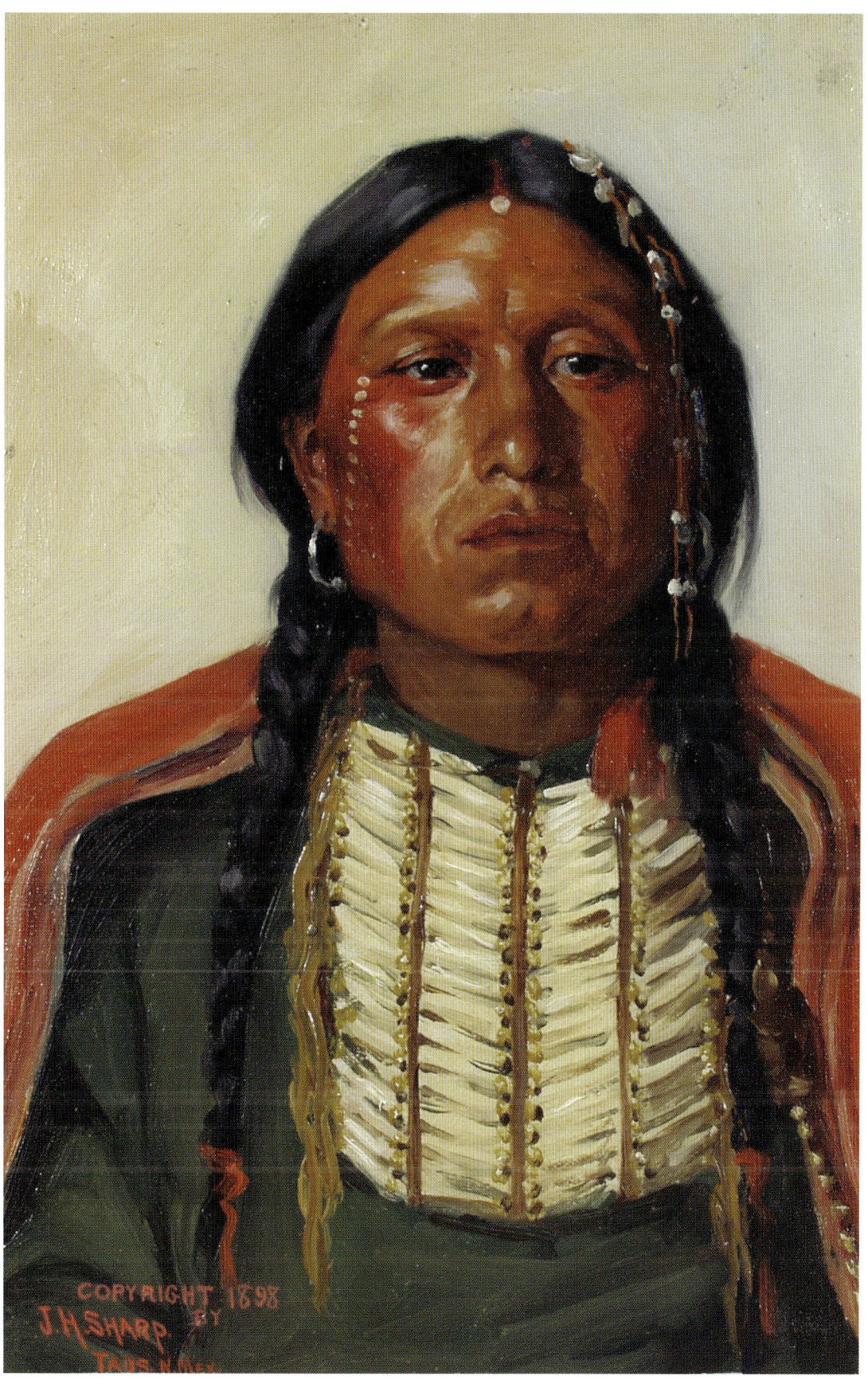

[PLATE 2.11] JOSEPH HENRY SHARP, *Soaring Eagle.* 1898, oil on canvas, 13 ⅝ x 9 ½ in.
Courtesy of the Phoebe A. Hearst Museum of Anthropology and the Regents of the University of California, Berkeley, California. 17-58

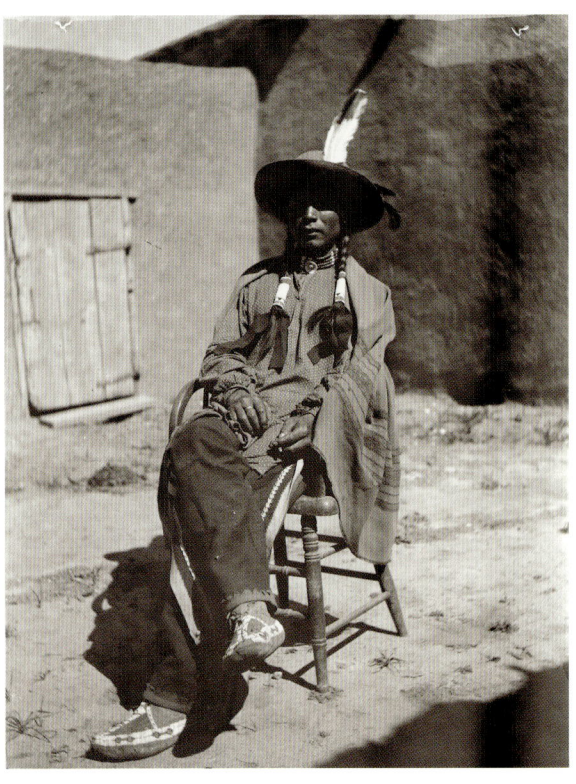

[PLATE 2.12]

JOSEPH HENRY SHARP

Concha

1898, photograph, b&w
C. M. Russell Museum,
Great Falls, Montana

extraordinary and common, a man who possessed his space with self-assurance, elegance, and nobility. What more could Sharp have wanted?

Sharp summarized his summer trips to Taos in two articles in *Brush and Pencil* magazine in 1899 and 1900.[31] In their pages both portraits, *Soaring Eagle* and *Concha*, were illustrated. With the articles, he was endeavoring to establish his identity as a painter of Indians as well as his territory in the Southwest. After he and Addie had returned to Cincinnati in the early fall of 1898, where he resumed his teaching, two of his American friends from Paris, Ernest Blumenschein and Bert Phillips, had arrived in Taos for the first time. Neither man mentioned Sharp having directly preceded them that year or acknowledged Sharp's earlier explorations of Taos in 1893 and 1897, but rather began proclaiming that they had in fact "discovered" the area. This may have persuaded the Sharps to look northward for additional options in 1899, and they headed for Montana and Crow Agency that summer.

On the northern plains, Sharp searched for another type of even more ideal Native figures, ones who were, as he later described them to Ewers, representative of "the great fighters of the No. West."[32] In 1891, several years before Sharp ventured into the region, Farny had produced his summative work on the theme of the Northern Plains Indians' fate. Following the tragic Wounded Knee Massacre of 1890, Farny created a painting, using Oglala Fire as his model. He titled the work *The Last Scene of the Last Act of the Sioux War* (location unknown) and it appeared as an illustration in *Harper's Weekly* [PLATE 2.14].[33] That work provided an opening for Sharp, and over the ensuing years he painted dozens of canvases depicting similar burial scenes.[34] But mostly Sharp grasped the opportunity to explore Montana in order to record not the melancholy denouement of a people but the living champions of Native resistance, especially the victorious survivors of the Battle of the Little Big Horn.

The venerated Cheyenne chief Two Moons was a prime example of his early subjects [PLATE 2.15]. Crow Agency, where Two Moons lived and Sharp first visited in 1899, became his northern headquarters, and by 1902 he and Addie were calling that spot their seasonal home. Sharp

31 Sharp, "An Artist among the Indians," 1–2, 6; J. H. Sharp, "The Chant," *Brush and Pencil* 5 (March 1900), 284–85.

32 JHS to Ewers, April 1939, Robert Taft Collection, Kansas Historical Society, Topeka, Kansas.

33 *Harper's Weekly*, February 14, 1891, p. 120.

34 An early example of this is his 1900 painting *The Great Sleep*, which he exhibited as his sole entry in the Fine Arts exhibition of the Pan-American Exposition in Buffalo, New York, in 1901. It was later sold to Phoebe A. Hearst for her private collection.

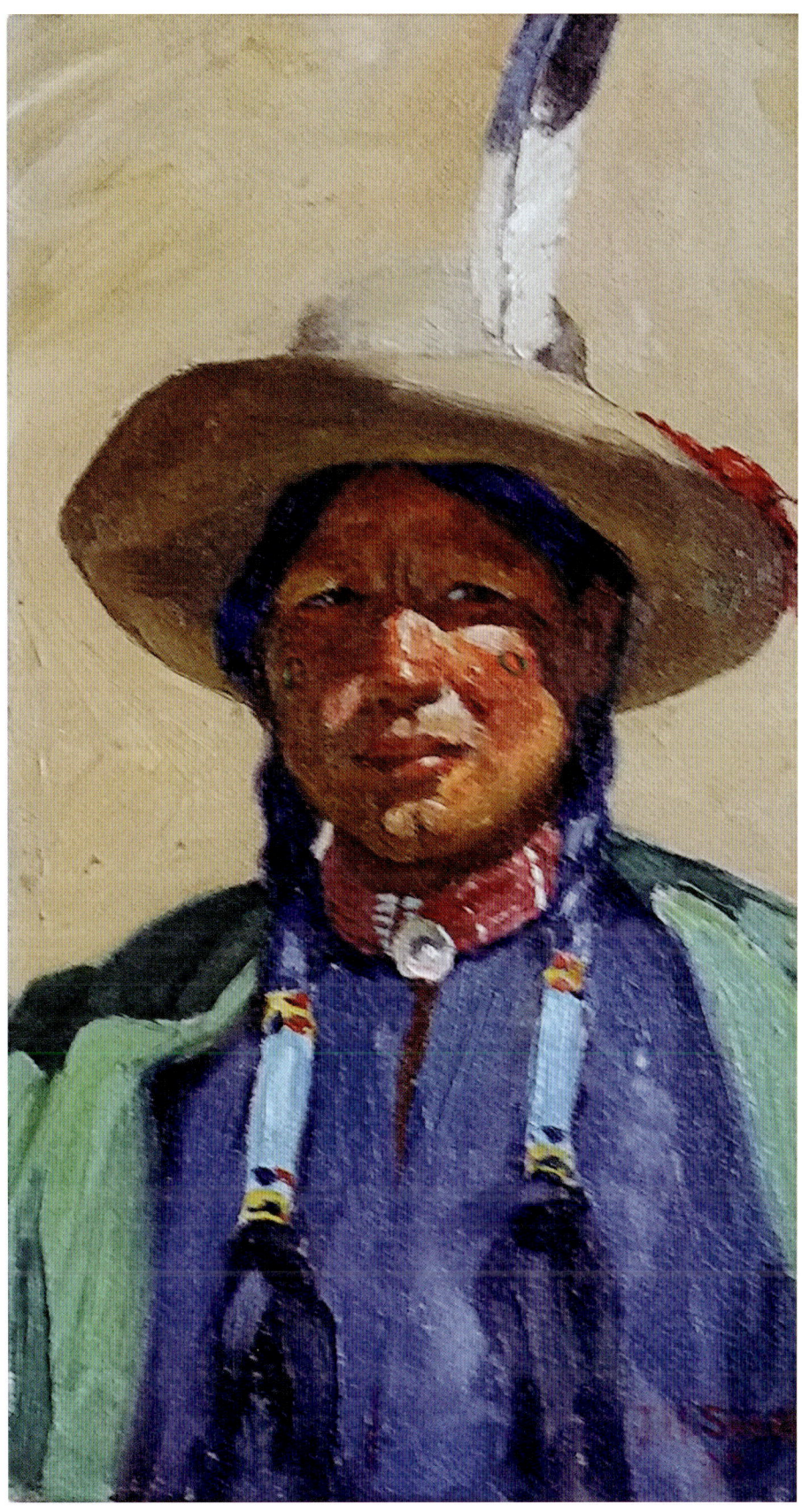

[PLATE 2.13] **JOSEPH HENRY SHARP,** *Concha.* 1898, watercolor on paper, 9 ½ x 6 in.
The Taos Art Museum, Taos, New Mexico

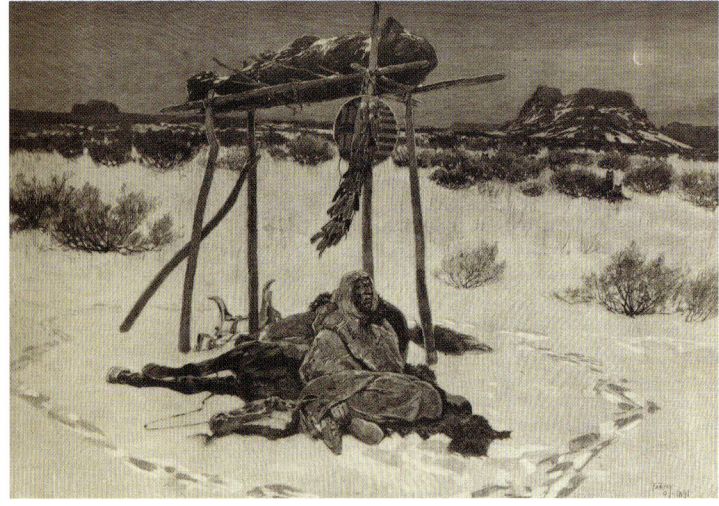

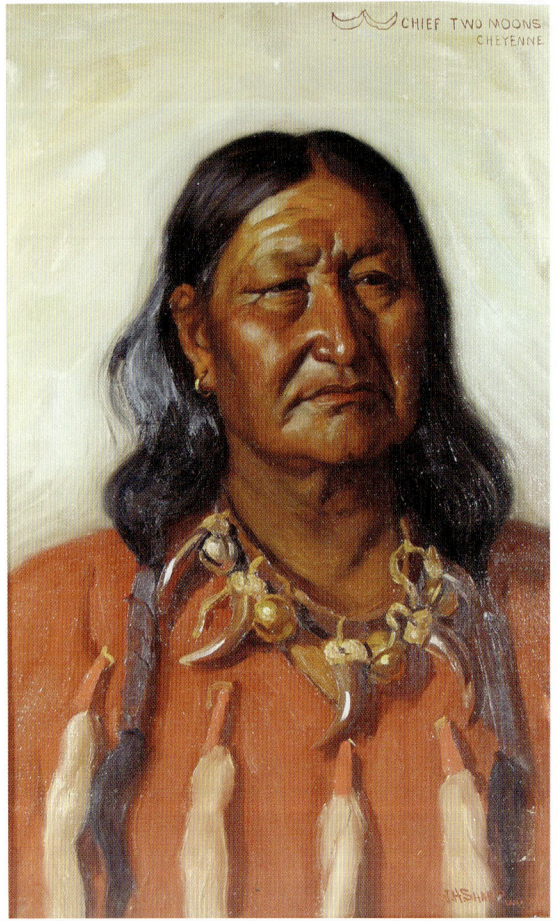

began by working in a room in the agency's only hostelry, the Server Hotel. In the three years between his first arrival and his settling into life at Crow Agency, Sharp created a host of portraits of the Indians of that region and the Southwest, enough to organize a significant exhibition that debuted in the fall of 1900 at the Cincinnati Art Museum.[35] It then traveled in various formats to venues such as the Detroit Museum of Art, the Pan-American Exposition in Buffalo, New York, and the Cosmos Club in Washington, DC. It was this circulating exhibition that really launched Sharp's career and, following substantial sales of his portraits and Indian scenes to the Smithsonian Institution, Joseph G. Butler Jr., and Phoebe A. Hearst, he was able to leave his teaching position at the Cincinnati Art Academy and his Ohio studio and move west.

Between 1902 and 1903 Sharp established two western studios, one at Crow Agency and the other in Pasadena at his sister's house. The Crow Agency studio was opened even before he had a permanent place to live there. It measured, as explained in an invitation he had printed for its opening [PLATE 2.16], only ten by fourteen feet and was followed shortly by a second studio about twice the size of the first [PLATE 2.17]. The interior of the second structure [PLATE 2.18] was published in a feature on Sharp in the *New York Herald* in 1906.[36] Crow Agency afforded a substantially reduced and a far more masculine, rustic environment than what he had become accustomed to in Cincinnati, but he said that the studio was "fine and warm" even in December and his experience there marked the "first time I ever had a place out here where I could stand up & work & walk back & see it."[37] He also reported that light spread more evenly in the expanded space and

[PLATE 2.14]

HENRY F. FARNY
(1847–1916)

*The Last Scene of the Last Act
of the Sioux War*

Illustrated in *Harper's Weekly*,
February 14, 1891, p. 120

---

35 *Indian: Portraits Painted from Life by J. H. Sharp* (Cincinnati: Cincinnati Art Museum, 1900). The exhibit included eighty-five portraits and western scenes dealing with the Cheyenne, Sioux, Apache, Pueblo, and Crow tribes.

36 See "A Studio on Custer Battlefield," *New York Herald*, December 23, 1906.

37 JHS to J. H. Gest, December 4, 1904, JHSC.

"won't get my things so dark."[38] The enlarged studio was bare bones, yet better lit and relatively commodious compared to the first iteration. Most important, it welcomed countless sitters from the Crow Nation, as well as, during Crow Fair, individuals from the ranks of the Cheyennes, Sioux, Blackfeet, and others.

Adjacent to his studio at Crow Agency was a large buffalo hide teepee that Sharp also used as a studio [PLATE 2.19].[39] He had purchased it from a prominent Blackfeet medicine man, Bull Child, around 1902, and the artist prized it as a rarity. In December 1904 Sharp wrote to his close friend Joseph Henry Gest, director of the Cincinnati Art Museum, that it had just snowed and that "my old skin teepee looks nice as a foreground."[40] Then, Henry Koch, the museum's treasurer, learned in 1905 about a second tepee structure inside the studio that Sharp had in Montana. "I am interested in firelight things now," Sharp wrote, "& have a little teepee interior rigged up in studio, where I can pose model by lamplight & work by daylight. Awfully hard, but lots of fun & interesting."[41] Sharp had come all the way to Montana to begin experimenting with mixed sources of light as learned from Velázquez a decade earlier. Still, there was

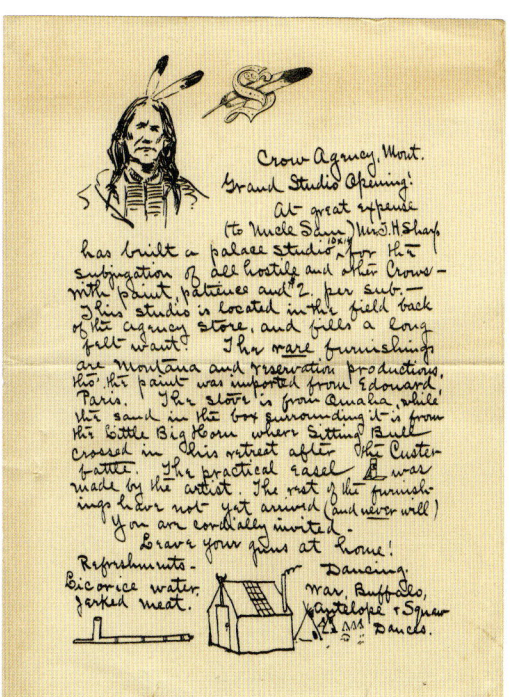

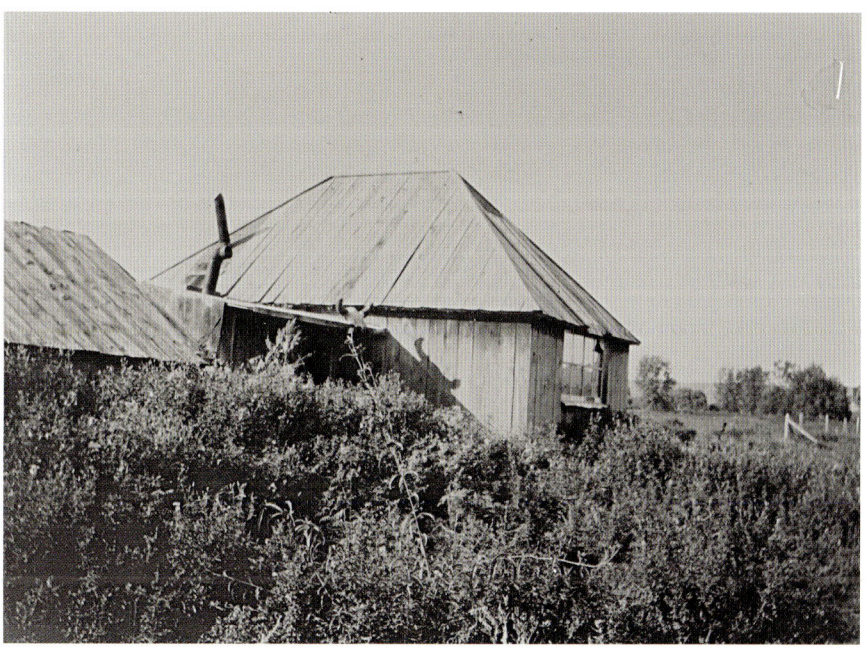

nothing in the Spanish Baroque master's lesson book that helped him with depicting light from a wood fire. For that, he needed counsel from his old

[PLATE 2.15]

JOSEPH HENRY SHARP

Chief Two Moons—Cheyenne

ca. 1899, oil on canvas, 18 x 12 in. Courtesy of the Phoebe A. Hearst Museum of Anthropology and the Regents of the University of California, Berkeley, California. 17-30

[PLATE 2.16]

JOSEPH HENRY SHARP

Grand Studio Opening Invitation

1902, pen on paper Harold McCracken Research Library, Buffalo Bill Center of the West, Cody, Wyoming. JHSC. Library Purchase. MS.22.1.18

[PLATE 2.17]

JOSEPH HENRY SHARP

Crow Agency Studio

1903, photograph, b&w C. M. Russell Museum, Great Falls, Montana. Gift of Mr. and Mrs. Gene Ball

---

38 JHS to J. H. Gest, October 29, 1904, JHSC.

39 Riebeth, *J. H. Sharp among the Crow Indians*, 44–45.

40 JHS to J. H. Gest, December 4, 1904.

41 JHS to Henry Koch, January 1, 1905, JHSC.

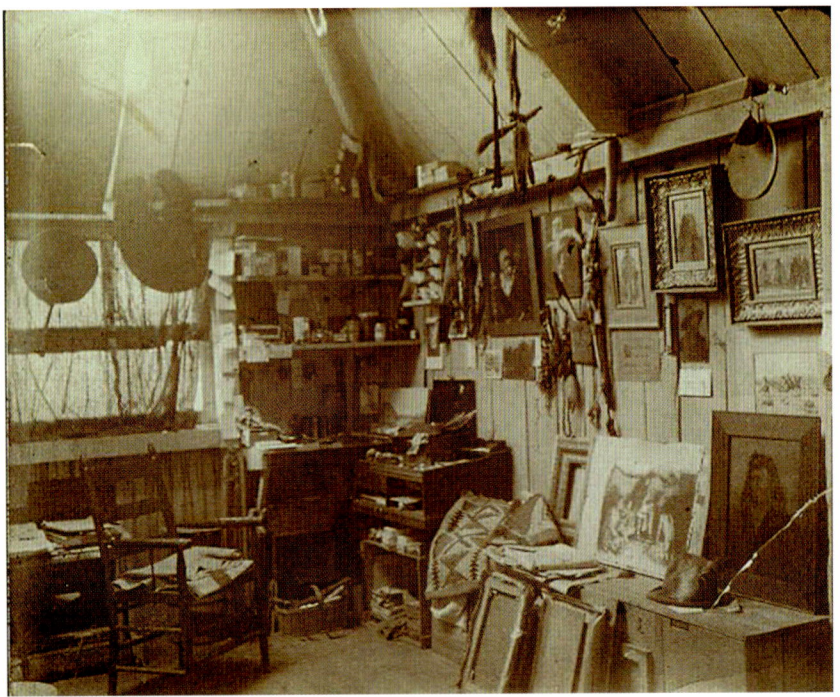

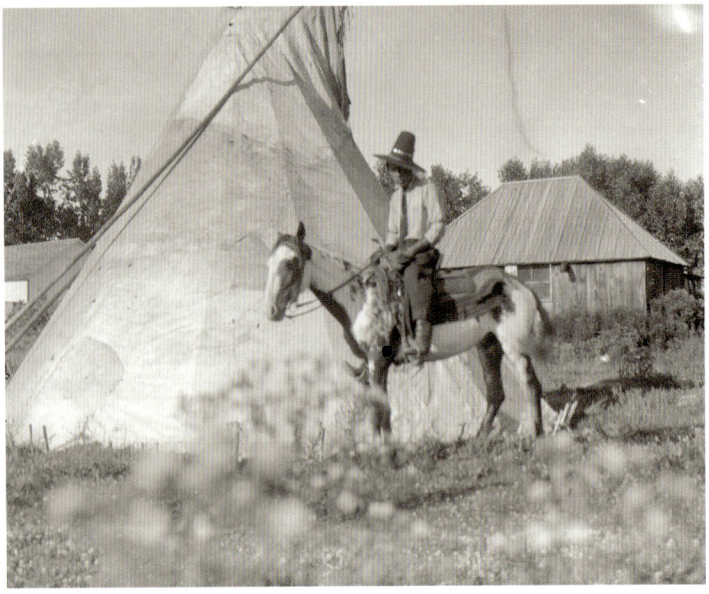

[PLATE 2.18]

UNKNOWN
PHOTOGRAPHER

Crow Agency Studio

undated, photograph, b&w
Harold McCracken Research
Library, Buffalo Bill Center of
the West, Cody, Wyoming. JHSC.
Gift of Mr. and Mrs. Forrest Fenn.
MS22.3.2

companion and teacher Frank Duveneck. He wrote his friend in early 1905 asking for technical advice and must have received some useful guidelines, as by 1906 he was turning out masterful firelit scenes such as *A Gift for Her Brave* [PLATE 2.20] that garnered welcome laudatory accolades from the critics.[42] The soft tones that he achieved with these firelight canvases harmonized with the Native people whose lives he so wished to reveal with candor and sympathy. "Thanks to him," wrote a Kansas City reviewer of an exhibit Sharp presented there in 1908, "the Indian becomes less of a tradition and more of a human being. Such pictures as a *Gift for Her Brave* and the *Death Spirit* (a similar interior scene picturing a father mourning a lost child [1905; Woolaroc Museum]) are telling glimpses, showing the joy and sorrw [sic] that alternate in the teepee."[43]

Sharp embraced the great outdoors in summer months, when he ranged from the boundaries of Glacier Park in the North, to southern Montana across the Big Horn River at the Crow Reservation, to open ranch land in Wyoming farther south. The vast northwestern landscape became his studio when he was not focused on portraiture and domestic scenes. And in winter, when temperatures could freeze the paints on his palette, he was equally enthused with the outdoors. His Montana friend and patron Charles Bair outfitted him with a sheep wagon that was called the "Prairie Dog" [PLATE 2.21]. This gave Sharp mobility and shelter as he explored reaches beyond the view afforded by his cozy studio window. News of the transportable atelier reached his hometown of Cincinnati, where a

42 JHS to Duveneck, March 8, 1905, Beinecke Rare Book and Manuscript Library, Yale
    University, New Haven, CT.
43 *Kansas City Star*, January 17, 1908, JHSC.

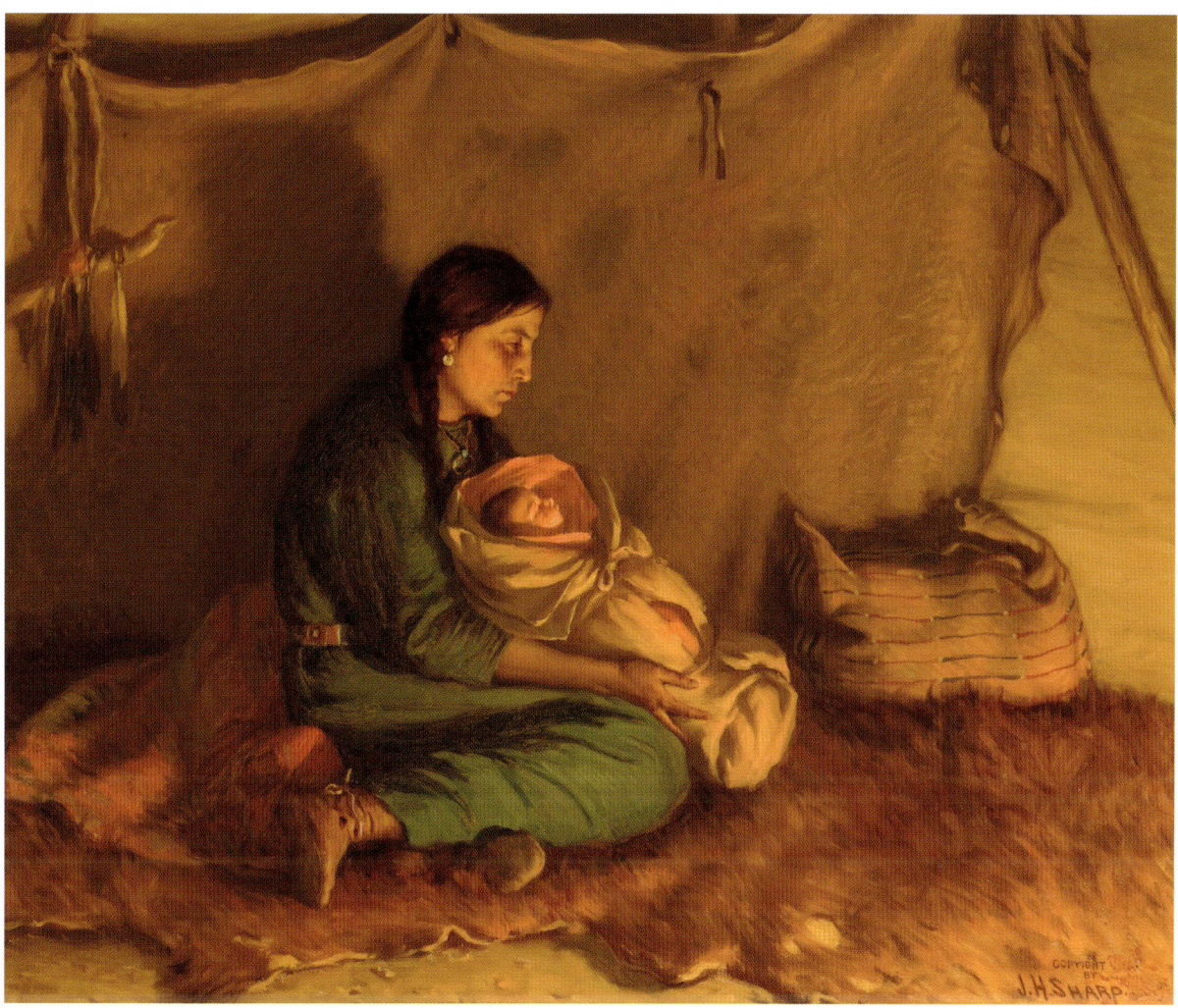

reporter proclaimed that Sharp, now undaunted, was able to brave thirty-below-zero temperatures "when the mood seizes him for painting."[44] The wagon featured a stove for warmth, a bed for naps, and a mica skylight to bring in natural light when he was not trudging through drifts of snow in search of the perfect spot to capture on canvas.

Perhaps the first painting Bair purchased from Sharp, *Winter Scene* [PLATE 2.22], was one of the results of the artist's explorations of the winter landscape. It was what Sharp referred to as one of his "light or atmospheric snow pieces."[45] These provided a set of challenges for the artist, both technical and psychological, very different from those posed by portraits or interior firelight scenes. Such velvety, proto-Impressionist works explored the temperature of light and were completed, as he said, as much as possible "directly from nature" with "little or no studio." These were artworks that Sharp convinced himself were re-creating "the true spirit of the West."[46]

[PLATE 2.19]

UNKNOWN
PHOTOGRAPHER

Crow Agency Teepee Studio

1903, photograph, b&w
C. M. Russell Museum,
Great Falls, Montana

[PLATE 2.20]

JOSEPH HENRY SHARP

A Gift for Her Brave

ca. 1906, oil on canvas,
32 ⅜ x 38 ¾ in.
Gilcrease Museum, Tulsa,
Oklahoma. Gift of the Thomas
Gilcrease Foundation, 1955.
0137.331

44 "No Steam-Heated Flat Artist."
45 JHS to J. H. Gest, December 4, 1904.
46 "Last of a Vanishing Race," *Kansas City Star*, January 17, 1909.

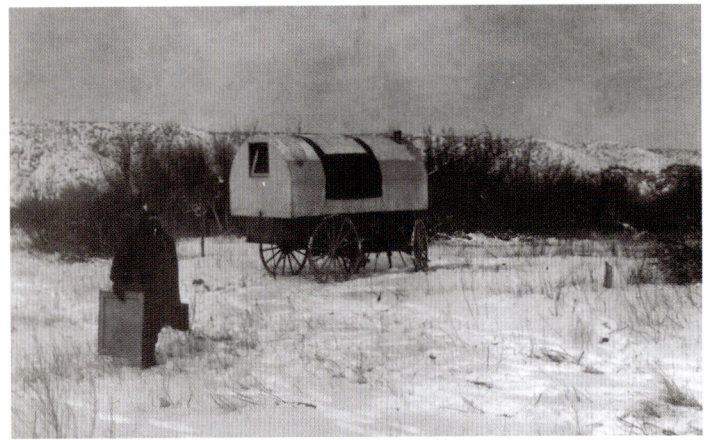

While the Sharps spent most of their winters at Crow Agency in the first decade of the twentieth century, they reserved their summers for Taos from 1903 on. In June 1906 Sharp wrote Gest that the couple had recently arrived in Taos, "our first love & stamping ground." It was here, among an ever-growing cadre of eastern, academic painters including Ernest Blumenschein, Eanger Irving Couse, Bert Phillips, and

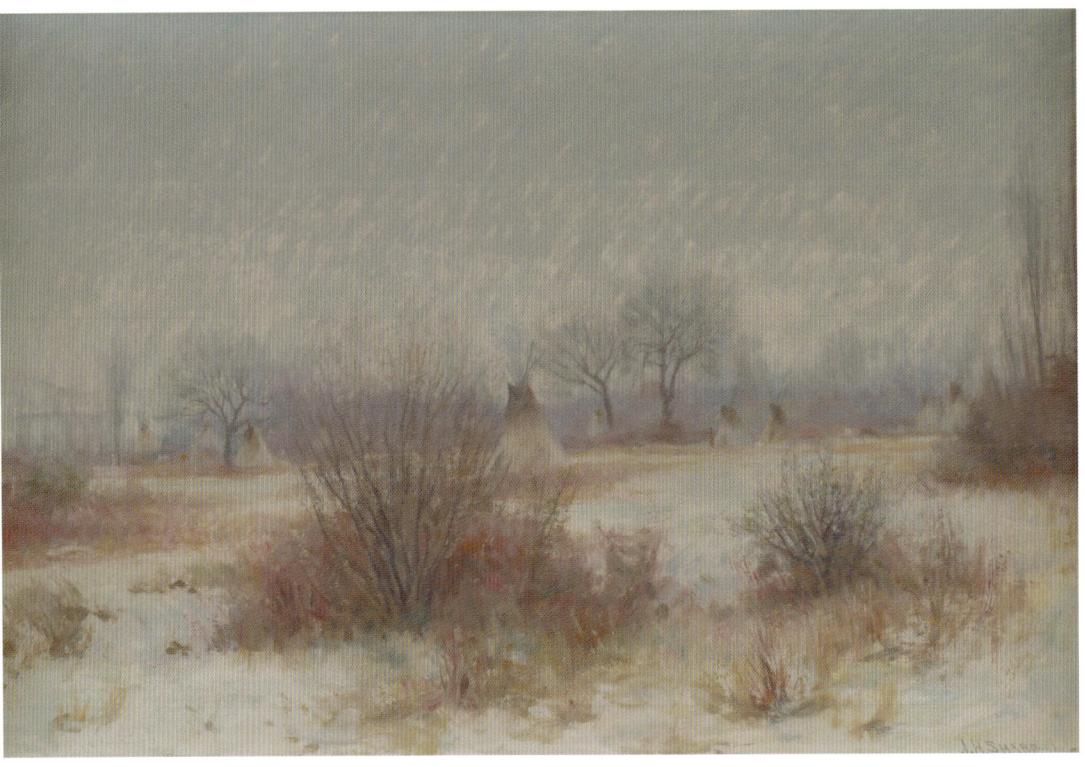

[PLATE 2.21]

UNKNOWN
PHOTOGRAPHER

Sharp and the Prairie Dog

undated, photograph, b&w
Harold McCracken Research
Library, Buffalo Bill Center of the
West, Cody, Wyoming. JHSC.
Gift of Mr. and Mrs. Forrest Fenn.
P.22.29

[PLATE 2.22]

JOSEPH HENRY SHARP

Winter Scene

ca. 1905, oil on canvas, 18 x 27 in.
Bair Family Museum,
Martinsdale, Montana

Oscar Berninghaus, that they truly felt at home. And "others are coming," he continued, "so there may be a Taos Colony a la Barbizon yet!" However, even with all this encouragement and comradery, Sharp at first found Taos a difficult place in which to concentrate. "This climate is killing the germ that the north fosters," he continued. "We are near 8,000 ft high, & mañana is the finest word they have here. It is the only place I never get tired of loafing."[47] Indeed, his production at that point was reduced by comparison. In an exhibition of more than fifty paintings he held in New York at the Fishel, Adler and Schwartz Gallery that fall, less that 10 percent of his work centered on New Mexico subjects.[48]

---

47 JHS to J. H. Gest, June 15, 1906, JHSC.

48 *Pictures by J. H. Sharp* (New York: Fishel, Adler and Schwartz, 1906).

In 1909 the Sharps purchased a former dance hall on Kit Carson Road, just up the street from the old scout's house. After lengthy efforts to repurpose that building as their new home, they also acquired a historic Penitente chapel next door. It was there that Sharp established his first serious Taos studio, one he called his "Bell Chapel" or "Chapel Studio" [PLATE 2.23]. Once he refurbished that structure, his southwestern output gradually increased. By 1912, when he organized an exhibition of paintings for a show at the University Club in Cincinnati, more than 20 percent of the offerings were Taos canvases and much of the Montana work was old inventory. His agreement with Hearst had been terminated in 1904 (though he continued to sell works to her until her death in 1919), and Butler's tastes were more focused on Taos subjects after 1912.[49] Sharp tried to liquidate his large stock of Northern Plains Indian portraits (about seventy-five in number) to the Smithsonian Institution in 1910, but the director, William Henry Holmes, demurred.[50]

It is a good thing that Sharp had his studio to distract his attention at this moment. Addie had become seriously infirm, and much of his attention was drawn to her, as well as his own, unsteady health. She had rallied during the summer of 1912, and thus he was able to produce several Taos chefs d'oeuvre in his studio. *The Broken Bow* [PLATE 2.24] was one example out of what he referred to as a pair of "life size figure" paintings that were "*better* than any former work."[51] *The Broken Bow* was a testament to cultural and familial endurance, a fresh and encouraging subject celebrating youth and growth rather than illness and confinement. Tragically though, Addie would die the next year, yet

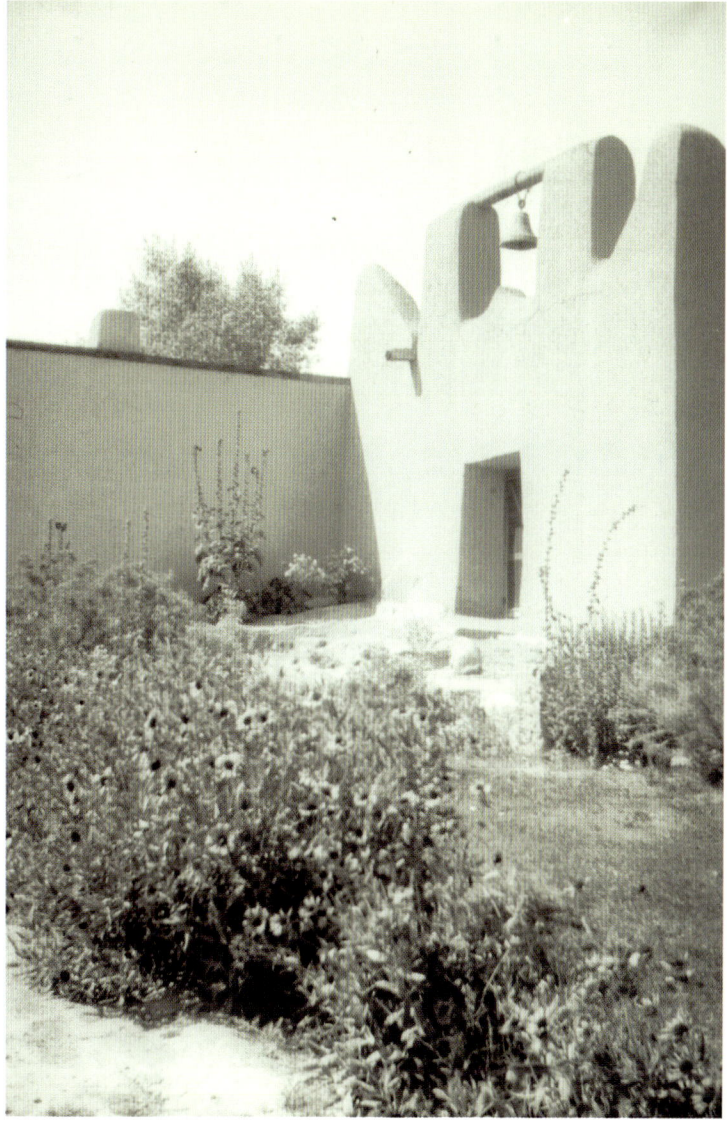

[PLATE 2.23]

UNKNOWN
PHOTOGRAPHER

Bell Chapel Studio

1924, photograph, b&w
C. M. Russell Museum,
Great Falls, Montana

49 See Marie Watkins, "Painting the American Indian at the Turn of the Century: Joseph Henry Sharp and His Patrons, William H. Holmes, Phoebe A. Hearst, and Joseph G. Butler, Jr.," PhD dissertation, Florida State University, 1999, pp. 272–74, 585–87.

50 See JHS to Holmes, December 4, 1910, William Henry Holmes artist file, AAA; and Holmes's reply on January 3, 1911, William Henry Holmes artists' file, AAA.

51 JHS to J. H. Gest, October 3, 1912, JHSC. The other painting in the pair is thought to be *Crucita—A Taos Indian Girl* (1913; Gilcrease Museum).

this painting carried Sharp's message of continuance into the future. It was a primary piece in a large show of his work at the University Club in Cincinnati that year and went on to be his featured painting at the National Academy of Design's annual spring exhibition in 1913.

Outside the walls of the Chapel Studio were gardens that had served as restoratives for Addie in her final years [PLATE 2.25] and that, with their luscious hollyhocks, would inspire Sharp to paint countless works, such as *Leaf Down at Studio Door* [PLATE 2.26], over the coming years of his long life. In Taos the gardens became a studio in themselves and painting them brought him great joy.

A couple of years after Addie died, Sharp married her sister, Louise. At about the same time, in 1915, he built an expansive, new, two-story adobe studio on the west side of his house, pitched his Blackfeet buffalo hide teepee next to it, and again filled the studio with Indian relics. When the painter, writer, and teacher Ernest Peixotto visited Taos in 1916, he was enthralled with Sharp's "new and large studio in the pueblo style, in which he now works and stores his rare and precious collections of baskets, mats and costumes." One might consider such a description as positive, but Peixotto preceded these comments with the conclusion that "ethnologically his work is of the greatest value," thus providing a sweeping dismissal of Sharp's earnest efforts to have his paintings considered as fine art.[52] It is difficult to know at what point Sharp began to become defensive about the moniker "ethnologist," which had endured since the early 1900s, but he gradually did. Many years later, he told John Ewers that he "never kept any detail record—didn't know what Ethnology meant!"[53]

Perhaps as a counter to Peixotto's assessment, Sharp donated one of his largest and most highly acclaimed recent works, *The Stoic* [SEE PLATE 1.20], to the new Fine Arts Museum in Santa Fe. The contribution was made directly on the heels of a gift by Robert Henri, of a life-size canvas titled *Dieguito* (1916; New Mexico Museum of Art).[54] Rubbing shoulders with Henri, Sharp wanted to be in proper company, and with the new museum, he sought a venue where his artifacts and his art would not be conflated.

What Sharp prized were reviews of his paintings that recognized creative genius. Such a work, set in Sharp's new studio, was an oil titled *The Red Olla*, of 1916 [PLATE 2.27]. His beloved model, Crucita, was posed in broad, clear light and seated on an adobe *banco*. She holds a peach-colored shawl in both hands and touches a water jar with her right hand. The gesture embodies grace and affection portrayed with a sense of personal, reserved interiority that Sharp allowed his model to enjoy. Crucita seems deep in thought. When *The Red Olla* was exhibited in Cincinnati in January 1918, his favorite art critic, Mary L. Alexander, acknowledged its importance immediately. "The Red Olla . . . is really a most beautiful arrangement of Crucita: the fascination this picture has for one springs from many sources

52 Ernest Peixotto, "The Taos Society of Artists," *Scribner's* 60 (August 1916): 258.
53 JHS to Ewers, August 8, 1948, JHSC.
54 "Art and Artists," *El Palacio* 4 (1917): 107.

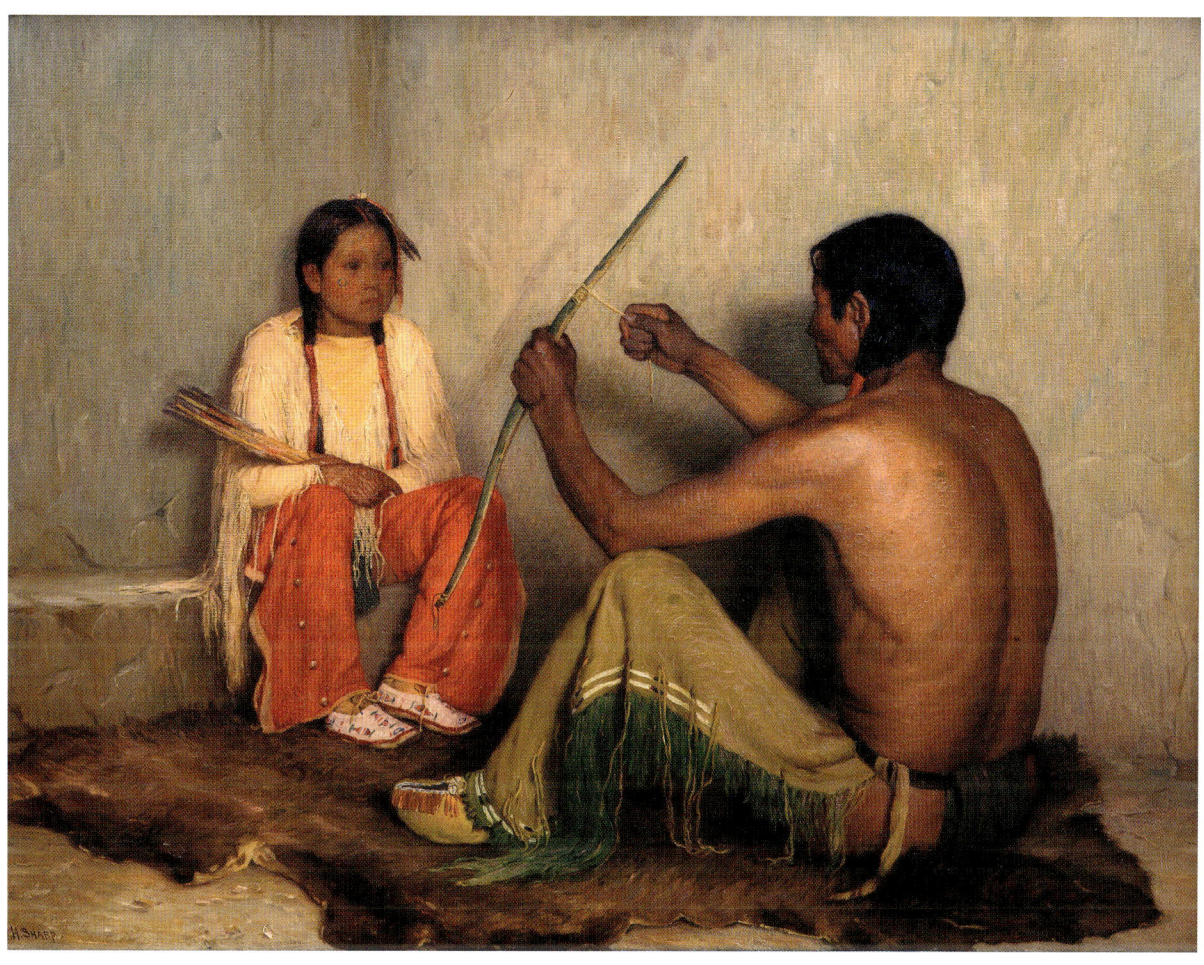

[PLATE 2.24] **JOSEPH HENRY SHARP,** *The Broken Bow, Father and Son.* ca. 1912, oil on canvas, 44 ½ x 59 ⅜ in. Buffalo Bill Center of the West, Cody, Wyoming. 7.75

while the beauty of Crucita fairly haunts one and the arrangement and harmony of line are almost Whistleresque in its statement."[55]

Sharp cherished his new space and it became a gathering place for him and his fellow Taos painters. With the teepee close at hand in the yard, he often abandoned Taos subjects and reinvented scenes of Northern Plains life reminiscent of his time in Montana [PLATE 2.28]. The teepee became a focal point for visitors too. A reporter from the *Christian Science Monitor* in 1919 was genuinely impressed by Sharp's Indian collection. "The Sharp studio is a veritable museum of Indian relics. Mr. Sharp owns what is perhaps the only buffalo-hide tepee outside a museum."[56]

By the early 1920s he and Louise had essentially abandoned the Crow Agency property. As early as 1919 he had written his patron Joseph Butler that "my health is so much under par that I am advised to forego the rigors of the Montana studio this winter, so we go to Pasadena instead."[57] His Crow Agency friend Carolyn Riebeth remembered their last year in Montana as 1923.[58] Pasadena would become his steady winter home, and the small studio behind the Sharps' house there, which they had previously purchased from his sister, became his new creative space. It was, as he later wrote, "about as large as the original one I had at Crow."[59] Despite the comfortable weather, Sharp painted very little in California. He was quoted as saying that "although he

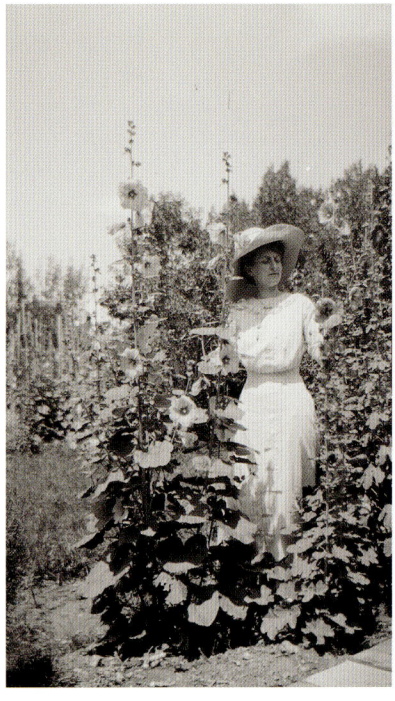

[PLATE 2.25]

UNKNOWN PHOTOGRAPHER

Addie in Her Garden

undated, photograph, b&w
C. M. Russell Museum,
Great Falls, Montana

[PLATE 2.26]

JOSEPH HENRY SHARP

Leaf Down at Studio Door

ca. 1928, oil on canvas, 22 x 18 in.
Gilcrease Museum, Tulsa, Oklahoma.
Gift of the Thomas Gilcrease
Foundation, 1955. 0137.349

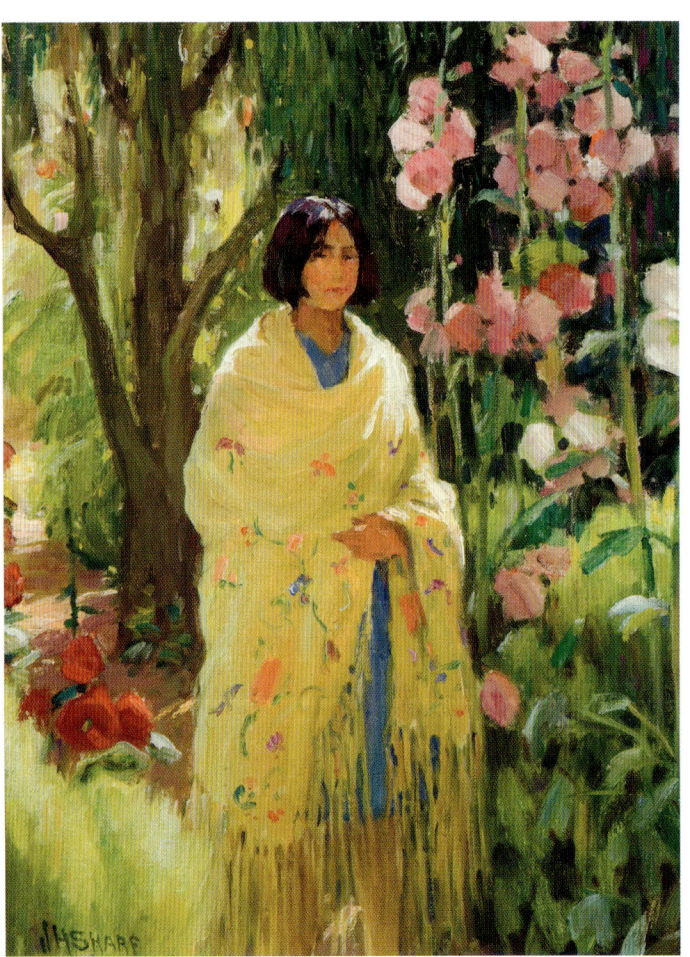

---

55 Mary L. Alexander, "Crucita, Beautiful Indian Girl, to Be Seen in Sharp's Exhibits," *Cincinnati Times Star*, January 12, 1918.

56 "A Unique Art Colony," *Christian Science Monitor*, February 10, 1919.

57 JHS to Butler, December 1, 1919, JHSC.

58 Riebeth, *J. H. Sharp among the Crow Indians*,

59 JHS to Mary Elizabeth Cornwell. December 19, 1933, JHSC.

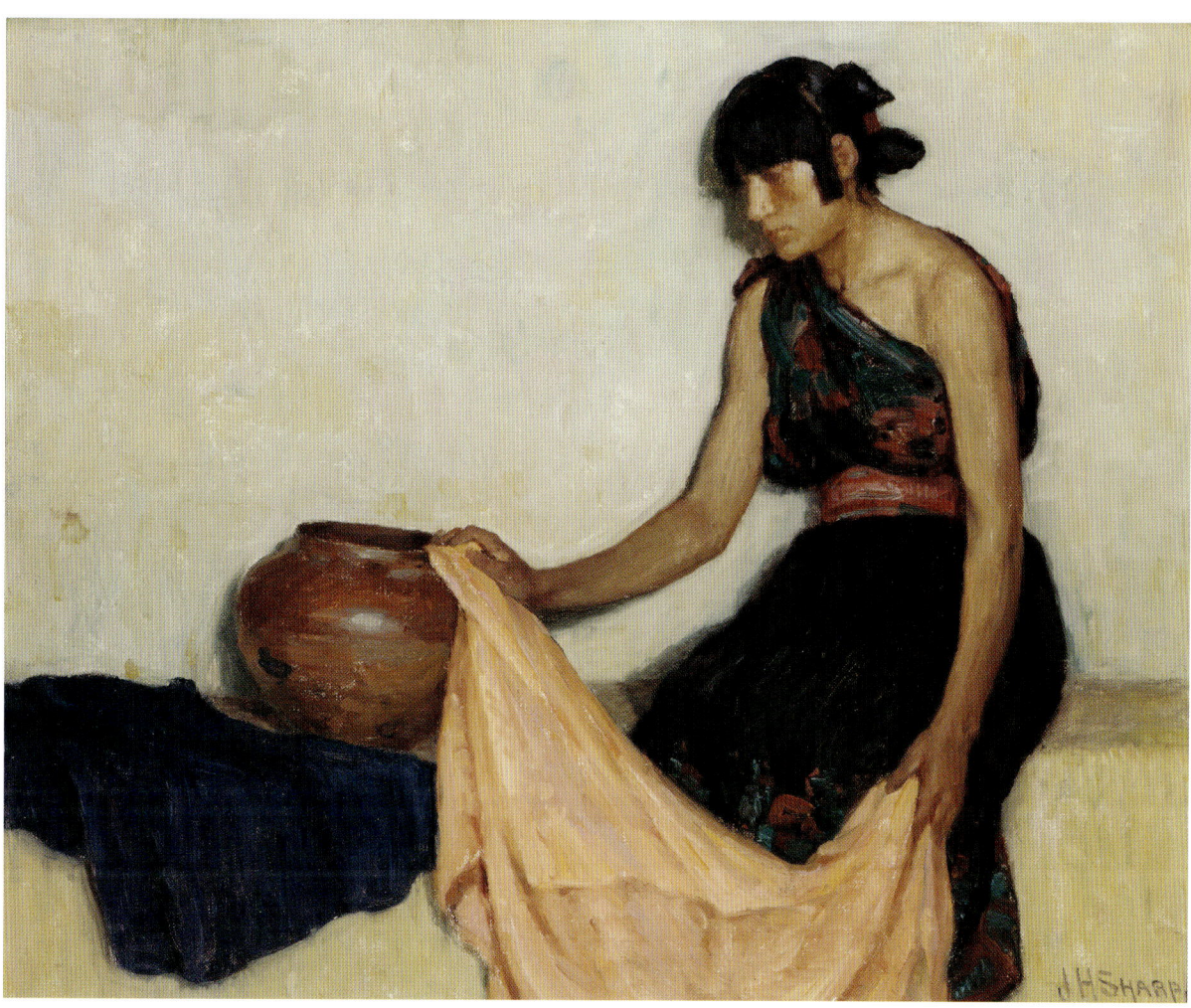

enjoys the country to the full, its painting possibilities do not appeal to him. 'It is apt to look too pretty on canvas.'"[60]

For summers, Taos had much to offer as a replacement for the open spaces of Montana. The Sharps lived in what might be considered an adobe compound, their property surrounded by high walls and sealed off with a robin egg–blue wooden entry gate. Still, Sharp found many intriguing subjects beyond those perimeters. In fact, the scene just outside his front gate captured his attention and became an extension of his studio. He made several paintings of it in the late teens and early twenties. *Kit Carson Road and House*, Taos is one such version [PLATE 2.29]. It featured his two favorite Pueblo female models, Crucita and Leaf Down, relaxing from their work to enjoy the sun-dappled street, the bustle of Indian passersby, and the early autumn light that brightened the huge cottonwood trees bordering the road. Sharp was also acutely interested in the fact that Kit Carson's house was just down the way on the right. The historical association pleased him greatly.

[PLATE 2.27]

JOSEPH HENRY SHARP

The Red Olla

ca. 1916, oil on canvas,
16 ½ x 20 ¼ in.
Denver Art Museum,
Denver, Colorado. 1989.148

---

60 M. R. C., "The Week in Art Circles," *Cincinnati Enquirer*, December 3, 1922. No images of the Pasadena studio are known to exist, and the house was demolished to make way for a freeway.

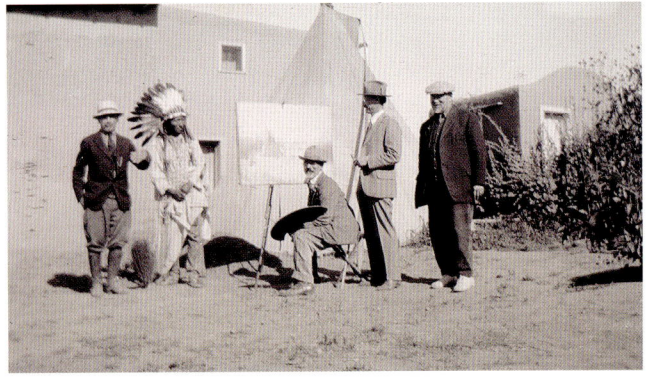

Further beyond his gate, Sharp enjoyed painting *en plein air* in the fields, arroyos, and aspen forests around Taos. So engaged was he with his environs—a vast, open-air New Mexico studio—that he requested to have photos taken of him painting in the field, portraits he used to promote his art shows in eastern markets [PLATE 2.30]. In 1922 he wrote to his old Crow Agency friend Samuel G. Reynolds that he and Louise had recently purchased an automobile. Now,

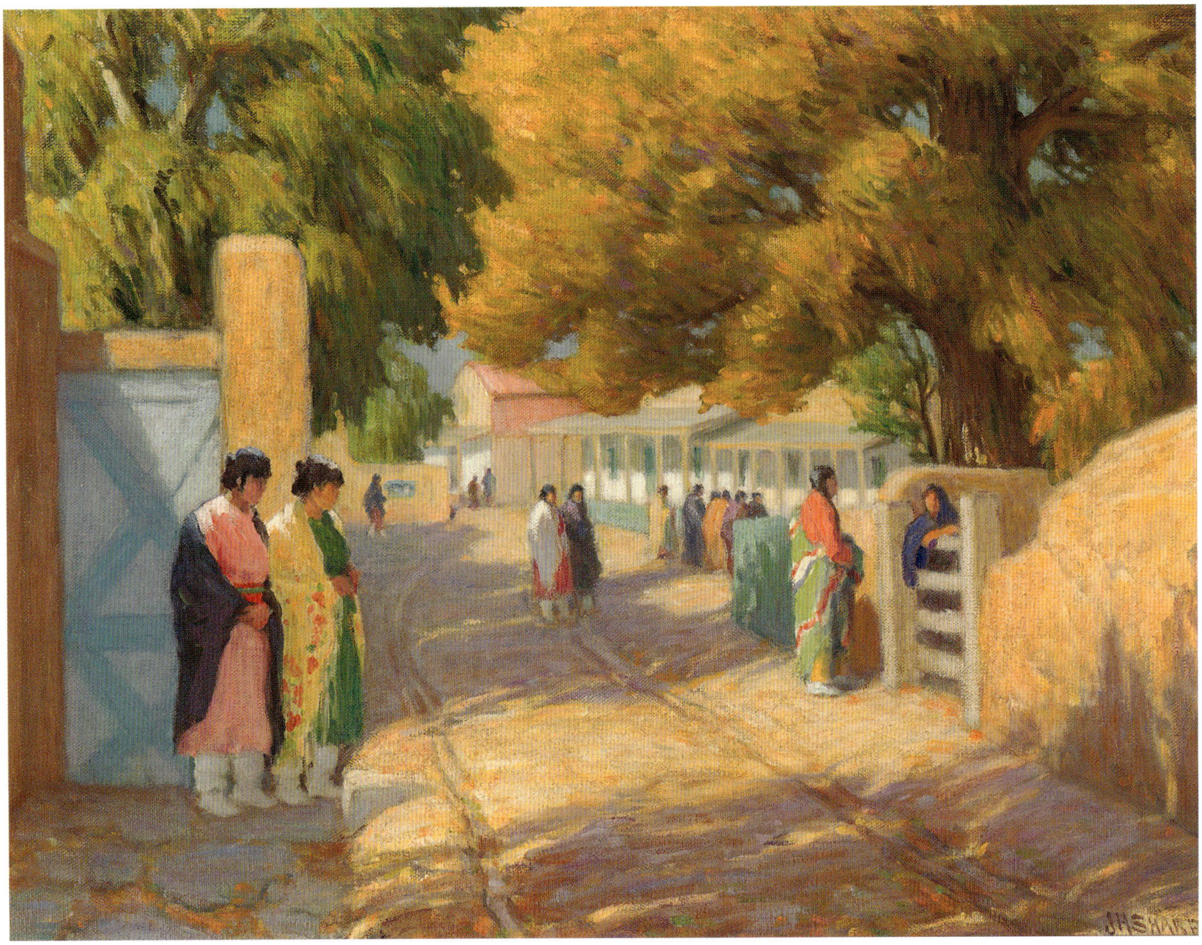

[PLATE 2.28]

UNKNOWN PHOTOGRAPHER

Sharp and Friends

undated, photograph, b&w
C. M. Russell Museum,
Great Falls, Montana. Gift of
Robert Luhn

Sharp wrote, "most work out of doors & stuff I wouldn't get otherwise." As a consequence, he could enthusiastically boast that "I work more than ever."[61] Of the sixty paintings in his annual Cincinnati winter exhibition that year, he included no fewer than eight listed collectively as "The Aspen Forest, New Mexico."[62] As reported in the local press, "Mr. Sharp has followed a new bent this year and that is to picture the wonderful

61 JHS to Reynolds, October 25, 1922, JHSC.
62 *Indian Paintings and Western Landscapes* (Cincinnati: Traxel's New Art Galleries, 1922).

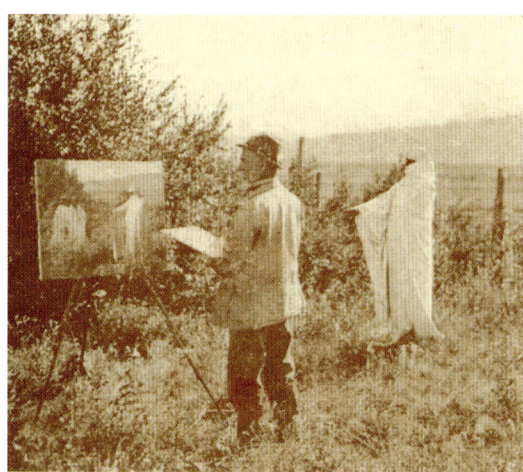

aspen that grow along the mountains of his beloved Taos."[63]

By the mid-1920s Sharp and his Taos studio had become synonymous. A signed photograph of him painting a canvas titled *His Record— Pointing with Pride* in 1921 [PLATE 2.31] shows him confidently returning the viewer's gaze and expressing his own pride of place and accomplishment. Sharp regarded himself as czar of his studio space and handed interested visitors photographs of himself at the easel as proof of his commanding presence. He would tell his friend Butler in 1925 that, regarding his artifact collection, he had sold most of his "surplus

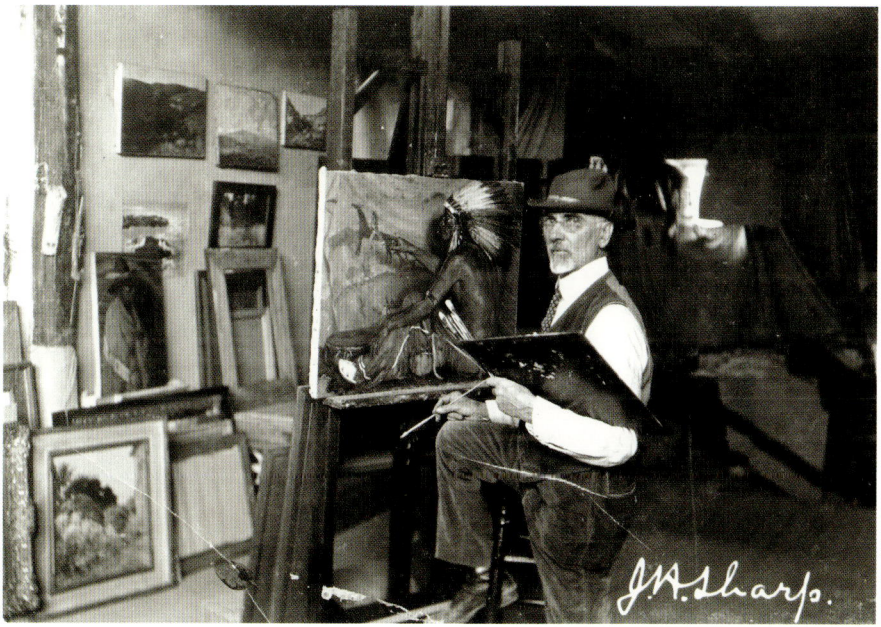

things, keeping all I need to work from and a few house decorations." He explained that his studio had been "burglarized several times while away in winter," so he cut back to just the essentials.[64] Among the artifacts that Sharp retained was a Sioux warbonnet he had purchased from a Crow man who had collected it following the Battle of the Little Big Horn.

[PLATE 2.29]

JOSEPH HENRY SHARP

Kit Carson Road and House, Taos

ca. 1925, oil on canvas, 25 ½ x 31 ½ in. Gilcrease Museum, Tulsa, Oklahoma. Gift of the Thomas Gilcrease Foundation, 1955. 0137.386

[PLATE 2.30]

UNKNOWN PHOTOGRAPHER

Sharp Painting in the Field

ca. 1920, photograph, b&w Harold McCracken Research Library, Buffalo Bill Center of the West, Cody, Wyoming. JHSC. Gift of Mr. and Mrs. Forrest Fenn. MS22.1.18

[PLATE 2.31]

UNKNOWN PHOTOGRAPHER

Sharp painting *His Record— Pointing with Pride*

1921, photograph, b&w Harold McCracken Research Library, Buffalo Bill Center of the West, Cody, Wyoming. JHSC. Gift of Mr. and Mrs. Forrest Fenn. P.22.167

---

63 Harold W. Coates, "More of the Outdoors, Less of Indians Is Seen in Exhibit of Year's Output of Paintings by Sharp at Gallery Here," *Cincinnati Commercial Times*, November 30, 1922.

64 JHS to Butler, September 9, 1925, JHSC.

[PLATE 2.32]

JOSEPH HENRY SHARP

The War Bonnet

ca. 1916, oil on canvas,
24 ⅛ x 20 ⅛ in.
Buffalo Bill Center of the West,
Cody, Wyoming. 24.61

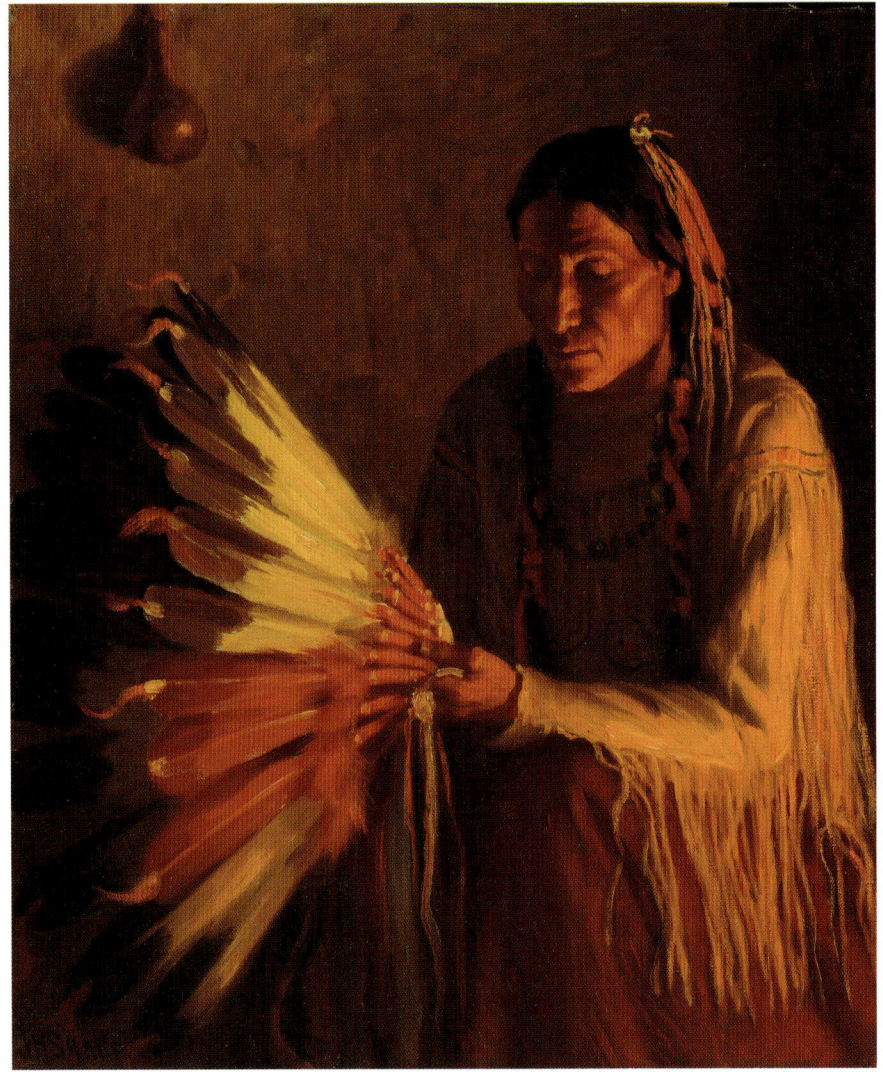

Sharp used this eagle feather hat in a good many of his paintings
produced both in Montana and later in Taos [PLATE 2.32].

In these same years, Sharp turned his studio into a motif for self-
portraits in paint, as well. Following a trip to France and Spain that the
Sharps took in 1922 and a second visit to the Prado Museum and the
Velázquez galleries there, the artist experimented several times with
inserting himself into paintings of the studio with his models. The most
accomplished and complex version of this self-promotional homage
to Velázquez's *Las Meninas* was *Studio Interior [A Corner of my Studio]*
[PLATE 2.33].[65] It pictures Crucita and her son Francisco enraptured by a
Pueblo song. As a neo-Baroque conceit, it sets the artist beside his models,
thus animating both parties and confirming their interdependence. It is as
if the three subjects were enjoying a creative, symbiotic relationship. The
models perform for the painter and he, in turn, records the recital in paint.
Although he was known to have painted only one formal self-portrait
[SEE PAGE 2], *Studio Interior [A Corner of my Studio]* and its companion

---

65 For a discussion of this work, see Riebeth, *J. H. Sharp among the Crow Indians*, 18.

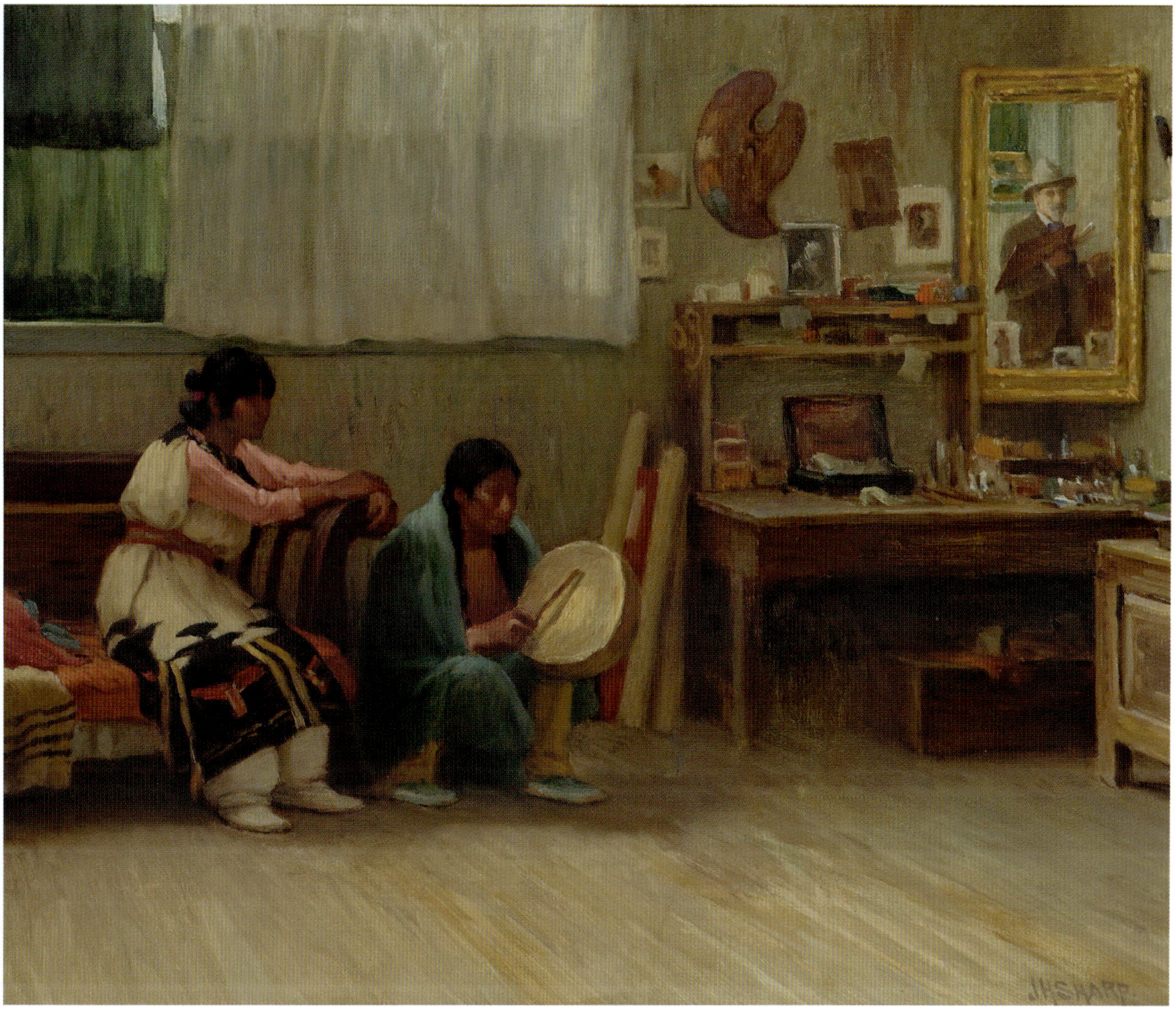

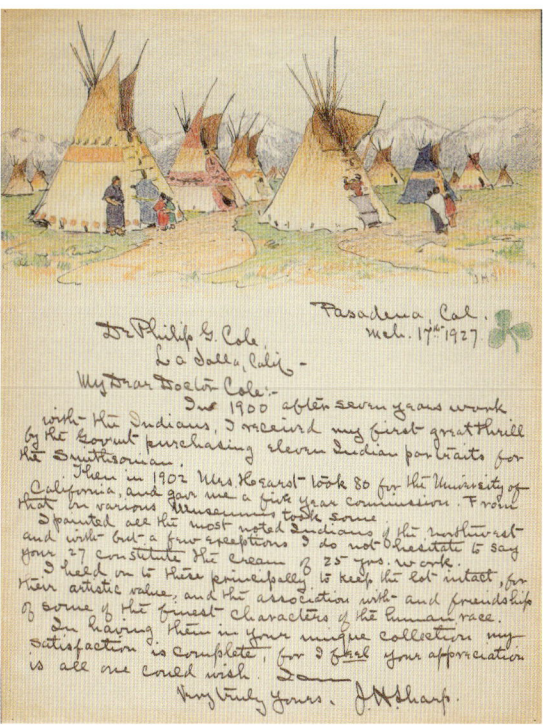

[PLATE 2.33]

JOSEPH HENRY SHARP

Studio Interior [A Corner of my Studio]

ca. 1925, oil on canvas,
20 x 27 ¹³/₁₆ in.
Phoenix Art Museum, Phoenix,
Arizona. Gift of the Carl S. Dentzel
Family Collection. 1985.136

[PLATE 2.34]

JOSEPH HENRY SHARP

Letter to Dr. Philip G. Cole

March 17, 1927, ink and
watercolor on paper, 11 x 8 ¾ in.
Gilcrease Museum, Tulsa,
Oklahoma. 1337.1046

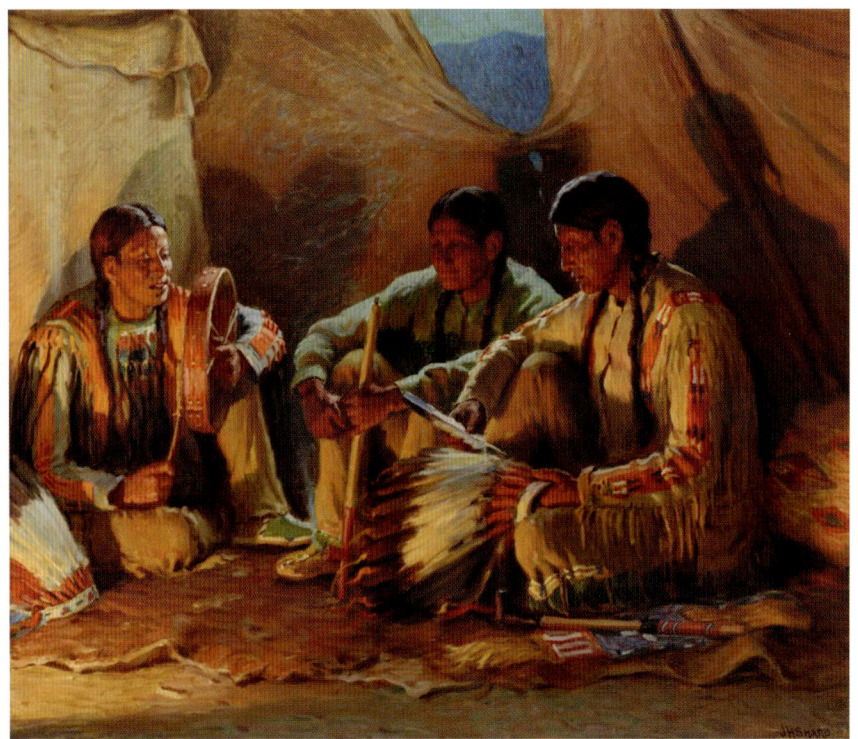

[PLATE 2.35]

JOSEPH HENRY SHARP

War Bonnet Song

ca. 1923, oil on canvas,
34 ¼ x 40 ¼ in.
Gilcrease Museum, Tulsa,
Oklahoma. Gift of the Thomas
Gilcrease Foundation, 1955.
0137.326

works, along with signed self-portrait photographs he had taken occasionally, illustrate his reliance on self-advancement.

Sharp was a master at promoting his paintings as well as himself. In 1927, when the collector Philip G. Cole of Brooklyn purchased twenty-seven of Sharp's old Indian portraits, it was a big relief for the artist. But Cole was given the impression, as Sharp would write in a letter accompanying the sale, that he had acquired "the cream of the crop." Although Sharp had endeavored to sell them several times before to Holmes, Butler, and others, he disingenuously advised the new patron that he had "held on to these principally to keep the lot intact, for their aesthetic value." What was touching and honest, though, was his explanation of how much he enjoyed living with the old portraits, treasuring "the association with and friendship of some of the finest characters of the human race [PLATE 2.34]."⁶⁶

Through the 1920s Sharp was happily working on multiple variations of light and mood in his studio. Often, he explored a combination of firelight and sunlight in complex figural compositions such as *War Bonnet Song* of 1923 [PLATE 2.35]. Such paintings were tour de force technical accomplishments, subtly exploring highlights and shadows cast over and by multiple sitters in close interior spaces.

By the early 1930s Sharp's studio collection had been pared down mostly to his current work and a select few remnants of artifacts he hung from the balcony at the end of the room, as in his portrait of Bawling Deer [PLATE 2.36]. His patrons were far-flung, but from time to time someone other than a troublesome tourist came to call. As Sharp phrased it in 1933 during the Depression, "There have been no picture sales in three years," and "I have to give over to the tourists who want to see a studio & . . . a real artist. Can't bluff the tourists unless we see their *car*, for once in a while some one *does* buy!"⁶⁷ He had learned the hard way when several years earlier, in 1926, he had ignored knocks at the door from John D. Rockefeller, Jr., who was calling to buy paintings. His next-door neighbor,

66 JHS to Cole, March 17, 1927, Joseph Henry Sharp Collection, Gilcrease Museum Library and Archives, University of Tulsa, Tulsa, OK.
67 JHS to Riebeth, August 15, 1933, JHSC.

Irving Couse, teased Sharp mercilessly that evening as, having been more alert and accessible, he had sold Rockefeller almost a thousand dollars' worth of paintings. Fortunately, Sharp was able to make some equally substantial sales to Rockefeller the next day.[68]

Through the 1920s and '30s, Sharp's studio interior gradually changed in character. Less and less did he depend on models for subjects. More often his attentions were focused on elaborate floral arrangements. These were easier on his aging eyes and cheaper than paying for models. Reviewers of his exhibitions began to notice the transformation as early as 1927. Although they felt that "Indians remain his master work," "Sharp seems at present less interested in painting Indians and more interested in painting flowers."[69] That propensity would only increase over the coming decade until in 1936 he would write fellow artist Joe Scheuerle that he "hadn't painted an Indian for over two years." "I just got tired of them after over 40 yrs." Instead, he said, "I've been painting a good deal of landscapes, still life (mostly flowers on big scale) & marines."[70]

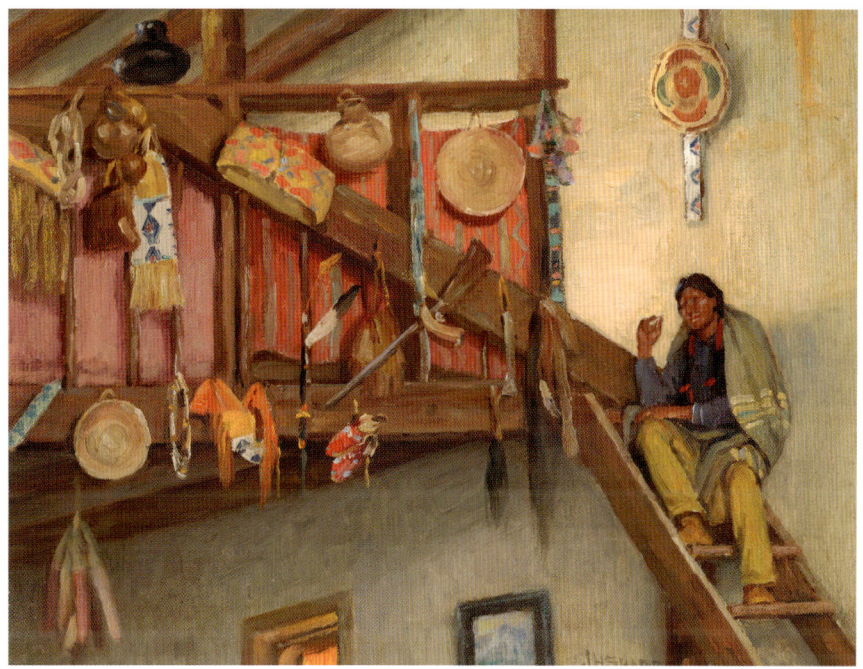

[PLATE 2.36]

JOSEPH HENRY SHARP

Bawling Deer, Taos

ca. 1925, oil on canvas,
15 x 18 ¾ in.
Gilcrease Museum, Tulsa,
Oklahoma. Gift of the Thomas
Gilcrease Foundation, 1955.
0137.340

The only reason he dipped his brush in paints to picture Indians at this point was to make some ready cash. He wrote Scheuerle again in 1937 saying that he was now forced to bring Indians back into his studio because he was "almost cleared out of salable stuff, so have to do some firelight & war bonnet potboilers. I have a lot of heads of the fine old fellows yet, but people (this generation) are only interested in a curious way, not as purchasers."[71] Sharp was burned out, and his patrons were inclined to indulge only in romantic reveries of firelit Indians.

This may explain the fact that his signature painting in 1934 was about Hispanics rather than Indians. Set in his old Bell Chapel studio, which had been converted to storage space in 1915, *The Passing of a Penitente* [SEE PLATE 1.27] was a rare departure from his typical choice of subject. Driven perhaps by historical imperatives such as Henry Farny's

---

68 Rockefeller to JHS, August 17, 1926, JHSC. Later that year Sharp sold Rockefeller $2,500 worth of Navaho blankets and some additional Nez Perce bags. See Rockefeller to JHS, October 21, 1926, JHSC.

69 "The Week in Art," *Cincinnati Enquirer*, December 4, 1927.

70 JHS to Scheuerle, October 13, 1936, JHSC.

71 JHS to Scheuerle, April 15, 1937, JHSC.

early directive for Sharp to study the Penitentes, their popularity among
the ranks of the other Taos painters, and the fact that his Bell Chapel
studio was once a Penitente church, Sharp created a clearly reverential
celebration of the sect's profound devotion to their religious beliefs and
practices. He gave the building a new life by recalling one of its original
functions. The two candlesticks pictured in the oil painting had stood on
the altar in the building when Sharp purchased it from the local Catholic
archbishop in 1909.

Sharp considered *The Passing of a Penitente* a major artistic
accomplishment at this time. When he presented it for sale in Cincinnati
at the Kreimer Gallery in the fall of 1935, it led the list of thirty-four works
in the catalogue and commanded a price of thirty-five hundred dollars,
more than twice the value of any of the other offerings.[72] Unfortunately,
tormented flagellants and somber funerals appear not to have been popular
in the mid-thirties, and the painting did not sell until a decade later when it
was acquired by the Tulsa oilman Thomas Gilcrease.

Sharp relied less and less on sales in Cincinnati after the mid-1930s.
Instead he maintained relationships with commercial art galleries in the
region, from the Blue Door Art Gallery in Taos and La Fonda in Santa Fe
to the O'Connor Gallery in Lubbock, Texas, and the McKenzie Gallery
in El Paso.[73] Sales through these venues over the following ten years were
steady but not particularly robust. In 1946 Sharp sent a letter to Mrs.
McKenzie containing a bit of astonishing news. He told her, with no little
surprise on his part, that "I sold all my remaining old Custer Battle & other
chiefs & warriors of the N. W. and several of the large ones to the Gilcrease
Foundation, Okla."[74] The old portraits, according to Sharp, numbered
seventy-five, and with that sale, he calculated that more than one hundred
of his old paintings were ensconced in museum collections where he
hoped they would remain forever.

Gilcrease visited Sharp's studio for the first time in October 1945.
The collector came to Taos with the primary intention of meeting Sharp,
the patriarch of the Taos Society of Artists. Before he left, Gilcrease had
promised to purchase eighty-eight paintings for $18,680.[75] The studio must
have looked rather lonely following the Gilcrease transaction.

Included in the incredible sale of artworks to Gilcrease was a painting
that, though smaller than *The Passing of a Penitente*, carried a similar message
of spiritual veneration. Titled *Rehearsal in the Estufa, Taos* [PLATE 2.37], it
was posed in 1946 in Sharp's studio but recalled sacred, exclusive ceremonials
that, as with the Penitente funeral, normally took place away from the
presence of women and out of view of Anglo observers. The figures, some
shadowed and others bathed in strong overhead light, suggesting a kiva door
above, are brought together in intense worship. The sophisticated use of light

72 *Hawaiian and Taos Paintings* (Kreimer & Brother Co., 1935).
73 Sharp's sales ledgers for 1947, for example, list six dealers outside Taos. JHSC.
74 JHS to McKenzie, March 26, 1946, JHSC.
75 Fenn, *Teepee Smoke*, 289. Some of the paintings were yet to be created.

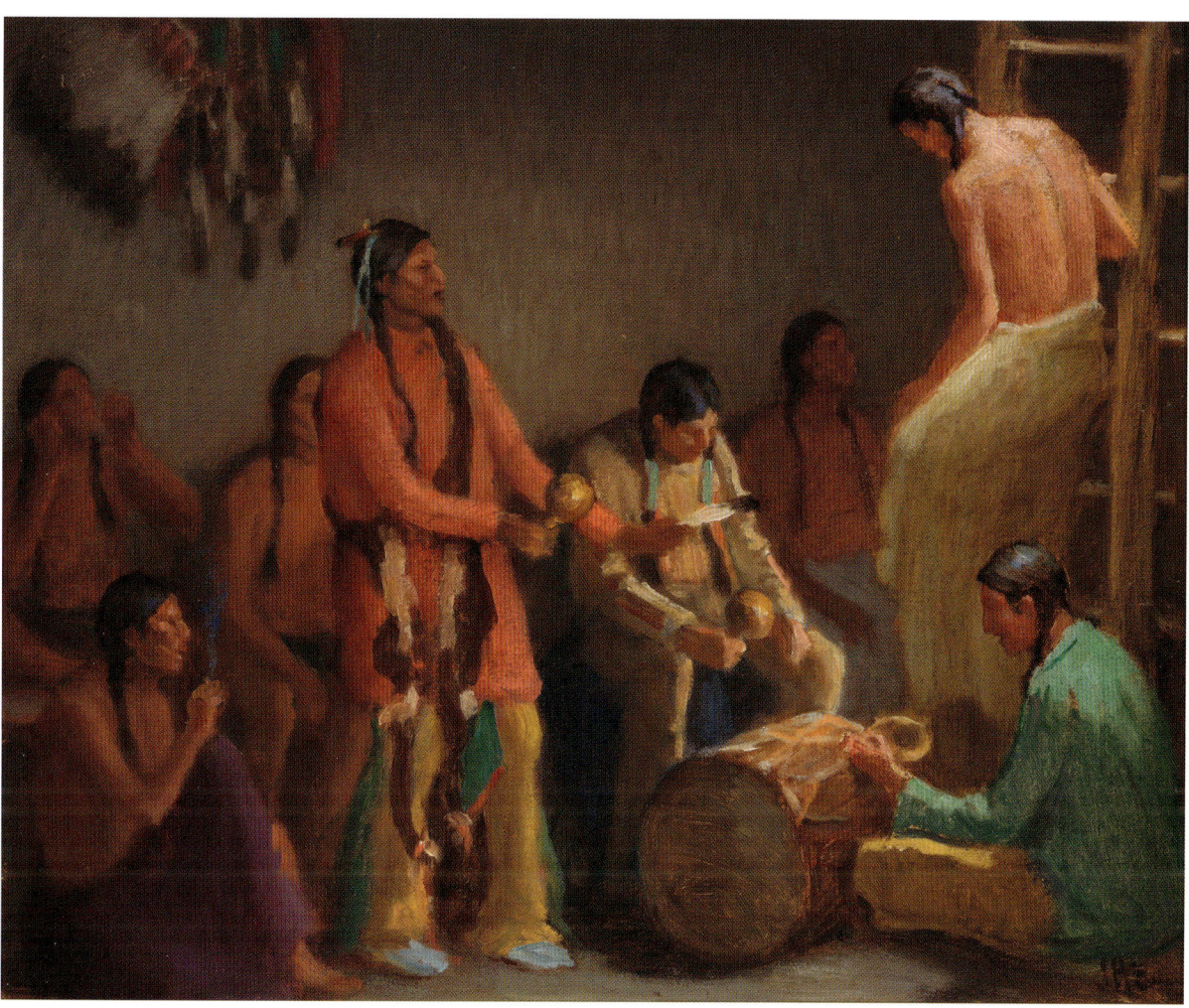

combined with rather rough modeling of forms suggests that this work was completed for better and worse during Sharp's mature, waning years.

Sharp's many studios—a rare buffalo hide teepee, a windowless art school attic space, a well-lit Munich apartment, an elegantly decorated atelier in Cincinnati, a simple adobe church in Taos, two flimsy wooden shacks at Crow Agency, a creaky sheep wagon on Montana's snowy prairie, and a comfortable and commodious adobe treasure house in Taos—all provided forceful, inventive environments, inspirational ambiance, sanctuaries for self-identification, and forums for social and intellectual intercourse that enabled Sharp to thrive and create. It is hard to say which, if any, he preferred, but collectively they assuredly shaped his art, his sense of being as an artist, and his legacy as one of the West's most ambitious, talented, and prolific painters.

[PLATE 2.37]

JOSEPH HENRY SHARP

Rehearsal in the Estufa, Taos

ca. 1946, oil on canvas,
17 ¼ x 21 ¾ in.
Gilcrease Museum, Tulsa,
Oklahoma. Gift of the Thomas
Gilcrease Foundation, 1955.
0137.348

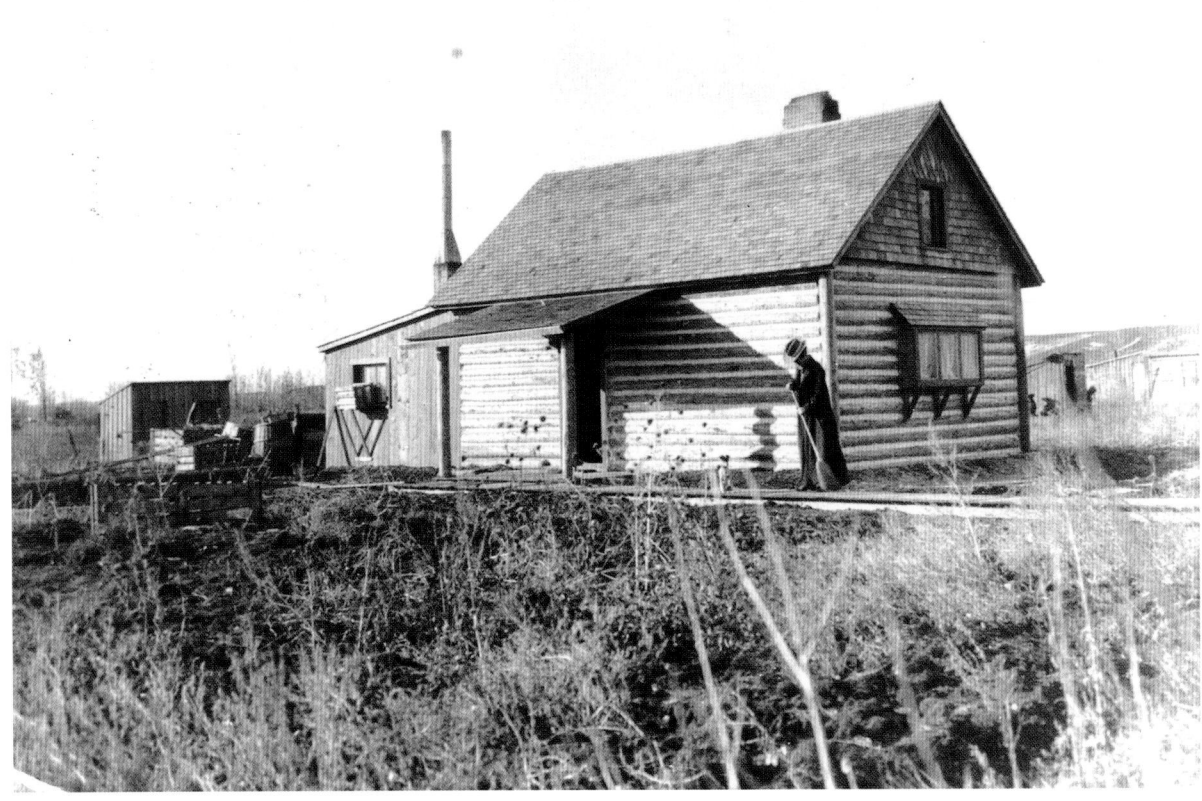

UNKNOWN PHOTOGRAPHER, *Addie Sharp Sweeping at the Absarokee Hut*. ca. 1908, photograph, b&w, 8 x 10 in.
Harold McCracken Research Library, Buffalo Bill Center of the West, Cody, Wyoming. JHSC. Gift of Mr. and Mrs. Forrest Fenn. P.22.531

Addie Sharp, wife of Joseph Henry Sharp, sweeps the boardwalk leading to the cabin that the Sharps had built at Crow Agency, Montana. The Sharps' terrier, named Frans Hals, watches. The Sharps enjoyed having visitors to the cabin, though Joseph wrote that it sometimes became a problem: "We had lots of company during (Crow) Fair and Mrs. Sharp worked herself to a frazzle cooking." Sharp to J. H. Gest, November 17, 1908, Box 1, Folder 3, JHSC.

SARAH E. BOEHME

ABSAROKEE HUT
THE JOSEPH HENRY SHARP CABIN

A sturdy log cabin, furnished with simple oak furniture and handsome Indian artworks, provided artist Joseph Henry Sharp an ideal setting for creating his works of art. Building this cabin on an Indian reservation on the plains of Montana offered tangible evidence of Sharp's belief that the appropriate environment would foster the making of art. For him, that ideal environment was genuinely American, inspired by the tenets of the Arts and Crafts movement and enriched by contact with American Indian cultures. Choosing to live on the Crow Indian Reservation in the midst of the subjects he portrayed, the artist named his cabin Absarokee Hut [PAGE 76] ("Absarokee" derived from the Crow People's word for themselves).[1] The cabin represented the artist's commitment to weaving together his life and his art into one seamless, richly patterned fabric.

Building the cabin in 1905 solidified Sharp's commitment to an art inspired by America, and specifically the American West. During his long and prolific career, Sharp produced most of his works in direct response to subjects in the West, primarily the Indians of the plains [PLATE 3.1] and of the Southwest. He also developed a relationship to the physical landscape of western regions [PLATE 3.2].[2] In artistic heritage, he followed the paths of other American artists who came west specifically to paint: George Catlin, John Mix Stanley, Albert Bierstadt, Thomas Moran, Frederic Remington, and others.

Unlike those earlier artists, all of whom visited the West but returned to the urban East to live, Sharp and a group of artists from his generation chose to settle and establish their studios in the heart of their inspiration. They broke a pattern of artistic migration to already-established art centers such as New York, Paris, and Rome, choosing

---

1 *Absarokee* is a variation of the name *Apsáalooke* or *Absaroke*, the Crow people's name for themselves. It means "children of the long beaked bird." For a tribal elder's account of the Crow people, see Joseph Medicine Crow, *From the Heart of the Crow Country: The Crow Indians' Own Stories* (New York: Crown, 1992). For a history of the Crow, see Frederick E. Hoxie, *Parading through History: The Making of the Crow Nation in America, 1805–1935* (Cambridge: Cambridge University Press, 1995).

2 The most comprehensive biography of Sharp is the monograph Fenn, *Teepee Smoke.* See also Fenn, *The Beat of the Drum and the Whoop of the Dance: A Study of the Life and Work of Joseph Henry Sharp* (Santa Fe: Fenn Publishing Company, 1983).

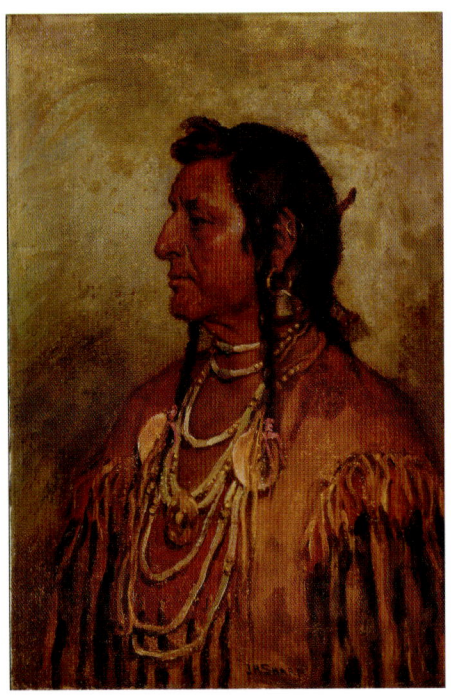

[PLATE 3.1]

JOSEPH HENRY SHARP

White Swan

ca. 1906, oil on canvas,
17 ⅝ x 11 ¾ in.
Buffalo Bill Center of the West,
Cody, Wyoming. 18.61

White Swan (1851 or 1852–1904)
was a noted Crow warrior and
an artist who recorded his battle
experiences in buffalo hide
paintings. The brother of Curly,
who had served as Custer's scout,
White Swan had been a scout for
Major Marcus Reno in 1876 and
continued scouting for the U.S.
Army at various times through
1881. Sharp recounted that
White Swan had been wounded:
"forehead crushed with war club
(deaf and dumb ever after) full
of bullet holes and knife cuts, but
none in his back!" White Swan
taught sign language to Sharp,
whose hearing was also impaired.
Douglas Bradley, *White Swan:
Crow Indian Warrior and Painter*
(Notre Dame, Ind.: Snite Museum
of Art, 1991)

instead to create new communities. Sharp first visited the small village of Taos, New Mexico, in 1893. He later commended it as a picturesque site to other painters. It became an artists' colony, attracting aesthetic immigrants in search of an American environment.[3] Sharp's early years in the West were divided between Montana, New Mexico, and California, but like the western settlers who built cabins, then packed up and moved on in search of better conditions, Sharp eventually left his home on the plains, succumbing to the magnetism of Taos. However, he took with him, quite literally, pieces of his Montana experience, and they continued to nourish his artistic career.

Almost forty years old when he discovered Crow Agency, Sharp found there a focus for his craft that established his identity as an American artist and initiated a period of independence in his career.[4] His departure point had been Cincinnati, Ohio, a significant regional artistic center in the latter half of the nineteenth century. From Bridgeport, Ohio, where he was born in 1859, and Ironton, Ohio, where he grew up, Sharp gravitated to Cincinnati for artistic training when he was fourteen years old. From its midwestern vantage point, Ohio looked both eastward to the metropolitan cities of the Eastern Seaboard and to Europe, and westward to the vast lands that still beckoned with promise. Sharp would venture in both directions. After initial training in the McMicken School of Design, he set out in 1881 on the first of several European trips for study and observation. In the Old World, he continued his artistic studies, learning technique, methods, and style. He also found inspiration in the Old Master paintings he saw in the museums and in the works and lives of contemporary European artists.

Sharp found that painting commissioned portraits offered the greatest promise as a career, both for patronage and for distinguishing himself among the many Cincinnati artists. He also obtained income as an instructor at the Cincinnati Art Academy. Yet he yearned for other possibilities, and the West was alluring. He cited youthful memories to explain his predilection for Indian subject matter. He recalled the excitement of seeing an Indian delegation, whose members were delayed at a nearby train station while on their way to Washington, DC.[5] Late in his life, when he was asked why he painted Indians, he referred to his

---

3   The artists' colony in Taos has been the subject of several important studies. For an exhibition catalogue that gives both biographical information on the artists and analysis of the environment, see Charles Eldredge, Julie Schimmel, and William H. Truettner, *Art in New Mexico, 1900–1945: Paths to Taos and Santa Fe* (New York: Abbeville Press, 1986). For an insightful patronage study, see Dean A. Porter, Teresa Hayes Ebie, and Suzan Campbell, *Taos Artists and Their Patrons, 1898–1950* (Notre Dame, IN: Snite Museum of Art; Albuquerque: University of New Mexico Press, 1999).

4   See my earlier study on Sharp, Sarah E. Boehme, "The North and Snow: Joseph Henry Sharp in Montana," *Montana The Magazine of Western History* (Autumn 1990): 32–47.

5   Robert Taft, *Artists and Illustrators of the Old West 1850–1900* (Princeton: Princeton University Press, 1983), 380.

youthful, romantic interest, but added, "Then when I came to know them I liked them for themselves. Perhaps they attracted me as subjects to paint because of their important historical value as the first Americans. Then the color of their costumes and dances, this no less attracted me."[6]

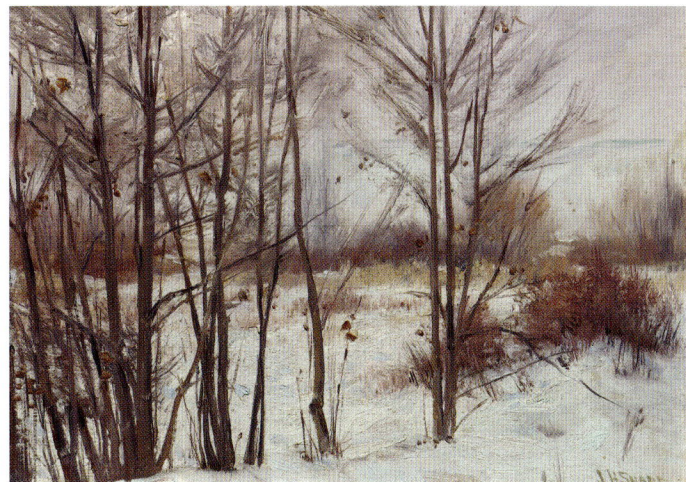

The Cincinnati artistic milieu also nourished this interest in American Indians. The same year that Sharp headed to the Old World, fellow Cincinnatian Henry Farny (1847–1916) set out for the Sioux agency at Standing Rock, North Dakota. The following year Sharp and Farny rented studios in the same building in Cincinnati. The younger artist would have seen the intriguing collection of Indian clothing and equipment that Farny used to decorate his studio.[7] Sharp soon created his own unique studio in Cincinnati, artfully arranging the exotic objects he collected on his European journeys in the space where he created his works.[8] Farny, both Sharp's mentor and rival, had carved out a niche for himself as a painter among the Plains Indians of the North. Sharp appears to have regarded Farny's position as the older, more established artist and avoided directly competing with him by going first to the Southwest. Sharp took his first trip to the American West in 1883, taking the train to New Mexico and Arizona, then going to California and up the coast to Washington.[9] When Farny effectively ended his traveling to the West, it opened up the northern plains to the younger artist. Concerning Sharp's trip to see Plains

[PLATE 3.2]

JOSEPH HENRY SHARP

The Winter Screen

ca. 1906, oil on canvas board, 9 ¾ x 13 ¾ in. Stark Museum of Art, Orange, Texas. Bequest of H.J. Lutcher Stark, 1965. 31.25.22

Sharp had residences in Crow Agency, Montana; Taos, New Mexico; and Pasadena, California. He often spent winters in Montana because he found it easier to hire models in the colder months and because he said the landscape was "too green" in summer. Sharp responded to the subtle grays, browns, and purples of the barren trees and brush, set off by the white with blues and yellows of the snow. Sharp traveled around the Crow Reservation and to other places in Montana and Wyoming, but he painted this scene "from my cabin backyard, Crow Agency, Montana," which he noted in an inscription on the verso. When he traveled outside his backyard, the artist used a sheepherder's wagon as a traveling studio. The artist wrote that he would "haul it to different localities and get several canvases each place. . . . Generally worked outside until cold froze the paint, then in and fired up." Sharp, quoted in *Joseph Henry Sharp and the Lure of the West* (Great Falls, MT: C. M. Russell Museum, n.d.), 24.

---

6 Sharp, quoted in Fenn, *Teepee Smoke*, 281.

7 Taft, *Artists and Illustrators of the Old West*, 219. For further discussion of Farny, see Susan Labry Meyn, *Henry Farny Paints the Far West* (Cincinnati: Cincinnati Art Museum, 2007).

8 Fenn, *Teepee Smoke*, 93–95. An undated clipping in one of Sharp's scrapbooks discusses the artist's Cincinnati studio: "It is thoroughly artistic in every detail and an air of comfort is suggested by the Moorish couch which occupies one end of the room under the balcony." JHSC. For analysis of another western artist's studio, see Peter Hassrick, *The Remington Studio* (Cody, WY: Buffalo Bill Historical Center, 1981).

9 The first trip would be followed by additional European study and work in Cincinnati, before the western experience would have a profound effect on Sharp's career. Another important event took place in the intervening years: on June 16, 1892, Joseph Henry Sharp married Addie Byram, a music student whom he had met at a Cincinnati Art Club event. Addie Byram Sharp would encourage her husband in his career and, by accompanying him to the western outposts, would make life more comfortable for the artist. That year Sharp also obtained a teaching position at the Art Academy of Cincinnati, providing a steady income.

Sharp's next encounter with the West was the following year, 1893, and it effectively commenced his specialization. He and his wife traveled to New Mexico with fellow artist John Hauser. While Addie stayed in Santa Fe, the two artists visited the pueblos (including Taos). As a result of this trip, Sharp produced several significant works, including *The Harvest Dance of the Pueblo Indians of New Mexico* and *The Turquoise Driller*, both of which *Harper's Weekly* published as illustrations, along with text written by Sharp. It appeared that Sharp had found a niche, portraying the customs, ceremonies, and lifeways of the traditional Pueblo Indians. During the 1890s, the Sharps spent time in Cincinnati, returned to Europe again for more study, and traveled to Taos again in 1897 and 1898.

Indians, a Cincinnati reporter wrote, "Until very recently few painters have had the temerity to invade this field so distinctly for years Farny's own."[10]

In 1899, as the nineteenth century drew to a close, Sharp, accompanied by his wife, Addie Byram Sharp, first visited the Crow Reservation in southern Montana. Its unique possibilities soon became the center of his attention. The Burlington Northern Railroad ran through the reservation, making travel there easy. (Farny had been invited out by Burlington Northern back when the line opened in 1883.) The Crow Reservation gave Sharp a base for visiting other Indian reservations in the region, including those of the Blackfeet, Cheyennes, Shoshones, Arapahos, and Sioux. This trip, and succeeding ones to the north, provided Sharp the opportunity to paint the Plains Indians, peoples whose traditional lives as nomadic hunters and warriors presented rich pictorial possibilities.[11] Popular dramatic performances in which war-bonneted Indians played a large role heightened Sharp's interests in the Plains Indians. He cited the "early Texas Jack Omohundro and Buffalo Bills shows" as influential.[12] He felt it was more urgent to depict the Plains Indians, rather than the Southwestern Indians, because the Plains culture and traditions were in danger of disappearing through the changes resulting from the decimation of the buffalo, the Indian wars, and the reservation system.

With the Crows, Sharp encountered a people known historically for the beauty of their clothing and for their horsemanship [PLATE 3.3].[13] The artist also found sources for his fascination with the Battle of the Little Big Horn. Because the Crows were traditionally in conflict with other Plains tribes such as the Sioux, they did not participate with those tribes in the battles against the U.S. military.[14] Rather, some Crow men served as scouts for the United States Army, the most famous instance being the Crow scouts who served with Lieutenant Colonel George Armstrong Custer and his battalion. The Battle of the Little Big Horn, the event in the Indian wars that so galvanized U.S. citizens in 1876 and afterward, fascinated Sharp as well. The battlefield was down the road from Crow Agency. Even though these events had brought changes that dramatically obliterated many elements of the Plains culture, the Crow held onto their ways as much as

10 Unidentified clipping, JHS scrapbook, JHSC.

11 John Ewers, "The Emergence of the Plains Indian as the Symbol of the North American Indian," in *Indian Life on the Upper Missouri* (Norman: University of Oklahoma Press, 1968), 183–203.

12 JHS to Thomas Gilcrease, n.d., photocopy, JHSC. If Sharp saw Texas Jack Omohundro and Buffalo Bill Cody together, it would have been in the 1870s when Sharp was a teenager. He certainly saw Buffalo Bill's Wild West, which William F. Cody began in 1883. The performances featured Plains Indians, primarily Sioux. In another, undated note to Thomas Gilcrease, Sharp said of Buffalo Bill Cody, "Saw him Frequently . . . saw him at all World's Fairs and Paris." Photocopy, JHSC.

13 See, for example, the commentary of early-nineteenth-century artist George Catlin, in *Letters and Notes on the Manners, Customs, and Condition of the North American Indians* (1841; reprinted, Minneapolis: Ross & Haines, 1965), vol. 1, p. 196. For a study of the Crows by one of Sharp's contemporaries, see Edward Curtis, *The North American Indian* (1909; reprinted, New York: Johnson Reprint, 1980), vol. 4, pp. 20–22.

14 Fred W. Voget, *The Shoshoni-Crow Sun Dance* (Norman: University of Oklahoma Press, 1984), 13.

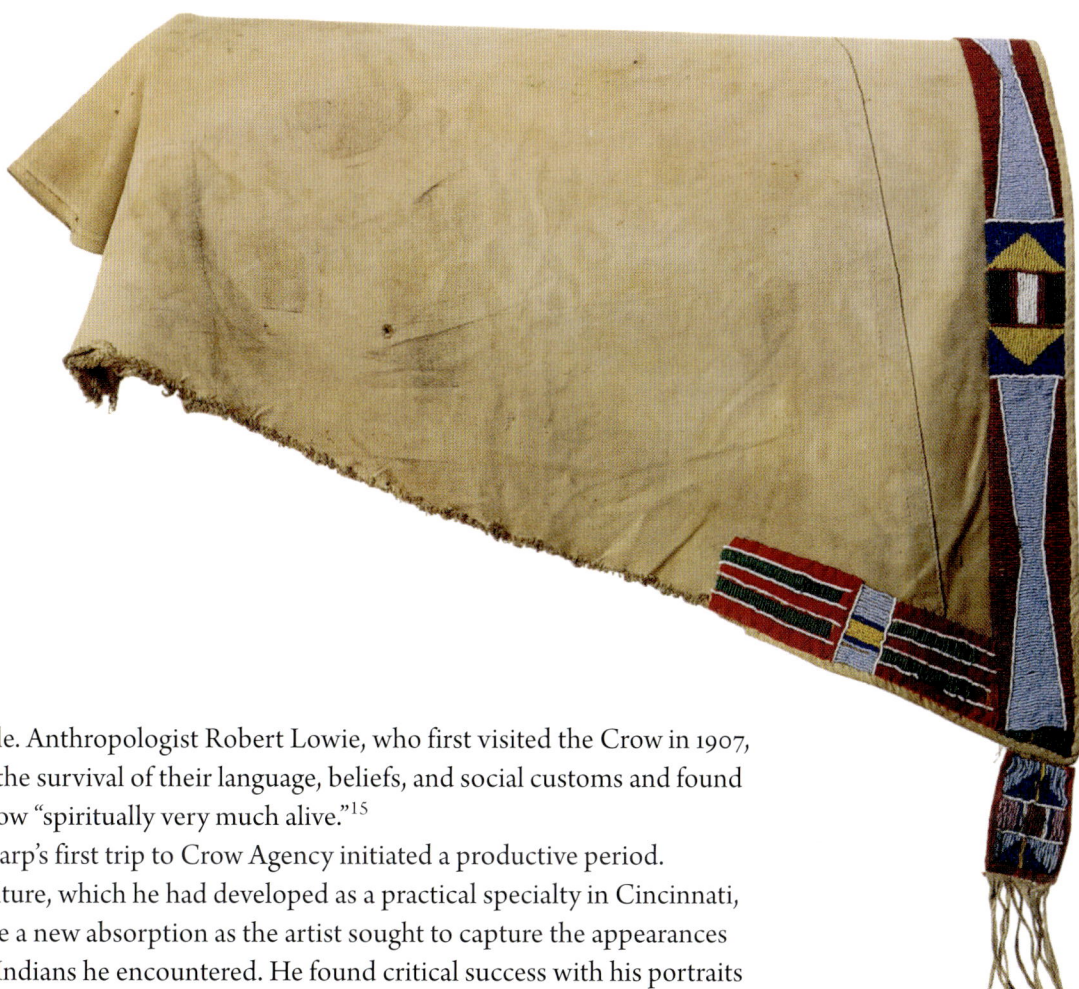

[PLATE 3.3]

UNIDENTIFIED CROW
ARTIST

Saddle Blanket

late nineteenth century, canvas
with beads, length 35 in.
Buffalo Bill Center of the West,
Cody, Wyoming. Gift of Mr. and
Mrs. Forrest Fenn. 19.00.246

possible. Anthropologist Robert Lowie, who first visited the Crow in 1907, noted the survival of their language, beliefs, and social customs and found the Crow "spiritually very much alive."[15]

Sharp's first trip to Crow Agency initiated a productive period. Portraiture, which he had developed as a practical specialty in Cincinnati, became a new absorption as the artist sought to capture the appearances of the Indians he encountered. He found critical success with his portraits of Indians and developed new sources of patronage.[16] When the artist sold a group of eleven Indian portraits to the Smithsonian Institution, the sale held special significance as government patronage of his work.[17] Returning to the West, he produced a large group of works for the Pan-American Exposition in Buffalo, New York. Through that forum he met the most important patron for his Crow Agency time, Phoebe Hearst. Encouraged by ethnologist Alice Fletcher, Hearst went to see his paintings, bought seventy-nine of them, and agreed to buy more on a yearly basis. Her contract with Sharp enabled him to resign from his teaching job in 1903 and move out west.

When Sharp first began visiting Crow Agency, he stayed at the Server Hotel. Soon needing a place to paint, he constructed a small, twelve-by-fourteen-foot studio. He found that space inadequate, however, and by

The Crow people are known for their horsemanship and for fine beadwork, which is usually done by the women. The beadwork on this saddle blanket features bold geometric designs of hourglass shapes outlined with white beads. On Crow beadwork, see Barbara Loeb, "Crow Beadwork: The Resilience of Cultural Values," *Montana The Magazine of Western History* (Autumn 1980): 46–59.

---

15 Robert H. Lowie, *The Crow Indians* (Lincoln: University of Nebraska Press, 1963), xvi.

16 Sharp sold Indian paintings to Joseph G. Butler Jr., who later founded a museum in Youngstown, Ohio, for his collection of American art.

17 An exhibition at the Cosmos Club in Washington, DC, led to this sale. Sharp succeeded in obtaining government patronage for his Indian paintings, whereas earlier artists such as George Catlin and John Mix Stanley had been unable to do so. William Henry Holmes, a former head of the Bureau of Ethnology, purchased the paintings that Sharp sold to the government for the United States National Museum, the Smithsonian Institution. As a scientist with an interest in ethnology, Holmes saw Sharp's work as valuable documents for the scientific study of the races.

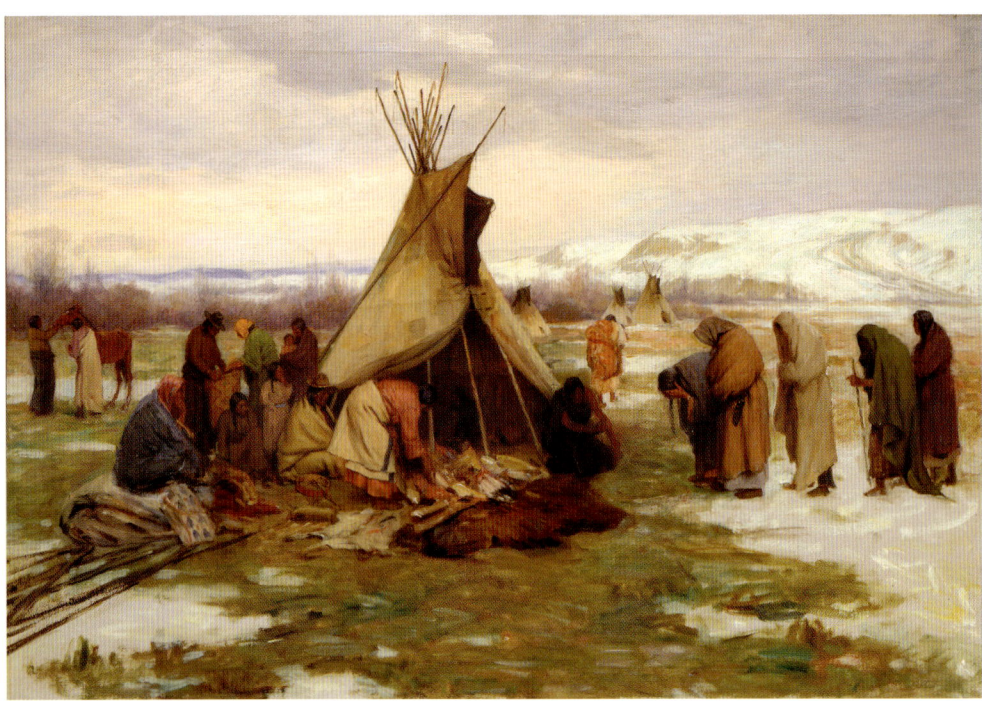

[PLATE 3.4]

JOSEPH HENRY
SHARP

Dividing the Chief's Property

ca. 1905, oil on canvas,
27 x 39 ⅜ in.
Buffalo Bill Center of the West,
Cody, Wyoming. 1.61

Sharp portrayed the mourners in a
procession that has the solemnity
of those carved on ancient funerary
monuments. This painting depicts
the custom of giving the deceased's
belongings to the mourners. While
at Crow Agency Sharp painted
several representations of burial
customs, such as this painting and
its pendant, *Burial Cortege of a
Crow Chief.* He also painted scenes
of the tree and scaffold graves
traditionally used by this tribe. In
portraying these scenes, Sharp took
the ethnologist's stance of interest
in customs. The quantity of death
scenes he painted could also signal
an acceptance of the belief that
Indian people were dying and
becoming a "vanishing race." The
Sharp paintings in the Buffalo Bill
Center of the West's collection that
were purchased with the Whitney
Purchase Fund are works that
Sharp left in his Montana cabin
and then gave to Carolyn Reynolds
Riebeth. They were purchased for
the Whitney Gallery of Western
Art in 1961.

October 1904 had built another studio, one that had more light and larger
dimensions (fourteen by twenty feet).[18]

Having a workspace while lacking a permanent living space was not an
adequate solution, and by April 1905 Sharp was planning to build "a little
shanty or bungalow."[19] Sharp gave a practical reason for building a home:
he wanted to be able to live year-round on the reservation. "I have . . . built
my 'hut' in just this spot because I wanted to paint the winter landscape
here as well as the Indians," he said, "to paint them day after day and
month after month."[20]

The ability to live on the reservation year-round opened up new
possibilities for the artist. Sharp was able to paint during the winter,
producing landscapes with the subdued tonalities of gray skies and the
softening effect of snow blanketing the natural forms. It also gave him more
occasions for portraying traditional patterns of Indian life [PLATE 3.4].
He wrote of expanding his subject matter beyond portraiture: "Now that
I have more time, I shall devote much of it to composition & pictures of
the poetry & legends as well as the home life of the Indians at present."[21]
In reality, he found he needed time living among his subjects to find the
poetic imagery he sought. The reservation system had changed Plains
Indian life, and Sharp, like most other artists, sought a picturesque image of
Indian life that looked back to past times. He was able to witness examples
of traditional Indian life, but his most productive experiences occurred
at special times, such as Crow Fair [PLATE 3.5]. In the autumn the Crow

18 JHS to J. H. Gest, October 29, 1904, photocopy, Box 1, Folder 3, JHSC.
19 JHS to J. H. Gest, April 20, 1905, photocopy, Box 1, Folder 3, JHSC.
20 "Our Home Department," *The Craftsman* (June 1906): 408.
21 JHS to Butler, March 14, 1904, Box 1, Folder 14, JHSC.

people came from all over the reservation to the campground near the agency, gathering for a fair and celebrations.[22] In 1908, when rain and then eight inches of snow postponed Crow Fair for a week, Sharp seized the chance to paint camp scenes among the Indians who had already set up their tipis in anticipation of the event.[23]

Yet it was more than simply being there year-round; an idealism undergirded the artist's move to the agency. Sharp sought to integrate his life and his work in the belief that "where we were working best we should also live best," and thus the house was to be "plain outside, comfortable within, near the work of our life, almost the essence of it."[24]

Sharp's decision to build at Crow Agency was supported by Samuel Guilford Reynolds, the agent who administered the U.S. government's policies at the reservation. Reynolds and his family became friends of the

[PLATE 3.5]

JOSEPH HENRY SHARP

Crow Indians Crossing River on Horseback

ca. 1906, photograph, b&w, printed posthumously from Sharp's negative, 11 x 13 ⅞ in. Harold McCracken Research Library, Buffalo Bill Center of the West, Cody, Wyoming. JHSC. Library Purchase. P.61.1.16

A procession of Crow riders fords the river going to the fairgrounds during Crow Fair.

---

22 Samuel Reynolds, in his Annual Report for 1906, wrote: "The Crow fair was organized for the purpose of working up a friendly competition in farming, gardening, and stock raising between the individual Indians and the Indians of one district with those of another. A fair was held in the fall of 1904 which was an absolute failure. We started anew in the fall of 1905 and called it the First Industrial Fair of Crow Indians. This was as much a success as the other was a failure, and the Indians as well as the employees are very proud of the event." Report of Agent for Crow Agency, *Annual Reports of the Department of the Interior* (Washington, DC: Government Printing Office, 1906). Crow Fair continues today, though not as an agricultural fair but as a celebration of Crow Indian life.

23 JHS to J. L. Hubbell, October 6, 1908, Box 1, Folder 11, JHSC.

24 "Our Home Department," 408.

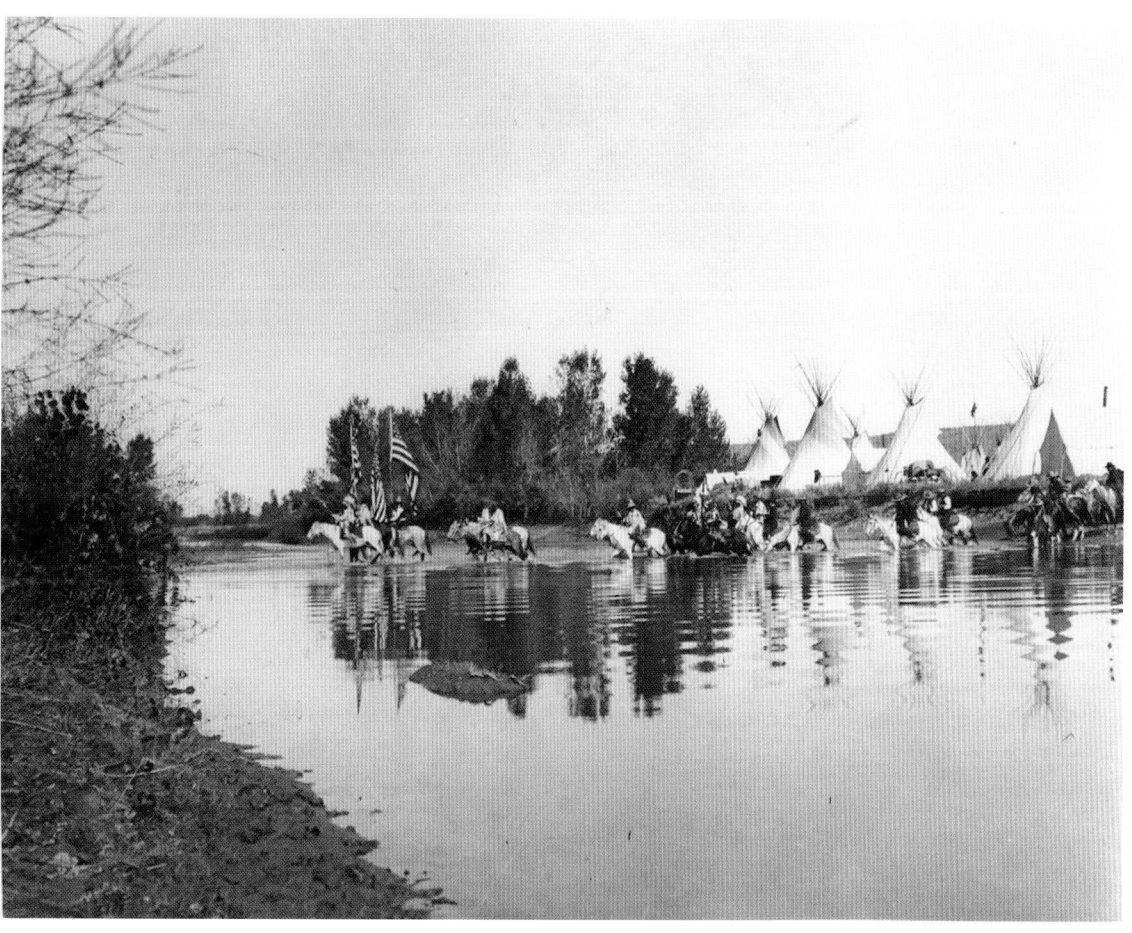

[PLATE 3.6]

UNKNOWN
PHOTOGRAPHER

Absarokee Hut, Interior

View showing fireplace, windows, and buffalo robe
Illustration in *The Craftsman* 10, No. 3 (June 1906): 410.
Syracuse University Library, George Arents Research Library for Special Collections, Syracuse, New York

In a letter Sharp sent with photographs of his cabin to *The Craftsman* magazine, published by Gustav Stickley, he wrote, "A great robe decorated with colored porcupine quills is on one wall; a buffalo skull over the fireplace, shields, skins, Navajo rugs, other Indian things and several pictures complete the decorations." "Our Home Department: A Real Lesson in Home Building," *The Craftsman* (June 1906): 411. Sharp avidly collected Indian art and during his life sold or traded objects from his collections to museums and other collectors. Today, the Gilcrease Museum, the Historic Southwest Museum, the Museum of the American Indian, the Cincinnati Art Museum, and the Buffalo Bill Center of the West are among the museums holding Native American art that Sharp once owned.

Sharps, and the agent encouraged the artist to settle on the reservation.[25] When Sharp started building his cabin in the first decade of the twentieth century, Crow Agency might have been remote from the centers of urban life, but it was no barren prairie. An eastern publication romantically, but inaccurately, described the cabin as "this little house standing alone in the heart of a great western plain."[26] The agency consisted of a small village centered on a tree-filled park.[27] Sharp deliberately chose to build a log cabin to emphasize the rustic character of his life in Montana. Although the log cabin was a form of architecture used in the region, it was by 1905 an outdated form for a permanent residence. The other houses at the agency were built of board lumber.

Sharp did not choose an architecture that identified himself with his subjects. The traditional Indian homes had of course been tipis, made first of buffalo hide and later of canvas. The government was encouraging reservation Indians to abandon traditional life and live in houses, so on the Crow Reservation the government built houses of surplus lumber and brick.[28] Although Sharp owned a buffalo hide tipi, he used it primarily as a prop for his paintings, not as a personal living space. He chose not to live like his subjects, but rather to harken back to the form of architecture used by white settlers coming into the West. In choosing the log cabin, he selected an architectural style that had come to symbolize the pioneer spirit and an American identity. Sharp designed the home as a one-room log cabin, with a "lean-to" for the bedroom and kitchen.[29]

Reynolds was instrumental in helping Sharp find assistance in building the cabin. Charles "Smokey" Wilson, an African American man who lived among the Crows and worked for the agency, supervised the work. According to the artist, prisoners in the agency jail, "mostly young men for minor offense and girls," provided labor.[30] Logs came from the reservation forest. The Burlington Railroad gave Sharp a load of "discarded old oak & oil-soaked ties" that he used for firewood.[31] Sharp and his wife, Addie, both worked on the cabin, and by November 1905 they were nearly ready to move into their new home. "We are going to move into our little log 'hut' in a day or two," he wrote Joseph Gest. "I've been tinkering around on the interior for three weeks, and have only painted twice, but hope to get at it again soon," he wrote. Although Sharp recited a list of ailments from the

25 Although it has often been repeated that Sharp's cabin was built through the authorization of Theodore Roosevelt, no documentation has ever surfaced to support that claim. Most likely the government authorization came from Reynolds. Fenn concluded that it was a private arrangement between Reynolds and Sharp. Fenn, *Teepee Smoke*, 166.

26 "Our Home Department," 408.

27 For more information on Crow Agency during the time of Sharp's residence and for personal reminiscences about Sharp from the Indian agent's daughter, see Riebeth, *J. H. Sharp among the Crow Indians*.

28 Riebeth, *J. H. Sharp among the Crow Indians*, 113.

29 When the cabin was moved to the grounds of the Buffalo Bill Historical Center, it was not possible to retain the lean-to.

30 JHS, "The Cabin," photocopy of handwritten document, Box 1, Folder 27, JHSC.

31 JHS, "The Cabin."

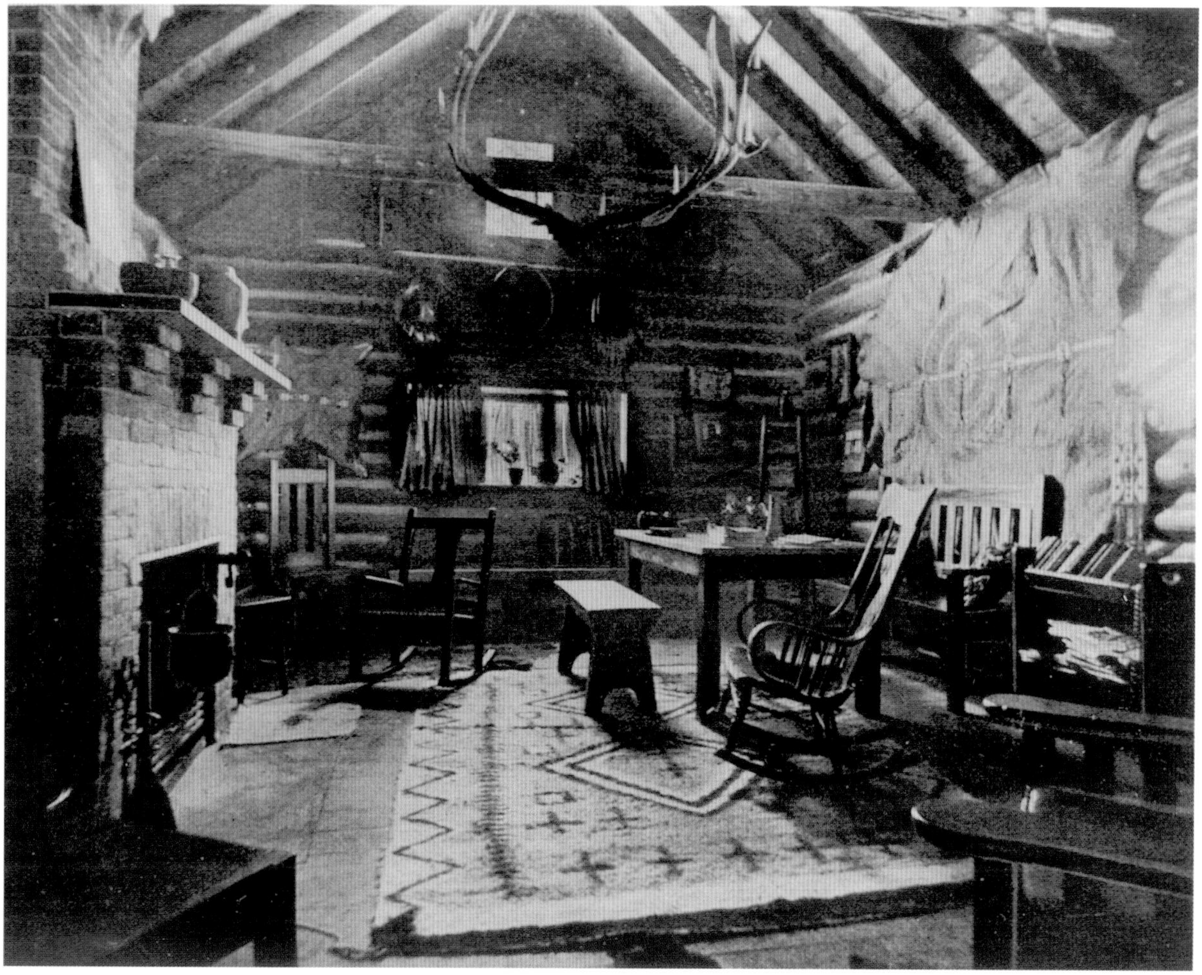

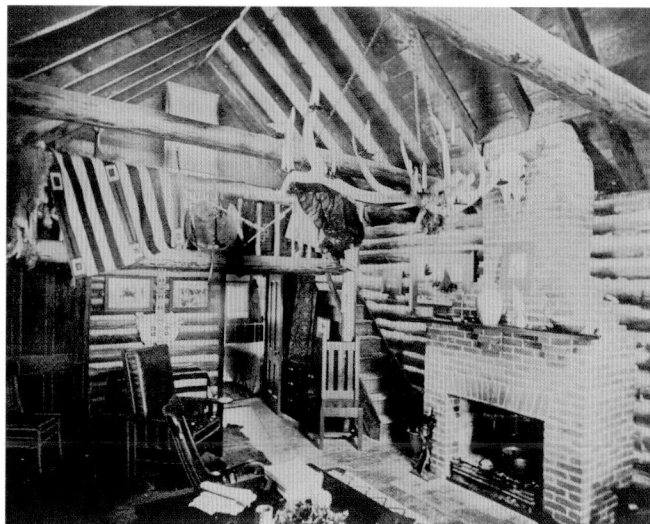

[PLATE 3.7]

UNKNOWN
PHOTOGRAPHER

Absarokee Hut, Interior

View showing candelabrum
and balcony
Illustration in *The Craftsman* 10,
No. 3 (June 1906): 409.
Syracuse University Library,
George Arents Research Library
for Special Collections, Syracuse,
New York

In *The Craftsman* article featuring
photographs and a description
of Sharp's cabin, the Absarokee
Hut was described as having
been "designed and partly
constructed by an artist deeply
in sympathy with Craftsman
aims and purposes." "Our Home
Department," 408.

work—"'calouses' on my hands, 'charley horses' in both arms and various cuts and bruises from the hatchet, saw, and chisel"—he nevertheless concluded, "It's lots of fun."[32]

Sharp had very definite ideas about how the interior of the cabin should look. "From the start we planned our house for comfort and for roominess, yet with the utmost simplicity and always with a view to harmonious effects so far as color and line were concerned."[33] He wanted a warm, cozy atmosphere and chose a palette primarily of browns, gray, and green. Sharp's concern for color and tone led him to treat the peeled logs with oil darkened with burnt umber. He noted that the woodwork on the doors and windows was stained even darker and the chinking was gray. A focal point of the large central room was a fireplace that heated the house and served as an alternate cooking fire with its "crane for bean pot and tea kettle" [PLATE 3.6][34] The bricks for the fireplace were scrap material from nearby Fort Custer, but Sharp found the color "sickly billious [sic]," so he stained each brick with turpentine and "a touch of Venetian red, and there is not the least suggestion of paint about them." Candles set in a large candelabrum made of elk antlers provided the interior light [PLATE 3.7]. Sharp fastened the candleholders to screw eyes, and then put them in drilled holes in the antlers. "This was a harder job than painting Indians!" he remarked.[35]

Although Sharp chose an architecture then identified with America, he nevertheless constructed some elements suggesting a European influence. Sharp disliked the coldness of the light coming through a high north window, so he painted the window to look like stained glass, "putzen scheiben."[36] The small cabin (with an interior of about fifteen and a half by twenty-four feet) was sixteen and a half feet high to the ridgepole, allowing enough height for a balcony at one end. Indian blankets and animal hides draped over the railing created sufficient privacy that the balcony could serve as a guest bedroom, occupied by Addie's visiting sister Louise, among others.[37] This seemed a recurring architectural feature meaningful to Sharp; he had a balcony in his Cincinnati studio and would have one in his Taos studio. He associated it with the European ateliers that provided him and his generation with examples of the artistic life. A newspaper critic visiting Sharp's Cincinnati studio described the balcony as "designed in miniature after those in Paris which are used as storerooms for the canvases, plasters, brushes &c., often indeed for the sleeping apartments of the artist."[38]

32 JHS to J. H. Gest, November 21, 1905, photocopy. Box 1, Folder 3, JHSC.

33 "Our Home Department," 408.

34 JHS to J. H. Gest, November 21, 1905.

35 "Our Home Department," 411.

36 "Our Home Department," 411. *Putzen scheiben* are "small, round panes with a bubble of glass in the center," according to Robert Haven Schauffler in "Meissen and Dresden," *Century Illustrated Monthly Magazine* 77, No. 6 (April 1909): 871.

37 Riebeth, *J. H. Sharp among the Crow Indians*, 59–60. After Addie Sharp died in 1913, Louise Byram became Joseph Henry Sharp's second wife, in 1915.

38 "Among the Artists," newspaper clipping, n.d., Sharp scrapbook, JHSC.

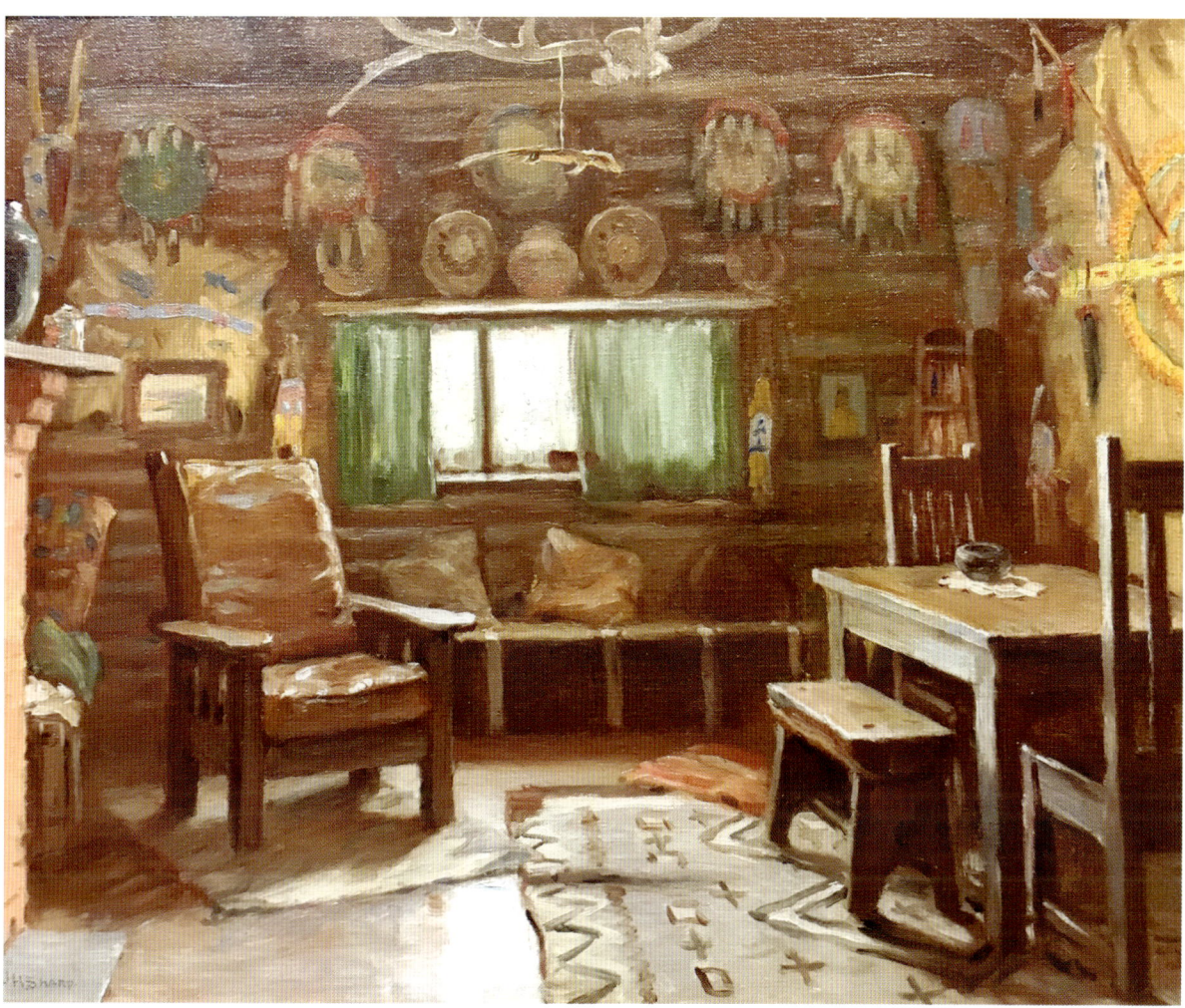

In planning the interior's appointments, Sharp chose an Arts and Crafts style. From his background in Cincinnati, he would have been aware of the growing movement, started in England by William Morris as a reaction against the industrial age and the excesses of the Victorian era. In a return to the virtues of earlier ages, the Arts and Crafts movement sought to promote good design and good craftsmanship.[39]

That Sharp intended his cabin as an exercise in the style can be seen in the letter he sent to *The Craftsman* magazine, the movement's leading U.S. periodical.[40] Gustav Stickley, the editor of *The Craftsman*, was the foremost American proponent of the Arts and Crafts style. In his Craftsman shops, Stickley sought to produce furniture and other decorative items that would be practical, simple in design, and honestly made. In his letter to the magazine, Sharp mentioned that the curtains and portieres, which were soft green, were from the Craftsman shop [PLATE 3.8]. He also wrote that

[PLATE 3.8]

JOSEPH HENRY SHARP

Interior of Sharp Cabin

ca. 1906, oil on canvas, 16 x 20 in. Lainey Jacobson Reynolds-Keene Collection. Image courtesy of Big Horn County Historical Museum, Hardin, Montana

Sharp probably painted this view of the interior of his Crow Agency cabin during the early years of his living there. He gave the painting to Carolyn Reynolds Riebeth, though he retained possession of it for many years. He had it in his living room in Taos, New Mexico, in the 1950s. Collector Thomas Gilcrease wanted to purchase it, and Sharp wrote to Riebeth asking her if she wanted to sell the painting. J. H. Sharp to Sissy [Carolyn Reynolds Riebeth], n.d. [notation concerning postmark in 1950s], Box 1, Folder 15, JHSC.

---

39 Robert Judson Clark, ed., *The Arts and Crafts Movement in America*, 1876–1916 (Princeton: Princeton University Press, 1972).

40 "Our Home Department," 408–12. The article never mentions Sharp's name. It refers only to an artist from Cincinnati whose paintings had been purchased by Phoebe Hearst. Sharp mentioned *The Craftsman* article in a June 15, 1906, letter to J. H. Gest, in which he told his friend that the June *Craftsman* would have pictures of the hut (JHSC).

[PLATE 3.9]

Roycroft Settee, ca. 1905, oak, height 40 in. 19.00.133

Trade Blanket, late nineteenth century, wool, length 70 in.

UNIDENTIFIED PLATEAU ARTIST

Corn Husk Bag, late nineteenth century, woven plant fiber, length 24 in. Buffalo Bill Center of the West, Cody, Wyoming. Gifts of Mr. and Mrs. Forrest Fenn.

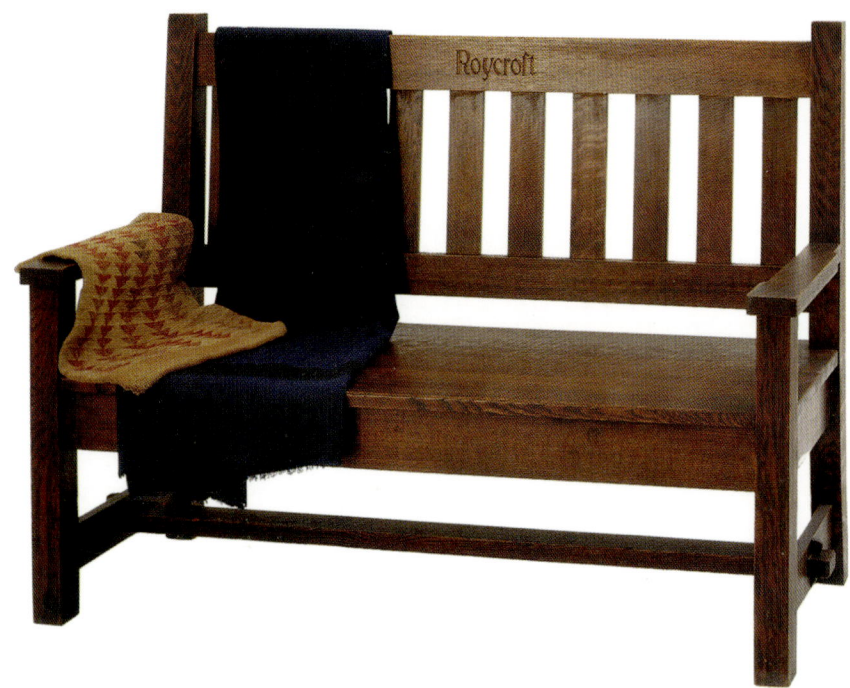

Sharp used Roycroft furniture in his Montana and New Mexico homes. The Roycrofters were an artistic community in East Aurora, New York, founded by Elbert Hubbard, a charismatic leader. The Roycroft village, devoted to producing well-designed objects, included not only shops for the workers but also activities for educational and cultural enrichment. Hubbard wrote, "Art is the expression of man's joy in his work, and all the joy and love that you weave into a fabric comes out again and belongs to the individual who has the soul to appreciate it." Elbert Hubbard, "A Social and Industrial Experiment," in *Roycroft Catalogue* (East Aurora, N.Y., 1902), 27.

The furniture and the artifacts used in the reinstallation of Absarokee Hut at the Buffalo Bill Center of the West are objects that were in Sharp's studio and residence in Taos, New Mexico, at the time of his death. Sharp had left Montana cabin furniture in the Taos cabin. Those pieces of furniture are now in private collections in Montana or their locations are unknown. Sharp ordered from Roycroft some of the same items of furniture for both of those residences. Jonathan Noffke provided documentation on the objects and countless other aspects of the installation at the Buffalo Bill Center of the West.

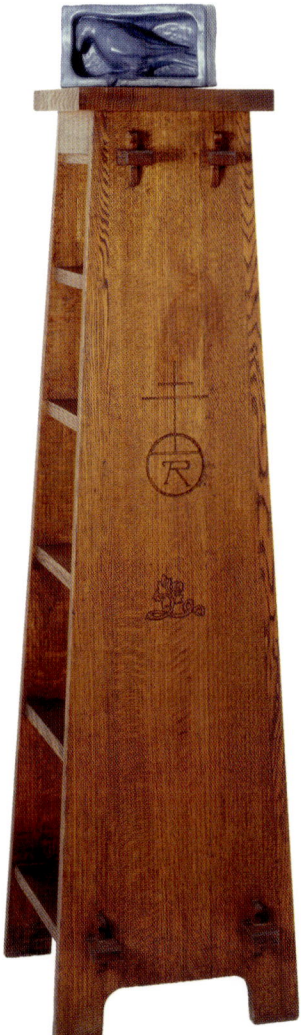

[PLATE 3.10]

Roycroft Magazine Pedestal

ca. 1905, oak, height 64 in. Buffalo Bill Center of the West, Cody, Wyoming. Gift of Mr. and Mrs. Forrest Fenn. 19.00.79

The furniture bears the incised Roycroft insignia of an R within an orb with a cross. A 1905 catalog of Roycroft productions described the furniture: "It is simple, solid, substantial, severe and rarely beautiful. It is distinguished—it has as much personality as a Rookwood vase." Quoted in Clark, *The Arts and Crafts Movement in America*, 45.

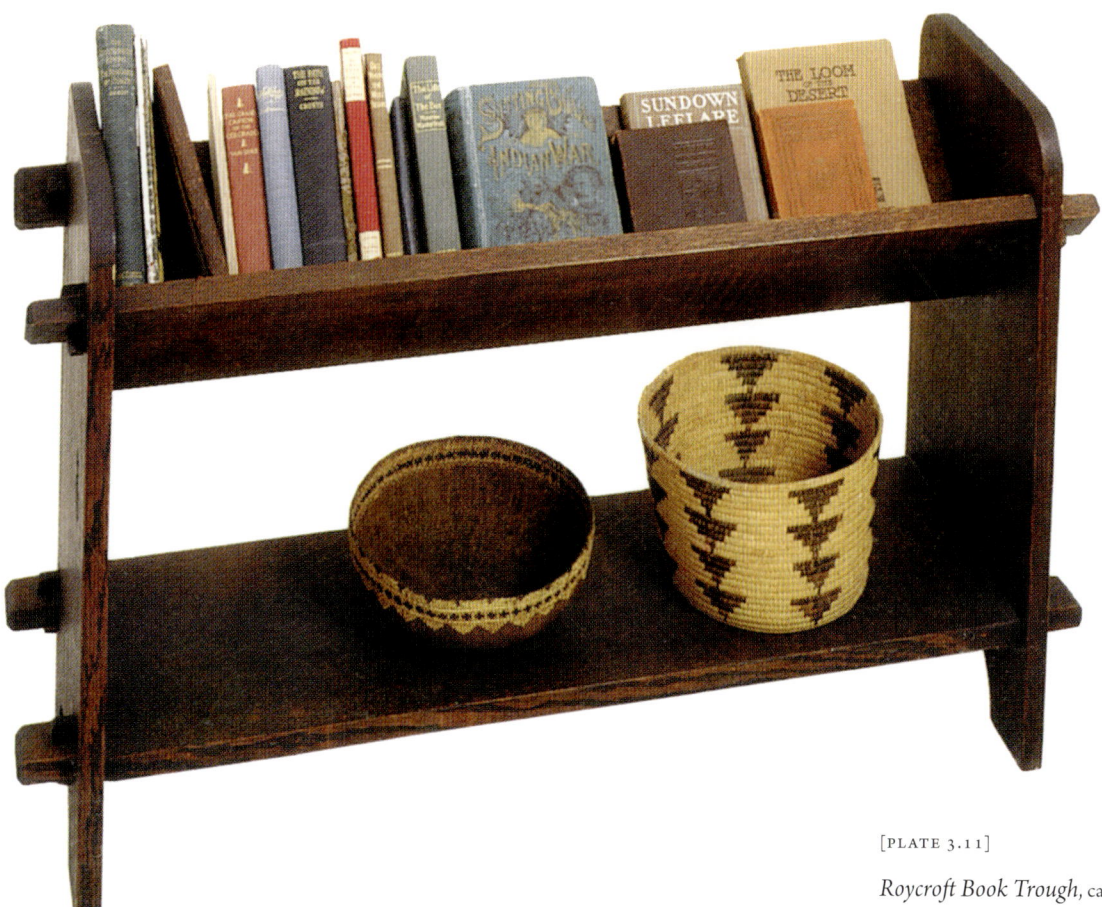

[PLATE 3.11]

Roycroft Book Trough, ca. 1905, oak, height 24 in.

UNIDENTIFIED KAROK ARTIST

Basket (bowl), late nineteenth century, twined plant fiber, height 4 in., 19.00.80

TOHONO O'ODHAM, PAPAGO

Basket, late nineteenth century, coiled plant fiber, height 6 in. 19.00.119

Books owned by Sharp, including some Roycroft publications. Loans and gifts from Mr. and Mrs. Forrest Fenn.

Buffalo Bill Center of the West, Cody, Wyoming. Gifts of Mr. and Mrs. Forrest Fenn.

Books with elegant typefaces and fine bindings were the Roycrofters' first productions, and Sharp collected such publications for his personal library, including *A Message to Garcia* by Elbert Hubbard (1914) and *The Myth in Marriage* by Alice Hubbard (1912).

the furniture was "dark oak, the table and one or two other pieces were made here, the book-rack is from the Craftsman shops."[41] With Sharp's directions, Louis Ballou, the agency carpenter, had made some furniture in the Arts and Crafts style. Sharp refrained from mentioning that most of the furniture came from a rival firm, the Roycrofters, founded by Elbert Hubbard [PLATE 3.9]. In a letter to his friend Gest in Cincinnati, Sharp had written, "Furniture all from Roycrofters. I helped steer Mr. Hubbard around the reservation for a couple days, he was very much interested in my work—we made a good trade, then he bought an extra picture."[42] Hubbard visited Crow Agency during one of his lecture tours to promote Roycroft ideals, giving Sharp the opportunity to trade several paintings for the sturdily built, simply lined furniture [PLATE 3.10 AND PLATE 3.11].

The Craftsman highlighted Sharp's cabin, even though it was not a pure Craftsman design, because it was an expression of Craftsman ideals: "a home inspired by the taste and needs of the people who are to live in it, built for comfort, arranged to afford the man who is to live in it the utmost

41 "Our Home Department," 411.

42 JHS to J. H. Gest, November 21, 1905.

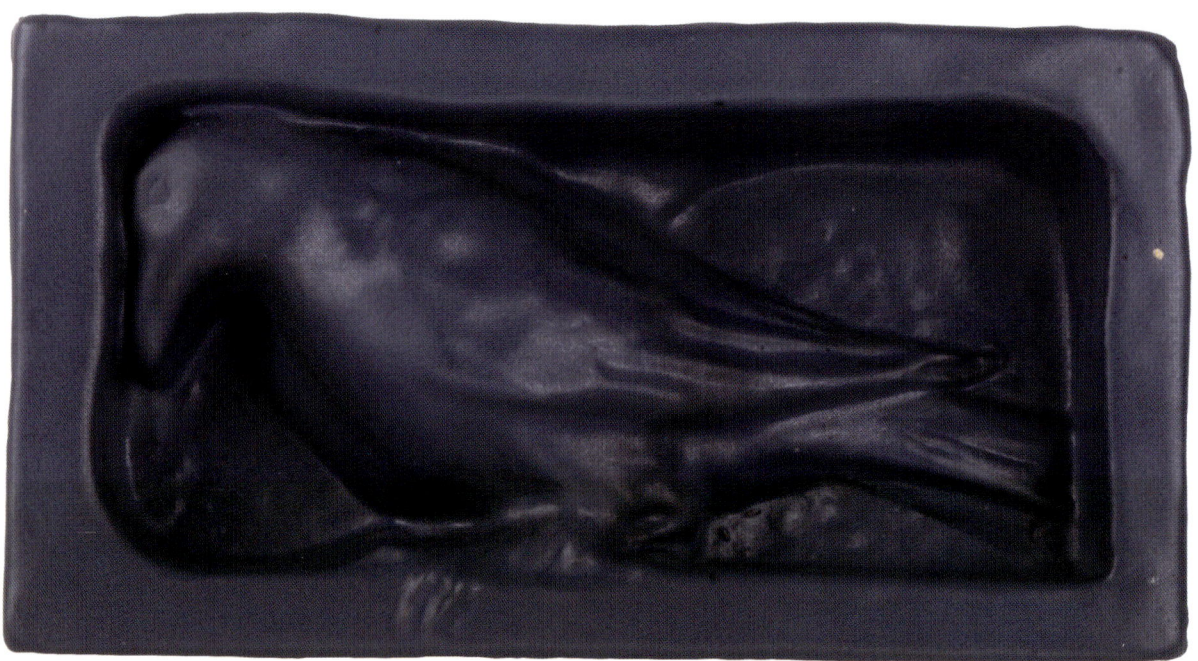

Rookwood Pottery Faience

ca. 1902, matte glaze architectural brick, height 6 in.
Buffalo Bill Center of the West, Cody, Wyoming. Gift of Mr. and Mrs. Forrest Fenn. 19.00.283

Carolyn Reynolds Riebeth, daughter of the Crow Reservation agent, remembered a Rookwood Pottery raven above the door of Sharp's cabin. The crow was the symbol of the Rookwood Pottery Company in Cincinnati, where Sharp was trained. "Absarokee is the Indian word for Crow," Sharp wrote. Riebeth, *J. H. Sharp among the Crow Indians*, 34; Sharp to J. H. Gest, December 15, 1908, Box 1, Folder 3, JHSC.

opportunities to pursue the work of his life contentedly and successfully and arranged so that the mistress thereof should find in it the maximum of brightness and convenience with the minimum of labor."[43] *The Craftsman* saw Sharp's cabin as an example of the reformation occurring in American architecture that spelled an end to the imitative style of building and the beginning of an age when simple charm and beauty would provide comfort and convenience.

Above the front door, Sharp placed a symbol of the cabin's name, a representation of a crow. He owned a Rookwood Pottery brick that portrayed the bird in low relief [PLATE 3.12]. The Rookwood Pottery Company was a Cincinnati ceramics firm that made art pottery. From his time in Cincinnati, Sharp might have had connections with Rookwood through students and other artists. The rook (or crow) was also a company symbol, so the brick had multiple associations for the artist, evoking his artistic early environment as well as his current one.

Sharp seemed to find the cabin comfortable, even in conditions that might have inhibited others. He usually came to Montana during the winter, saying he found it too green in the summer. In a letter written in ink that was pale from having been frozen, Sharp reported in January 1906, "It was 16 [degrees] below zero last night, but is fine & clear & exhilarating."[44] Ten years later, upon heading back to Crow Agency after a week of painting near Sheridan, Wyoming, he reported that the "cold has been intense . . . 6 degrees to 33 degrees below zero all the time." Pledging that next year he would charge more for his snow scenes, he still concluded that "sunshine and air is great tho!"[45]

---

43 "Our Home Department." 408.
44 JHS to J. H. Gest, January 22, 1906, Box 1, Folder 3, JHSC.
45 JHS to J. H. Gest, January 18, 1916, Box 1, Folder 3, JHSC.

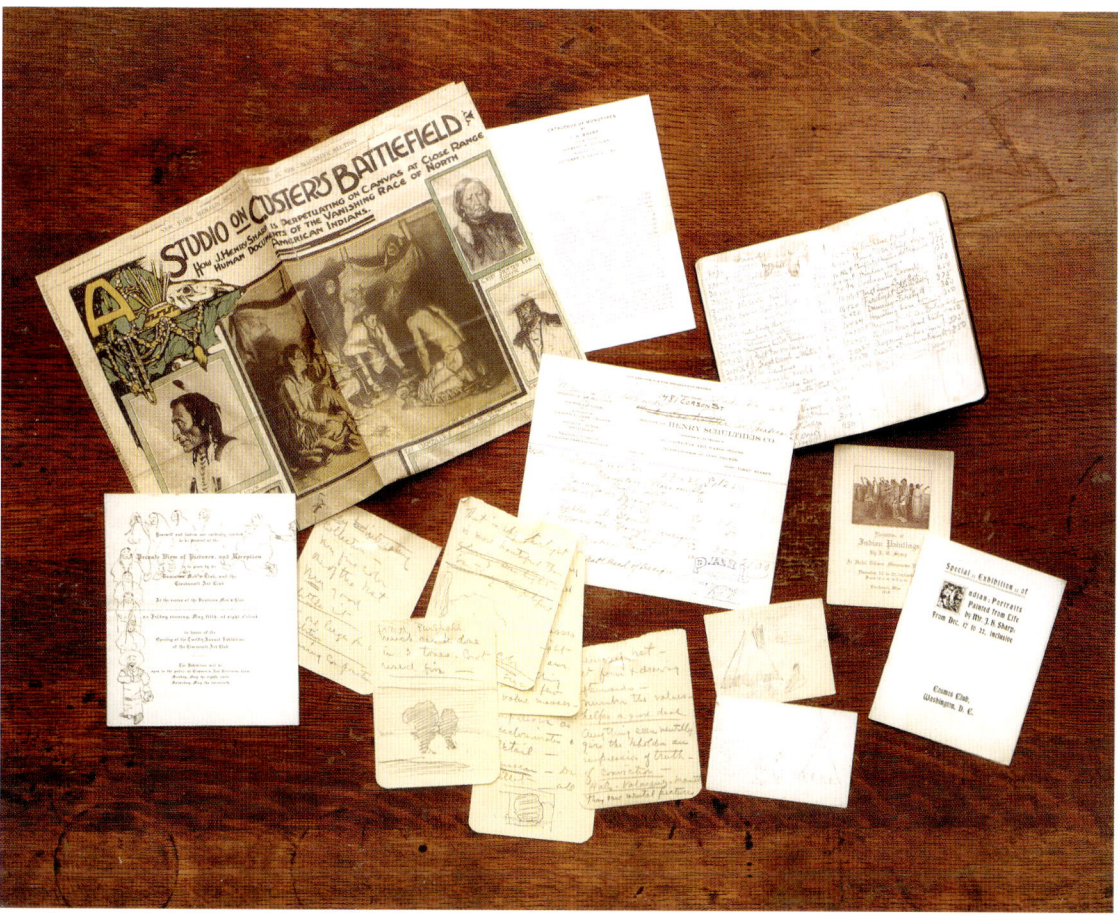

For an artist who played an active role in the Cincinnati art scene and seemed to thrive on the stimulation of an artistic community, Crow Agency might seem too isolated. Yet Sharp was highly productive there, and he found nearby sources for exhibiting and selling his works. As early as 1900 he mounted exhibitions, sponsored by Sheridan, Wyoming, bookdealer Herbert Coffeen [PLATE 3.13]. The artist gained attention and the *Sheridan Post* declared, "Mr. Sharp is one of the few American artists who sees that the great art of America must come from the west."[46] Sharp also held exhibitions and sold paintings in Billings, Montana. He made contact with other artists when possible. Sharp took up photography as an aid to his work and traveled around the agency with photographer Fred Miller. He often visited a former student from Cincinnati Art Academy days, Fra Dana (née Dinwiddie), who lived on a ranch in Parkman, Wyoming, near Sheridan. Sharp wrote of Dana that she "paints well and is a fine critic."[47] In Sheridan he also met and offered advice to cowboy artist Bill Gollings. When Sharp traveled up to Great Falls, Montana, in 1907, he visited Charles M. Russell, "a nice fellow."[48] Sharp was at Crow Agency during the filming of a movie based on the story of Hiawatha, produced by

[PLATE 3.13]

Newspaper Clipping, Account Book, Exhibition Lists and Invitations, Receipt, Notes, and Sketches

Harold McCracken Research Library, Buffalo Bill Center of the West, Cody, Wyoming. JHSC. Gifts of Mr. and Mrs. Forrest Fenn

Materials such as these from Sharp's career document the paintings he exhibited, as well the critical reception they received. Due to a childhood accident and infection, Sharp was deaf, and he carried a notepad for holding conversations with people. Sharp to Mr. Koch, January 1, 1905, photocopy, Box 1, Folder 3, JHSC.

---

46 "Famous Pictures of Indian Life," *Sheridan Post*, May 4, 1909.

47 JHS to J. H. Gest, November 20, 1907, Box 1. Folder 3, JHSC.

48 JHS to J. H. Gest, July 22, 1907, Box 1, Folder 3, JHSC.

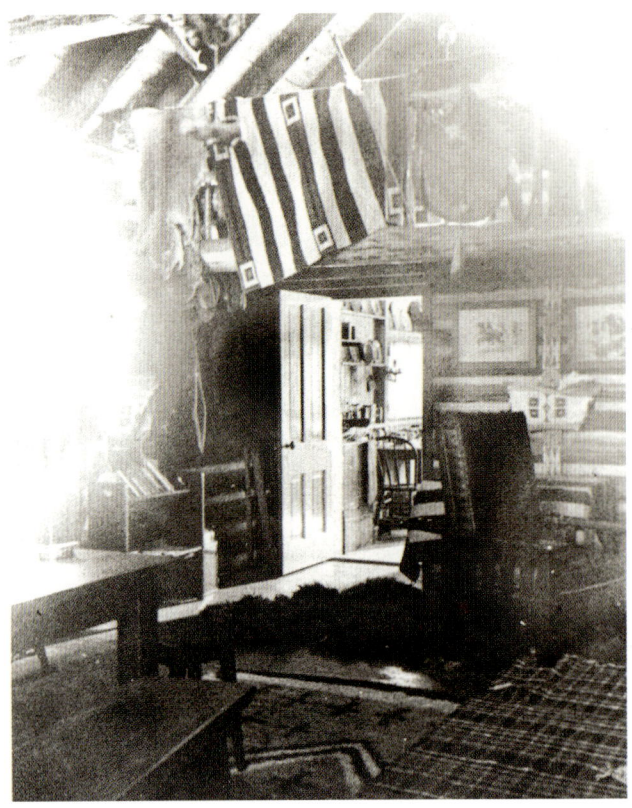

[PLATE 3.14]

UNKNOWN
PHOTOGRAPHER

Absarokee Hut (Interior)

ca. 1908, photograph, b&w
Buffalo Bill Center of the West,
Cody, Wyoming. JHSC. Gift of Mr.
and Mrs. Forrest Fenn. P.22.1443

This photograph shows the
Schreyvogel prints along with many
of the Indian art objects Sharp
collected. Sharp took pride in his hut
and made numerous photographs to
show his friends in Cincinnati. "We
had some negatives made of our
house, but they are bad, and have to
try over again," he wrote. "Have sent
for some non-halation plates—the
windows fog it so, and the flashlight
I do not like, I still hope to send you
one before we return." Sharp to J. H.
Gest, January 22, 1906, photocopy,
Box 1, Folder 3, JHSC.

Rodman Wanamaker and ethnologist Joseph
Dixon.[49] Other artists passed through Crow
Agency, including Frederic Remington and
Charles Schreyvogel. Two platinum prints
by Schreyvogel, given to Sharp and probably
intended as emblems of fellowship, found their
way onto the walls of the hut [PLATE 3.14].
My Bunkie (ca. 1900; Buffalo Bill Center of the
West) represented the comradeship between
cavalry bunkmates, and *How Kola!* (1901;
Buffalo Bill Center of the West) chronicled
a moment of reciprocated mercy between
enemies in the midst of war.[50] Schreyvogel's
military narratives from the Indian wars,
belonging to the past, added to the cabin's
rustic air. Sharp's other items of decor in the
cabin signaled a different relationship with
Indian peoples [PLATE 3.15].

Sharp's letter to *The Craftsman* magazine
emphasized the collection of Indian artifacts
that he used to decorate the cabin, including
a buffalo robe, shields, skins, Navajo rugs,
pottery, and baskets [PLATE 3.16]. Sharp's Indian collection correlated
with those ideals of the Arts and Crafts movement in the United
States that looked to Native American works of art as sources of
inspiration. Indian arts were lauded as examples of art whose design and
craftsmanship bloomed from the soil of America.[51] Sharp exemplified
that ideal by surrounding himself with such prime examples of Indian
craftsmanship as an early Chief Blanket, a Two Grey Hills rug, and
extraordinary pieces of quillwork and beadwork. For his collection,
he sought early Indian artworks not obviously influenced by modern
life. After seeing a collection of baskets that artist Frank P. Sauerwein
obtained at Hubbell Trading Post in Ganado, Arizona, Sharp wrote to
J. L. Hubbell offering to trade paintings for Native art. He specifically
wanted Hopi baskets that were "fine and artistic" and that used natural,
vegetable dyes rather than commercial dyes.[52] He expressed a similar
preference in blankets and rugs: "In the modern blankets I like the grays
& natural browns & whites. I have quite a number of fine old ones—

49 Fenn, T*eepee Smoke*, 192–93. See also Joseph K. Dixon, *The Vanishing Race: The Last Great
Indian Council* (New York: Doubleday, 1913).

50 James D. Horan, *The Life and Art of Charles Schreyvogel* (New York: Crown, 1969), 25, 28.
For another interpretation of *How Kola!* see Alex Nemerov, "Doing the 'Old America,'" in *The
West as America: Reinterpreting Images of the Frontier*, ed. William H. Truettner (Washington,
DC: Smithsonian Institution Press, 1991), 297–98.

51 See "Indian Blankets, Baskets and Bowls: The Product of the Original Craftworkers of This
Continent," The Craftsman (February 1910).

52 JHS to J. L. Hubbell, July 6, 1908, photocopy, Box 1, Folder 11, JHSC.

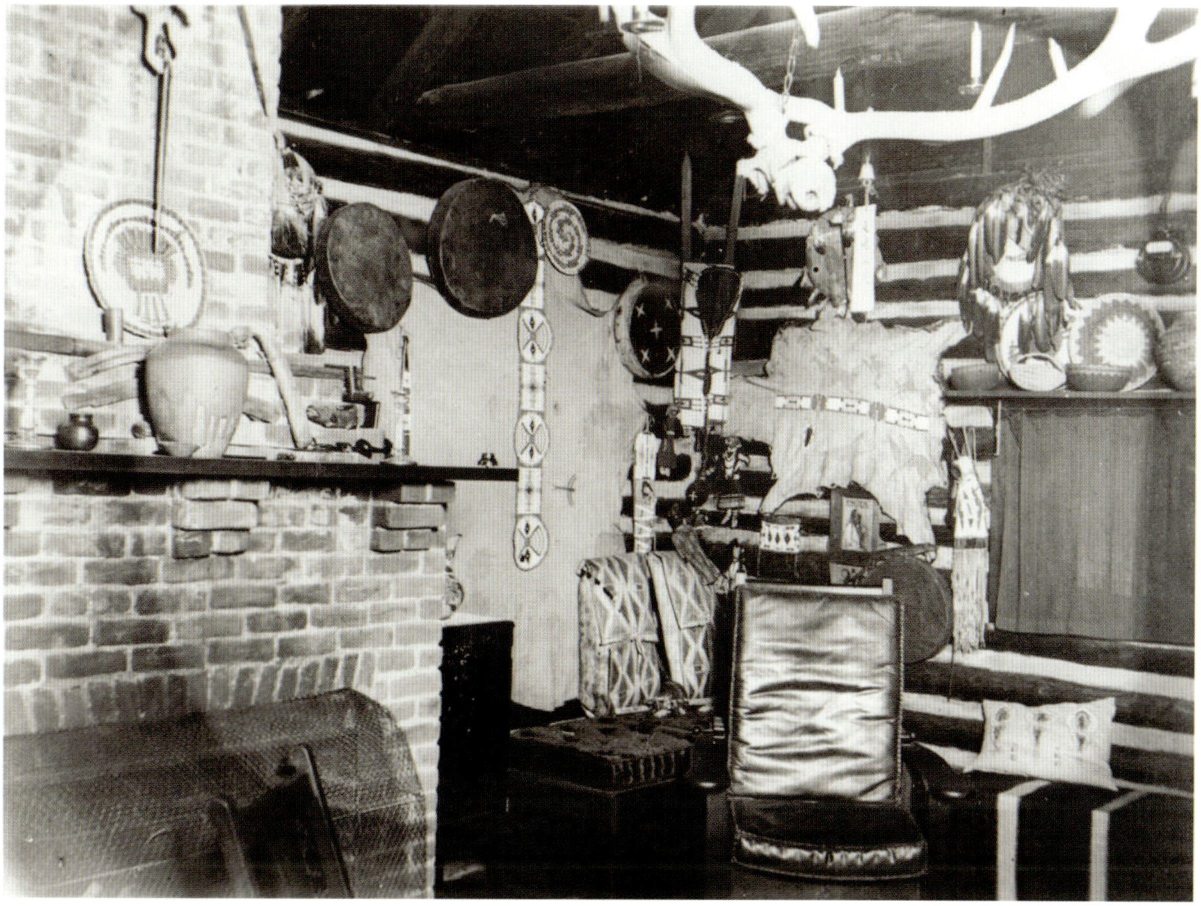

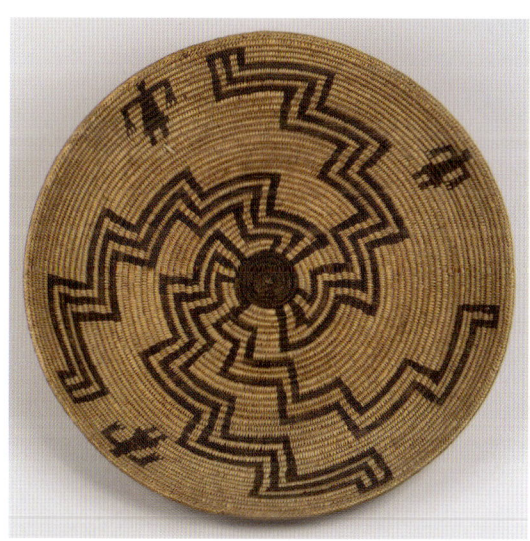

[PLATE 3.15]

UNKNOWN
PHOTOGRAPHER

Absarokee Hut (Interior)

after August 1911,
photograph, b&w
Buffalo Bill Center of the West,
Cody, Wyoming. JHSC. Gift of Mr.
and Mrs. Forrest Fenn. P.22.1062

Sharp hung an elk hide with
painted dragonfly and a beaded
blanket strip on the wall beside the
large fireplace. Flat Iron, a Sioux
from Pine Ridge who visited Crow
Agency, gave Sharp the elk hide.
The artist used it as a backdrop in
many of his paintings. The framed
cover of *Pacific Monthly* magazine
dates this photograph sometime
after August 1911.

[PLATE 3.16]

UNIDENTIFIED APACHE
ARTIST

Basket

late nineteenth century, coiled
plant fiber, diameter 16 ¾ in.
Buffalo Bill Center of the West,
Cody, Wyoming. Gift of Mr. and
Mrs. Forrest Fenn. 19.00.125

An article in *The Craftsman*
exemplifies the appreciation for
this type of Indian art: "The best
baskets . . . are made by the Pima
and Apaches, who excel in this
art as markedly as the Hopi and
Navajos excel in the making of
blankets. . . . The real Indian basket
is something to bring despair to
the 'arts and crafts' basket maker,
because it is a form of handicraft
as nearly perfect as any that exists."
"Indian Blankets, Baskets and
Bowls: The Product of the Original
Craftworkers of this Continent,"
The Craftsman (February 1910):
590.

Chief and other designs, so the modern dyes of reds, yellows, greens &c. would not hit me at all."[53] He was willing to consider blankets with red "if the red is good & quiet in design, & not loud & noisy, & raw common red."[54]

Sharp also expressed in his paintings a reverence for Indian art. In works such as *The War Bonnet* (ca. 1916; Buffalo Bill Center of the West) he depicted an Indian solemnly contemplating an object of beauty, the dramatic eagle feather warbonnet. Sharp would pursue this theme in his paintings in Taos, posing his southwestern models in reverie in the presence of Indian artworks. Sharp and his colleagues in Taos appreciated Indian artworks for their artistic value, not merely as curiosities. In commenting on the quality of some older baskets and pottery that he identified as choice, museum-quality pieces, he referred to their artists as "real old masters."[55]

Sharp's motives for living among the Indians, collecting Native arts, and portraying Indians were primarily aesthetic rather than scientific. His decision to live on a reservation parallels the contemporaneous practices of American anthropologists who were basing their research on field studies among Native Americans, but he did not try to compile a comprehensive analysis of Indian life. Sharp personally had the inclinations of a collector, the desire to acquire both in quantity and quality. His collection of Indian artifacts was substantial and eventually supplied several American museums with important acquisitions, but he documented the history only of some pieces in his collection late in his career. His paintings, especially those from the early western years, were often appreciated for their ethnological content, and Sharp certainly realized the effects that estimation could have on selling his paintings to patrons such as the Smithsonian and collector Phoebe Hearst. His style of painting, grounded in observation and studies of nature, gave a realistic appearance to his works. Yet Sharp's intentions were more poetic than documentary, and he disavowed being an ethnologist.[56] Even with his early portraits, his concerns were more emotive than factual. In 1937, as the Great Depression continued to affect art sales, Sharp lamented to another artist about the lack of interest in his portraits: "I have a lot of heads of the fine old fellows yet, but people (this generation) are only interested in a curious way, not as purchasers. Very few of the present generation know anything of the Indian, the romance, dignity & beauty of their life, & care less."[57]

Sharp's attitudes toward the Indians among whom he lived were born of his own time and of his position as an artist. For him, Indians were first of all models, and he complained when they did not meet his expectations. He preferred to paint Plains Indians but found an inducement in the Southwest: "cheap models." He wrote back to

---

53 JHS to J.L. Hubbell, July 27, 1908, photocopy, Box 1, Folder 11, JHSC.

54 JHS to J.L. Hubbell, September 9–10, 1908, photocopy, Box 1, Folder 11, JHSC.

55 JHS to Butler, September 28, 1925, photocopy, Box 1, Folder 13, JHSC.

56 Boehme, "The North and Snow," 35.

57 JHS to Scheuerle, April 15, 1937, photocopy, Box 1, Folder 6, JHSC.

Cincinnati that the other Taos artists paid "50 cents a pose for what
I always have to pay two dollars for in the North. Fine for figure
compositions but very few have the interesting faces & history of the old
plains fighters, so 'me' for the North & snow!"[58] Although he preferred
the picturesqueness of the Plains Indians and romanticism of the aged
warriors, he found he had increasing difficulty in finding Plains Indians
to model for him. He began turning more to painting landscapes and
spending his time in Taos.

Sharp's pervasive sympathy toward his Indian subjects led him
to support the preservation of Indian culture. "It is a great pity the
government compels the children attending school to wear government
shoes," he wrote. "The mothers complained to me that the white man's
shoes made the foot crooked—and living in the white man's house was
stuffy."[59] He protested a regulation requiring Indians to cut their hair,
pleading for their rights to preserve their own religion.[60] His appreciation
for Indian art and his romantic, poetic view of Indian life brought a
consciousness of cultural values to a larger audience. One of the reviewers
of his paintings cast his painting career in a reformist light:

> In these days when we are discussing the problems of emigration
> . . . it might be well for those of us who are the descendants of the
> early emigrants to turn to the real Americans. . . . The home of
> the brave it has ever been, but not a land of the free to those early
> braves who were and whose descendants are the true Americans.
> . . . Mr. Sharpe [sic] is one of those artists who believe that we
> "Americans" do not understand the real Americans and has
> devoted his career in art to telling the story of the Redman. Not in
> a pedantic manner, but always he tells the story of the Indian in so
> poetic a manner and with such intriguing colors that our interest is
> at once aroused—and then a better understanding.[61]

Sharp's separation from Absarokee Hut was gradual but ordained by
several factors. In December 1908 a cinder from the fireplace damaged one of
his eyes, causing a temporary halt to his painting and great anxiety about his
future. He confided his concerns to fellow Cincinnati artist Joe Scheuerle:

> Can you realize what it is to be blind in one eye for near a year the
> other one weak from the strain, & the nerves giving you fear all the
> time you would loose [sic] the other, and to see in a way the most
> beautiful & paintable things in the world & not work. To never
> have the anticipatory feeling when squeezing paint tubes—the
> hope that you may really & truly paint something good this time
> [PLATE 3.17]?[62]

58 JHS to J. H. Gest, June 15, 1906, photocopy, Box 1, Folder 3, JHSC.

59 JHS, "The Women," manuscript, n.d., JHSC.

60 JHS to Office of Indian Affairs, January 21, 1902, photocopy, JHSC.

61 Alma May Cook, "Real American Studied: Artist Paints in Quaint Indian Towns," *Los Angeles Express*, September 5, 1922.

62 JHS to Scheuerle, Oct. 3, n.d., photocopy, Box 1, Folder 6, JHSC.

While at Crow Agency, Sharp continued to order his paints from Cincinnati. He was particular about the paints he used, ordering specific brands for certain colors. "When I have Eduard yel. ochre on my palette it seems I always get a better Indian head." JHS to Mr. Koch, January 1, 1905, photocopy, Box 1, Folder 3, JHSC.

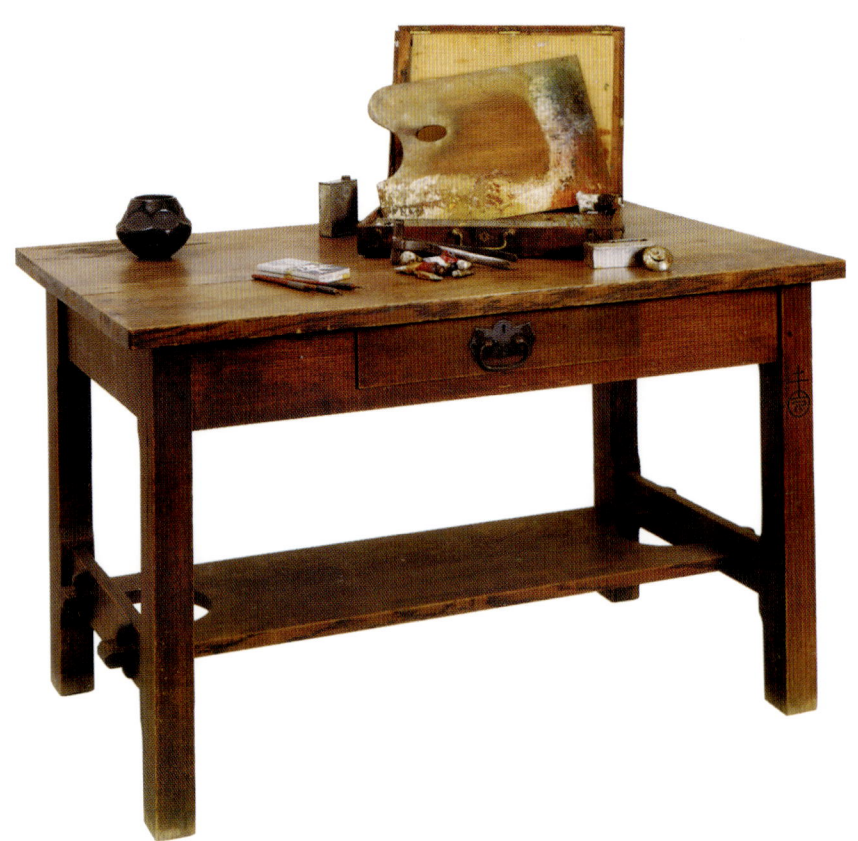

Sharp's beloved wife, Addie, was in poor health too, suffering from "nervous prostration." In search of a healthier climate, the couple spent time in Pasadena, California. Addie Sharp died in the spring of 1913, and although her husband had recovered his sight enough to rejuvenate his painting career, he had less commitment to Montana. His friend and supporter Samuel Reynolds had resigned as agent in 1910. The succeeding agents, who were not especially interested in having an artist in residence on the reservation, sought possession of the cabin as a residence for clerks since it was on government land. Sharp tenaciously held onto the cabin, renting it to a young couple, with whom he stayed when he visited the agency in 1914, and he continued to visit the area into the early 1920s. Sharp believed that the structure was rightfully his since it had been built for him and he had made improvements on it. When it appeared he could obtain legal title to it, he urged Samuel Reynolds to bid on it for him: "There is a good deal of sentiment connected with the old cabin—your building it & the lively interest we all took doing it—the happy years Addie & I had there, the doggie & all, that it would break my heart to lose it."[63]

Sharp finally obtained the title to the house and land, but sentiment was not enough to bring him back. Too many changes had occurred for the cabin to mean what it had in Sharp's earlier life and art. In Taos, New

---

63 JHS to Samuel Reynolds, October 25, 1922, photocopy, Box 1, Folder 1, JHSC.

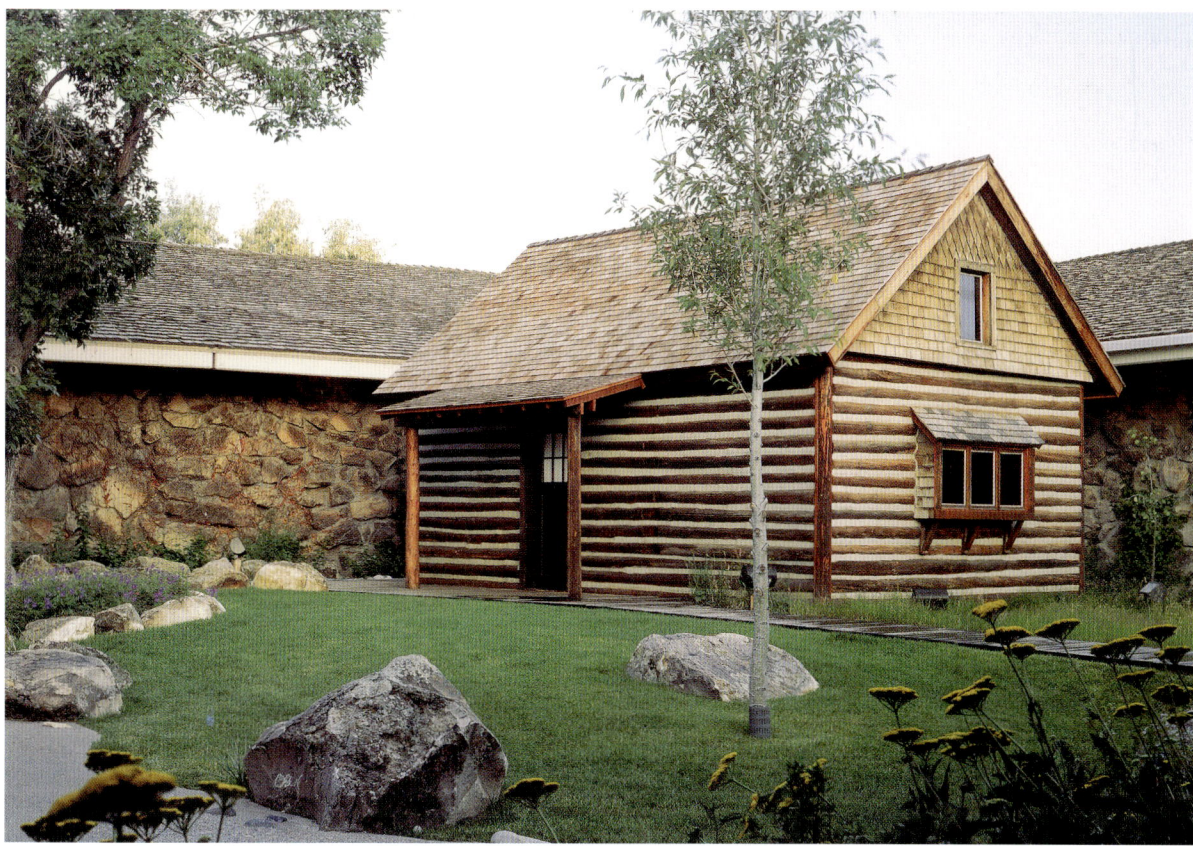

Mexico, he had created another ideal environment, again using Roycroft furniture and a rich assortment of Indian art, including many objects he had gathered while living in the North.

Sharp sold the cabin in 1934 and it remained in private hands for several decades. While doing research on Sharp, author and art gallery owner Forrest Fenn located the cabin and purchased it in order to preserve it. He and his wife donated it to the Buffalo Bill Center of the West in 1986. The cabin was moved to the Center, reconstructed, and installed in a garden adjacent to the Center's Whitney Western Art Museum [PLATE 3.18]. Absarokee Hut stands as an embodiment of the ideals of artist Joseph Henry Sharp.

[PLATE 3.18]

DEVENDRA SHRIKHANDE
PHOTOGRAPHER

Absarokee Hut: Joseph Henry Sharp Cabin

As installed in a garden of the Buffalo Bill Center of the West, photograph, color
Buffalo Bill Center of the West, Cody, Wyoming.

The log cabin was moved to the grounds of the Center in 1986 and is preserved as an example of the artist's environment.

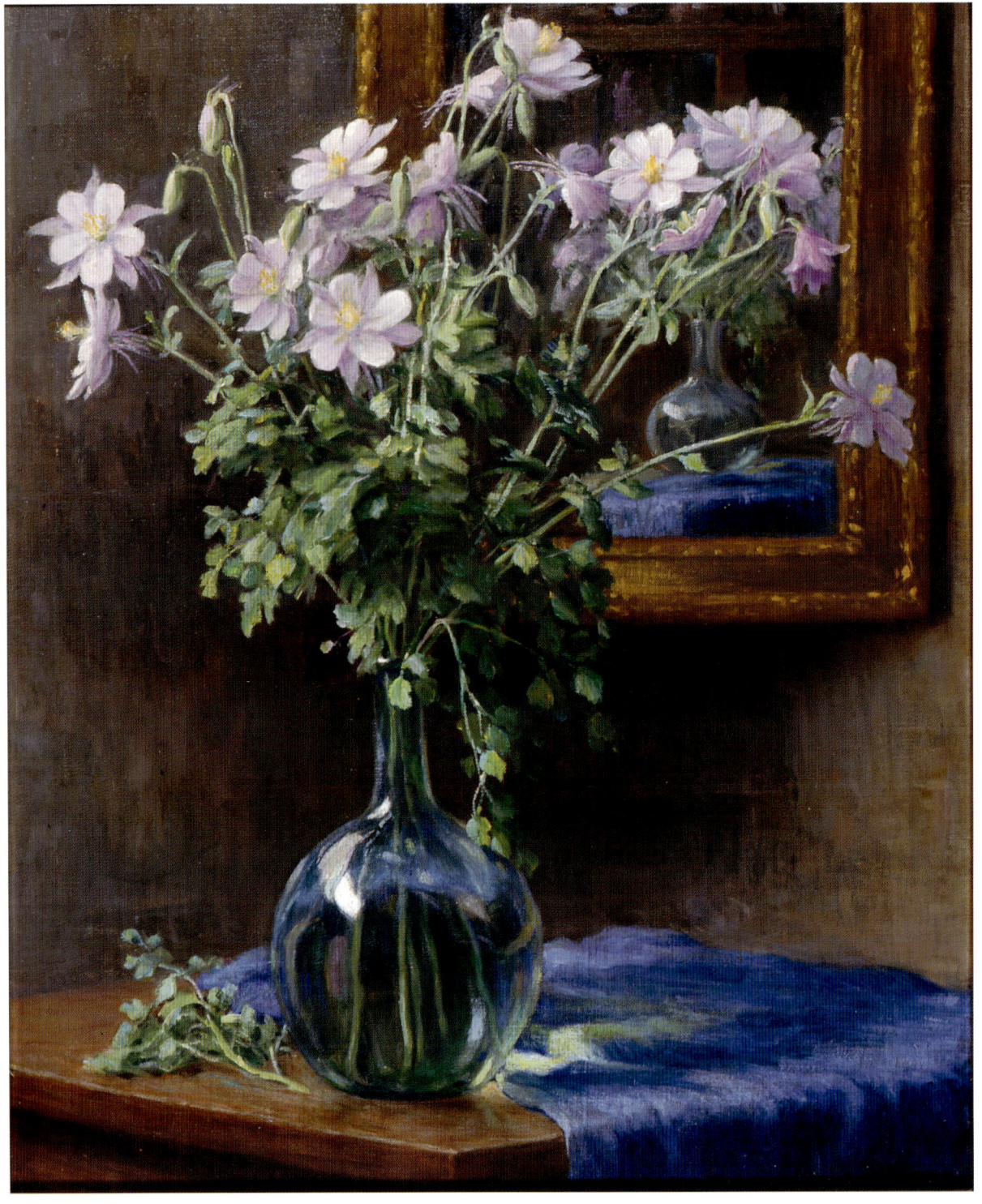

JOSEPH HENRY SHARP, *Columbine.* 1909, oil on canvas, 30 x 25 in. Image courtesy of Thomas Minckler Fine Arts, Billings, Montana

KELIN MICHAEL

STYLE, COMPOSITION, AND SUBJECT MATTER
JOSEPH HENRY SHARP AND THE INFLUENCE OF EUROPEAN ARTISTIC TRAINING

Joseph Henry Sharp was a prolific American artist active through most of his life, which spanned the Civil War and both world wars. Much of his work was strongly influenced by his European training, which he undertook sporadically between 1881 and 1896. Although his work showed great skill and ingenuity, he never settled on one defining style during the course of his career. This chapter explores Sharp's ability to adapt to the changing landscape of American art by examining how the artist combined European artistic trends with western American subject matter.

Sharp showed an interest in and propensity for art from a young age. Although his family came from wealth, hard times befell them during Sharp's childhood. This, however, did not deter his parents from providing their children with a classical education that emphasized the arts. At about age twelve, Sharp suffered permanent, eventually complete hearing loss due to an accident.[1] As his hearing declined and he could no longer understand his teacher, Sharp began doodling in his notebooks during class. When this habit continued, Sharp had to forfeit participation in traditional schooling.[2] His mother, a lover of the arts, encouraged him to pursue his artistic talents instead. A few years after his accident, at age fourteen, Sharp left his hometown of Bridgeport, Ohio, and moved to Cincinnati with the hope of enrolling in the McMicken School of Drawing and Design. Once he arrived in Cincinnati, he stayed with relatives, worked to save the money required to enroll, and entered the school in 1874.[3]

---

1 See Fenn, *Teepee Smoke*, 32. Sharp was playing "skin the cat" and, while hanging from a bridge, fell into the river below. Someone pulled him from the water and brought him to his mother, who rolled him over a barrel to expel the water from his lungs. This act saved his life, but the event led to an ear infection that resulted in deafness.

2 "A Biographical Sketch of Joseph Henry Sharp," in *The National Cyclopedia of American Biography* (New York: James T. White and Company, Publishers, 1901), 1.

3 "A Biographical Sketch of Joseph Henry Sharp," 1.

Between 1874 and 1896, Sharp split the time he spent in training between Cincinnati (transitioning to a teaching role in 1892) and Europe. This training ultimately influenced his aesthetic, composition, and choice of subject matter, helping inform what scholar Joan Carpenter Troccoli has called his "eclectic cosmopolitan style," a style that revealed the different facets of his artistic training in combining multiple traditions with his own innovation.[4]

The art school Sharp attended in Cincinnati progressively incorporated a number of European styles and techniques and promoted a culture that valued European study. In 1873, one year before Sharp's arrival, the established artist Frank Duveneck (1848–1919), who would become Sharp's mentor and lifelong friend, returned to the McMicken School. After completing his four-year study in Europe at the Royal Academy of Fine Arts in Munich with honors, Duveneck brought a number of European influences back to McMicken.[5] In Munich, Duveneck had studied under Gustave Courbet (1819–1877), Wilhelm Leibl (1844–1900), and Wilhelm von Diez (1839–1907), under whose influence Duveneck embraced what became known as the Munich Style. The Munich Style, characterized by the use of chiaroscuro, rich impasto, a dark palette, rapid brushwork, and unsentimental realism, was most popular between 1850 and 1918.[6] These qualities distinguish *The Turkish Page* [PLATE 4.1], one of Duveneck's best-known paintings. Duveneck adopted these characteristics through direct observation of Courbet, Leibl, and von Diez's own works of art and through study of their technical and philosophical teachings. Paintings such as Courbet's *A Burial at Ornans* (1849–1850; Musée d'Orsay), Leibl's *Sleeping Savoyard Boy* (1869; State Hermitage Museum), and von Diez's *Dead Deer* (before 1875; National Gallery of the National Museums) demonstrate the qualities that came to define Munich's Royal Academy in the second half of the nineteenth century.

Duveneck's evolving style and technique were influenced not only by his professors at the Royal Academy but also by other contemporary and historical painters, whose work hung in the Alte Pinakothek and

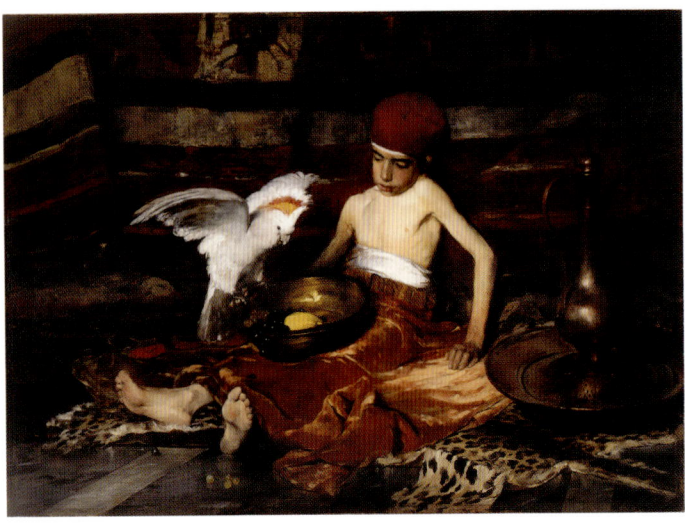

[PLATE 4.1]

FRANK DUVENECK
(1848–1919)

The Turkish Page

1876, oil on canvas,
42 x 58 ¼ in.
Pennsylvania Academy
of the Fine Arts, Philadelphia,
Pennsylvania. Joseph E. Temple
Fund. 1894.1

---

4 Joan Carpenter Troccoli, "J. H. Sharp," *Persimmon Hill* 18 (Winter 1990): 10.

5 Fenn, *Teepee Smoke*, 33.

6 See Alison Hokanson, "Catalogue Entry: Franz von Stuck's *Inferno*," The Met, https://www.metmuseum.org/art/collection/search/749639. While Duveneck adhered closely to the Munich Style, not all art that came out of Munich followed suit. Artists such as Franz von Stuck (1863–1928) played with characteristics of the Munich Style and combined them with elements from artistic movements such as Art Nouveau. Studying at Munich from 1881 to 1885 and teaching there from 1895 to 1928, Stuck would have been at the academy just before Sharp arrived in 1886 and a few years after his second departure from Munich in 1889.

the Neue Pinakothek, museums affiliated with the Royal Academy.[7]
In these institutions, Duveneck was exposed to the work of Peter Paul
Rubens (1577–1640), Diego Velázquez (1599–1660), Sir Joshua Reynolds
(1723–1792), Rembrandt van Rijn (1606–1669), Frans Hals (1582–1666),
and Édouard Manet (1832–1883), among others.[8] These artists' styles
and compositions would particularly influence Duveneck's use of visible
brushstrokes and contrasting tones. Duveneck also looked to several
contemporary movements, including the Barbizon School, which
promoted the practice of painting directly from nature; the Marées, known
for their monumental composition and deep impasto; and the Realists
(a movement of which Courbet was a leader), who strove to depart from
academic convention (the tight, linear forms of Neoclassicism, and the
emotional aestheticism of Romanticism).[9] Duveneck brought these
influences back to Cincinnati just before Sharp's arrival at McMicken.

———————————

Cincinnati was, at this time, a regional center of artistic life that
featured progressive alternatives to academic tradition. Sharp found
inspiration and encouragement in this untraditional environment.
During Sharp's studies at McMicken, between 1874 and 1881, Duveneck,
John Henry Twachtman (1853–1902), Henry Farny (1847–1916), Robert
Frederick Blum (1857–1903), Kenyon Cox (1856–1919), and Edward
Potthast (1857–1927) were experimenting with new ideas of style and
subject matter, even working with nude models, a practice more typical
of Paris schools.[10] The director of McMicken, Thomas Satterwhite Noble
(1835–1907), after facing a student revolt, eventually came to support
this progressive atmosphere.[11] In an effort to align the Cincinnati art
school more closely with European practices, he instituted a life class
at McMicken in 1877, though nude models were only allowed during
night classes.[12] He took a sabbatical in 1881–83 to study in Munich, the
influence of which is evident in his painting *The Polish Exile* (1882;

———————————

7 Robert Neuhaus, *Unsuspected Genius: The Art and Life of Frank Duveneck* (San Francisco:
   Bedford Press, 1987), 7.

8 Neuhaus, *Unsuspected Genius*, 12.

9 Neuhaus, *Unsuspected Genius*, 8, 10, 12.

10 See Marie Watkins, "Joseph Henry Sharp: 'Painter of Indians' (1859–1953)," unpublished
    manuscript, 1. At this time, working with nude, especially female, models was not typical in
    American art academies.

11 See Bruce Weber, "Frank Duveneck and the Art Life of Cincinnati, 1865–1900," in *The
    Golden Age: Cincinnati Painters of the Nineteenth Century Represented in the Cincinnati
    Art Museum* (Cincinnati: Cincinnati Art Museum, 1979), 25. This student uprising is
    documented in an article from the *Cincinnati Commercial Tribune* (March 21, 1915) titled
    "Revolt in Old Art School Led by Famous Painters," by Charles A. Elliot. Elliot, who had
    been a student at the academy, tells how Kenyon Cox and Alfred Brennan, both disciples of
    Duveneck, fought for the inclusion of a life drawing class in the fall of 1875.

12 Minckler, *In Poetic Silence*, 12; Weber, "Frank Duveneck," 25–26.

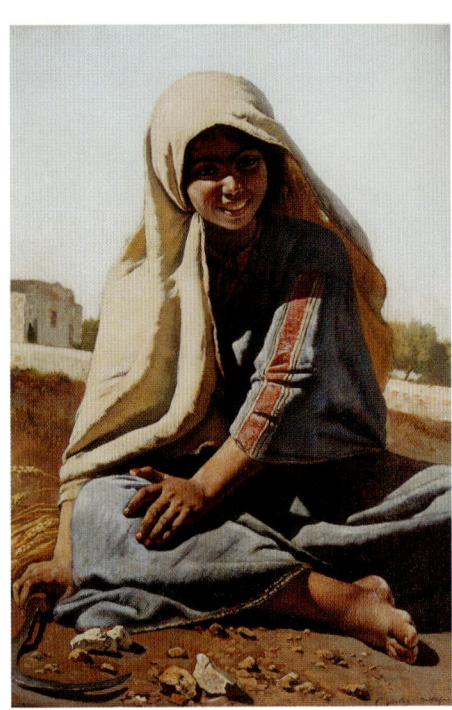

private collection).[13] While in Cincinnati, Sharp studied diligently, participating in day and night classes focused mainly on drawing.[14]

Once he had gained some small degree of prominence in the Cincinnati community, Sharp garnered the attention of Matthew Sommerville Morgan (1837–1890), an established illustrator and lithographer, who suggested he travel abroad to strengthen his education.[15] In 1881 Sharp took his own journey across the Atlantic to directly benefit from European artistic training. He sailed for Europe and enrolled at the Royal Academy in Antwerp that fall.[16] Sharp's decision to study at Antwerp was somewhat unusual. While the Antwerp academy was hardly a disreputable school, American artists at this time gravitated toward the Royal Academy in Munich. While it is impossible to know exactly why Sharp chose Antwerp, the school's reputation for its focus on humanity and the use of common people as subjects may have influenced his decision. Indeed, those values influenced later

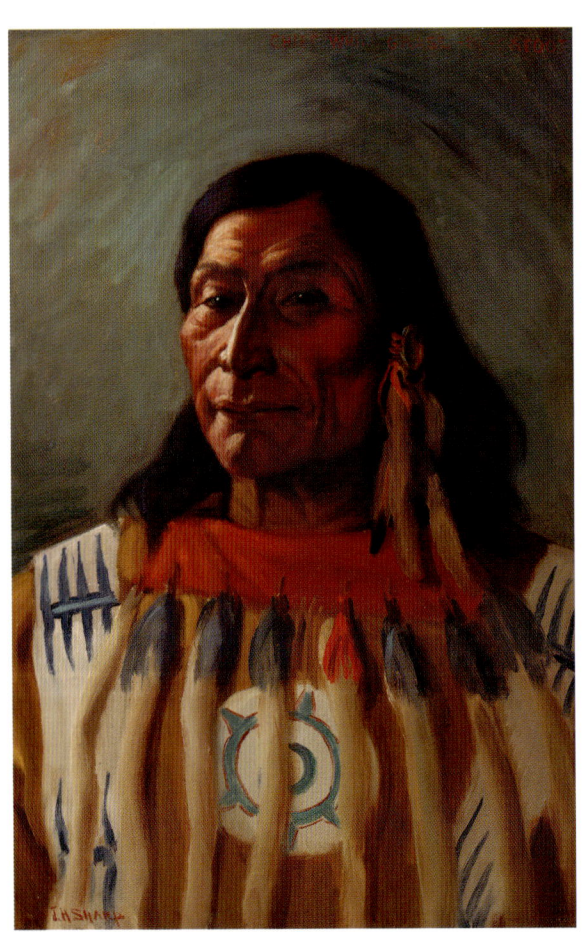

13 See Weber, "Frank Duveneck," 26. This sabbatical was possibly commenced by a series of angry letters published in the *Cincinnati Commercial Tribune* shortly before his departure. See Letter to the Editor from "Trebor," *Cincinnati Commercial Tribune*, June 19, 1881, p. 2. These letters "complained of the School's lack of a regular life class and of Noble's rigid antagonism 'to any method of instruction other than that taught at the school he represents.'"

14 See Peter H. Hassrick and Elizabeth J. Cunningham, *In Contemporary Rhythm: The Art of Ernest L. Blumenschein* (Norman: University of Oklahoma Press), 16–17. In the Art Academy of Cincinnati catalogue (formerly the McMicken School of Drawing and Design), courses taken in 1892–93 by Ernest Blumenschein, a contemporary of Sharp, are listed as "Illustration," "Pen Drawing," and "Drawing—Head from Casts and from Life—Second Grade." Weber, "Frank Duveneck," 27. The first oil painting class offered at McMicken was taught by George E. Hopkins and wasn't instituted until Noble was on his sabbatical, between 1881 and 1883, when Sharp was already in Antwerp.

15 Unidentified author, "Joseph Henry Sharp," n.d., 4 (note in top right corner: "Found among Blanche C. Grant's papers"), Box 2, Folder 22, JHSC.

16 "A Biographical Sketch of Joseph Henry Sharp," 1.

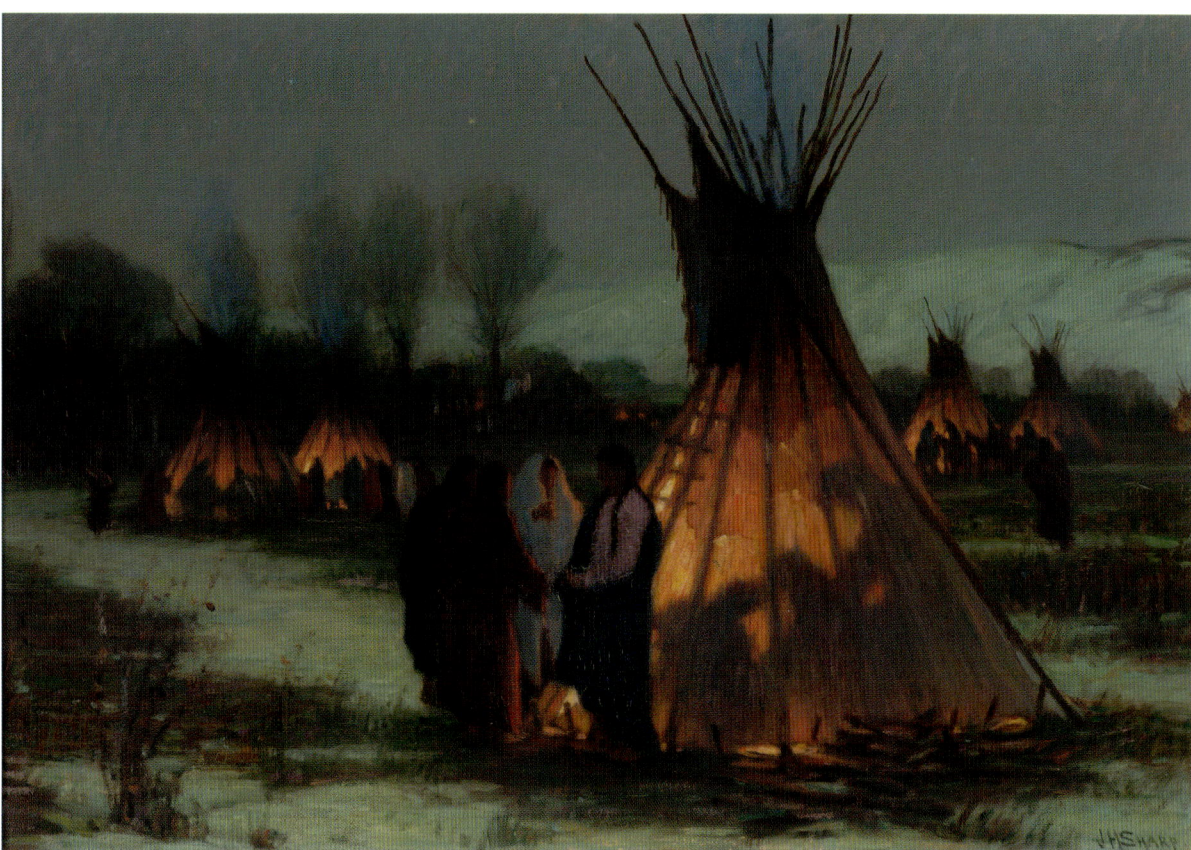

[PLATE 4.4]

JOSEPH HENRY SHARP

Crow Teepees at Night

ca. 1927, oil on canvas,
23 ⅝ x 33 ¾ in.
Gilcrease Museum, Tulsa,
Oklahoma. Gift of the Thomas
Gilcrease Foundation, 1955.
0137.548

French painters and Realists.[17] Sharp's own interest in depicting the human condition would later manifest in his paintings of indigenous peoples of the American West.[18]

Apart from Antwerp's focus on common humanity, Sharp may also have been attracted by the presence of the artist Charles Verlat (1824–1890), the renowned Belgian animal and portrait painter.[19] Verlat's portraiture and genre scenes often included or emphasized "exotic" peoples, as in *Jeune fille de Bethlehem* [PLATE 4.2]. In Cincinnati, Sharp had found work as a portrait painter that allowed him to earn income while honing his craft. Studying with Verlat would have allowed the young artist to enjoy a European education under a well-known portraitist at less expense than at a more famous school such as Munich. Based on similarities in their choice of subject, Sharp's exposure to Verlat's work during his time in Antwerp may have inspired his later Indian paintings. For example, in *White Grass, Blackfoot* [PLATE 4.3], Sharp's portrait of an indigenous man, he plays with the effect of light and shadow, just as Verlat does in *Jeune fille*.[20]

---

17 Fenn, *Teepee Smoke*, 37.

18 See Scrap Album 1, Box 4, JHSC. Addie Sharp writes of their interest in the humanity of the West in an undated, untitled newspaper clipping: "We are in love with the West. It is full of human nature and thoroughly American, and the older I grow the more I care for poor, old human nature. It is so real. For a long time I wondered where the real was. We had it in our art, but not among people. Out here we find it unadulterated."

19 "A Biographical Sketch of Joseph Henry Sharp," 1.

20 Sharp's use of light was not praised by everyone. The critic Philip Hale wrote that Sharp's portraits looked "greasy." *Boston Herald*, January 19, 1903.

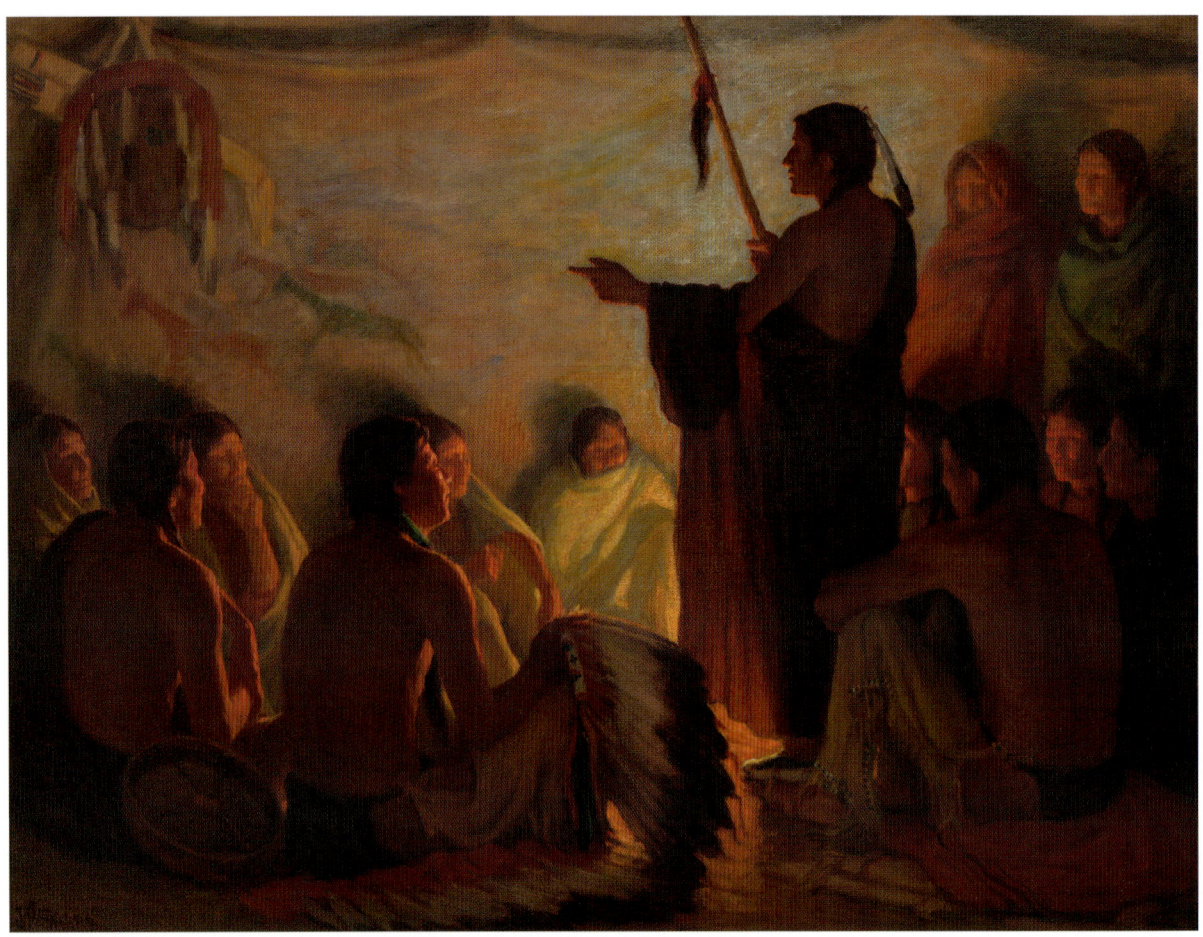

[PLATE 4.5] JOSEPH HENRY SHARP, *The Orator.* ca. 1912, oil on canvas, 35 ½ x 45 ⅜ in.
Gilcrease Museum, Tulsa, Oklahoma. Gift of the Thomas Gilcrease Foundation, 1955. 0137.338

At the Royal Academy in Antwerp, Sharp studied in a strict academic discipline that progressed from drawing to painting classes.[21] This experience complemented his less structured, more innovative training in Cincinnati. In the winter of 1881, he participated in the "Antiek" class offered by the artist Polydore (Pierre) Beaufaux (1829–1905).[22] In the course, which was taught in an amphitheater, students drew from plaster casts of antique sculpture. Beaufaux would place the objects in question under a strong gas light, allowing the students to complete studies in high relief.[23] This practice is likely to have led to Sharp's lifelong infatuation with the emphatic effects of different lighting, as demonstrated in his portrait *White Grass, Blackfoot* and works such as *Crow Teepees at Night* [PLATE 4.4] and *The Orator* [PLATE 4.5], among countless others.

Completion of this "Antiek" class allowed Sharp to progress to the painting courses offered at the academy. He entered the class titled "Natuur" (Life), taught by Verlat, in May 1882 and began developing his understanding of the human form.[24]

There were drawbacks to studying at Antwerp, however. Overall, the school hosted a strong bias toward Realism and toward the idea that history painting was the highest form of art.[25] There was therefore little room for students to experiment with combinations of subject matters, compositions, and styles. Thus, after studying at Antwerp, many students went on to continue their schooling in Paris in order to benefit from greater diversity, as Sharp himself did more than ten years later.

In addition to his formal classes at Antwerp, from the onset of his European training, Sharp was exposed to the work of the established sixteenth- and seventeenth-century painters, including Anthony van Dyck (1599–1641), Rubens, Rembrandt, Velázquez, and Hals. In fact, Antwerp had been Rubens's home. Sharp especially admired and emulated the Flemish painter's use of color, light, energy, and tension.[26] Drawn to these artists' works while traveling during breaks from the Antwerp academy, Sharp made copies of paintings by Rembrandt, van Dyck, and Velázquez.[27] Sharp was particularly drawn to Velázquez's realism, use of light, and method of painting directly from life. Sharp sought to imitate Hals's and

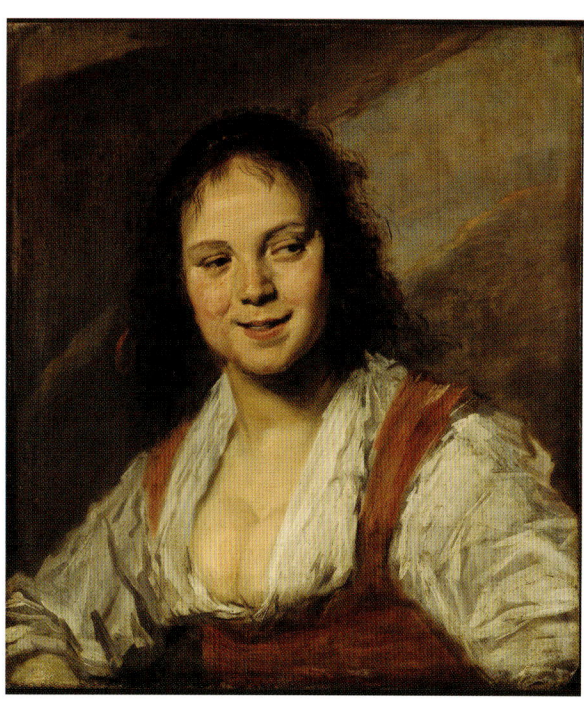

[PLATE 4.6]

FRANS HALS, L'ANCIEN
(b. Belgium, 1582–1666)

Gypsy Girl [La Bohémienne]

1628, oil on canvas,
22 ⅞ x 20 ½ in
Musée du Louvre,
Paris, France. M.I. 926
© RMN-Grand Palais / Art
Resource, NY

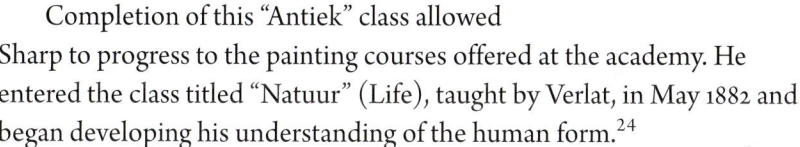

---

21 Minckler, *In Poetic Silence*, 12.

22 Perhaps "Polydore" took his Greek name because the curriculum at Antwerp was so influenced by the classical tradition.

23 Minckler, *In Poetic Silence*, 13.

24 Minckler, *In Poetic Silence*, 13.

25 Minckler, *In Poetic Silence*, 14.

26 Fenn, *Teepee Smoke*, 37.

27 Minckler, *In Poetic Silence*, 16; Fenn, *Teepee Smoke*, 93.

Rembrandt's use of the visual brushstroke. Sharp loved Hals' portraits, such as *Gypsy Girl* [PLATE 4.6], and he admired the economic use of brushwork with which this artist captured the fleeting movement and the essence or soul of his subjects.[28] In Sharp's portrait of Judge Shorty White Grass, his incorporation of these influences is apparent in both his ability to capture subtle facial expression and in his application of loose, broad brushstrokes.[29] Sharp internalized these numerous new elements and influences, and concluded his year of study in Antwerp in 1882.

Sharp returned to Cincinnati, where he remained for several years, enrolling once again in courses at McMicken. He resumed his established relationship with his mentor and friend Duveneck, and, in addition, became drawn to the artist Henry Farny and his work. In fact, in a magazine article written by Sharp himself, he acknowledges the effect Farny had both on him and on his oeuvre.[30] Farny had been influenced by Albert Bierstadt (1830–1902) in Düsseldorf and attended the academies in both Düsseldorf and Munich between 1867 and 1870.[31] In Munich, Farny studied alongside Duveneck, while also taking classes from Wilhelm Leibl. It was by way of this German training that Farny acquired his signature technique, which combined the drab, stylized realism of Düsseldorf with the freer brush strokes characteristic of the Munich School.[32] Of greater interest to Sharp than Farny's style, however, was his eventual choice of subject matter: western Native Americans.[33]

Inspired by the growing market for Indian paintings, Farny traveled up the Missouri River in 1881 to produce sketches, take notes and photographs, and collect artifacts.[34] Upon Farny's return to Cincinnati from the West

28 Fenn, *Teepee Smoke*, 86; Minckler, *In Poetic Silence*, 16.

29 See Carolyn Reynolds Riebeth, "Some Memories of J. H. Sharp" (Billings, MT: Parmly Billings Library, 1969), 2. Sharp's dedication to Hals was so strong that he gave his dog the nickname Franzel after the Dutch painter.

30 Sharp, "An Artist among the Indians," 1.

31 According to a letter sent from Farny to his mother, Bierstadt invited him to dinner and, while complimenting his rapid artistic progression, suggested that he continue his studies for another year. He also states that Bierstadt suggested Farny come with him to the Rocky Mountains after finishing his studies. See Farny to his mother, November 1 [no year, likely 1868], Henry Francois Farny Papers, Reel 1233, AAA.

32 Vitz, *The Queen and the Arts*, 180.

33 Although Farny and Duveneck were both American artists (French-born American in Farny's case), it is imperative that one examine their influence on Sharp's work, as they were both integral in the development of his style and subject matter. In addition, as they both participated in the European art academy system, their influence resonated with Sharp much as had the artists who affected him during his studies in Europe. It is also interesting to compare the stylistic trajectory of Sharp's friend and contemporary John Hauser with that of Sharp's own work. While both were greatly influenced by Farny, Hauser stuck much closer to Farny's subject matter *and* style, while Sharp broke away from Farny's tighter, detail-oriented handling of paint to craft his own variable hybrid style. See JHS to Robert Taft, April 1937, Taft Papers. In fact, Sharp, while he admired Farny in certain respects, thought "all his pictures interesting but not [those of] a great artist."

34 See Brigitte M. Foley, "Joseph H. Sharp's Cincinnati and Oscar E. Berninghaus's St. Louis: The City as Patron," master's thesis, University of Notre Dame, Department of Art, Art History, and Design, April 1995, 28. Farny would take documentary photographs and make sketches in order to return east and paint his larger canvases. See "Henry F. Farny," Smithsonian American Art Museum, https://americanart.si.edu/artist/henry-f-farny-1490. His western travels inspired more than one hundred paintings over the course of his career.

and Sharp's return from Antwerp, Sharp expressed an interest in going west himself to paint American Indians. This decision may have been partially spurred by his time in Antwerp, and specifically by his Belgian professor Verlat's depictions of "exotic" peoples. At first, Farny tried to dissuade Sharp from going west, as he had found painting Indians quite lucrative and did not want the talented young Sharp encroaching on his business.[35] However, when Farny saw Sharp's determination, he eventually pointed him to the Southwest, providing him books on the Pueblo Indians. As Farny typically painted the Plains Indians, perhaps he viewed this as a reasonable compromise.

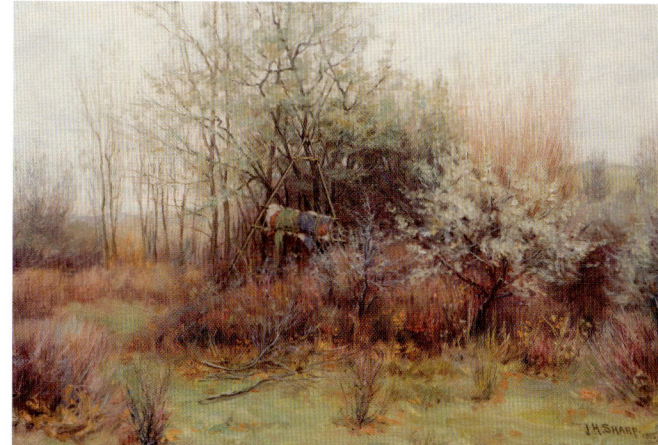

[PLATE 4.7]

JOSEPH HENRY SHARP

The Grave of a Crow Child

1905, oil on canvas,
19 x 26 ⅞ in.
Gilcrease Museum, Tulsa,
Oklahoma. Gift of the Thomas
Gilcrease Foundation, 1955.
0137.332

Armed with his new knowledge of the Pueblo cultures, Sharp went west for the first time in summer 1883, to New Mexico and then up the West Coast. This trip was his first opportunity to combine his European training with a singularly American subject matter. This excursion proved transformational and altered Sharp's entire career trajectory. During this trip, however, Sharp produced only drawings, no paintings; thus it is impossible to assess if the combination of American subject matter and European training showed any immediate effect in his completed painted works. It is clear, however, that the experience changed him. The change is evident by observing the shift in the artist's choice of subject matter throughout the rest of his career.

———

Upon returning to Cincinnati from the West, Sharp quickly grew bored painting society portraits and found the profession of portrait painting somewhat stifling as it left little room for creativity or experimentation with style.[36] The works he produced during this period are technically impressive (e.g., *The Neophyte*, [1883; Butler Institute of American Art]), but they lack any visible signs of a development of personal style and composition. They largely reflect the combination of influences on his artistry up to that date. Sharp seemed aware of this fact himself, and after enrolling in a night drawing class at McMicken in the fall of 1885, he concluded that he needed to return to Europe to enrich his training.[37] As McMicken was a drawing-centered academy, Sharp felt he needed to turn elsewhere for further instruction in

———

35 Boehme, "The North and Snow," 34. While Farny may have dissuaded Sharp from going west due to business matters, as the two were close, he may also have been acting in a paternal capacity, warning Sharp against the dangers of traveling west as a deaf man.

36 Fenn, *Teepee Smoke*, 44.

37 Fenn, *Teepee Smoke*, 47. See also Weber, "Frank Duveneck," 29. Although Charles Hopkins had taught an oil-painting class at McMicken in the early 1880s, Noble did not institute an advanced class in oil painting at the academy until 1893. Perhaps this further explains why Sharp left Cincinnati for Europe.

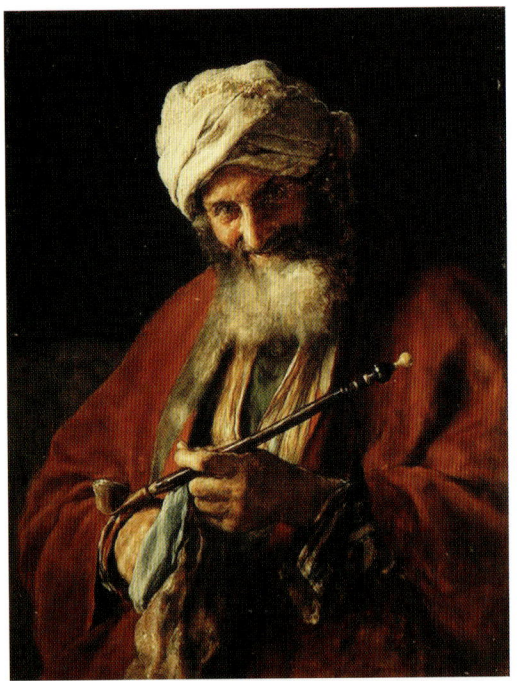

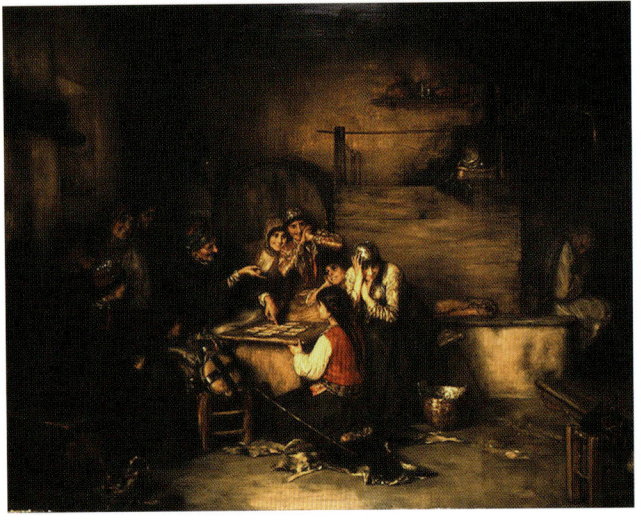

painting.[38] He did not return to Antwerp, however. Instead, on October 18, 1886, he enrolled at the Royal Academy in Munich, as his mentors and influences from Cincinnati Duveneck, Farny, and Twachtman, as well as many other aspiring American artists, had done before him.[39]

Sharp's educational experience in Munich was both similar to and different from his experience in Antwerp. The disciplined progression of studies was much the same. Students participated in courses beginning with drawing studies of antique sculpture and live models, advancing to painting mostly portraits, and ending with more specific master classes.[40] Here, however, a strong sense of style was imposed, the same "Munich Style" with which Sharp was already familiar through Duveneck's work. While Sharp's training at Antwerp had expanded his knowledge of technique, use of lighting, and the historic European artists, his training at the Munich academy refined these skills. It did so by working within one style, the Munich Style, which emphasized the artist's spontaneous and direct reaction to a subject. Perhaps the most striking difference between Sharp's education in Antwerp and that in Munich was the Munich School's rejection of moral and historical painting as the pinnacle of artistic subject matter, preferring instead to emphasize the importance of realism and painting from everyday life.[41] Sharp's dedication to the Munich School's preferred subject matter is evident in his later scenes of Indian life. *The Grave of a Crow Child* [PLATE 4.7], for example, demonstrates Sharp's attention to the way Indians experienced birth,

[PLATE 4.8]

NIKOLAOS GYZIS
(b. Greece, 1842–1901)

Middle Easterner Man with Pipe

ca. 1873, oil on panel,
15 7/8 x 12 1/4 in.
National Art Gallery—Alexandros Soutzos Museum, Athens, Greece. Bequest of Eleni Christomanou.
P.407

38 Minckler, *In Poetic Silence*, 11.

39 "Matrikelbücher," Akademie der bildenden Künste München, https://matrikel.adbk.de/matrikel/mb_1884-1920/jahr_1886/matrikel-00303; "A Biographical Sketch of Joseph Henry Sharp," 1.

40 See Rachel Berenson Perry, *William J. Forsyth: The Life and Work of an Indiana Artist* (Bloomington: Indiana University Press, 2014), chapters 2 and 3. Forsyth attended the Royal Academy in Munich between 1881 and 1888. Multiple references to letters written by Forsyth and included in Perry's work detail his process of studying drawing and then painting at the academy. Minckler, *In Poetic Silence*, 16, 18.

41 Minckler, *In Poetic Silence*, 16. See also Edward Paxton Harris and Jerry Glenn, *Straight White Shield: A Life and Works of John Hauser (1859–1913) with a Catalogue Raisonné* (Bellevue, KY: MicroPress, Inc., 2012), 16. After Karl von Piloty became director of the academy in 1874, he "widen[ed] the scope of accepted subject matter and encourage[d] more personal and colorful approaches to realism." See "Chronicle," Akademie der Bildenden Künste München, https://www.adbk.de/en/akademie-en/archive/chronicle.html. During the "Prince Regent Age," between 1886 and 1912, Munich reoriented itself, becoming a home to a number of budding Modernist artists, including Wassily Kandinsky, Paul Klee, and Giorgio De Chirico. In this way, while Sharp participated in a controlled curriculum, the atmosphere at Munich was much more innovative than that at Antwerp.

life, and death, while simultaneously providing a clear example of his ability to paint landscapes from life in multiple styles—in this case, Tonalism.[42] Here, in addition to the influence of the Munich academy, Sharp looks back to his Cincinnati influences, mainly Twachtman's Impressionistic and Tonalist works.[43]

In addition to the Munich Royal Academy's broader influence, Sharp also drew inspiration from his professors. In Munich, Sharp studied pastels with the Greek painter Nikolaos Gyzis (1842–1901).[44] Under Gyzis, he mastered the medium and learned classical techniques of modeling and composition with a focus on genre and still-life painting (Gyzis, *Study for the "Crafts"* [1895-1899; National Art Gallery, Greece]).[45] Gyzis's influence is clear from the stylistic range that Sharp exhibited across his career and from his choice of subject matter and composition. Throughout his own work, Gyzis transitioned from a slightly tighter, more controlled version of the Munich Style to a looser, more impressionistic brushstroke. He also experimented with interior, emanating light sources and vivid applications of color. This progression can clearly be seen in three of his works: *Middle Easterner Man with Pipe* [PLATE 4.8], *The Fortune Teller* [PLATE 4.9], and *Poppies and Tulips* [PLATE 4.10].

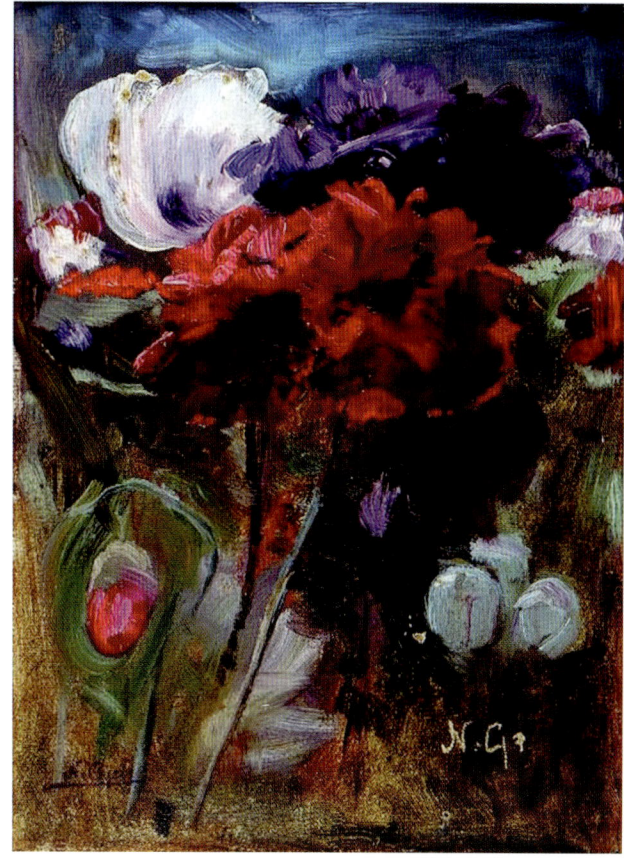

[PLATE 4.9]

NIKOLAOS GYZIS
(b. Greece, 1842–1901)

The Fortune Teller

1885, oil on panel,
28 ½ x 36 ½ in.
National Art Gallery—Alexandros
Soutzos Museum, Athens, Greece.
Bequest of Antonios Benakis.
P.1858

[PLATE 4.10]

NIKOLAOS GYZIS
(b. Greece, 1842–1901)

Poppies and Tulips

1885, oil on panel,
28 ½ x 36 ½ in.
Emfietzoglou Gallery Museum,
Athens, Greece

---

42 Another way Sharp's work demonstrates the Munich influence is in his near complete avoidance of moral, historical, and religious subject matter. Works by Sharp devoted to these subjects are few and far between and include *The Oil Promoter*, *Penitente Flagellants*, *Black Robe*, and *Playing the Game*.

43 See Boehme, "The North and Snow," 46. Sharp was often compared to landscape artists of the American Impressionist school such as Twachtman, rather than other painters of Indians.

44 "Matrikelbücher"; "A Biographical Sketch of Joseph Henry Sharp," 1. See "Gyzis Nikolaos," National Gallery of Greece, http://www.nationalgallery.gr/en/painting-permanent-exhibition/painter/gyzis-nikolaos.html. Gyzis himself studied under Karl von Piloty at Munich, this experience perhaps accounting for his less traditional painting style and broad range of subject matter, including genre painting, still life, and portraiture, and his transition to more idealistic-allegorical subjects in his later work. An example of such a work can be seen in *Behold the Bridegroom Arriving* (1899–1900; National Gallery of Greece). Sharp would have entered the Munich academy as Gyzis was experimenting with this style, a precursor of *Jugenstil*, the German equivalent of Art Nouveau. Susanne Boeller, "Two American Painters in Munich: Walter Ufer and E. Martin Hennings," in *A Place in the Sun: The Southwest Painting of Walter Ufer and E. Martin Hennings*, ed. Thomas Brent Smith (Norman: University of Oklahoma Press, 2016), 14.

45 Minckler, *In Poetic Silence*, 15. See Scrap Album 1, Box 4, JHSC. Farny even noted "that Sharp is the ablest man with the crayon he ever knew." Farny quoted in *Denver Rocky Mountain News*, December 1898. An additional newspaper article from April 1894 states that pastel is "a medium which the artist is a master of." "Art and Artists," clipping, n.d. JHSC. An example of Sharp's pastel work can be seen in his portrait *Little Beaver, Sioux* in the Autry Museum of the American West, Los Angeles (no. 22).

Notably, both Gyzis and Sharp demonstrated fluidity in style, color, and subject matter over the course of their careers. As Sharp began to travel to Crow Agency in Montana, he continued to paint Indian portraits but turned largely to scenes of daily life.[46] Examining Gyzis's *The Fortune Teller* and Sharp's *The Orator* side-by-side, one may observe the professor's influence on the student's experimentation with interior

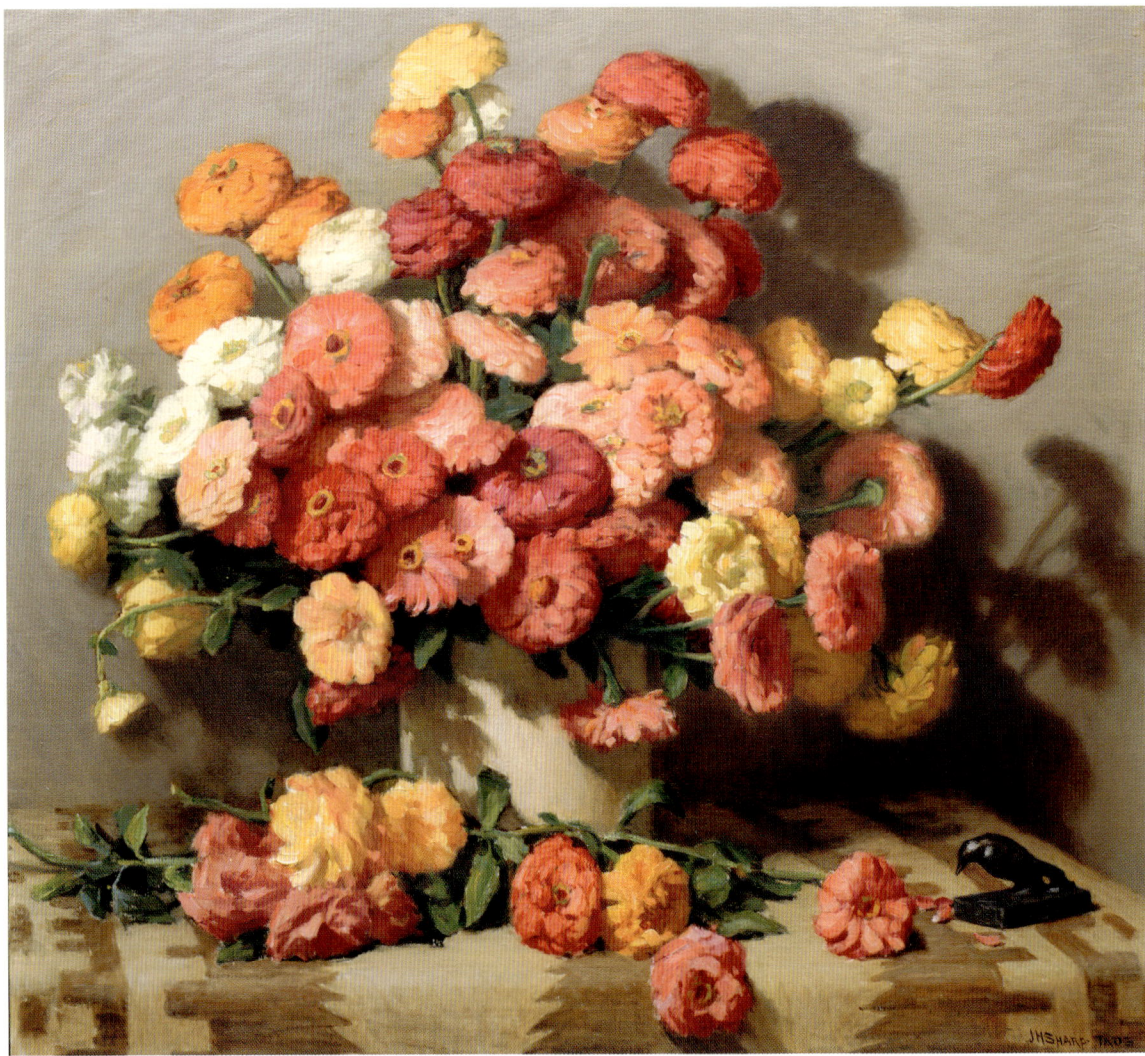

lighting and group scenes.[47] The figures in the two paintings participate in different activities, yet in both, directional light emanates from a position slightly offset from the center of the composition, illuminating the figures from within and creating a strong contrast of light and dark tones. Interestingly, Sharp also turned to his longtime friend and mentor Duveneck for advice concerning firelight scenes, demonstrating his desire

46 Sharp spent almost every winter in Montana between 1902 and 1910 and continued to visit sporadically until 1923.

47 In scenes and compositions like this, Sharp also looks to such Old Masters as Gerrit Dou (1613–1675) and especially Georges de la Tour (1593–1652), seventeenth-century artists who played with the effects of a sometimes-hidden interior light on surrounding figures. Sharp would have encountered their work on multiple occasions throughout his European training.

to "get it right." In a 1905 letter to Duveneck, Sharp writes:

> "Before you go will you please tell me how to paint a firelight interior? What medium is best for such a thing, scotch and soda, or castor oil! I've been using Hatfields washed petroleum, but either that don't work right or it has been washed too much. It may be the tints I used arn't mixed right, what will harmonize with cerulean blue, mauve pink, DeCamp brown and orange chrome?"[48]

In his interior firelight scenes, we see a clear example of Sharp combining inspiration and advice from multiple influences. The final parallel can be seen in Sharp's later floral still-life work and Gyzis's *Poppies and Tulips*. In the latter work, Gyzis turns to a much brighter and vibrant palate and employs a loose, impressionistic style of paint handling. Sharp does much the same thing in his work *Zinnias*, applying an economy of loose, broad strokes of paint. In addition, if one compares *Zinnias* [PLATE 4.11] to *The Orator*, one can see that Sharp chooses a much livelier palate for his floral still life, resulting in a strong departure from the darker, shadowy palate of the Munich Style.

Although Sharp did not study under Leibl himself, as Duveneck had, Leibl's circle of influence at Munich remained a huge presence within the academy. This is especially true of Leibl's practice of painting alla prima, wet on wet, typically in one sitting. By the time Sharp studied at Munich, the academy had undergone a shift from the darker palette of the 1870s (when Duveneck had studied under Leibl) to the stronger lighting, colorful palette, and forceful realism of the 1880s.[49] Sharp would go on to embody these aesthetics, often together, especially in Indian portraits such as *White Grass, Blackfoot*.

Despite the significant impact the Royal Academy had on his technical ability and style, Sharp did not stay there long. After only a year of study in Munich, Sharp, along with his friend and fellow painter John Hauser (1859–1913), decided that the curriculum was too strict and the art scene too dull. The two painters thus left to travel, likely to Paris.[50] Little is

---

48 JHS to Duveneck, June 16, 1905, Beinecke Rare Book and Manuscript Library, Yale University Library.

49 Minckler, *In Poetic Silence*, 16–18.

50 According to the article "Society's Outing" in the *Cincinnati Enquirer* from July 17, 1887, Sharp "arrived in New York early Thursday morning on steamer Westernland. . . . Mr. Sharp will spend two months in the United States and return to Paris for the coming year." The latter statement indicates that he returned to the United States briefly in summer 1887. "Among the Artists," in *The Criterion: An Illustrated Magazine* of October 1887, confirms Sharp's return to the United States and relates his intention to return to Munich and then move on to Paris.

Another *Enquirer* article, from September 25, 1887, states that "Mr. J. Henry Sharp leaves to-morrow for New York, whence he sails for Germany for another winter at the Munich Art School"—documenting his return to Europe and suggesting that perhaps his time in Paris did not begin until early 1888. Marie Watkins, "Joseph Henry Sharp: The Early Years, 1874–1903" (book manuscript in preparation). See Scrap Album 1, Box 4, JHSC. An undated article titled "Treasure Troves from an Artist's Studio" from the *Cincinnati Commercial Gazette* states that "a young Cincinnati artist, Mr. J. H. Sharp, who has been studying for the past two years in Paris and the Royal Academy of Munich, is enjoying a very pleasant holiday with his friends in the city."

documented from Sharp's first time in Paris (beginning in late 1887 or early 1888), save that he may have spent time studying in the city, perhaps at the Académie Julian, a school founded by Rodolph Julian in 1867 that catered largely to foreigners and French students who could not pass the rigorous entrance examination of the École des Beaux-Arts. While it cannot be definitively determined if this brief period in Paris had a direct influence on Sharp's work at this time, he did later return to the Académie Julian for further study in the 1890s. This period at the Académie would act as a catalyst for the merging of influences in the remainder of Sharp's work.

———————

Sharp returned briefly to Cincinnati in 1888.[51] However, he quickly returned to Munich for the opportunity to study under the historical and genre scene painter Carl von Marr (1858–1936).[52] He remained in Munich until 1889.[53] The fact that Sharp left the United States again, to study with von Marr, implies that the latter artist must have been important to Sharp and may have had a powerful effect on his work. In particular, von Marr advocated for painting directly from nature, in plein air.[54] The Barbizon School and the Impressionists, other influences on Sharp's work [SEE PLATE 2.3], also promoted this practice. Furthermore, von Marr taught his students to pay close attention to detail, use accurate color, and create a sense of immediacy in their paintings.[55] All of these tenets are demonstrated in von Marr's large, 1898 painting *Adoration of the Christ Child* [PLATE 4.12], a work with which several of Sharp's paintings show close parallels. In particular, the softness of von Marr's rendering of this scene is echoed in the softness of Sharp's work in, for example, *The Orator*. While Sharp utilizes muted complementary hues (with red and green tones creating an intimate atmosphere), in contrast to von Marr's angelic yellows and blues, neither painting employs hard edges or harsh contrasts. Instead, the color contrast in both paintings deepens the soft contours in each scene, creating a sense of dynamism and intimacy. Furthermore, while brushstrokes are clearly visible in each work, the paintings are much tighter than those of many of Sharp's teachers and influences (including Duveneck) who employed the

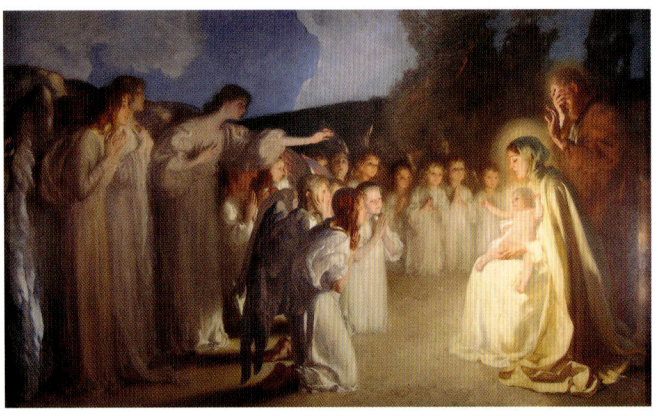

[PLATE 4.12]

CARL VON MARR
(1858–1936)

Adoration of the Christ Child

ca. 1898, oil on canvas,
94 x 159 in.
Museum of Wisconsin Art, West
Bend, Wisconsin. Gift of the
Constance Dentzler Estate

51 "Treasure Troves from an Artist's Studio." A mention that Sharp had been studying for two years in Europe places the article roughly in 1888, as Sharp began his studies in Munich in October 1886.

52 "Matrikelbücher"; "A Biographical Sketch of Joseph Henry Sharp," 1.

53 Manifest from SS *Alaska*, Port of Departure: Liverpool, England/Queenstown, Ireland, Port of Arrival: New York, June 10, 1889. "Men and Things about Town," *Cincinnati Enquirer*, November 11, 1889, confirms that by that date Sharp was back in the United States (Marie Watkins "Joseph Henry Sharp").

54 Minckler, *In Poetic Silence*, 22.

55 Fenn, *Teepee Smoke*, 59.

Munich Style. Lastly, both scenes, once again, display an internal light source, allowing the respective artist to experiment with the effects of light from angles less conventional than those produced by external light sources.

The work Sharp produced during this second, Munich-focused European period demonstrates a newfound, albeit short-lived propensity for the pure Munich Style. The pencil sketch *Man Seated, Looking Right* [PLATE 4.13] reflects the type of technical instruction Sharp incorporated in his painting during his time at the Munich Royal Academy.

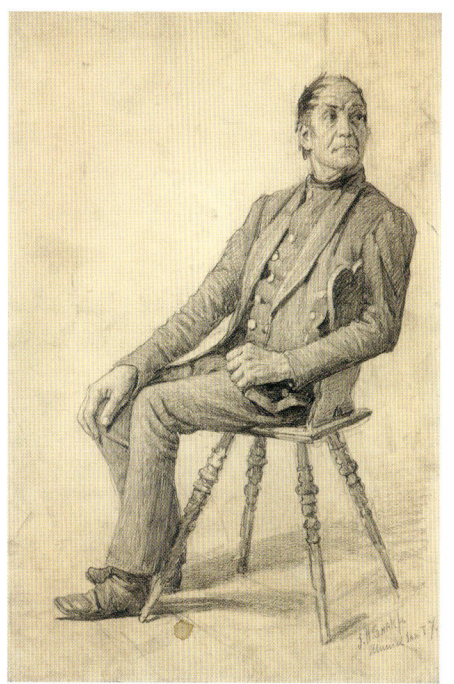

Sharp returned to Cincinnati as a student in 1889; in 1892 he became a professor at the Cincinnati Art Academy, where he taught life classes.[56] Sharp's European training, however, was not finished. Sharp garnered renown for his paintings *Fountain Square Pantomime* (1892; Cincinnati Art Museum) from 1892 and *The Harvest Dance* [SEE PLATE 2.2] from 1893, and he gained attention for his Indian portraits, one of the first of which appears to have been *Coming Deer, Taos* (1893; Gilcrease Museum). Yet he felt as though he was missing something. After traveling to the West again in the summer of 1893, this time with his new wife, Addie, and friend and fellow painter John Hauser, Sharp noticed that something was preventing him from authentically portraying his subject matter, particularly Indians, despite his accumulated arsenal of techniques. He realized that he was limited by his practice of producing sketches in situ, then using those sketches to paint larger finished works later in a studio setting.

Upon his return to Cincinnati at the end of the summer of 1893, therefore, Sharp paused his teaching career in order to complete further study in Europe to refine his plein air painting skills. Through his connection with museum director J. H. Gest, he was granted leave to study for two years with the understanding that this training would allow him eventually to make a greater contribution to the Cincinnati Art Academy.[57] In a letter to Gest of March 15, 1894, Sharp thanked the school's board for granting him leave and promised to devote time to "conscientious study" while he was away.[58] He left for Europe in the summer of 1894 and, after traveling to Antwerp and Italy for a few months, began his study in Paris in the fall, ultimately splitting his time between the Académie Julian and the Académie Colarossi.[59]

The previous time Sharp had been in Paris, in 1881, the Realist movement led by Duveneck's teacher Courbet was waning and Impressionism was on

[PLATE 4.13]

JOSEPH HENRY SHARP

Man Seated, Looking Right

1887, pencil on paper,
14 x 9 5/16 in.
Cincinnati Art Museum,
Cincinnati, Ohio. X1962.31

---

56 "A Biographical Sketch of Joseph Henry Sharp," 1. The McMicken School of Design, founded in 1869 as a department of the University of Cincinnati, became the Cincinnati Art Academy in 1887, then became the museum school of the Cincinnati Art Museum.

57 Fenn, *Teepee Smoke*, 86.

58 JHS to J. H. Gest, March 15, 1894, Box 1, Folder 2, JHSC.

59 "A Biographical Sketch of Joseph Henry Sharp," 1.

the rise.[60] By the time Sharp returned to study in Paris in 1894, Impressionism and other, more modern movements were at the forefront of the art scene, even though Realism still held some importance in the contemporary art world. Sharp's presence in Paris during this liminal artistic moment, combined with his study at Belgian, German, and French schools, profoundly influenced the development of his own personal style, aimed at authentically portraying Indian cultures and their environment.

The Académie Julian offered a much more liberal course of study than Antwerp and Munich did, in an attempt to achieve a more "sincere" approach to art. This approach attracted Sharp. While there, Sharp studied under the celebrated professors Jean-Paul Laurens (1838–1921) and Jean-Joseph Benjamin Constant (1845–1902).[61] Laurens, one of the last major followers of the French Academic style, frequently worked with historical or religious themes with a highly realistic technique (e.g., *Saint John Chrysostom and Empress Eudoxia* [1893; Musée des Augustins]). He extended the techniques of his own teacher Jean-Léon Gérôme (1824–1904), who was a painter and sculptor of the academic style. Gérôme also influenced and taught many American painters in the mid- to late nineteenth century, including Cincinnati's own Kenyon Cox (1856–1919).[62]

Laurens would often tell students to return to drawing casts, citing Jean-August-Dominique Ingres's (1780–1867) sentiment that "drawing is the foundation of art."[63] He also advised the close study of anatomy in order to understand how the body functioned in its parts and as a whole.[64] During and after his career, Sharp has often been called a master draftsman and has been commended for his portrayals of the human body, due no doubt in large part to Laurens's strict standards of drawing and advice on studying anatomy.[65] For Sharp, though, no traditional academic instructor, however well regarded or talented, could satisfy his stated purpose for returning to Europe—to find a more innovative influence.

Sharp's second instructor, Constant, was less traditional than Laurens in both style and subject matter. Like Sharp, Constant sometimes worked as a portrait painter, and in this area, in addition to plein air painting, Sharp hoped to refine his skills. Constant's work spanned a broad range of subject matter, from grim and violent genre scenes to bright and alluring farm scenes.

60 Interestingly, both of these movements were influenced in part by the Dutch schools of the 1850s.

61 "A Biographical Sketch of Joseph Henry Sharp," 1.

62 See H. Barbara Weinberg, *The American Pupils of Jean-Léon Gérôme* (Fort Worth: Amon Carter Museum, 1984), 58–59. Gérôme's oeuvre encompassed historical and mythological painting, portraiture, and Orientalism.

63 Alphaeus P. Cole, "An Adolescent in Paris: The Adventure of Being an Art Student Abroad in the Late 19th Century," *American Art Journal* 8, No. 2 (November 1976): 112.

64 See Cole, "An Adolescent in Paris," 114. Alphaeus Cole, who studied under Laurens and Constant, would attend free lecture courses offered at the École des Beaux-Arts, where one had the opportunity to draw directly from bones and corpses.

65 Carl Schaefer Dentzel, *Joseph Henry Sharp and the Lure of the West* (Great Falls, MT: C. M. Russell Museum, 1980), 6–7; Jon De Lack, "J. Henry Sharp—Painter of Indians," Society, November 6, 1913, p. 11; J. F. Earhart, "Indian Paintings by Sharp Are Placed on Exhibition," unidentified newspaper clipping, November 29, 1916, JHSC; "Sharp's Indians and a Sculpture Exhibit," unidentified newspaper clipping, May 9, 1908, JHSC.

His work has a lively, yet detailed appearance, a quality that Sharp emulated in much of his output.[66] Much as Sharp's travels west had inspired him to paint Indians, Constant's travels to Morocco in 1872 had inspired him to paint that country's citizens, in an Orientalist style.[67] In *Head of a Moor* [PLATE 4.14], Constant captures the intensity and personality of his subject through brightly colored, loose brushwork— the parallels with Sharp's portrait of Judge Shorty White Grass are clear. While Sharp's paint handling is typically somewhat controlled and soft, the stylistic reference to Constant is not lost. Even with this inspiration, in Constant, Sharp had not yet found the spark that would lead him to produce an authentic representation of the American West.

While the Académie Julian may have been better known than the Académie Colarossi, it was at Colarossi that Sharp found a professor who truly spoke to him as an artist, pushing him individually to refine his work. In a letter to Gest penned from Paris in 1896, Sharp compared the effects his teachers had on his training at the Académie Julian versus the Académie Colarossi. In one passage, Sharp detailed his experiences with the Paris professors and singled out one whom he found particularly influential. "The greater variety of knowledge in the teachers," he wrote,

> the greater the opportunity of talented students having their individuality developed. For instance, in my study here (in the school's I have drawn nearly *all* the time) I found the man that did us the most good was not Jean Paul Laurens, Benjamin Constant or Gustav Courtois, but Girardot a younger man, who criticises in the night class. He not only saw where my weakness was, but he fought me week after week and month after month and not until a month ago did I get any kind of compliment from him, and the next week after that compliment I took the Concour medal passed on by another Prof. I give you my own illustration to prove that if a teacher and pupil is earnest he, the pupil, will sooner or later find the one who will develop his individuality and crush his weaknesses. This illustration does not belittle what I consider the greatest artists and teachers in Paris (Laurens and Constant) but proves that some men are better for certain failings than others, hence the greater variety in the method of the teachers the better opportunity for the student to get what he most needs.[68]

Sharp studied under Gustave-Claude-Etienne Courtois (1852–1923)

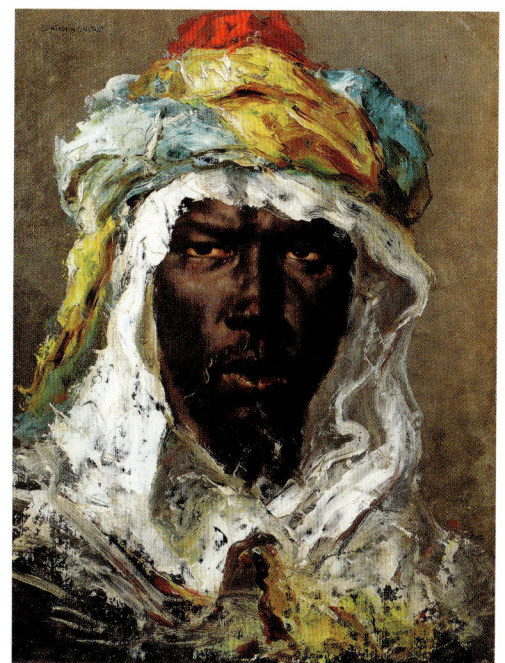

[PLATE 4.14]

JEAN-JOSEPH BENJAMIN CONSTANT
(b. France, 1838–1921)

Head of a Moor

1875, oil on paper mounted on canvas, 17 ¾ x 13 ¾ in.
Collection of Mr. Laurence Graff

66 See "John-Joseph Benjamin Constant," National Gallery of Art, https://www.nga. gov/collection/art-object-page.75181.html. Constant was an admirer of Eugéne Delacroix (1798–1863), as evident in his choice of palette and his painterly surface.

67 "John-Joseph Benjamin Constant."

68 JHS to J. H. Gest, April 21, 1896, Thomas Minckler Collection.

and J. André Castaigne (1861–1929) at Colarossi; the other professor whom Sharp mentioned in the letter is Louis-Auguste Girardot (1856–1933), a French Orientalist painter and lithographer who had studied at the École des Beaux-Arts. Girardot taught night classes at Colarossi, and Sharp learned much from him, as the letter to Gest indicates.[69] Looking at Girardot's work, it is clear that Sharp drew from this teacher's subject matter (once again, non-European peoples and their lives), use of lighting, and composition. *Femme du Riff* [PLATE 4.15], for example, showcases the dramatic lighting, portraiture, and "exotic" subject that influenced Sharp's work. In *Tétouan, cimetière israélite* [PLATE 4.16] and *La lumière du souvenir* (1893; Musée du Louvre), Girardot balanced Middle Eastern and North African figures with landscape in ways Sharp soon took up in order to portray the lives of western Native Americans, their pueblos, and their teepees.

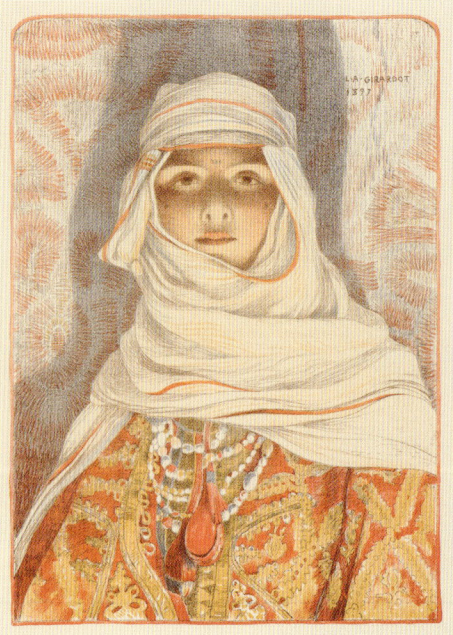

[PLATE 4.15]

LOUIS-AUGUSTE GIRARDOT
(b. France, 1856–1933)

Femme du Riff from L'Estampe moderne, no. 1, 1897

lithograph (one of a set of four), Imprimerie Champenois, Paris, lithographer, 12 9/16 x 9 1/8 in. Museum of Modern Art, New York, New York. Gift of Mr. and Mrs. E. Powis Jones. 342.1958.1 Digital Image © The Museum of Modern Art/Licensed by SCALA / Art Resource, NY

Sharp supplemented his study in Paris with a trip to Spain and North Africa in the summer of 1895. Accompanied by Duveneck, Sharp made this excursion a formative experience. As he wrote to Gest: "The year's trip to Europe, with an extra year's leave of absence enabled me to make the pilgrimage to the shrine of Velázquez with Mr. Duveneck, which was of inestimable value."[70] Sharp and Duveneck visited Madrid, specifically the Prado, where each artist produced four full-sized copies of works by Velázquez along with several smaller copies.[71] As noted earlier, Sharp had already encountered historic European artists and created copies of

69 Marek Zgórniak, "Polish Students at the Académie Julian until 1919," *RIHA Journal* 0050 (August 10, 2012), n49.

70 JHS to J. H. Gest, May 28, 1903, Box 1, Folder 3, JHSC.

71 This conclusion is based partly on a photo of Sharp's studio featuring a nude figure, thought to be Addie, and partly on a copy of *Margarita de Austria, Infanta of Spain* (attributed to Velázquez when Sharp was copying works at the Prado and now attributed to Velázquez's son-in law Martínez del Mazo). The original painting is a little over seven feet tall, making the figure of Margarita about four feet in height. Comparing the figure of Margarita to that of Addie in the photo of Sharp's studio reveals that Margarita cannot be more than two or three feet high at most. "A Biographical Sketch of Joseph Henry Sharp," 1. See also Fenn, *Teepee Smoke*, 91. The full-sized copies made by Sharp included *Martinez Montanes* (a portrait of the sculptor by that name) and *Don Fernando, Prince Balthazar*, and the idiot *Calabazas* (portraits of the sons of Philip IV).

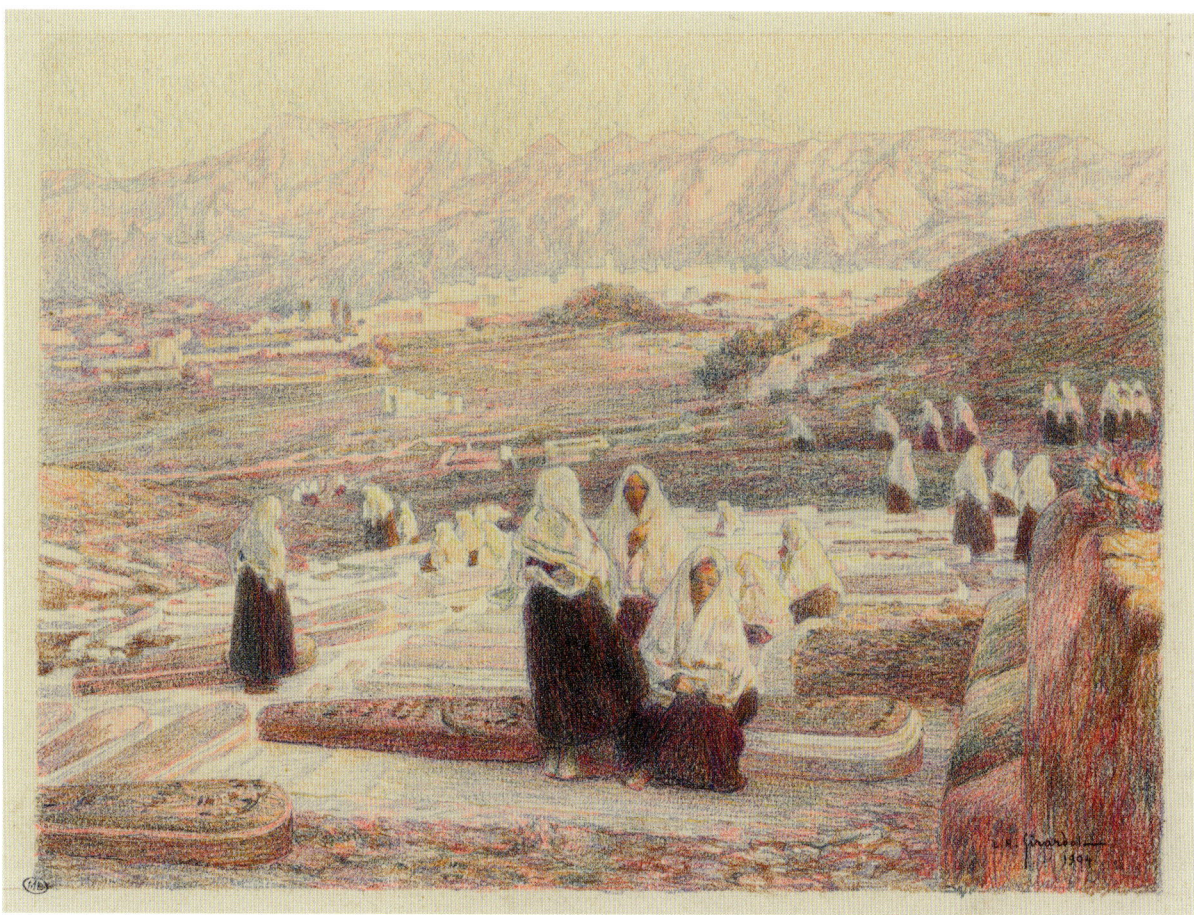

[PLATE 4.16]

LOUIS-AUGUSTE
GIRARDOT
(b. France, 1856–1933)

Tétouan, cimètiere israélite

1904, colored crayons on paper,
7 ¾ x 10 ½ in.
Musée d'Orsay, Paris, France
© RMN-Grand Palais / Art
Resource, NY. Photograph by:
Michel Urtado

their works. This experience in 1895, however, led to an exhibition of the copies back in Cincinnati, solidifying Velázquez's role in the establishment of Sharp's career.[72] Sharp also continued to display these copies in his Cincinnati studio [PLATE 4.17], and later in his house in Taos, signifying their importance and inspirational role in his artistic milieu.

When in 1938 Sharp looked back on the whole of his European training, he wrote: "Munich gave me a good foundation in drawing and technique, which sticks too closely to this day. Did not know much about art when I was there. Just that going to Europe was the thing to do and finish off. On return to Europe in 1895–96 to Paris—instead of Munich because the fellows were all criticizing the Munich school as old fashioned and wanting more modern training."[73] While he considered his training at Munich invaluable and foundational, in Paris he found a vibrant artistic community that fostered experimentation with style, composition, and subject matter. This supportive environment, coupled with his continued exploration of historic European artists and paintings, allowed Sharp to complete his training in a way that set him up for success in painting the American West.

---

72 See unidentified newspaper clipping, n.d. Box 3, Folder 3, JHSC. The exhibition likely took place in late 1896 at the Cincinnati Art Museum.

73 JHS, reminiscence in unidentified letter, May 29, 1938, Mary R. Schiff Library and Archives, Cincinnati Art Museum.

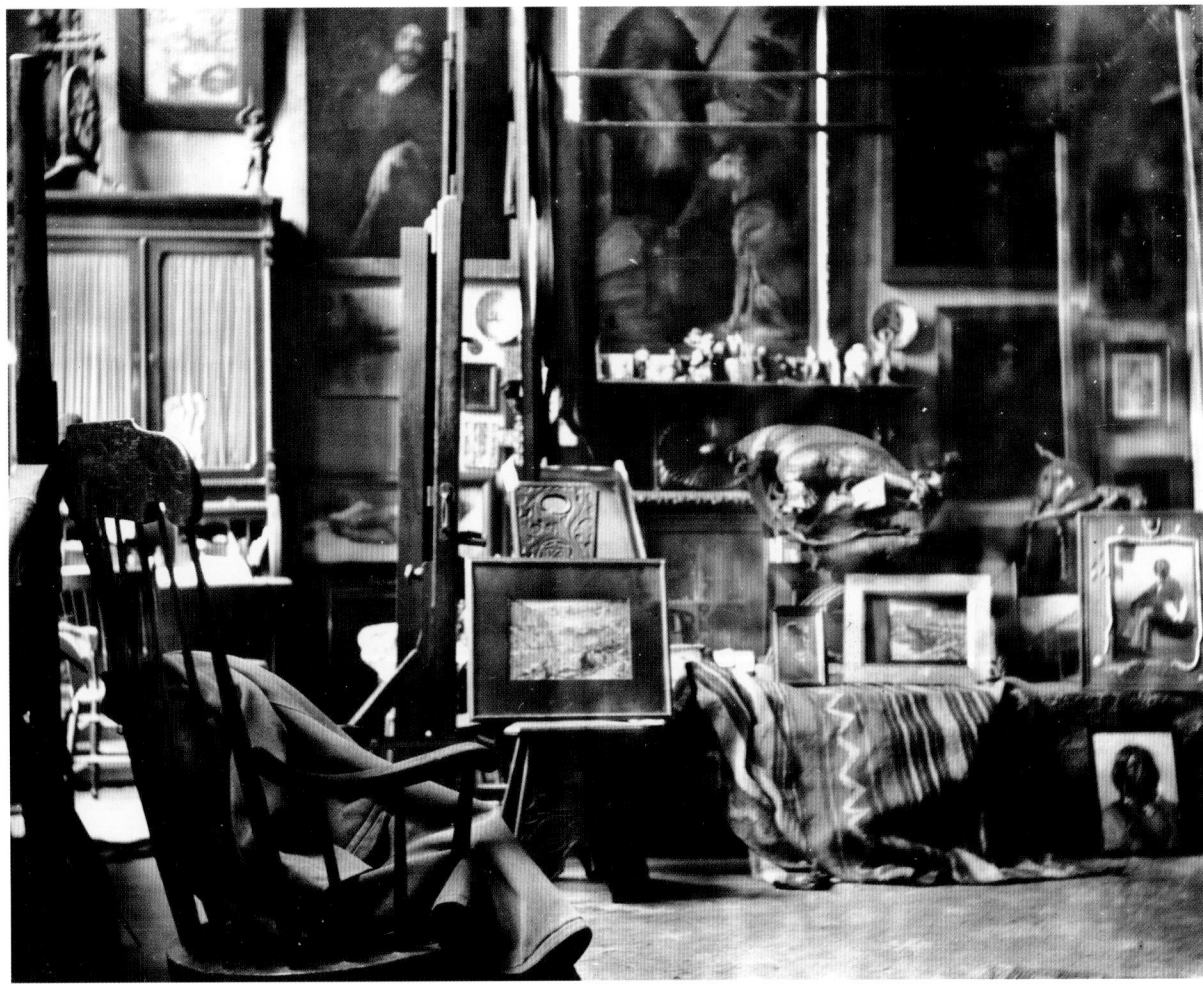

[PLATE 4.17]

UNKNOWN
PHOTOGRAPHER

*Sharp's Studio in
Cincinnati, Ohio*

ca. 1896, photograph, b&w,
7 ⅞ x 9 ⅞ in.
Harold McCracken Research
Library, Buffalo Bill Center of the
West, Cody, Wyoming. JHSC.
Gift of Mr. and Mrs. Forrest Fenn.
P.22.96

After Sharp's final period of training in Europe, the range of his ability
to integrate characteristics from specific artists and movements while
managing to infuse each work with his own originality began to emerge.
In this way, he cultivated a constantly shifting style that never remained
stagnant. Sharp often painted *en plein air*, and he took the sentiment
behind Realism and the Munich Style and conveyed it through a softer,
more emotive style, generated by his use of impressionistic color and
paint handling and informed by his internal desire to authentically portray
the American West.[74] In his eulogy of Sharp, fellow Taos Society of
Artists painter Ernest Blumenschein said that Sharp's "indefatigable labor
developed his technical skill to a point where he could put up his easel and
paint with great speed what ever his eye could see."[75]

To create portraits that effectively emulated the personalities of

---

74 Sharp preferred painting *en plein air* to the extent that he would paint outdoors in Montana
during the winter months until his paints were affected by the below-freezing temperatures.
Sharp told the *Kansas City Star* in 1909, "My landscapes were painted direct from nature,
with little or no studio work, and I tried to put into them the true spirit of the West." Untitled
article, *Kansas City Star*, January 17, 1909, Box 3, Folder 2, JHSC.

75 Blumenschein eulogy for JHS (1953), pp. 7–8, Ernest Blumenschein Papers, 1873–1964,
AAA.

the Indians he painted, Sharp needed to take a slightly innovative route compared to other artists who painted Indians, such as Farny. Sharp tackled this challenge in two ways, by painting quickly, alla prima, with broad strokes of color (a combination of the Munich Style and Impressionism) and by using photography to capture his American Indian sitters for later reference.[76] In the late nineteenth and early twentieth centuries, the use of photography as a painting tool would have been slightly controversial in European academic practice. Photography had a complicated relationship with academic painting and Impressionism, competing with the two as a representational medium struggling to be considered as art in its own right.[77] In the 1890s when Sharp traveled to Europe to improve his portraiture skills in Paris, traditional preparatory sketches, not photographs, were still used as a compositional aid, though his mentor Farny used photos in this way. Farny represented the United States' more lenient opinion of photography's place in the art world.

In the American West, this history of conflict between painting and photography did not exist to the same extent as in Europe, where the academies enforced much more established practices among artists. Too, in the American West, photography was being used not only as documentary medium but as a narrative one as well, capturing symbolism and detail, much like painting.[78] This American use of "narrative photography" allowed Sharp more leeway in the way he incorporated the medium into his painting practice. He thus not only used photography to capture images of Native American sitters for later reference but brought together characteristics of Realism and Impressionism and used photography as a compositional aid, aligning the competing media to create his landscape and genre paintings. The result was a combination of European and American practices and yielded portraits and compositions that appeared detailed, yet enlivened, the subtle movement of the surface effected by Sharp's specific combination of techniques and characteristics he learned in Europe [SEE PLATE 4.3].

Sharp continued to paint Indian portraits, and in 1899 he traveled to Crow Agency in Montana for the first time. Curator Sarah Boehme writes that "among the Plains Indians of the north [Sharp] found subjects appropriate for the character studies he had experimented with in Europe and in his travels with Duveneck."[79] As he began to expand his subject

---

76 Painting quickly was not just an aesthetic choice for Sharp but a practical one as well. "Though the plains Indians are not disinclined to pose, . . ." Sharp observed, "you must never count upon getting a second sitting from any of them. Almost all my portraits are painted from one sitting. I did not understand this and other peculiarities of the Indian in the first four years of my experience and as a result I accomplished very little." "Uncle Sam's Official Painter of Indians," *Leslie's Weekly*, January 3, 1907, Box 3, Folder 2, JHSC.

77 For more on this complicated relationship, see Peter Galassi, *Before Photography: Painting and the Invention of Photography* (New York: Museum of Modern Art, 1981); and Beaumont Newhall, *The History of Photography* (New York: Museum of Modern Art, 1964).

78 Martha A. Sandweiss, "Undecisive Moments: The Narrative Tradition in Western Photography," in *Photography in Nineteenth-Century America*, ed. Martha A. Sandweiss (Fort Worth: Amon Carter Museum, 1991), 99.

79 Boehme, "The North and Snow," 34.

matter beyond portraiture, Sharp retained the versatile brushwork, realism, and dramatic lighting of the Munich Style, but started combining these elements with the Orientalist compositions and scenes, vibrant colors, and impressionistic tendencies he observed while studying in Paris. Branching out to paint pure landscapes as well as landscapes including scenes of daily life, Sharp found himself employing varying combinations of the styles, subject matter, and compositions he had been exposed to in European academies and museums.

Sharp's work exhibits no clear trajectory, or progression, of style across his career. He continually took up and dropped certain stylistic tendencies depending on each painting. One constant presence in his work after returning from study in Paris, however, is his continued interest in Impressionism. In a letter to Gest on March 28, 1898, Sharp suggested that he and Gest go to see the paintings of Mr. and Mrs. Pope, which he says include "1 Monet, 2 Manet, 2 Cassatt, 2 Degas, etc.," and added that he wanted to convince the couple to loan these works for a future exhibition.[80] Sharp's continued engagement with Impressionist art demonstrates that his taste as a viewer visually manifested in his own work, particularly in his landscape paintings such as *Morning in Aspen Forest* [PLATE 4.18].

Sharp did not draw purely on the Impressionists, however. He also looked to artists who embodied Post-Impressionism, Romanticism, Realism, and Tonalism. Depending on the day, weather, subject, and place, Sharp let the environment dictate the visual outcome of the painting. His range of influence beyond the Munich Style and Impressionism can be seen in the Tonalist-slanting, Realist work *The Grave of a Crow Child* [SEE PLATE 4.7] and the Post-Impressionist-styled *The Lament for the Dead* [SEE PLATE 1.5], among many others.

After his last visit to Montana in 1923, something changed for Sharp. He began to grow tired of painting Indians, even though he knew he must continue, as they were some of his most marketable works.[81] Thus, although he continued painting his signature subject matter, the 1920s and 1930s saw an exponential increase in Sharp's output of floral still lifes, chronicled meticulously by Thomas Minckler in his book *In Poetic Silence: The Floral Paintings of Joseph Henry Sharp*, as well as the completion of a series of self-referential works. In these works, Sharp attempted to remain in dialogue with the mounting Modernist movement and drew inspiration from his earliest European training, specifically regarding Dutch painting.

It was the Dutch, particularly in the late sixteenth and seventeenth centuries, who made still-life painting a genre in its own right.[82] During Sharp's European training, especially in Antwerp and Munich, he was exposed to several Dutch painters, including Hals and Vermeer, but

---

80 JHS to J. H. Gest, March 28, 1898, Box 1, Folder 2, JHSC.

81 JHS to Mary Cornwell, September 5, 1933, Box 1, Folder 17; JHS to Scheuerle, October 13, 1936, Box 1, Folder 16; JHS to Scheuerle, April 15, 1937, Box 1, Folder 16, all in JHSC.

82 See Minckler, *In Poetic Silence*, 195. Still life has been an artistic subject since Greco-Roman times; however, the Dutch term *still-leven* was not coined until the 1650s.

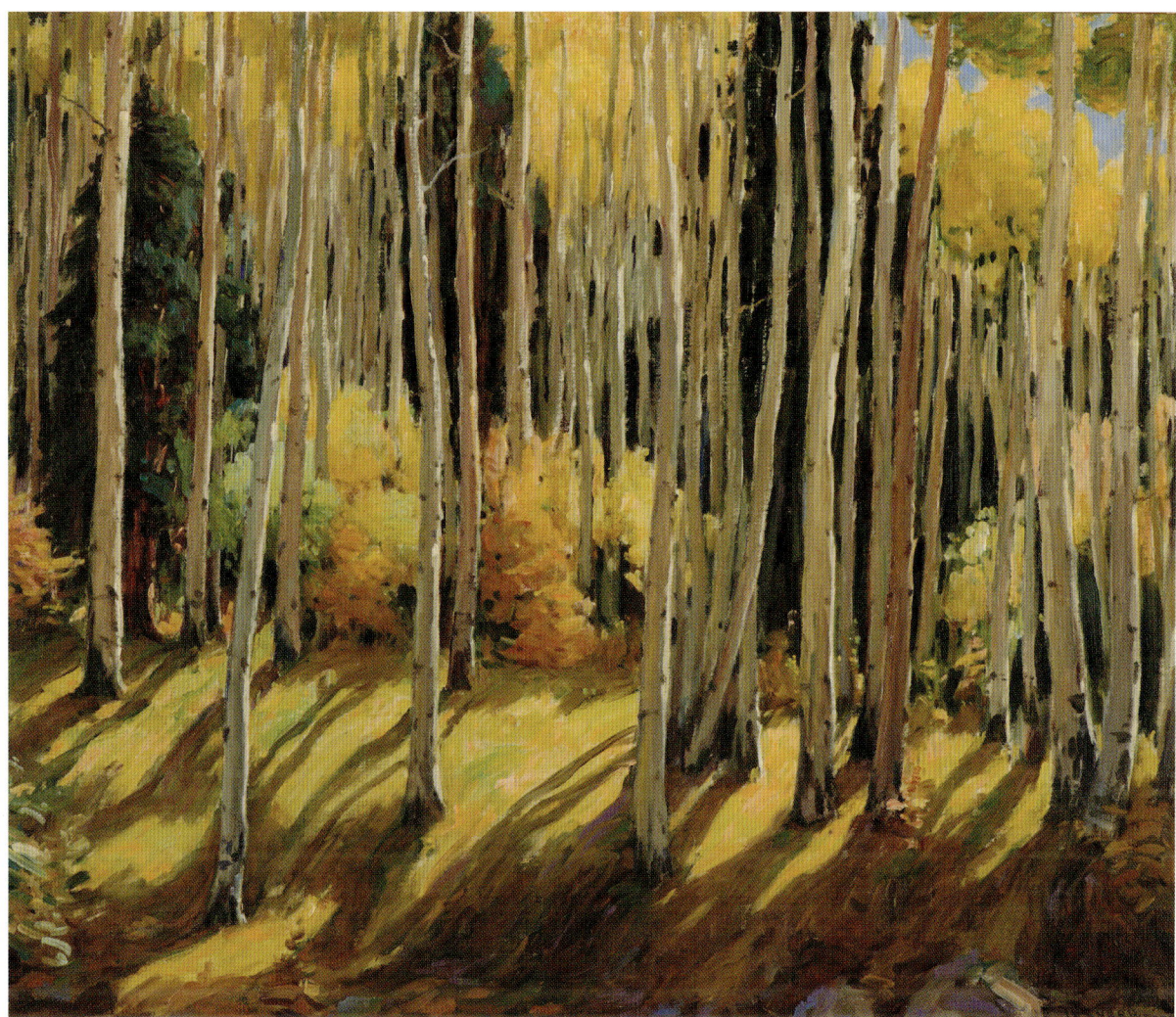

more specifically to Dutch still lifes.[83] In his Indian paintings, both portraits and landscapes with scenes of daily life, Sharp had little need to incorporate this particular artistic influence into his work. However, as he shifted his focus later in life, Sharp dipped back into this store of visual knowledge for inspiration.

A 1922 trip to Europe reinvigorated Sharp's interest in Velázquez and opened his eyes to new direct influences, including Dutch still life. During this trip he returned to the Prado and was struck again by Velázquez's 1656 painting *Las Meninas*. Sharp's self-referential series of canvases echo the perspective Velázquez takes in depicting himself in *Las Meninas*, in the act of painting a portrait whose subjects (the king and queen of Spain, Philip IV and Mariana of Austria) can be seen in the mirror at the back center of the work.

Furthermore, while Sharp's works that feature himself are not strictly still lifes, they emulate aspects of the Dutch masters' work. An example of such a work that Sharp would have seen at the Prado is Clara Peeters's

[PLATE 4.18]

JOSEPH HENRY SHARP

Morning in Aspen Forest

ca. 1935, oil on canvas, 29 ⅜ x 35 ⅝ in. Gilcrease Museum, Tulsa, Oklahoma. Gift of the Thomas Gilcrease Foundation, 1955. 0137.320

---

83 In a November 22, 1909, letter, Sharp mentioned to Joe Scheuerle that he had been looking "at the Dutch pictures in Met Museum," further solidifying his continued interest in Dutch paints. In fact, at the time, the Met was in possession of a few paintings by none other than Frans Hals. Box 1, Folder 16, JHSC.

1611 painting *Still Life with Flowers, Gilt Goblet, Dried Fruits, Sweets, Biscuits, Wine, and a Pewter Flagon* [PLATE 4.19], which features several obscure portraits of Peeters reflected in various surfaces of the objects in the painting.[84] Sharp's 1925 painting *Studio Interior [A Corner of My Studio]* [SEE PLATE 2.33] utilizes this motif, as one can see the artist's reflection in the mirror at the right corner of the image. While others of Sharp's self-referential series feature the artist more prominently, *Studio Interior* allows the viewer to observe Sharp's understanding of the subtlety employed by Dutch practitioners like Peeters.

Peeters' painting demonstrates the Dutch motif of placing images of the artist specifically within still lifes. While Sharp does not partake of this practice in *Studio Interior*, the development of his floral still lifes saw the occurrence of this motif later on in combination with another seventeenth-century Dutch theme: *vanitas*. In Dutch still life, *vanitas* works were symbolic and showed the fleeting quality of life, the certainty of death, and therefore, the futility of pleasure. Sharp's painting titled *Columbine* [PAGE 98] manifests this theme through the depiction of a few slightly wilted flowers and a fallen stem lying on the table. At first glance this image seems a quintessential Sharp floral still life. However, there is one slight difference: the artist has added a vague depiction of himself reflected in the vase.[85] Here, in contrast to *Studio Interior*, Sharp almost completely hides the painting's self-referential aspect. However, as seen in Peeters's still life, the Dutch often opted for this more obscure portrait rendering. Thomas Minckler astutely points out that in portraying himself in this way, Sharp solidifies his commitment to the genre of still life as an artist who knows its history, not just someone who dabbles in the subject.[86]

In a few of his other still lifes, Sharp extends the theme of *vanitas* by including small objects. *Zinnias*, for example, features a miniature figure of a crow and a Navajo blanket. In combination with the fallen petal that rests against the statue, a symbol for loss or death, the painting as a whole likely acts as a metaphor for the decline of the Indian people, particularly the Crows, as indicated by the presence of the black figurine.[87] Here, not only does Sharp pay respect to his European influences, but he does so in a way that specifically incorporates commentary on the situation of his western American subject matter.

In terms of style, Sharp's still lifes retain much of the qualities seen in his landscapes and Indian scenes. The appearance of his works in this genre remains rooted in his European schooling. One sees the draftsmanship underlying his compositions and the controlled application of paint, and

---

84 Celeste Brusati, "Stilled Lives: Self-Portraiture and Self-Reflection in Seventeenth-Century Netherlandish Still-Life Painting," *Simiolus: Netherlands Quarterly for the History of Art* 20, Nos. 2–3 (1990–91): 168. This particular painting by Peeters hangs in the Prado, where Sharp could have accessed it during the time he copied works of Velázquez, Goya, and El Greco with Frank Duveneck in 1895.

85 Minckler, *In Poetic Silence*, 98.

86 Minckler, *In Poetic Silence*, 5, 100.

87 Minckler, *In Poetic Silence*, 105.

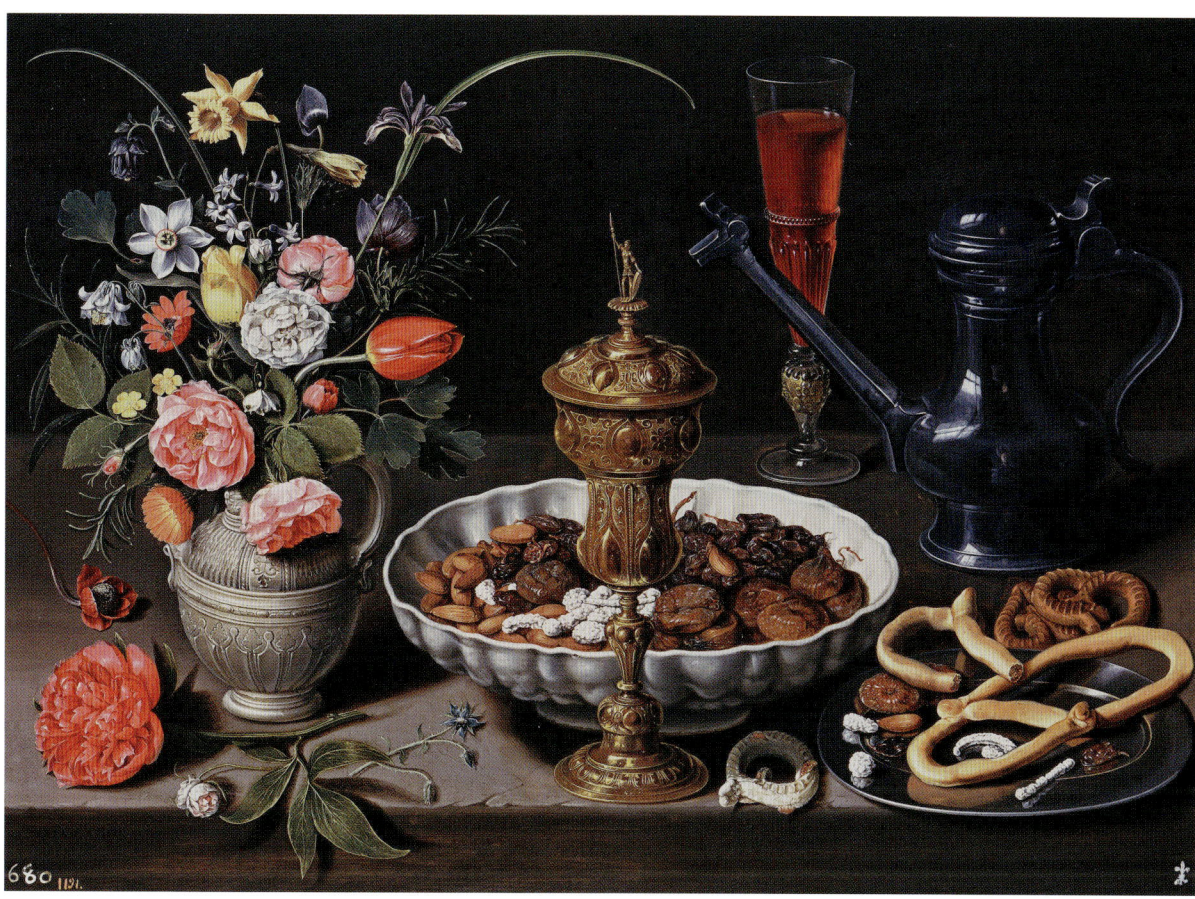

his visible brushstrokes and use of vivid colors and textures continue to suggest the influence of Impressionism. By this point, however, Sharp began to encounter the rising popularity of Modernism. While other western American artists—for example, Georgia O'Keeffe (1887–1986) and fellow Taos Society of Artists painter William Victor Higgins (1884–1949)—explored Modernist techniques in their works, Sharp remained resistant.[88] When Gest inquired whether he would return to teach in Cincinnati, Sharp wrote back on August 8, 1926, expressing frustration:

> You should have a younger man than I any way. You know whatever I do is done with all my heart and energy, and I wouldn't last four weeks. Besides I am old fashioned now, like Mr. Noble, and can't get with it tho I try mighty hard to keep in the swim. Students nowadays like all the young artists want stuff with the punch, and if it has that it has everything, and I still acknowledge there should be beauty and draftsmanship, values, tone . . . , etc., tho I realize any one of these can be carried too far too. It is maddening when a fellow knows how a thing ought to be done, how to do it, and ordinarily with his knowledge should do it and can't!![89]

Interestingly, Georgia O'Keeffe's and Sharp's floral periods coincided

[PLATE 4.19]

CLARA PEETERS
(b. Flemish, 1594–1659)

*Still Life with Flowers,
Gilt Goblet, Dried Fruits,
Sweets, Biscuits, Wine and
a Pewter Flagon*

1611, oil on panel,
20 ½ x 28 ¾ in.
Museo Nacional del Prado,
Madrid, Spain / Art Resource, NY

88 Charles Eldredge, Julie Schimmel, and William H. Truettner, *Art in New Mexico, 1900–1915: Paths to Taos and Santa Fe* (New York: Abbeville Press, 1986), 14.

89 JHS to J. H. Gest, August 8, 1926, Box 1, Folder 2, JHSC.

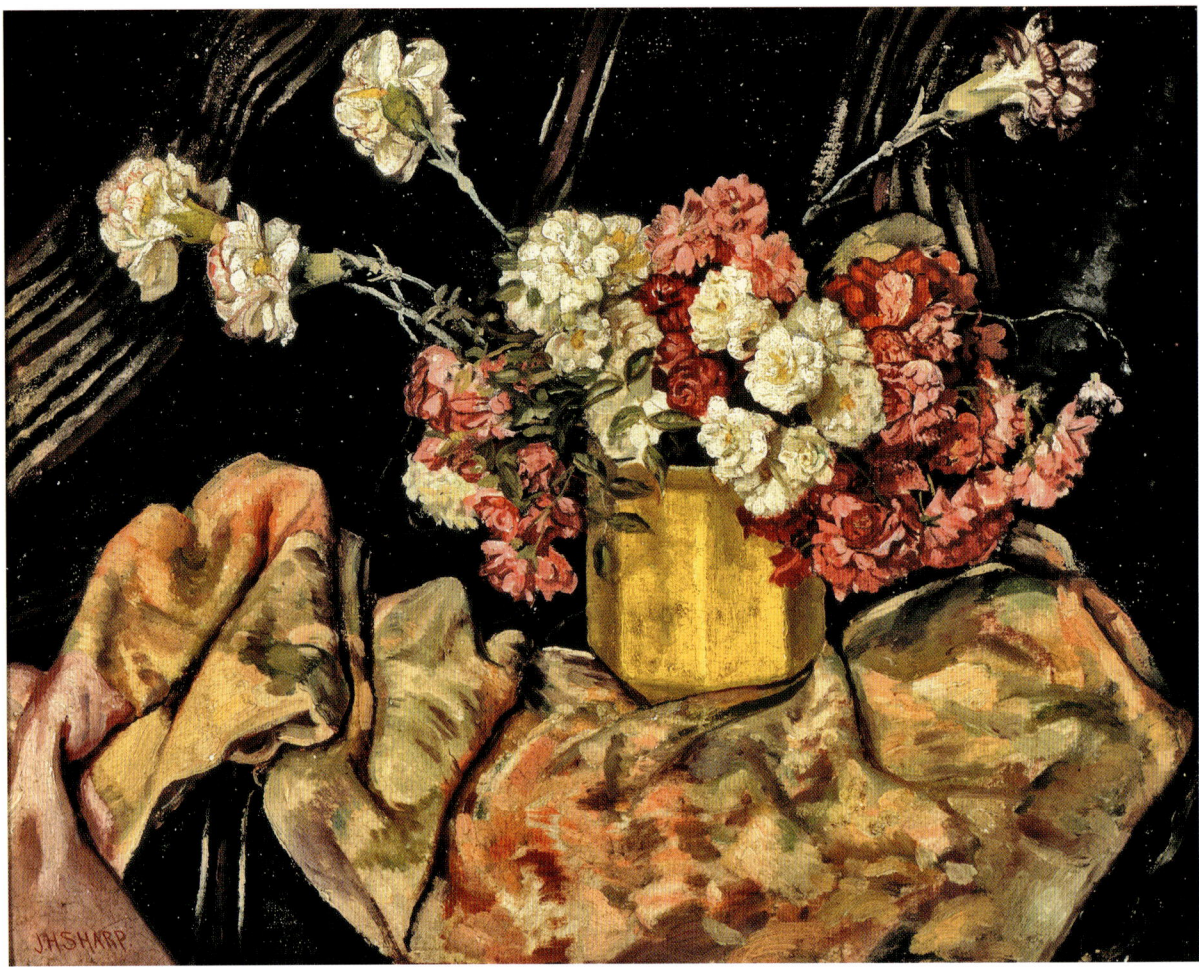

[PLATE 4.20]

JOSEPH HENRY SHARP

Carnations

oil on canvas, 16 x 20 in.
Image courtesy of Thomas
Minckler Fine Arts, Billings,
Montana

in time and geography, and it is in their stark differences that we can physically see Sharp's resistance to the emerging Modernist tendencies of the Immaculates and the Precisionists.[90] Only one known floral still life by Sharp exists that demonstrates his desire to at least investigate Modernist style. The painting, titled *Carnations*, shows a much more stylized floral still life than his other paintings of similar subject matter. Here, Sharp's treatment of the scene appears in a style closer to that of Higgins. While no other Sharp painting that resembles the Modernist *Carnations* [PLATE 4.20] is known, the painting demonstrates Sharp's continued determination to experiment with combinations of styles. In fact, Sharp referred to his works as "experiments" more than once in letters to his friends and colleagues.[91] Even in the final phase of Sharp's career, spanning the 1920s to his death in 1953, the artist managed to find new and different ways to incorporate aspects of his European training into his painting

---

90 Minckler, *In Poetic Silence*, 203.

91 See, for example, JHS to Mary Cornwell, Thanksgiving, 1934, Box 1, Folder 17; JHS to Butler, May 2, 1902, Box 1, Folder 13; JHS to J. H. Gest, August 7, 1908, Box 1, Folder 2, all in JHSC.

Blumenschein's eulogy, though at points it seems to slight Sharp, is nevertheless telling:

Problems of art which we often discussed did not bother him. He accurately reproduced what was before him. And some of these paintings will live as long as paints last on canvas. He was the reporter, the recorder of absolute integrity of the American Indian. . . . He will go down in history with Russell and Remington and the few early artists of Indian life. In trying to arrive at real values in our group of Taos artists I sometimes wonder if our ambitious attempts along tough art lines will be worth as much to the world as the honest un-varying recordings of this simple man. . . . We will never see another just like Henry Sharp.[92]

In the end, Sharp's European training at multiple points in his early artistic career equipped him with a repertoire of historical and contemporary styles that he drew upon throughout his career, but never in a formulaic or entirely predictable way. In the words of John Jellico:

"There is no easy way or clever formula for [Sharp's] kind of art. His is an enduring art. In all of it there is a sincere feeling of purpose and a craftsmanship one seldom encounters in his search for good art. The quality of Sharp's paintings is the result of an innate skill so deep as to deceive many who are apt to look for surface trickery—the art of Joseph Henry Sharp is timeless."[93]

Sharp achieved this timeless, truthful quality in his paintings by allowing his subject matter to speak for itself. Ultimately, it was Sharp's craftsmanship, straightforwardness, and desire to authentically portray the American West, alongside his extensive European training, that permitted him to become such a versatile artist with an ever-evolving, multifaceted style.

---

92 Blumenschein eulogy, 1.

93 John Jellico, "Joseph H. Sharp, 1859–1953," *Artists of the Rockies and the Golden West* 7 (Spring 1980): 98.

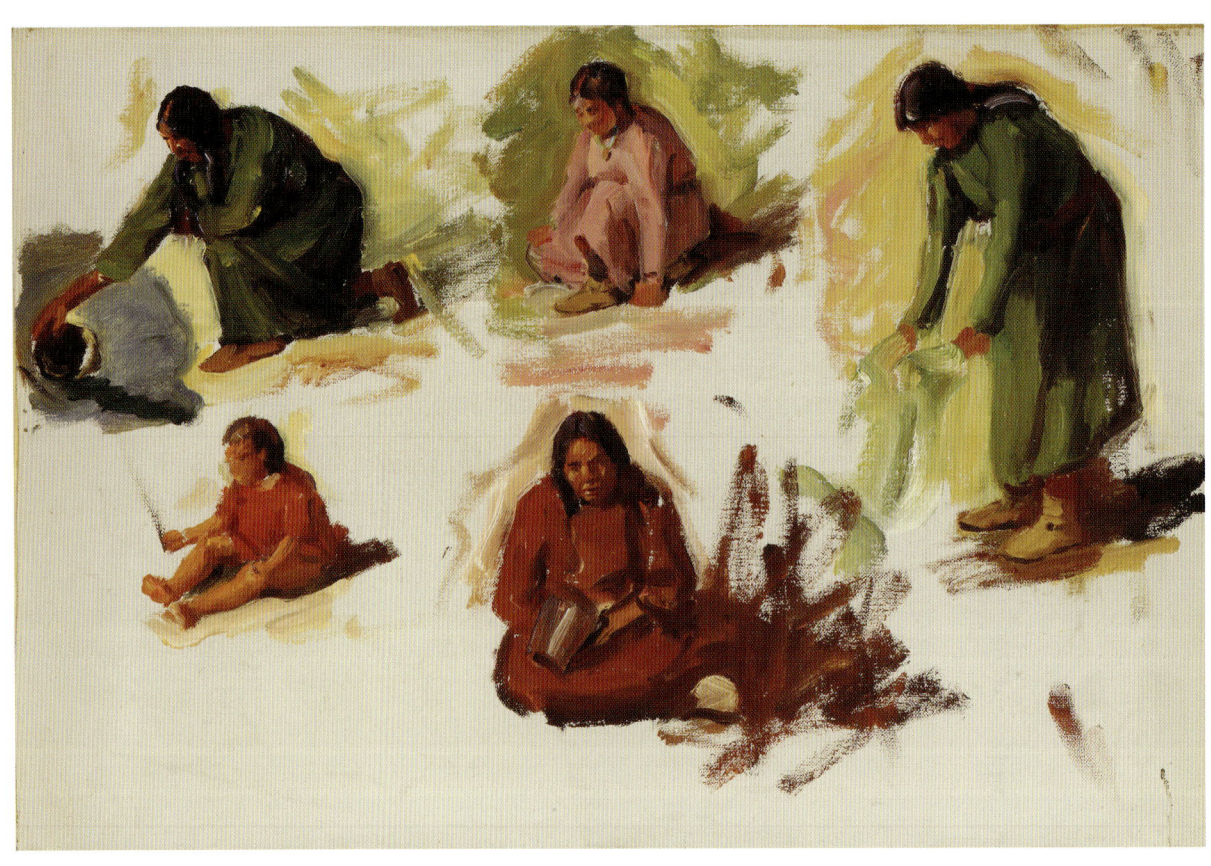

JOSEPH HENRY SHARP, *Crow Women.* ca. 1905, oil on canvas, 14 ⅛ x 21 ⅛ in.
Buffalo Bill Center of the West, Cody, Wyoming. 7.61

JOSEPH HENRY SHARP
CHRONOLOGY, 1859–1953

1859 Born in Bridgeport, Ohio, September 27

1873 Enrolls, at age fourteen, in McMicken School of Drawing and Design, Cincinnati

1879 Exhibits *An Artist's Attic* in the Cincinnati Industrial Exposition

1881 Travels to Europe and enrolls, at age twenty-two, in Academy of Fine Arts, Antwerp

Studies with portrait master Charles Verlat, who offered *Antiek* (classical antiquities) class in 1881 and *Natur* (life) class in 1882

1882 Returns to Cincinnati and rents studio in building at 30 W. Fourth Street, Ogden Building (Whittredge's old studio)

He comes under influence of Henry Farny

1883 Travels west for the first time—Santa Fe, Albuquerque, Tucson, California, and Northwest Coast

1885 Enrolls in drawing class at Cincinnati Art Academy (previously McMicken School of Drawing and Design)

Travels with John Hauser to Europe—Antwerp, then Germany

1886 Enrolls in Royal Academy, Munich, studies under Nikolaos Gyzis (master of classical techniques)

Influenced by Wilhelm Liebl (*alla prima* technique) and his old friend Frank Duveneck (with whom he may have formally studied)

Moves to Paris and enrolls in the Académie Julian

He and Hauser live in Montmartre

1888 Returns to Cincinnati briefly and then travels back to Munich to study under Carl von Marr (plein air painting)

1889 In fall, leaves Munich for good, resettles in Cincinnati and resumes his old studio

1890 Helps found the Cincinnati Art Club

1892   On June 16, he marries Addie Byram

Takes a position at the Cincinnati Art Academy teaching life drawing

1893   With Addie in tow, visits New Mexico once more

Joins John Hauser in Santa Fe, Sharp and he travel to the San Juan Pueblo to see the San Geronimo ceremonies (*Harvest Dance* and *Turquoise Driller* result) and then on to Taos

1894   Large exhibition (over a hundered canvases and watercolors) in his studio of Cincinnati-related subjects

Also has first one-man show at Traxel and Maas Gallery, with about thirty mostly western (New Mexico) paintings included, and a major joint exhibition at the fourth annual Cincinnati Art Club show at the Cincinnati Art Museum

In May, sells Cincinnati Art Museum his *Harvest Dance* for $500

Studio partly filled with what he calls, in a 1925 letter to Butler, works by the "real old Masters," Indian artisans

Takes a two-year leave from his teaching duties

Sails for Europe with Addie (June 28) to take more classes at the Académie Julian (studies with Benjamin Constant and Jean-Paul Laurens), lives at 15 Rue Campagne in Paris

1895   In the spring, he meets up with Duveneck and goes to Spain and studies in the Prado Museum

Receives a silver medal at the Académie Colarossi and exhibits three works in Paris Salon

1896   Returns from Europe with one hundred crates of paintings

Enlarges his studio and hosts a one-man show, *Studio of J. H. Sharp*, in November–December

Exhibits in Chicago with newly founded Society of Western Artists (Farny and Duveneck, founders, and Blumenschein, Hauser, Lundgren, and Sharp, members)

1897   Resumes teaching life class at Cincinnati Art Academy

At end of term, sublets studio to Duveneck and makes his first of many annual summer trips back to Santa Fe and Taos

1898   Sets up his first studio in Taos

1899   Changes routine and travels to Crow Agency in Montana to paint for the summer

Makes his first art sale to Joseph G. Butler, Jr. (the portrait *Ogalalla Sioux Indian Scout* probably from a Cincinnati Art Club exhibit in December)

1900   Butler buys eleven more paintings; *Brush & Pencil* publishes a long article on him and his art with eleven illustrations

Visits the Sioux around Pine Ridge, South Dakota and then Seattle and Alaska in August (*Seattle Post*, 8/7/00)

October, traveling show of Indian portraits begins at the Cincinnati Museum, then to The Carnegie, Pittsburgh (Andrew Carnegie buys a portrait)

November, presents exhibition in Sheridan, Wyoming (*Sheridan Enterprise*, 10/27/00)

Exhibits at the Paris Exposition

1901   January, displays portraits at the Detroit Museum of Art (*Detroit News-Tribune* 1/20/01), then in February, St. Louis Art Museum (*St. Louis Globe* 2/20/01)

He and Addie spend part of summer among the Blackfeet

August, is in Seattle exhibiting his painting and *Mourning Her Brave* is a sensation at Texas State Fair, Galveston

Joins group of ethnographic artists including Herbert Vos, E. W. Deming, and F. A. Verner in a show at Ethnology Building at Pan-American Exposition in Buffalo, New York; wins a silver medal

W. H. Holmes purchases eleven paintings from Sharp's December Cosmos Club exhibition for Smithsonian Institution

Phoebe A. Hearst purchased seventy-nine Indian portraits for the University of California, Berkeley

Hearst also commissions him to paint fifteen more paintings per year for five years

Exhibits one Indian portrait in Fine Arts Exhibition in 1900 Paris Exposition

1902   May, Sharp resigns from the Cincinnati Art Academy after ten years' teaching there

Visits Blackfeet, Sioux and Flathead tribes

Electing to *live* among his subjects, a novel idea, he tries painting on Crow Agency (living at first at the Server Hotel) to fulfill Hearst commission

Leases land at Agency for his future studio and house

In the spring, the Sharps visit Henry's sister in Pasadena, and establishes a studio at the rear of the house (which he uses off and on over many winters to come)

Participates in joint exhibition at National Arts Club, New York; some critics begin to question the artistic quality of his portrait work … the theme too narrow (*NY Sun* 12/2/02)

1903   Joint exhibit travels to St. Botolph Club in Boston (*Boston Herald* 1/19/03)

Dedicates first, small studio (10 by 14 feet) at Crow Agency

Continues to paint among the Blackfeet and Flathead Indians

1904   Travels to California in May to show Hearst paintings to pick from (she selects twelve)

Visits the Zuni and Navajo in the Southwest and the Shoshone and Arapaho in Wyoming

October 29, reports that new, enlarged Montana studio in Crow Agency is ready (14 by 20 feet)

1905   Tries firelight scenes to add variety to his work (Letter to Koch 1/1/05) and finds them difficult; asks Duveneck for help

In the spring, visits the Blackfeet again

Over the summer and perhaps fall, he works on his house on Crow Agency, Absarokee Hut

September, sees his first Crow Fair

1906   The Sharps start annual pattern of winter in Montana and summer in Taos, what he calls "our first love"

July, to Grand Canyon, then San Francisco to repair Hearst's paintings damaged by earthquake

December, two firelight scenes are included in a favorable feature article (*N Y Herald* 12/23/06); *The Gamblers* and *A Gift for Her Brave*, both featured

December, open one-man show at Fishel, Adler & Schwartz in New York City

1907   Exhibits again at Cosmos Club with assessment of a fine artist as well as an ethnographic painter (*D C Evening Express* 1/5/07)

Buys land at Crow Agency

Meets Charles Russell in Great Falls and would have seen his log cabin studio (built in 1903)

September, visits Grand Canyon

Visits Shoshone and Arapaho Reservation, Wyoming (letter to Gest 11/20/07)

November, visits Fra Dana at her ranch, Parkman, WY

1908   February, first known mention of portable Montana sheep wagon studio, the "Prairie Dog"

Buys former dance hall and adjacent house on Kit Carson Road in Taos for his first house and studio, next door to Couse's; land and house cost $480

Important traveling exhibit goes to Cincinnati, Indianapolis, and St. Louis

1909   January, opens one-man show at Swan Gallery, Kansas City

March, visits Helena, Montana, sells several works (*Treasure State* 3/6/09)

March, holds exhibition in Sheridan, Wyoming

Purchases Penitente Chapel in Taos for $250

1910   Moves full-time to Taos; by June, has completed his "Chapel Studio," and house "nearly so"

Addie's health begins to deteriorate

Buys his sister's house in Pasadena for winter stays (1481 Corson Street)

1911   March, sells King Gillette, Brooklyn, Massachusetts, nine portraits for $2,800

1912   Productive summer in Taos; completes *The Stoic* and *Broken Bow* (Sharp to Gest 10/3/12)

Major exhibition at the University Club, Cincinnati (eighty-eight western works)

1913   Addie dies in April

Invited to submit six canvases to Panama-California Expo (Sharp to Gest 10/19/14)

1915   Builds new studio in Taos

Marries Louise Byram, Addie's sister

Founding member of Taos Society of Artists

Exhibits major works in San Diego (Panama-California Exposition) and San Francisco (Panama-Pacific Exposition)

1918   Landscapes and floral compositions begin to dominate Sharp's work

1919   December, writes Butler—bad health and won't go to Montana this winter; goes to Pasadena instead

1920   Sharp praises new Museum of New Mexico for "encouraging all schools and 'isms'" with its open-door policy

1921   Ambassador Hotel in Santa Barbara burns and Sharp loses twelve to 115 paintings

1922   Sells Butler two large works, *Ration Day* and *Young Chief's Mission* for the new museum

Buys a car to avail himself of landscape painting opportunities

December 27, he and Louise sail for Europe; France and Spain

1923   Last year Sharps spent winter at Crow Agency

Sharp elected president of TSA but soon declines to serve

1925   Starts a series of self-portraits picturing him in his studio mirror

1926   John D. Rockefeller, Jr. visits Taos studio and purchases four paintings for nearly $1,000

Makes final trip to Crow Agency for one hundredth anniversary of Battle of Little Big Horn; studio still standing

Turns increasingly to still lifes because of eyesight problems

1927   Sells twenty-seven Indian portraits to Dr. Philip Cole

Has show at Traxel Art Galleries in which floral paintings prevail

1930   First of many trips to Hawaii (others in 1932, '34, '35, '37, and '38)

1931   Sends 95 old Indian portraits to his California agent, Grace Nicholson, for her to sell

1933   Sharp tells Carolyn Riebeth that he wishes to sell Crow Agency house; reports having had no art sales in three years

Don Fernando Hotel in Taos burns down; Handyman, Alois, saves twenty-one of his paintings

1934   Sharp files quit-claim to sell Couse all his Taos property for $1; thereafter, the Couses to pay the Sharps a periodic fee for the rest of their lives and to take possession of his house and studio at Louise's death

1935   Sells Crow Agency properties

1939   Oklahoma oilman Frank Phillips begins buying large numbers of Sharp's Indian portraits and genre scenes

1945   Meets Oklahoma oilman, Thomas Gilcrease, for first time as a visitor to his Taos studio

Gilcrease eventually buys 250 works by Sharp, along with many artifacts

1949   Gilcrease Foundation hosts a comprehensive retrospective exhibition comprising 236 paintings

1952   Leaves Taos in August for the last time, saying farewell to New Mexico (*Santa Fe News* 8/3/52)

1953   Dies in Pasadena, August 29, at 94 years old

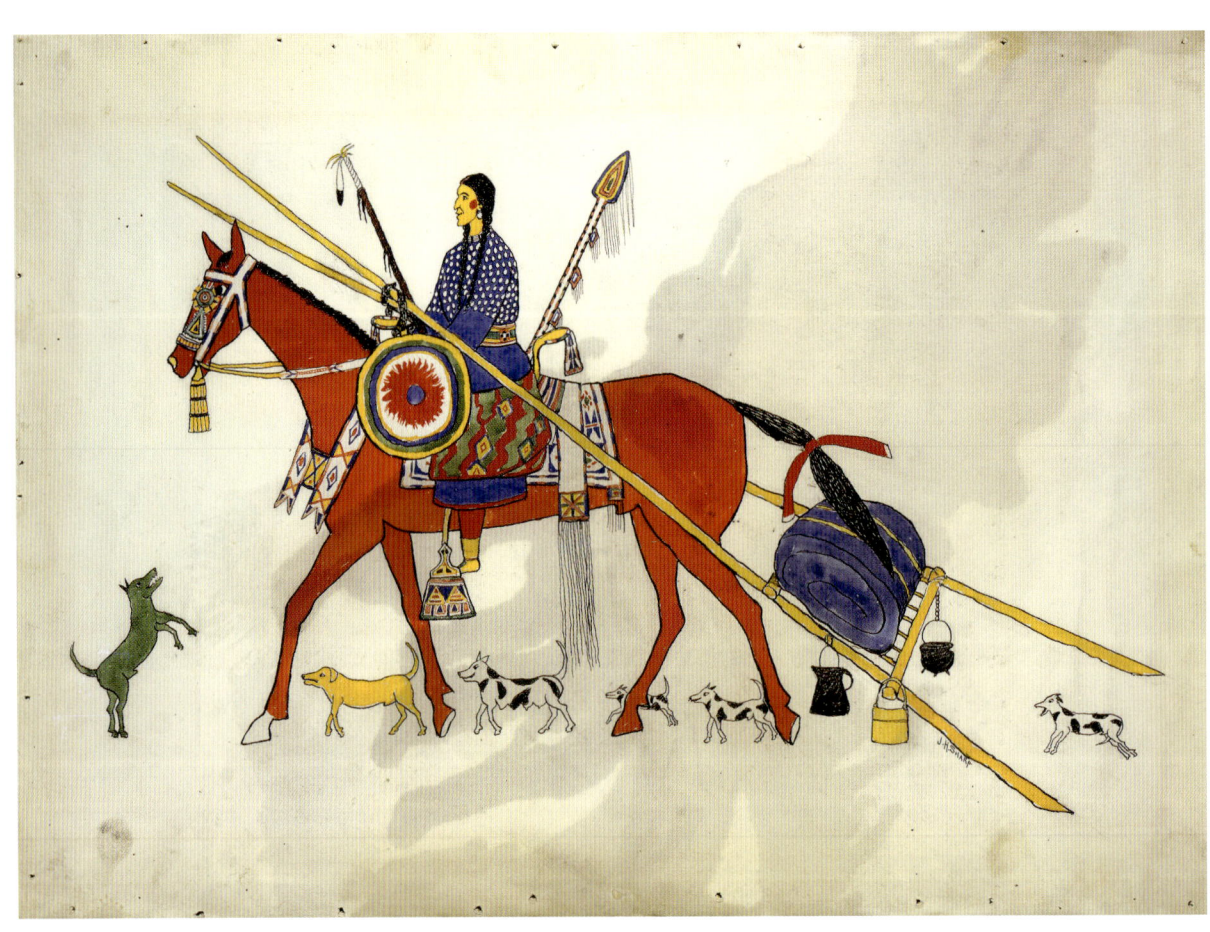

JOSEPH HENRY SHARP, *Going to Trade with E.A. Richardson.* 1905, watercolor on paper, 12 ½ x 22 in.
Buffalo Bill Center of the West, Cody, Wyoming. 11.61

SELECTED BIBLIOGRAPHY
ARCHIVAL COLLECTIONS

Blumenschein, Ernest, Papers, 1873–1964. Archives of American Art, Smithsonian Institution, Washington, DC.

Farny, Henry Francois, Papers, 1839–1941. Archives of American Art, Smithsonian Institution, Washington, DC.

Sharp, Joseph Henry, Collection. MS 22, McCracken Research Library, Buffalo Bill Center of the West, Cody, WY.

Taft, Robert, Papers. Kansas State Historical Society, Topeka.

PUBLISHED SOURCES

"Among the Artists." *The Criterion: An Illustrated Magazine*, October 1887.

Bickerstaff, Laura M., *Pioneer Artists of Taos*. Revised edition. Denver: Old West, 1983.

"A Biographical Sketch of Joseph Henry Sharp." In *The National Cyclopedia of American Biography*. New York: James T. White and Company, Publishers, 1901.

Boehme, Sarah E. *Absarokee Hut: The Joseph Henry Sharp Cabin.* Cody, WY: Buffalo Bill Historical Center, 1992.

———. "The North and Snow: J. H. Sharp in Montana," *Montana The Magazine of Western History* (Autumn 1990): 32–47.

Boeller, Susanne. "Two American Painters in Munich: Walter Ufer and E. Martin Hennings." In *A Place in the Sun: The Southwest Painting of Walter Ufer and E. Martin Hennings*. Edited by Thomas Brent Smith, 7–19. Norman: University of Oklahoma Press, 2016.

Brusati, Celeste. "Stilled Lives: Self-Portraiture and Self-Reflection in Seventeenth-Century Netherlandish Still-Life Painting." *Simiolus: Netherlands Quarterly for the History of Art* 20, Nos. 2–3 (1990–91): 168–83.

Carter, Denny. *Henry Farny*. New York: Watson-Guptill, 1978.

Cassidy, Ina Sizer. "Art and Artists of New Mexico." *New Mexico Magazine* (August 1932).

Coke, Van Deren. *Taos and Santa Fe: The Artist's Environment, 1882–1942.* Albuquerque: University of New Mexico Press, 1963.

Cole, Alphaeus P. "An Adolescent in Paris: The Adventure of Being an Art Student Abroad in the Late 19th Century." *American Art Journal* 8, No. 2 (November 1976): 111–15.

Davies, Laura A. "An Indian Painter of the West." *El Palacio* 8, No. 5 (September 1, 1922): 65–69.

De Lack, Jon. "J. Henry Sharp—Painter of Indians." *Society*, November 6, 1913, pp. 11–13.

Dentzel, Carl Schaefer. *Joseph Henry Sharp and the Lure of the West.* Great Falls, MT: C. M. Russell Museum, 1980.

Dippie, Brian W. *The Vanishing American: White Attitudes and U.S. Indian Policy* Middletown, CT: Wesleyan University Press, 1982.

Eldredge, Charles, Julie Schimmel, and William H. Truettner. *Art in New Mexico, 1900–1915: Paths to Taos and Santa Fe.* New York: Abbeville Press, 1986.

Elliot, Charles A. "Revolt in Old Art School Led by Famous Painters." *Cincinnati Commercial Tribune*, March 21, 1915, p. 8.

Ewers, John C. *The Blackfeet: Raiders on the Northwestern Plains.* Norman and London: University of Oklahoma Press, 1958.

Farr, William E. *The Reservation Blackfeet, 1882-1945: A Photograph History of Cultural Survival.* Seattle and London: University of Washington Press, 1984.

Fenn, Forrest. *The Beat of the Drum and the Whoop of the Dance.* Santa Fe: Fenn Publishing Co., 1893.

———. *Teepee Smoke: A New Look into the Life and Work of Joseph Henry Sharp.* Santa Fe: One Horse and Land Cattle Co., 2007.

Foley, Brigitte M. "Joseph H. Sharp's Cincinnati and Oscar E. Berninghaus's St. Louis: The City as Patron." Master's thesis, University of Notre Dame, Notre Dame, IN, 1995.

———. *A Retrospective Exhibition of the Work of Joseph Henry Sharp.* Cincinnati: Mary Ran Gallery, 1996.

Grafe, Steven L., ed. *Lanterns on the Prairie: The Blackfeet Photographs of Walter McClintock.* Norman: University of Oklahoma Press, 2009.

Grant, Blanche C. *"When Old Trails Were New."* New York: Press of the Pioneers, 1934.

———. Taos Today. Taos, NM: n.p., 1925.

Guheen, Elizabeth, ed. *The Charles M. Bair Family Museum Collection*. Martinsdale, MT: Charles M. Bair Family Museum, 2011.

Hassrick, Peter H., and Elizabeth J. Cunningham. *In Contemporary Rhythm: The Art of Ernest L. Blumenschein*. Norman: University of Oklahoma Press, 2008.

Hokanson, Alison. "Catalogue Entry: Franz von Stuck's *Inferno*." The Met, 2017. https://www.metmuseum.org/art/collection/search/749639.

Jellico, John. "Joseph H. Sharp, 1859–1953." *Artists of the Rockies and the Golden West* 7 (Spring 1980): 90–99.

"John-Joseph Benjamin Constant." National Gallery of Art, n.d. https://www.nga.gov/collection/art-object-page.75181.html.

"Henry F. Farny." Smithsonian American Art Museum, n.d. https://americanart.si.edu/artist/henry-f-farny-1490.

Leavitt, Virginia Couse. *Eanger Irving Couse: Image Maker for America*. Albuquerque: Albuquerque Museum, 1991.

———. *Eanger Irving Couse: The Life and Times of an American Artist, 1866–1936*. The Charles M. Russell Center Series on Art and Photography of the American West, vol. 34. Norman: University of Oklahoma Press, 2018.

Luhan, Mabel Dodge. *Taos and Its Artists*. New York: Duell, Sloan and Pearce, 1947.

"Matrikelbücher." Akademie der bildenden Künste München. https://matrikel.adbk.de/matrikel/mb_1884-1920/jahr_1886/matrikel-00303.

"Men and Things about Town." *Cincinnati Enquirer*, November 11, 1889.

Meyn, Susan Labry. *Henry Farny Paints the Far West*. Cincinnati: Cincinnati Art Museum, 2007.

Minckler, Thomas. *In Poetic Silence: The Floral Paintings of Joseph Henry Sharp*. Phoenix: Settlers West Galleries, 2010.

Montana Historical Society. *Joe Scheuerle and His Remarkable Indian Gallery*. September 2018–September 2019. Exhibition catalogue.

National Gallery of Greece, http://www.nationalgallery.gr/en/painting-permanent-exhibition/painter/gyzis-nikolaos.html, Accessed on July 12, 2018.

Neuhaus, Robert. *Unsuspected Genius: The Art and Life of Frank Duveneck.* San Francisco: Bedford Press, 1987.

Newhall, Beaumont. *The History of Photography.* New York: Museum of Modern Art, 1964.

O'Connor, Nancy Fields, Barbara Novak, William Stapp, Joe Medicine Crow, and Dr. Margot Liberty. *Fred E. Miller: Photographer of The Crows.* Carnan VidFilm, Inc.: University of Montana, 1985.

———. "The Pueblo Turquoise Driller." *Harper's Weekly* 37, (June 9, 1894): 549.

Perry, Rachel Berenson. *William J. Forsyth: The Life and Work of an Indiana Artist.* Bloomington: Indiana University Press, 2014.

Porter, Dean A., et al. *Taos Artists and Their Patrons.* Notre Dame, IN: Snite Museum of Art, 1999.

Riebeth, Carolyn Reynolds. *J. H. Sharp among the Crow Indians, 1902–1910: Personal Memories of His Life and Friendships on the Crow Reservation in Montana.* El Segundo, CA: Upton and Sons, 1985.

———. "Some Memories of J. H. Sharp." Billings, MT: Parmly Billings Library, 1969.

Sandweiss, Martha A. "Undecisive Moments: The Narrative Tradition in Western Photography." In *Photography in Nineteenth-Century America.* Edited by Martha A. Sandweiss, 99–129. Fort Worth: Amon Carter Museum, 1991.

Schimmel, Julie, and Robert R. White. *Bert Geer Phillips and the Taos Art Colony.* Albuquerque: University of New Mexico Press, 1994.

Sharp, Joseph Henry. "An Artist among the Indians." *Brush and Pencil* 4, no. 1 (April 1899): 1–7.

———. "The Harvest Dance of the Pueblo Indians of New Mexico." Harper's Weekly 37 (October 14, 1983): 981–83.

———. "The Chant." Brush and Pencil 5 (March 1900): 284–85.

Smith, De Cost. *Red Indian Experiences.* London: George Allen & Unwind Ltd.,1949.

Smith, Sherry L. *Reimaging Indians: Native Americans through Anglo Eyes, 1880–1940.* Oxford: Oxford University Press, 2000.

"Society's Outing." *Cincinnati Enquirer,* July 17, 1887, p. 14.

Taft, Robert. *Artists and Illustrators of the Old West, 1850–1900.* New York: Charles Scribner's Sons, 1953.

Taggett, Sherry Clayton, and Ted Schwarz. *Paintbrushes and Pistols: How the Taos Artists Sold the West*. Santa Fe: J. Muir, 1990.

"Trebor." "Letter to the Editor." *Cincinnati Commercial Tribune*, June 19, 1881, p. 2.

Trenton, Patricia. *Picturesque Images of Taos and Santa Fe*. Denver: Denver Art Museum, 1974.

Troccoli, Joan Carpenter. "J. H. Sharp." *Persimmon Hill* 18 (Winter 1990): 8–15.

———. *Painters and the American West*, Volume 2. Denver: American Museum of Western Art, 2012.

"Uncle Sam's Official Painter of Indians." *Leslie's Weekly*, January 3, 1907.

Vitz, Robert C. *The Queen and the Arts: Cultural Life in Nineteenth-Century Cincinnati*. OH: Kent State University Press, 1989.

Watkins, Marie. "Joseph Henry Sharp: 'Painter of Indians' (1859–1953)." Unpublished manuscript.

———. "Joseph Henry Sharp: The Early Years, 1874–1903." Manuscript in preparation.

———. "Painting the American Indian at the Turn of the Century: Joseph Henry Sharp and His Patrons, William H. Holmes, Phoebe A. Hearst, and Joseph G. Butler, Jr." PhD dissertation, Florida State University, 2000.

Weber, Bruce. "Frank Duveneck and the Art Life of Cincinnati, 1865–1900." In *The Golden Age: Cincinnati Painters of the Nineteenth Century Represented in the Cincinnati Art Museum*, 23–33. Cincinnati: Cincinnati Art Museum, 1979.

Weinberg, H. Barbara. *The American Pupils of Jean-Léon Gérôme*. Fort Worth: Amon Carter Museum, 1984.

Wierich, Jochen, ed. *Enchanted Visions: The Taos Society of Artists and Ancient Cultures*. WA: Northwest Museum of Arts and Culture, 2005.

White, Robert R., ed. *The Taos Society of Artists*. Albuquerque: University of New Mexico Press, 1998.

Zgórniak, Marek. "Polish Students at the Académie Julian until 1919." *RIHA Journal* 0050 (August 10, 2012).

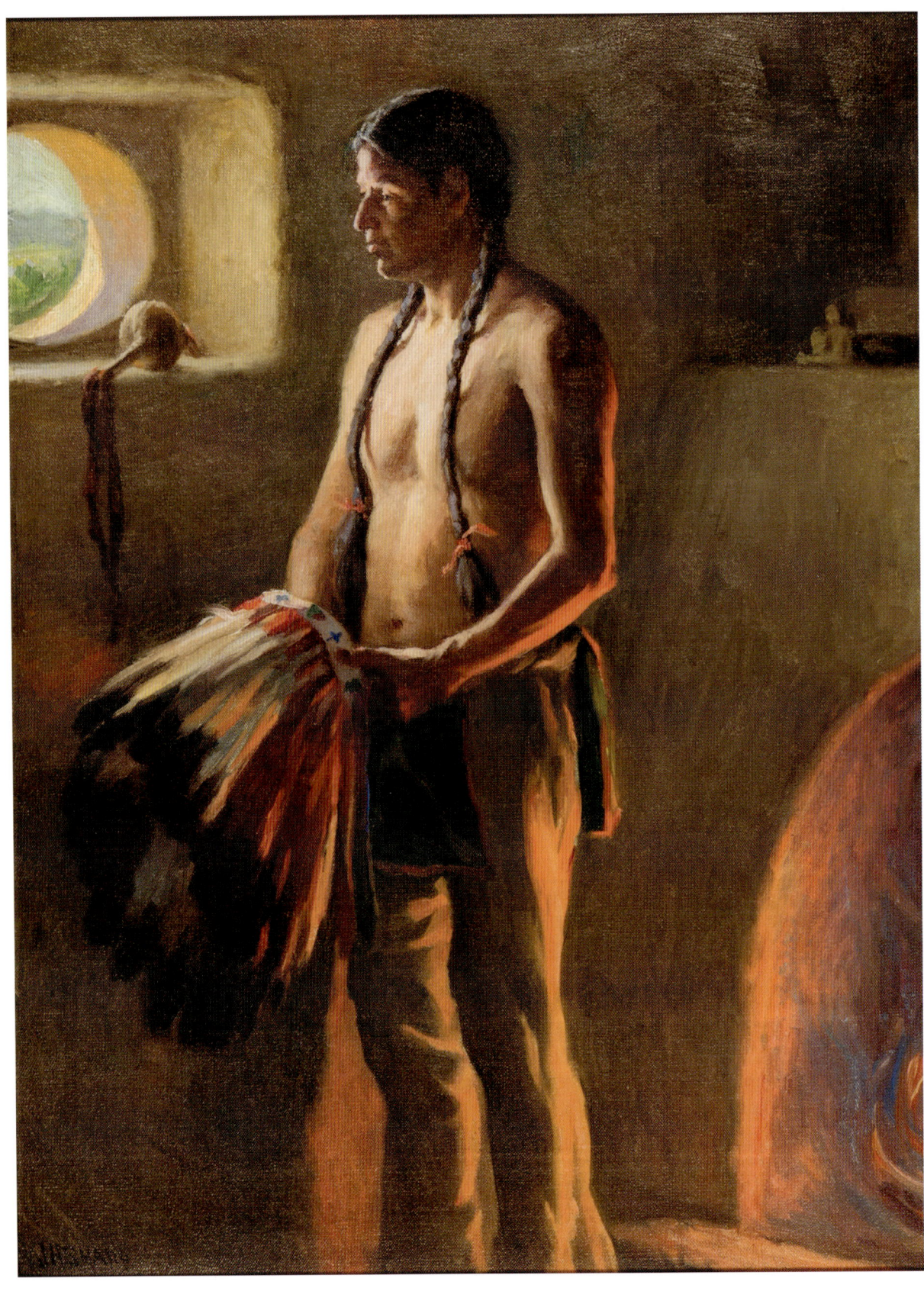

JOSEPH HENRY SHARP, *At a Pueblo Window.* ca. 1919, oil on canvas, 24 x 18 in.
The James Museum of Western & Wildlife Art, St. Petersburg, Florida

INDEX